78°   80°   82°   84°   86°   88°

D1452479

N

ARCTIC OCEAN

FORT SEA

VICTORIA ISLAND

OF   FRANKLIN

STEF

Vilhjalmur Stefansson at Dartmouth College, 1959

STEF

A Biography of
VILHJALMUR STEFANSSON

Canadian Arctic Explorer

WILLIAM R. HUNT

University of British Columbia Press
Vancouver
1986

ALSO BY WILLIAM R. HUNT
To Stand At the Pole (1981)
Alaska: A Bicentennial History (1976)
Arctic Passage (1975)
North of 53 (1974)
Dictionary of Rogues (1970)

STEF: A BIOGRAPHY OF VILHJALMUR STEFANSSON,
   CANADIAN ARCTIC EXPLORER

© The University of British Columbia Press 1986
   All Rights Reserved

This book has been published with the help of a grant from the Social Science Federation of Canada, using funds provided by the Social Sciences and Humanities Research Council of Canada. The author acknowledges with thanks the generous support of the Nova Corporation of Alberta, arranged by Senior Vice-President, Dianne Hall, towards the publication of this book.

PHOTO CREDITS

Dartmouth College and National Film Board of Canada, frontispiece; Richard Finnie, Plates 29, 30, 31, 32; Arnold Liebes Collection, California Academy of Sciences, Plate 3; Public Archives of Canada, Plates 4, 5, 6, 13, 14, 15, 16, 17, 18, 19, 20, 21, 22, 23, 24, 25, 26, 27, 28; University of North Dakota, Plates 1, 2.

Canadian Cataloguing in Publication Data

Hunt, William R., 1929-
   Stef

   Bibliography: p.
   Includes index.
   ISBN 0-7748-0247-2

1. Stefansson, Vilhjalmur, 1879-1962. 2. Explorers — Canada — Biography. 3. Arctic regions — Discovery and exploration — Canadian. I. Title.

G635.S7H85   1986   917.19'9042'0924   C86—091059—8

ISBN 0-7748-0247-2
Printed in Canada

To Marie Elsner, our good Omi

Contents

Acknowledgments

Material for this book came from a number of centres of polar research, notably the Stefansson Collection, which was the explorer's own library and is housed at the Baker Library, Dartmouth College; the Center for Polar Archives of the National Archives; the Public Archives of Canada; the Elmer E. Rasmuson Library of the University of Alaska; and, finally, the Scott Polar Research Institute. Librarians of these splendid institutions have been uniformly helpful. My thanks in particular to Erika Parmi (Stefansson Collection); Franklin Burch and Alison Wilson (Polar Archives); Dr. Ian McClymont and J. F. Kidd (Public Archives); and Harry King (Scott Polar Research Institute). Erika Parmi's unfailing assistance at Dartmouth before her retirement has been extremely important. She and others at the Baker Library have made my work there pleasant, and Mrs. Parmi has responded to letters many times. The substantial aid to publication of Dianne Hall of Nova is deeply appreciated.

Several competent women typed this manuscript with intelligent care and accuracy, particularly Kathleen Aamodt, Sheila Finch, Mary Hayes, Susan Hoffman, Judith Smith, and Judy Stephenson. Mary Hayes helped me tremendously by a speedy, careful typing of the first draft, while Susan Hoffman and Judith Smith cheered me down the home stretch while typing the final draft.

Several readers helped with suggestions and corrections: Evelyn Stefansson Nef, John Bockstoce of the Dartmouth Historical Society's Old Whaling Museum at New Bedford, Richard S. Finnie, Paul Neff, Gordon Smith of Ottawa, and my friend and colleague, Claus M. Naske. Richard Finnie and Gordon Smith went far beyond the conventions of courtesy in their exceedingly close scrutinies of the text in its first draft.

My work has benefited by conversations or correspondence with William S. Carlson, Elmer Harp of Dartmouth, Evelyn Stefansson Nef, Terris Moore, Alan Innes-Taylor, Trevor Lloyd of McGill University, Alan Cooke, George Rogers of the University of Alaska, Lawrence Gould of the University of Arizona, Richard Slobodin of McMaster University, Richard S. Finnie, Lowell Thomas, and Gordon Smith.

Mrs. Charles Smith graciously gave her permission to use her parents' papers—the Rudolph Anderson collection—housed in the Public Archives of Canada.

Bob Carlson and Chick Hartman of the Institute of Water Resources, University of Alaska, are appreciated for their support. They are sensitive to what a university is all about.

My thanks to Dennis Rawlins for permission to use the C. Henshaw Ward papers in the Center for Polar Archives of the National Archives; Edward Stafford for permission to use the Peary papers at the same place; Evelyn Stefansson Nef for permitting use of the papers at the National Archives and Dartmouth, and to her and her husband, John U. Nef, for receiving me at their lovely Georgetown home several times.

On the first of several research visits to the serenity of the Baker Library, Dartmouth College, my wife worked with me. A travel grant from the American Philosophical Library aided the completion of this work.

And, last of all but first in importance, I am indebted to Shirley Milligan and Walter Kupsch of the University of Saskatchewan for reading, editing, and worrying with me for a long time. Shirley Milligan, in particular, has shared intensely in this project with others of the Northern Studies Institute and the *Musk-Ox*.

Preface

A century after Stefansson's birth I sat in the Baker Library of Dartmouth College and listened to tapes recording some of his last reflections on personal and professional matters. By that time the path from Fairbanks, Alaska, which was my home, and Hanover, N. H., where Vilhjalmur and Evelyn Stefansson lived from 1952 to 1962, had become familiar to me. Dartmouth seemed the right place for an Alaskan to learn about Stefansson, particularly since John Ledyard, a Dartmouth college drop-out who sailed with Captain James Cook, had been the first white American to set foot in Alaska.

The tapes impressed me. Stefansson's memory at eighty was acute, and he responded clearly to queries — many of them on familiar topics — with his accustomed gusto. Knowing and sympathetic, he was also quick to make his point and reinforce his argument. He was, as he always had been, certain of his facts and certain, too, of how he wanted to handle his arguments. Of course, these few tapes are not of major importance, but the mountain of correspondence and other original material in the Baker Library and the Public Archives of Canada are ample documentation of his long and fruitful life.

What kind of a man was Stefansson at eighty? What kind of a man was he at twenty? How does one explain his significance in the history of his time? This book is one assessment.

I thought about all I had read over several years and the people I had consulted who had something to say about Stefansson. A number of individuals disliked him or his ideas, or his manner of presenting them, or for various other reasons regarded him unfavourably. Others remembered him with respect and cherished his memory. Naturally, most people know him only through his books and lectures and are not particularly aware of his personal and professional controversies.

My perspective on Stefansson and his thesis about living in the North has probably been affected by twelve years of residence in Fairbanks — a subarctic community where life goes on just as it does in more temperate climes. I do not know whether other prejudices have influenced my interpretation of the man and his work, but certainly I have felt no compulsion to be either censorious or acclamatory. One of his last writings was the introduction to a book on the explorer Adolphus Greely; in it, Stefansson wrote, "[he] has been given the gift not to be for, against, or charitable, but just to tell everything that he has space for, if it is pertinent and interesting."

. A biographer reading what were almost Stefansson's last words senses a firm directive: can I be neither for nor against, avoid charity, and tell only the pertinent and interesting? I have tried hard to follow Stefansson's prescription. I have not considered him as a forgotten man who needs rehabilitation, nor as a wronged one who requires defence from his enemies. What I have learned in the course of this work is that many people are more eager to crtiticize the work of others than to praise it, if only because the condition for praise is a somewhat fuller understanding of the matter in question. We are not too quick to make heroes, which is perhaps a good thing, yet we are unhappy because we lack models whom we can respect and emulate. Often I think of H. L. Mencken's point of view: he respected all those who did their work well, regardless of whether the work ranked among the more preferred activities, or even whether it were the kind of work he would have liked to do.

Vilhjalmur Stefansson was a talented man whose achievements as an explorer and ethnologist entitled him to the recognition he had as a leading expert on the Arctic until his death in 1962. Between 1906 and 1918 he became famous for his explorations in the Arctic. He played a unique and active role as publicist and promoter of the North for the rest of his life. He was a prodigious scholar, a prolific writer, and a popular lecturer, who more than any other individual focused public attention on a vast region and its potential.

In the course of his career Stefansson sparked a good deal of controversy. His detractors questioned his achievements, decried his theories, and tried to dismiss him as merely an exploiter of the public's thirst for sensationalism. There were ample grounds for animosity and misunderstanding, particularly in some exploration and Canadian government circles, where personal differences, rivalry, and jealousy created and nourished ill feeling. Stefansson did make mistakes, and his aggressiveness bruised the sensibilities of many members of that tight little world of regional experts.

Yet the controversies in which he was so often embroiled, whether colourful or tragic, should not dominate the story of this singular man. Although I have treated the conflicts that related to Stefansson's explorations fully, his work after 1918 is as significant, and perhaps even more important than his accomplishments in the field. I do not mean to suggest that his professional life ought to be divided into two parts; such a separation would do a disservice to the unity of his life's work. In fact, Stefansson is most interesting for qualities that express his essential unity of purpose, formed early and reflected in all aspects of his personal and professional life. Certain circumstances directed him toward exploration, yet long before he was to discover new lands, he had found the direction for channelling his aspirations, harnessing his genius, and utilizing his opportunities. As in any life there were false starts and setbacks, but Stefansson never lost his way. His life was artistically whole, well lived, purposeful, useful to society, and satisfying to himself.

Illustrations

[following page 142]

Maps

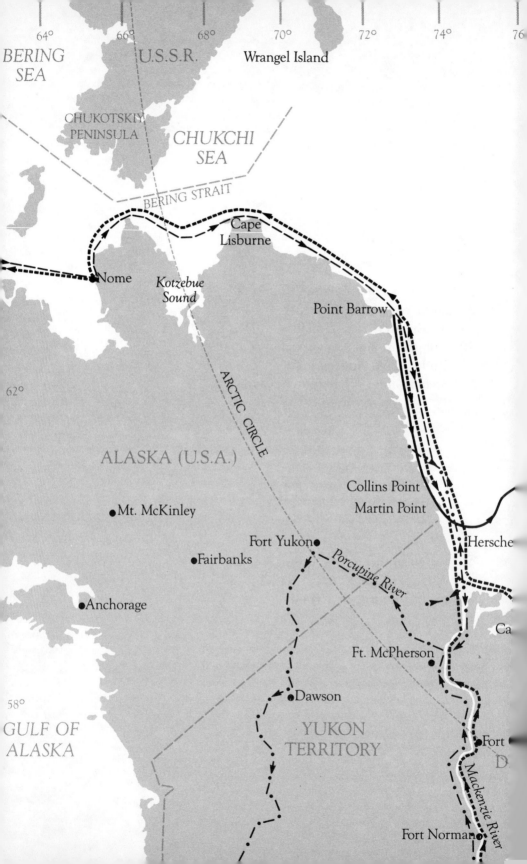

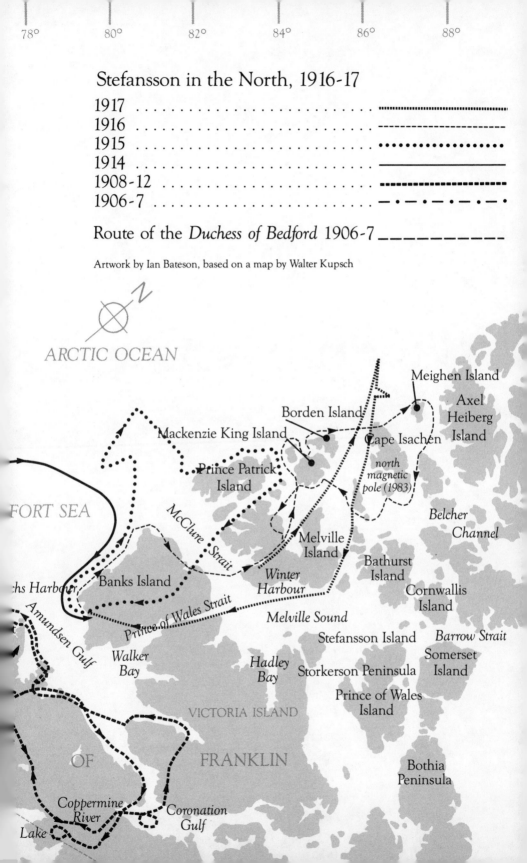

Stefansson in the North, 1916-17

1917	····················
1916	------------------
1915	••••••••••••••••••
1914	——————————————
1908-12	▬▬▬▬▬▬▬▬▬▬▬▬
1906-7	—·—·—·—·—·—

Route of the *Duchess of Bedford* 1906-7 ——————

Artwork by Ian Bateson, based on a map by Walter Kupsch

CHAPTER I

An Unlikely Profession

A S A CLASS, explorers are a bizarre group marked by strong personal characteristics: egotism, courage, tenacity—and ruthlessness. Essentially they are adventurers, driven by their passion to reach some geographic point regardless of the effort required. They are players in a great game that commands a huge public following, a game enlivened often enough by cut-throat competition, acrimony, and the threat of disgrace. In daring much, they risk much. Even in success their record can be belittled or besmirched; even at the pinnacle of public acclaim, they wear their laurels uneasily. Fame swiftly won can be as swiftly lost as new record-seekers surpass old goals.

Men obsessed by the extraordinary achievements of exploration are not noted for even temperament. That great trio of nineteenth-century African explorers—David Livingstone, Henry Stanley, and Richard Burton—for all their qualities of genius, were also neurotics. Devotion to their goals and desire for public recognition drove them to unreasonable conduct and savage vilification of their rivals and detractors. Similarly, the leading arctic explorers, Robert Peary and Roald Amundsen, revealed in their last years a vindictiveness and lack of grace that appalled even their friends. Of these five men only Burton was a scholar as well as an explorer, and yet, despite the wider range of his intellectual interests, he was a tortured character, biased and unstable, much given to black rages and self-hatred. We do not know what these men really sought in their wanderings, but if their goals were geographic records alone, their accomplishments did not reward them with personal fulfilment.

Although explorers and their patrons pay lip service to science, the systematic gathering of knowledge usually takes a distant second place to attaining a particular record. In earlier arctic explorations, this meant striving for a new farthest north and, ultimately, the North Pole. Explorers, as a rule, depend upon public support, and so they seek to hold public interest by sensational achievement, for their exploits appeal to sporting, rather than to intellectual appetites. This aspect of exploration creates great tensions and produces some unsavoury performances: exaggerated claims, devious behaviour, even outright frauds. But for all its questionable aspects, exploration is essential, and major geographic goals have to be reached before a more orderly and thorough assessment of a region, its people, and resources can commence.

This brief explanation helps place Vilhjalmur Stefansson. Although he differed greatly in temperament and approach from Peary, Amundsen, Stanley, and Burton, he was a part of the same extraordinary spurt of exploration effort during the last decades of the nineteenth century and the early years of the twentieth. As time went on, science did catch up with sport, but not before explorers had grasped all the major geographic records. Only then could the sober dictates of science assert priority. Finally, the traditional explorer who was part freebooter, part public performer, and—yes—part scientist, passed reluctantly from the main stage of history.

Most explorers create controversy. It is inherent in their competitive characters and in the nature of their pursuit; the fiercer disputes die hard. Today, many years after the events, scholars and enthusiasts still question the ethics of Amundsen's challenge to Scott for the South Pole and, even more vehemently, the justice of Peary's and Richard Byrd's respective places in the polar record book. Stefansson's career sparked controversy as well, and certain aspects of it smolder still. Some of his contemporaries dismissed him as a charlatan and sensationalist, even questioning the effectiveness of his field work. Such reservations are still expressed by some critics, particularly in Canada, where his detractors have had more influence than in the United States or in Europe.

Enough time has passed since Stefansson retired from active field work in 1918 to provide a perspective on the controversies generated by his field activity. Presumably the historical record is now virtually complete. Public archives safeguard the papers of participants whose impressions are open for inspection and whatever enlightenment they can provide.

There is not yet the same perspective on the second part of Stefansson's career, since he only died in 1962. Until then he was a lecturer, writer, and propagandist, espousing a view of the North which, as events unfolded, seemed much less visionary and far-fetched than it had appeared in the 1920's. It would be foolhardy to try to assess in definitive terms the extent of Stefansson's impact on the popular conception of the North yet. Certainly, however, the swift pace of northern development justifies a strong interest in the man who advocated that expansion so strenuously.

In 1879, the year of Stefansson's birth in rural Manitoba, two arctic explorations attracted attention. One, the successful navigation of the Northeast Passage by Adolf Nils Nordenskjold, indicated significant progress; the other, the disastrous attempt by the *Jeannette* on the Pole via Bering Strait and the Chukchi Sea, again demonstrated the perils of the unknown and reaffirmed the popular image of the Arctic as threatening, remote, and desolate.

Neither the Stefanssons nor their neighbours in the Canadian Icelandic community at Arnes, Manitoba, paid any attention to such distant activities. They were hard-scrabbling farmers trying to wring a living from a land that sternly resisted their efforts at cultivation. Their New World colony was certainly no Eden. Had a local soothsayer announced the birth of a future prophet of the North, they would probably have been dismayed. Their move to Canada had failed to reward them with abundance, so they were still looking for the Promised Land—and not to the north, either. Endless work and uncertain returns were constant strains, intensified by the harsh weather of the northern plains.

The Stefanssons were among the 250 colonists recruited by the Canadian government in 1877 who settled on government land north of Winnipeg. Over the first two winters New Iceland, as the settlement-at-large was called, fared poorly. Many colonists, including two of the Stefansson children, died from malnutrition, scurvy, and an epidemic of smallpox. Unfortunately, the site chosen for settlement was on low-lying land, too near a lake and streams that overflowed during the second spring, washing away the settlers' garden plots and flooding the floors of their crude log huts.

In 1881 Johann Stefansson took his wife, two sons, and two daughters to North Dakota, where many of the Manitoba Icelanders had resettled. This time the colonists chose a site in Pembina County above the flooded plain of the Red River Valley. Stefansson established his family's dwelling in the little community of Mountain. Life was still hard, but at least it was an improvement on their first harrowing years in the New World.

Young Stefansson was educated in the Icelandic tradition. An itinerant teacher taught him to read, and by the age of five or six he had mastered the entire Old Testament. The Icelanders enjoyed having some family member read aloud on winter evenings. Stefansson recalled, "What we read most often were the Icelandic sagas, narratives composed mainly in Iceland and preserved only there."[1] Later Stefansson attended school, where he learned to speak English, although the family continued to speak Icelandic at home. For reasons of economy, the school year was usually limited to three to four months, but at times he could extend his period of schooling by walking to another school when the one nearest the family farm closed. In all, Stefansson completed only twenty-seven months of primary school education, a meagre background for academic development had other sources of intellectual support been lacking.

Fortunately for Stefansson, literature and ideas were respected in his home. The Icelanders where Lutherans—serious, yet relatively tolerant; disputations about doctrine and the role of the church were as important to them as worship. And no amount of hard work could take priority over the Icelanders' deep-seated faith in learning. As much as they loved their own language and heritage, the old sat down with the young to study English.

Stefansson's father had a progressive view of life. He inclined towards reforming church doctrines so that Lutherans could cope more effectively with the modern world. In politics as well, he expressed liberal views, always voting the Democratic ticket because "he always belonged to the minority and Dakota was hopelessly Republican."[2] But the boy's richest heritage lay in the characteristic Icelandic love of learning, which he learned from his father. "A typical Icelandic intellectual environment had been transplanted without much change from the homeland to the Dakota prairies."[3] Although his father read only Icelandic, his reading was comprehensive because most of the classics of the world's literature had been translated and published in his native tongue. Reflecting on his father in later years, Stefansson found much to commend in his strength of character. "No amount of ridicule or social pressure could have induced him to modify either his beliefs or his expression of them. Pressure, in fact, was likely to have the opposite effect."

This trait in his father was not mere contrariness but rather, "an attribute of his nature, and I perhaps understand it because I, too, possess it in some degree."[4]

Johann Stefansson died in 1892 when his youngest son was thirteen. Vilhjalmur related the shock of his father's death to a neighbour, recalling that the sound of the earth thudding on his father's coffin caused him to break loose from his grieving family and run until he was exhausted, far into the woods where he could be alone.

Left with little means of support, the family had to split up. Vilhjalmur was taken in by his married sister. His brother and sisters left the family farm to find other means of making a living. Life remained spartan, but not without the amenities of family and community affection; it was a healthy, robust, outdoor life, and for Vilhjalmur, if not for his brother and sisters, it was enriched by his increasing joy in learning. He had an intellectual vitality that was wanting in his older brother Joe, a likeable, humorous, but lackadaisical fellow, and the others. Quiet and sensitive, he worked hard at farm chores like most of his contemporaries, but he revelled in his brief school sessions.

All his life he would regard learning with wonder and delight. While he could learn more and more, there was always the certainty that, happily, his appetite could never be sated. He was the product of an environment that was more notable for its physical rigour than for intellectual cultivation. Many advantages have been ascribed to western frontier life, but, with justice, it is not usually argued that nineteenth-century farmers enjoyed splendid educational opportunities. To attain learning Stefansson and his neighbours worked against the formidable handicaps of a meagre primary school system, family poverty, and remoteness from cultural centres. Insufficient formal education often proved to be an insurmountable obstacle.

Young Stefansson, with his rich literary background, his head full of Biblical and Norse lore, now began to read voraciously. In this early blossoming, he eagerly followed wherever intellectual pleasures beckoned. Later on he would agonize over his choice of career, but as a teenager, it was enough to know that whatever he was to do a university education was indispensable.

CHAPTER 2

The University Years

A T THE AGE OF EIGHTEEN, after investing in a seven-dollar suit, Stefansson was left with a cash reserve of fifty-three dollars; but he was ready for the greater world. He rode a train, for the first time, to Grand Forks, where he entered the State University of North Dakota. He could not be admitted to the college until he had made up for his scanty formal education by completing the four-year preparatory course, but he was permitted to reduce this time by taking examinations in history and other subjects as he mastered them.

Stefansson arrived after the fall term had begun, as he was to do each succeeding year because he needed to take advantage of the opportunities to make money working on farms in late summer and early fall. He was, nevertheless, well received by President Webster Merrifield, who respected students of Icelandic descent, knowing they generally did well. Besides, the fledgling university needed students.

The combined enrolment of preparatory school and college, some three hundred, occupied the two campus buildings, and most students boarded in town. Stefansson earned his keep at a family boarding house in return for caring for two milk cows and tending the wood stove. This favourable arrangement did not last long because the youth, polite and pleasantly mannered in ordinary social intercourse, grew hot and disputatious in defence of ideas. When his landlady overheard him praising Darwin's theory of evolution and criticizing the Lutheran church, she dismissed the radical student from her household. She "thought highly of her cows," mused

Stefansson, "and did not want them tended by anyone with views like mine."[1]

He soon found other lodgings and applied himself eagerly to his studies. After two years' work he was sufficiently prepared to enter fully into college life. The transition came as a relief to Stefansson, who was irritated by preparatory school drilling and the condescension with which lower year students were treated.

In July 1899, before he returned as a freshman, Stefansson took his first teaching job. A friend predicted at the time that "his eleven kids knowing no English now will by the time you get through with them, be studying XYZ of the English classics."[2]

For the rest of that summer, he worked on a farm. The return to physical work was good for him, and he kept in touch with others who shared his intellectual awakening. Their letters strengthened their bonds of friendship. There was always reading to comment upon as well as the work-a-day world: Herbert Spencer and haymaking. "Next week," wrote Stefansson, "I have a contract for shocking seventy-seven acres of rather light grain at twelve dollars and will send the ten dollars I owe you."[3] And so the friends cheered each other on in their new endeavours.

These stints of teaching and hay-shocking helped ease his financial problems. When Stefansson began his third year, taking freshman courses while completing some preparatory work, he also found a good part-time job: "My oar is in the lock pretty firmly now. I get twenty cents per hour for my work as assistant in our biology laboratory—ten to twenty hours a week."[4] He got his room free for assuming the responsibility for ringing the study bell at the boys' dormitory. As agent for a city steam laundry, he got fresh washing. All the money he needed to raise was ten dollars per month for his board.

Thus, before he reached the age of twenty Stefansson had completed two years of work, taught his first school term, and identified his intellectual heroes, declaring that "Spencer, Darwin, and Hugo mean more to me than geometry or political economy." Spencer's social theories had taken American intellectual circles by storm in the post-Civil War period, and Stefansson echoed the thrill which stirred many people over the implications of Darwinian evolution for human society. For Stefansson, this discovery was the highlight of the summer of 1899. "Is it not beautiful?" he wrote to a friend. "It is a skeleton key to the secrets of the universe...its depth and breadth—its omnicomprehensibility....Spencer is the giver and interpreter of the universe."[5]

Stefansson, too, longed to interpret the universe, not only as a scientist, but also as a poet. The power of poetry to express feeling enthralled him, and at the time he could imagine nothing could be more important than composing verse.

Among his student poems "A Philosopher at Twenty" stands out. It was well received by his fellow students when the school newspaper printed it. Eventually the poem was translated into Icelandic and published both in Canada and in Iceland, as were some of his other poems. In "Philosopher," the poet affirms the supremacy of love, "For love is the law, the master force that makes the world akin." Even world fame as a hero could not compare:

> *'Tis glorious on a world-wide stage*
> *To wear a hero's crown,*
> *That shines with the gems of mighty deeds,*
> *With the gold of a fair renown.*
> *But every prize this world holds out,*
> *Or has since the work began,*
> *We renounce for the love of the woman we love,*
> *And the life of a common man.*

In the end, the poet having failed to win this love, settles for "work that is strong and true."[6]

Poets, however, can have fun as well. In "Love Sonnets of a College Man," the singer insults a rival:

> *Be true, my Dove. Don't go with him. You bet*
> *That if you do there'll be the deuce to pay!*
> *He can't write sonnets, has no chink, nor wit.*
> *You'll drop me cold for such a Johnny? Nit!*

What is the use of being a poet, the young man moans, "I've gloried her in sonnets worth a prize/And he, not I, gets all the goo-goo eyes."[7]

His "Ode of Welcome" to freshmen exhorted them just to be themselves, and avoid mimicking upper classmen: "For many a mode, but fit for long-eared asses, is caught from Paris, and from upper classes."[8]

On the college level, he found courses were better, but not as good as he and his friends thought they should be. They also resented restrictions on their social and extra-curricular activities, and on occasion they rebelled.

Stefansson was exasperated by certain professors, whose lectures seemed artificially structured and arid. He felt deeply that learning is somehow akin to personal inspiration. Why, he wondered, did teachers reduce wisdom to a set of rules to be mastered mechanically? Why did they insist upon hammering "a few old fogey ideas" in their students' heads rather than suggesting new concepts?[9] His teachers felt his disdain, and no doubt understood his problems as little as he did theirs. It shocked Stefansson to be called intolerant and arrogant, yet he was. He was less critical after his own teaching apprenticeship, but he never abandoned his original stance nor his conviction that schools foster much that needs to be unlearned.

Stefansson revealed more of himself to his friends than to his teachers. They shared their uncertainties about the meaning and purpose of life and about their own roles in society. Their advocacy of particular ideas and assertions of firm purpose tended to alternate with confessions of doubt. Writing to a friend, Stefansson apologized for some rudeness of expression that had upset her. It was not his rudeness that distressed her, she replied, but "your intense and fervid self-depreciation." Don't apologize for yourself, she said, and "please consider me your friend in *every way*."[10]

Stefansson's school friends and even his professors often predicted that the young North Dakotan would accomplish great things. Understandably, however, their predictions lacked definition. Guessing the field of Stefansson's future endeavour was more difficult than simply agreeing that he possessed unusual talents that he would be likely to exploit successfully.

Stefansson himself was not sure what course he ought to pursue. Literature intrigued him more than politics and economics: possibly he would become a writer of some kind. Although he abandoned his early aspiration to be a poet, his efforts helped him develop a sinewy, forceful prose style. He also showed a marked aptitude for linguistics and probably could have become a distinguished professor had he chosen to be one. But, finally, his strong scientific inclination pushed him "towards sciences that have a direct bearing upon the phenomenon of life and society," he told his good friend Valdi Thorvaldson, then studying at the University of Manitoba. Still, he believed "that no science has more fascination than that of astronomy, and there the strongest mathematical intellect finds full scope," and he was attracted to physics because it had "a more direct bearing upon the necessities and luxuries of life, and while no less truly scientific, is more likely to bring a material reward."[11] Valdi's reply was shrewd: one should take a "bird's eye view of several sciences and let natural aptitude, more than pecuniary or other considerations determine your future course."[12]

Thorvaldson and Stefansson shared a contempt for materialism. They refused to measure success primarily in dollars and cents: "If your views were *such*, Valdi, we might do well to take a post-graduate course in a business college."[13] But if they rejected materialistic aims, they were practical. Often their friends were forced to drop out of university for want of money, and this angered Stefansson. He warned Valdi to stay in school. "As far as financial matters are concerned, we can both become Ph.D.'s in any college in America or Germany before we are thirty."[14] Even a college freshman could see that loans and scholarships existed in plenty for deserving students.

Agonizing over choice of vocation formed an essential part of his college experience, and discussing it contributed more to establishing a bond among his classmates than did sharing notes on geometry. Such esteem as Stefansson, the student, gained among his peers was no mean tribute. In his autobiography he joked about winning popularity at school by appearing to be lazy about studying, yet his friends often expressed their regard for his capacity to work.

And so the North Dakota years passed—happily, for the most part. Stefansson waited on tables, pulled stumps, harvested, sold correspondence courses, worked on the national census, and taught. Hard work caused him no anxiety, and it did not interfere with his studies, his wide reading in diverse fields, or with those extra-curricular activities he considered important, such as the Scandinavian society of which he was secretary.

Along with his recognized flair for poetry and his personal popularity, Stefansson gained a reputation as an outstanding debater, a hobby which was to influence his career directly within a few years. All these successes did not encourage humility or submissiveness, and his teachers at North Dakota were beginning to find him a pernicious influence. Although he did not join the late night drinking parties that some of his friends enjoyed, because of his shows of disrespect for the faculty, he worried the professors. His chief offence occurred in a German class in which he helped out some scholars who were more preoccupied with football than with their recitations. Among the students it seemed a good joke on a professor who was unaware that Stefansson was answering for others, but the faculty saw no humour in such mockery. Someone had to go, and it was not destined to be the absent-minded professor. Hence, while he was still a junior classman, and despite his excellent record, Stefansson was suspended by the university. His absence from classes to take on the job of a school principal who had become ill provided the official justification for his removal, but university officials privately informed him that the students were getting out of hand and that the faculty considered him to be a ringleader. His fellow students wanted to protest his case, but the ebulllient Stefansson felt that a mock funeral would be more fun. Friends conveyed him from the campus in a wheelbarrow to the accompaniment of solemn music and the simulated weeping of his black-clad "widow" and other mourners. Later the president assured him that he could return if he were willing to conform, but Stefansson decided against going back.

Stefansson worked for a time as a newspaper reporter and even ran, unsuccessfully and not too seriously, for the office of state superintendent of public instruction. But he wanted an academic degree, and he began to shop around for a school that had an accelerated program. He settled on the University of Iowa where he was allowed to move at his own pace, taking exams in individual subjects rather than by attending classes. He graduated from the University of Iowa in 1903, at the same time as his North Dakota class.

Stefansson's dismissal from the University of North Dakota might have had serious consequences for one less committed to study. The episode did not chasten him particularly; rather, it provided a chance to prove that a determined man could overcome obstacles set before him by people in authority, and, more than anything, his expulsion created in him a sense of independence. Nor did the experience embitter him towards the university. He later exchanged letters with the president and some members of faculty, and they, to their credit, wrote good letters of recommendation for him when he applied to graduate school. Years later, North Dakota became the third university to grant him an honorary degree, and Stefansson accepted the tribute with pride.

During his debates, Stefansson had attracted the attention of Unitarian churchmen in Winnipeg. They invited him to Winnipeg as a conference delegate and later asked him to attend a church conference in Boston. Since the Unitarians had gained members from among the Icelandic Lutherans of Manitoba and North Dakota, they hoped to woo men of Stefansson's calibre into the ministry. The western leaders were impressed with his performance in Boston and assured him of their assistance if he ever decided to enter the Unitarian ministry.

Stefansson remained bound to his friends of the University of North Dakota's class of 1903 by strong ties of affection. With Mary Brennan, Charles Hamel, Percy Crewe, Stefansson, and others of the 45-member freshman class who shared adventure—memories of spring mornings on the tennis courts, summer garden parties, chapel services, junior proms, and intense talks, always remained fresh as new grass in their minds. How they taked then, in wonder and hope of their ideals and aspirations, and how they settled all the lofty problems of religion and daily practicalities that so torment the young. College life was real life to these students, although their teachers seemed to treat them as "big children in a make-believe routine" from which they would some day graduate into reality. "We knew those days and ardent attachments to each other that made Ruth's story modern and real—'Thy people shall be my people, and whither thou goest, I will go,' " remembered Mary Brennan.[15]

Mary Brennan Clapp, later a poet and college English professor, was one member of the 1903 class who kept the bond secure among the North Dakota graduates over many decades. It helped Stefansson to have Mary to visit and to carry on a correspondence with. Her sensitivity was more acute than that of their other classmates, and her memory was prodigious. Over fifty years later she recalled her first day at college—smartly dressed in her high school commencement dress as were all the other girls—keen for new impressions. She remembered Stefansson vividly—tall and blond in a blue suit, blue tie, tan shoes, leaning against a wall, one hand in his pocket, the other "gesticulating effective punctuation to his conversation."[16]

There was no undisputed leader in that class. Mary was the best writer; Stef, sometimes called "Windjammer" by his friends, could not be surpassed in debate. "We were all too self-centered and opinionated to want a leader." Close friends like Mary missed him when he was away and were delighted with his presence, sensing the edge and lustre he brought to their group; he gave an "added vitality to friendly rivalry in scholarship; vividness to those great dreams we had of doing and being something in the future," she recalled in her memoir.[17]

By 1903, Mary knew Stefansson's character very well; she understood his gifts for friendship and fun and his way of thinking, as well as his determination to get a larger grasp of the ideas that his classwork and reading aroused, feverishly "trying to understand big things that some of us only vaguely sensed." He had his detractors even before the faculty expelled him—students who resented his quick replies in class and his easy victories over their hard-fought arguments: "Those who prophesied a dire end for bluffers called him 'Will-yell-more.' And over in Davis Hall when a girl could think of no expletive expressive enough, she resorted to Vilhjalmur!"[18]

After he graduated from Iowa, the Harvard Divinity School offered him a scholarship sponsored by the Unitarian church. Stefansson was not sure he had any interest in the ministry, and he accepted the scholarship only after asserting that he considered religion as folklore—that is, as a legitimate branch of anthropology—and that he would study it in this context. A liberal administration and his Unitarian patrons acceded to his view. During his first year at Harvard, Stefansson's genius attracted the attention of the Anthropology Department as well as that of the Peabody Museum director, and he was awarded a fellowship in anthropology. Although some Divinity faculty members influenced his thinking greatly, he knew, after a year's study, that he would be miscast in the ministry.

At Harvard Stefansson became intrigued by aspects of diet—an interest he was to retain all of his life. His mother told him that in her Icelandic village people had never heard of toothache nor of tooth decay. Their diet consisted of milk products, meat, and fish; they seldom ate cereals and bread. In the summer of 1904 Stefansson voyaged to Iceland with a grant to investigate the relationship between tooth decay and cereal-eating. His research supported his theory that cereals were detrimental to dental health, and in later years he would write more on the subject.

In 1905 Stefansson travelled to Iceland again for more field work, and the next fall Harvard appointed him a teaching fellow. He also found time to report for the *Boston Evening Transcript* and to write some scholarly articles on Icelandic literature and history. His first technical publication was quoted by the journalist, H. L. Mencken, in his study, *The American Language.*[19]

While he was at Harvard, the editor of the *North Dakota Student* asked Stefansson for an article on Harvard, and Stefansson complied. President Merrifield congratulated him on his graduation from the University of Iowa and provided him with a letter of recommendation to several graduate schools. Earlier he had suggested that Stefansson ought to try for an eastern university that was steeped in an atmosphere of age and tradition the young man would appreciate. The president could not resist warning his former student that eastern university instructors "will insist on regular and systematic work as the most punctilious of those at North Dakota, and you'll see the value."[20] Probably after Stefansson was accepted in graduate school Merrifield's advice about the need for regular and systematic work was unnecessary, because he was no longer in the awkward position of having to face a standard preparatory and college curriculum.

Stefansson did not immediately like Harvard as well as the University of Iowa, although he recognized Harvard's superiority as a university. He complained, as any western student might, of the attitude that prevailed at Harvard. "They are awfully conceited here...and know of no school but Yale, though some have heard it rumoured that there are others somewhere far away."[21]

More important to Stefansson was the high level of instruction offered at the Divinity School where certain teachers were to affect his future career more profoundly than those whom he had encountered earlier at North Dakota or Iowa or even later.

Dr. Samuel McChord Crothers, a Harvard University preacher, often expressed deep scepticism about the value of formal education, arguing that some institutions should exist for unlearning false doctrines taught at others. Crothers's thesis affected Stefansson's approach to established knowledge and encouraged his ingrained suspicion of accepted truths.

Another professor who influenced him was Ephraim Emerton, whose lectures on ecclesiastical history introduced Stefansson to conflicts produced by rigid dietary rules that prohibited eating the flesh of certain animals and alerted Stefansson to the general significance of food prejudices. Later he would learn that such prejudices could affect the organization and execution of expeditions, and sometimes create onerous limitations.

George Foot Moore also contributed to Stefansson's interest in diet by analysing the prevalent belief that "a man is what he eats." It was then that he understood why medical schools taught that eating meat made people fat; later he would appreciate why Eskimo murderers ate their victims' livers. Moore's liberal views on religion impressed his students. He professed to feel sorry for Robert G.

Ingersoll, the man so often condemned in Stefansson's youth for his attacks on Christian beliefs, on the ground that he was wasting energy trying to kill what was already dead. Stefansson marvelled that a professor of religious history could utter such profane remarks without provoking a storm of protest.

The fourth Divinity teacher to influence the young man was William Wallace Fenn, an effective interpreter of various philosophies. It was Fenn who originally urged Stefansson to become a Unitarian minister, arguing that the ministry would give him opportunities to do good for mankind. Fenn, more than anyone else, quieted Stefansson's doubts about Christianity by suggesting that the desire for reform ought to come from within, rather than be imposed from without. But as much as Stefansson admired Fenn, he found doctrinal disputes arid and meaningless, and he looked for approaches to wisdom and understanding less fraught with inherent contradictions. Stefansson admired the intellectual discipline employed by scientists, yet he preferred to study man directly and in broader terms than science offered or theology allowed. Anthropology did not have the prestige of biology, physics, and the other natural sciences, yet it seemed the only possible course of study for one of Stefansson's predilections.

In moving to anthropology Stefansson was stimulated by the department head, Frederic Ward Putnam, who doubled as director of the Peabody Museum. Putnam discovered that he had an unusual student who had not only read both Latin and Icelandic sources in order to determine the diet of early Icelanders, but who also could carry out field work directed to the same end. He encouraged Stefansson to remain with the department by appointing him a teaching fellow. Putnam's objections to the growing obsession in universities with graduate degrees delighted Stefansson, who was more than willing to study and teach without worrying about examinations and other degree prerequisites. It pleased Putnam to point out that renowned scholars such as George Lyman Kittredge, the Shakespeare critic, and William James, the philosopher, lacked graduate degrees, and he sneered at students who felt compelled to grind along until they earned such standing.

Stefansson suffered a great sorrow in 1904 when Valdi Thorvaldson died of a ruptured appendix. The loss of the talented young man grieved him particularly because he could have been saved had the ailment been diagnosed in time. A week after Thorvaldson's death Stefansson made the saddest journey of his young life when he accompanied Valdi's body to the Icelandic community on the west shore of Lake Winnipeg for burial.

While Stefansson was plugging along at Harvard in 1906, reading and teaching, a young Danish naval adventurer, Ejnar Mikkelsen, was suffering what he and other would-be explorers regarded as the most agonizing aspect of that hazardous occupation: fund-raising. He and his partner, American geologist Ernest de Koven Leffingwell, were veterans of the 1902-1904 Ziegler-Baldwin North Pole expedition, but they had gained no fortune. Usually impoverished, explorers have to hustle for patronage before they can embark on their expeditions, and great explorers have often given voice to their financial woes in heart-rending terms. Roald Amundsen insisted that no one except an explorer could appreciate the exquisite agony that fund-raising involved, and for all his justly deserved fame, the burden of constantly having to seek support almost ruined him. Hubert Wilkins said that he felt like a beggar or charlatan when obliged to make speeches to prospective donors.

On slight evidence, Mikkelsen had developed a theory that undiscovered lands still existed in the Arctic, north of Alaska, and he resolved to find them. However, money to finance an expedition had to be found first. His fellow Danes thought him an irresponsible fanatic or worse when he solicited contributions to the search: "The rich in fact were mostly so shocked at the stupidity of my going to them for a contribution towards an expedition to Alaska that they were almost bereft of speech."[22]

Furthermore, he had lost the patronage of Queen Alexandra by rashly telling a newsman that his ice travel plans would require the sacrifice of sled dogs. Alexandra's role as patroness of the Society for the Prevention of Cruelty to Animals created a conflict that worked against Mikkelsen's scheme.

Undeterred, Mikkelsen went to England, where the tradition of exploration flourished. President Clements Markham of the Royal Geographical Socierty assured him that he would eventually become accustomed to pleading for funds. He cautioned Mikkelsen not to be discouraged and reminded him that "it isn't for ourselves we do it, but for the cause."[23] This was good advice and Mikkelsen felt less like a beggar and more like a benefactor of mankind.

With the aid of the Royal Geographical Society and a few generous individuals, notably the father of his partner, Mikkelsen eventually pulled together a modest purse. he then moved on to New

York to solicit funds from American millionaires for what was now called the Anglo-American Polar Expedition. Alexander Graham Bell and President Theodore Roosevelt helped a little, along with other individuals and the American Geographical Society, but Mikkelsen's troubles were not over. When he priced ships on the Pacific Coast, he found his treasury was still inadequate. By this time, however, he had lost some of his youthful sensitivity, so he sent wires to all the wealthy patrons in America and England whom he had been unable to see previously. Amazingly, the philanthropist, John D. Rockefeller, who was not known to be a supporter of exploration, gave him $5,000, a sum that he called "an impudence reward," and which, fortunately, proved to be sufficient.

It was in this tradition of "shoe-string" funding of Arctic expeditions that Stefansson was to be introduced to the North. The circumstances by which he joined Mikkelsen and Leffingwell were entirely fortuitous, but they ended Stefansson's student life forever and launched him on his professional career.

CHAPTER 3

First Arctic Venture

ALTHOUGH the purpose of the expedition was geographical discovery, one backer insisted that a qualified ethnologist should accompany the group to study any natives who might be encountered in newly discovered land. They applied to Harvard, and Stefansson was recommended. His mentor Putnam advised him to travel to the Arctic overland in order to avoid a long, unproductive sea voyage on the expedition's schooner. Since the Anglo-American Polar Expedition could only fund one-half of Stefansson's land travel costs, Putnam secured money from the Peabody Museum and the University of Toronto to cover transportation expenses, stipulating that Stefansson was to study the Mackenzie River Indians as well as collect artifacts for the Peabody and Royal Ontario Museums.

Stefansson crossed Canada by rail, reaching Edmonton in April 1906. In the company of a Hudson's Bay Company trader and a Church of England missionary, he travelled in a horse-drawn wagon for two days to Athabaska Landing. From there a stern-wheel steamer conveyed the party north on the Athabaska River. After thirteen days the steamer reached Grand Rapids Island, 250 miles north of Edmonton, where the passengers were transferred to a river scow.

By this time Stefansson had encountered several aspects of the North that he disliked intensely: "One thing was the scourge of the mosquitoes, the awfulness of which no one who has not traveled toward the Arctic Circle could possibly imagine." He disliked the hot summer days as well. At Grand Rapids the temperature soared to 103°F in the shade. "The third disturbing element was our constant confrontation with the cruelty of the Indians and some of the white population to their dogs."[1] The Indians enjoyed decking their dogs in bells and fancy harnesses, but they beat them into cringing submission before setting out on a journey and refused to feed them in the summer when their hauling services were not required.

At Fort McMurray the travellers transferred to another sternwheeler which carried them downriver to Athabaska Lake and into the Slave River. They crossed Great Slave Lake on a steamer and entered the Mackenzie.

Downriver, where the Arctic Red River joins the Mackenzie, Stefansson saw his first Eskimos and was much more favourably impressed than he had been with the Indians whom he encountered earlier. He was aware of the adverse effects periodic famine had on the northern Indians and observed the consequences of their long period of contact with Hudson's Bay Company traders and other whites. "Along the Mackenzie there was a distinct, though polite, tendency among the Hudson's Bay Company servants to keep the Indian in his place," he remarked, "and this discrimination tended to show its effect in the demeanor of the forest natives."[2] He found that Eskimos, on the other hand, generally exhibited good spirits and worked willingly, while remaining gentle, untrammelled, and self-possessed. Although, the Eskimo people of the Mackenzie Delta had been trading with whites for years, most of them retained their independence because they still relied on traditional subsistence hunting.

The young ethnologist could not then have been aware how significant was the impression which he formed so swiftly. His journey to the Arctic had come about by chance, yet from his earliest contacts with the Eskimo people he was fascinated with their life. In years to come he lived among them at various times, observing their customs with diligence and appreciative understanding, and he was a renowned interpreter of their culture in his numerous books and periodicals. Many other whites have described the Eskimo before and after Stefansson's time, but no one's observations have been more widely read.

On 30 July 1906, Stefansson continued his journey and took passage from Fort McPherson in an Eskimo's whaleboat bound for Herschel Island near the Canada-United States boundary, where he expected to join Leffingwell and Mikkelsen. When steam auxiliary vessels were introduced in 1880, it became the custom for ships to winter over in the Arctic rather than return to San Francisco with an incomplete load. And at that time Herschel Island became an established whaling community.

In its heyday, the island—eight miles long and two to four miles wide—was a lively place, the only community in the western Arctic where whites gathered in any numbers. The island's importance to whalers was owing to a sandspit that jutted from its southwestern shore and provided a sheltered harbour where ships could lie in safety. The Beaufort Sea or, for that matter, the entire Arctic Ocean, did not offer many such havens.

At the time of Stefansson's visit, whaling was not the brisk pursuit it had been earlier when fleets of a hundred ships and more followed the retreating ice pack into Bering Strait and penetrated the Arctic. The San Francisco whaling fleet had decreased to eight steamers and two sailing ships. The market for oil had declined, and baleen was no longer in demand—by 1914 it was selling for only seventy-five cents a pound, a drop that effectively ended commercial whaling in the Arctic.

Stefansson described Herschel Island as "a little 'Sea Wolfey,' " a reference to the ruthless, marauding seamen depicted by Jack London in his novel, *The Sea Wolf*. Stefansson had been told yarns of unpunished murders and villainous skippers of "Hells Afloat." He accepted such chronicles with a grain of salt, knowing all the while that they held a grain of truth. But the seamen "are worse in their dealings with native women," Stefansson reflected in his diary: "Last winter Wona came to Whittaker [the missionary] complaining that her eleven-year-old daughter had been enticed out to a ship. Whittaker went out to find her screaming in the cabin with her pants, etc., off. Newth (captain of the *Jeannette*) said they were wet and took them off so she wouldn't catch cold. Newth's wives were usually from eleven to fifteen years old."[3]

A post had finally been established by a party of Royal North West Mounted Police who barged down the Mackenzie River to Herschel Island in 1903. By summer the Mounties, under Sgt. Edward F. Fitzgerald, were ready for whalers steaming into Herschel's harbour. The Mounties confiscated most of the liquor which the sailors carried ashore, and three truculent men were arrested and jailed. One whaler fired a revolver at Fitzgerald and missed—luckily, he was too drunk to shoot straight. A Mountie knocked out the steward of one ship when he refused him entry. After these early episodes, things had settled down.

In addition to manning the island and other arctic stations, the Mounties made a taxing patrol each winter. A party of police and interpreters mushed from Dawson to Fort McPherson, a post 475 miles distant above the delta of the Mackenzie River. These patrols took about a month to reach McPherson and another month for the return trip. Gruelling as these journeys were, they were important in convincing natives, traders, and trappers that they were subject to surveillance.

Stefansson's meeting with Roald Amundsen, then on his epic Northwest Passage voyage was a stimulating event. Amundsen must have enjoyed Stefansson's company because he gave him sleeping quarters on the little *Gjøa* before starting the final leg of his voyage on 11 August. Stefansson thought Amundsen and his seven-man crew, "a splendid set of men."[4]

On Herschel Island Stefansson met one character—the trader Christian "Charlie" Klengenberg, who lived up to the legend of Jack London's Sea Wolf. He arrived at Herschel with a small power schooner, the *Olga,* which he had stolen from another trader at Herschel. Klengenberg plundered a storehouse to provision the schooner and then sailed east to Victoria Island. Once ashore, the *Olga*'s crew made merry with hootch that they distilled from sugar and flour. The party got out of hand, and when the skipper began to berate his chief engineer, the seaman reached for his gun. But Klengenberg beat him to the draw and killed him.

On the return voyage to Herschel Island, three other crew members disappeared. Klengenberg reported the missing men to the Mounties, and to Stefansson, who had been asked to record the testimony. Klengenberg explained that one of his seamen had died of natural causes and two others had fallen through thin ice. The surviving crewmen corroborated his account of the deaths until Klengenberg secretly left the island in a whaleboat to forestall further inquiries. Then the seamen changed their stories.[5] The sailor who was said to have died of natural causes, they claimed, actually died in chains in the schooner's hold, and the two other missing men disappeared while walking on the sea ice with the captain. Interestingly enough, these men were the only witnesses of Klengenberg's fatal duel with the engineer.

The sailors excused giving false testimony earlier by saying that when the *Olga* had come in sight of Herschel Island, Klengenberg had called them on deck and said, "Boys, you know the penalty for killing five men is the same as for killing four. You know what has happened to the four of you who are not here today. The same thing will happen to the first man who tells on me, and maybe to the second and third."[6] This little speech encouraged the sailors to confirm their skipper's story, at least until he departed from Herschel. In 1907 Klengenberg was acquitted after a murder trial in San Francisco despite his men's testimony against him.[7]

Beyond the interest of their own history, Klengenberg and his crew played a momentous role in Stefansson's career when they reported having seen Eskimos with European features on Victoria Island. As one of the goals of his expedition, Stefansson intended to make a voyage to Victoria Island in order to observe its inhabitants, and Klengenberg's information enhanced the importance of making the trip.

Whaling men on Herschel Island discounted Klengenberg's story, but Stefansson talked to the Eskimo seamen aboard the *Olga*. The native sailors confirmed Klengenberg's information: "These strange people have knives and other implements of native copper, which of itself marked them off from the western Eskimos." According to Klengenberg, some of them had blond hair and blue eyes. The Eskimos on the *Olga* agreed "that several of the Victoria Islanders looked...as if they were white men in Eskimo clothing."[8]

Could such an unknown people actually exist? "The only suspicious thing about it," Stefansson thought, "was that it seemed too romantic to be true."[9] Yet, he reflected, if these Eskimos did exist, he might be the first trained white person to observe them. What a thrill for an anthropologist—and what an opportunity for scholarly recognition! Now, perhaps, his youthful dreams of becoming another Darwin would be closer to realization. After all, the first man to discover any significant natural phenomenon—whether planet, plant, or principle—would be sure to achieve celebrity.

Stefansson speculated as to whether the Victoria Island, or "Copper Eskimos" as they came to be called, were descended from the Norsemen who occupied Greenland in medieval times and subsequently disappeared. Theoretically, the possibility existed. Another polar mystery concerning people who had disappeared also required investigation: perhaps the survivors of Sir John Franklin's expedition had settled among these Eskimos. No wonder Stefansson found "all this was fascinating to ponder upon and made me watch all the more eagerly for the arrival of our schooner, the *Duchess of Bedford,*" which was yet to appear. He promised himself not to lose any sleep in his excitement over the news, but he said later, "the problem of the blond people never left my mind."[10]

Meanwhile, what should be done? Autumn brought the close of navigation in the Arctic, and still no news of the *Bedford* reached Herschel Island. Stefansson had no interest in remaining among the Mounties and whalers of Herschel, so he sailed east in a whaleboat with Alfred H. Harrison and a number of Eskimos. Harrison, a British would-be explorer, and Stefansson got along well. Originally, Harrison had planned to travel from the coast to Banks Island in search of undiscovered land. Since the Eskimos were reluctant to travel over sea ice and the white whaling men also believed such a route to be extremely dangerous, Harrison was unable to recruit companions and was compelled to abandon his plan. "Harrison...was fifteen years ahead of his time," Stefansson noted. "When he proposed to the whalers and the Cape Bathurst Eskimos that they should sell him an outfit and have some of them accompany him on this journey, they thought him crazy."[11]

The whaleboat party halted at Shingle Point, fifty miles east of Herschel Island, and Stefansson decided to stay with the Eskimos there. He had to remain within convenient distance of Herschel in case a message arrived from Leffingwell and Mikkelsen. Besides, he wanted to live with the Eskimos as a native. "You can never live in your own house as a neighbor to people of a strange race and expect to get an intimate view of their lives through visiting them no matter how frequently," he observed.[12] And certainly close contact with the natives was necessary if he hoped to master their language.

For Stefansson, taking up the study of the difficult Eskimo language was not simply a matter of expediency. The value of learning Eskimo had not been apparent to earlier arctic explorers, and few white men had made the effort. A common arctic trade jargon served well enough as basic communication for explorers and traders, and even the veteran polar explorer, Robert Peary, mistook the jargon for the natives' language. When he heard Eskimos speaking among themselves, he assumed that they had a "secret" tongue which they used when they did not wish to be understood by white men. Even among well-known ethnologists of the day, there were few who had mastered the language of the people whom they studied.

Stefansson, however, belonged to that happy breed of men who understood the importance of language as a means of providing access to foreign cultures. His discovery of the joys of language study was another offshoot of his youthful education. Reading sagas and eddas had awakened his consciousness to all that was beautiful, honourable, and heroic in human endeavour. Missing an opportunity to absorb himself in learning the Eskimo tongue would have been as unthinkable to Stefansson as neglecting the language of his youth, as many of his friends sharing his Icelandic heritage had done.

In his narrative, *Hunters of the Great North,* Stefansson described his experience in detail. Like most people he had certain food prejudices: he detested seafood, for instance, an aversion that presented an awkward circumstance at Shingle Point, which was located there because of its fishing industry. Eventually, after prolonged and stubborn resistance, Stefansson's stomach made the adjustment to a fish diet. His acculturation occurred all the more switfly because the Eskimos' stock of canned goods and flour had not been replenished by whalers that season.

As autumn wore on, Stefansson learned much from the Eskimos. He hunted seal and polar bear with them, and under their tutelage he became an expert dog-team driver. He observed the environment of the natives as well as every aspect of the world in the Arctic closely. Each item of Eskimo clothing, each piece of equipment they used, the shelters they inhabited—all attracted his meticulous attention. Not only did he record this data in his notebooks, but he also mastered their hunting techniques and learned how to use their tools.

In October 1906, Stefansson set out for Tuktoyaktuk, a coastal village one hundred miles east of Shingle Point because he had been given to understand that a family there lived entirely in the traditional manner. He stayed with an Eskimo named Ovayuak in a typical dwelling that was framed and supported by driftwood, then embanked and roofed with earth. Light entered through an opening in the roof covered with translucent strips of polar bear intestine, augmented by four seal oil lamps which also provided heat.

Over the stimulating weeks of winter Stefansson gradually discarded certain prejudices. When no salt was available, he discovered that he could enjoy fish without it. He also dispelled to his own satisfaction the idea that the absence of sun in the winter caused mental depression. "I began to realize that the Eskimos regarded this period as their vacation time," he recorded, adding that they enjoyed the greater leisure imposed by the darkness.[13]

The months passed easily. In March 1907 Stefansson heard that the *Duchess of Bedford* had wintered at Flaxman Island, to the west of Herschel. In April he sledded there along the coast, finding on arrival that Leffingwell and Mikkelsen were away on their sea ice exploration. The expedition physician, George Plummer Howe, and other members related the events of the previous year to him.

The voyage of the *Duchess of Bedford* to the Arctic had been eventful, and Stefansson must have been relieved that he had travelled overland. Leffingwell and Mikkelsen had many problems caused by crew members who were hired on the Pacific Coast. The leaders only understood when they reached Seward Peninsula in Alaska why the seamen had been willing to sign on for one or two years for a share in the ship in lieu of pay. Once there, four crew members stole ashore and made a dash for the goldfields of Nome, the site of a major new strike. This desertion would have finished the expedition but for the timely arrival of the U.S. Revenue Marine cutter *Thetis*. The ship's commander, Captain O.C. Hamlet, sent ten of his men in pursuit of the gold-crazed deserters and loaned four seamen to the *Bedford* to help get the ship north.

At Jabbertown, just east of Point Hope on the Chukchi sea coast, Mikkelsen and Leffingwell arranged a rendezvous with the *Thetis*.[14] Captain Hamlet took the erring *Bedford* crew into custody and held court aboard his ship. After recording their testimony, he ordered the seamen put ashore, a decision that seemed harsh to Mikkelsen, although there was little else Hamlet could do, knowing how dangerous it would be to go into the western Arctic with a mutinous crew. One of the seamen who did not care to cast his lot among the four hundred Eskimos of the Point Hope region asked if he could remain aboard the *Thetis*. This man was Storker Storkerson, "a brilliant seaman" according to Mikkelsen, and a man who was later to become Stefansson's dependable travelling companion.[15]

The *Bedford* continued her voyage east in the company of the *Thetis*. At Barrow the expedition landed for a visit with Charlie Brower, the veteran trader of the Alaskan Arctic. Captain Hamlet had more serious work to do, boarding whaling vessels that were anchored off Barrow to investigate reports that Eskimo girls and women were being held aboard. They discovered one skipper who had five girls in his cabin, the eldest of whom was only thirteen years of age.

Brower, for almost fifty years the genial host of Stefansson and other callers at Barrow, filled an important role in the Arctic.

Born in New York in 1863, he was a seaman for seven years before setting out for San Francisco at the age of twenty-one. At that time whalebone was fetching five dollars a pound, so Brower turned down a job offer from the local fire department and sailed north. His first job was digging coal at Cape Lisburne where, for a few years, there was commercial mining, chiefly for the Nome market. Most of the coal was taken by whalers and other ships which passed into the Chukchi Sea en route to the eastern Arctic. Large ore veins cropped out on the beach, one of which Brower measured and found to be fourteen feet; several others extended to nine feet.

A San Francisco whaling company hired Brower to help establish a shore whaling station at Point Barrow. There he married two Eskimo women—the second after the death of his first wife. He reared a large family, hunted whales, and ran a store. When Stefansson first met Brower in 1908, the village of Barrow had a population of four hundred Eskimos and a few whites, mostly whaling men, missionaries, and schoolteachers. The other white men communicated in the trade jargon that was understood by the Eskimos with whom they had frequent contact.

Ice stopped the *Bedford* near Flaxman Island, a small body of land about 150 miles west of the Canadian boundary, effectively ending the voyage. The crew removed the vessel's superstructure to build a hut on shore, and when the ice broke up the damaged schooner sank.

The loss of the *Bedford* was a setback to the search for undiscovered land in the Arctic Ocean. But Mikkelsen, Leffingwell, and Storkerson travelled safely with dogs one hundred miles out to sea on the ice. However, they did not discover any land north of Alaska, as Stefansson was to find later north of Canada's mainland. However, they did discover that the Arctic Ocean was not as shallow as was commonly believed—thirty miles offshore their two thousand-foot sounding wire no longer reached the sea floor.

After the ice party returned, the Anglo-American Polar Expedition was officially broken up. Mikkelsen went "Outside" by way of Nome, Fairbanks, and Valdez; Leffingwell decided to stay at Flaxman Island and do geological work, and Stefansson remained there as well until the following July. Leffingwell worked alone until 1914, mapping the arctic coast between Point Barrow and the Canadian border while conducting a geological investigation of the region. His analysis of what is now called permafrost (permanently frozen ground) was the first accurate report on this phenomenon ever published, and his report of oil seepages along the coast precipiated an oil "rush" to the North in 1921.

Leffingwell and Mikkelsen broke up their expedition reluctantly for lack of a ship and money. They could not persuade Storkerson to join them on a second sea exploration over the ice. Storkerson insisted that he would never travel again on sea ice, and Mikkelsen assumed that his refusal was the result of fear. More likely Storkerson preferred to have substantial payment for his services.

Mikkelsen asked Stefansson to remain another year in order to continue his explorations north of Alaska, while Leffingwell suggested that he stay to assist in a geological survey of the Endicott Mountains. "Had Leffingwell and Mikkelsen been able to agree on cooperating at either of these enterprises, I should doubtlessly have stayed with them," Stefansson wrote later, "but as one had his heart set on the mountains and the other on the sea ice I could not please one without displeasing the other, so I thought it better on the whole to sever my connections with this expedition and to try to organize one of my own the following year."[16]

Although he could as easily interest himself in sea ice exploration as in a geological survey, Stefansson's chief ambition was to continue his study of the Eskimo language. What he had already learned during his first year in the Arctic only whetted his appetite. Although nothing had gone according to his original plan and although he had been totally independent of the Anglo-American Polar Expedition until shortly before its termination, he found satisfaction in his accomplishments. Most important to him was the lure of reports of that little-known group of Eskimos. "My heart was neither in the mountains nor on the sea ice but rather in the mystery of the strange people with blond faces and copper weapons whom Klengenberg had reported from Victoria Island."[17]

During the summer Stefansson did some archaeological work on Jones Island near the Colville River Delta, eighty miles west of Flaxman Island, later catching passage on the whaler *Belvedere* for Herschel Island. From Herschel, Stefansson started south, forcing a swift pace to head off a misleading message to Leffingwell's and Mikkelsen's families. In the mistaken belief that the explorers had perished on their sea trip, someone sent the false news via ship. Stefansson travelled south on foot with two Indian packers to the Bell River, where he built a raft and floated downstream to the Porcupine River. Eventually, he reached a native camp where he persuaded an Indian to take him in his canoe to the Yukon River. At Fort Yukon he took the river steamer *Hanna* and sailed south to Eagle, but he did not arrive in time to intercept the erroneous report of disaster. However, he managed to save the mens' grieving families a further two months' mourning. Had Stefansson not gone to Eagle at that time, the news of the ice party's safe return could not have been telegraphed until the whalers could leave word at Nome on their return voyage to San Francisco.

The journey was similar to Roald Amundsen's trip the winter before when he telegraphed the news that he had successfully navigated the Northwest Passage. Stefansson would have enjoyed his trip more had he not been forced to hurry. Nevertheless, his pleasure in the North was growing all the time. He observed that "the wooded river, with vistas of mountains, snowless but bare, was calmly beautiful. Sometimes a moose would stand and look at me from a distance of only a boat length, but show no signs of fright."[18]

After completing his mission at Eagle, Stefansson caught a river steamer for the next leg of his journey, voyaging to Whitehorse, Yukon Territory, then over the White Pass and Yukon Railroad to Skagway, where he could take passage either to Seattle or Vancouver. Although he travelled in comfort, the trip seemed tedious because of his eagerness to get to New York and begin raising money for another expedition and also because he disliked having to depend on others for transport "after a year of almost no kind of transportation but my own feet."[19]

The idea of a new expedition grew on him as he thought about the Arctic and the popular conception of it. Why did people see the Arctic only as a battleground for the daring voyages of bold explorers, imprisoned by snow and ice, rather than as a unique and diverse region in which an ancient culture had evolved? It was as if there had been a conspiracy to depict the Arctic merely as a setting for the heroic exploits of a few intruding adventurers—a sort of arena in which imported talents and courage could be tested.

Such a limited conception of the North offended the student of ethnology. Surely, Stefansson reasoned, the importance of the Arctic lay in its people and resources, and attention should be directed to them rather than to exploration alone. Voyages of discovery were necessary, of course, yet to Stefansson they often resembled sport more than science. If a blank spot on a map were a disgrace to mankind, what about certain Eskimos' complete lack of knowledge of geography? Merely drawing a line on a map from any point to the North Pole did little to erase such ignorance. After the public sensation of a journey had died down, he reflected, perhaps it might be observed that man's *useful* knowledge really had not materially expanded. One need not be an explorer to contribute to knowledge; one should be able to interpret what is known for a greater audience. Stefansson decided that after he had educated himself further in arctic lore, eventually he might be able to shed some light on the essence of the North.

Once Stefansson reached the Yukon River, he neglected to keep his diary; the settled parts of Alaska and the Yukon were too civilized to capture his interest. He felt that he had served his apprenticeship, and he burned to go back to the North. It seemed to him that prospects for a successful career awaited him in the still uncrowded field of the Arctic. Best of all, aside from his ethnographic successes, he rejoiced in every aspect of his experience: the sled travel, the amicable Eskimos, and the atmosphere of the North. From this time on, Stefansson's course was clearly set.

CHAPTER 4

The Clash of Eskimo and White

IN NEW YORK Stefansson moved in the Judson Annex, an inexpensive Greenwich Village hotel. He enjoyed the bohemian atmosphere of the village and the occasional company of writers and show people. His circle included poets Olivia Dunbar and Ridgeley Torrence, who shared his admiration for William Vaughn Moody's poetry.

The American Geographical Society allowed Stefansson desk space, and there he wrote several popular articles on his northern journey for *Harper's* and contributed scholarly pieces to the society's *Bulletin*, the *American Anthropologist*, the *Journal of American Folklore*, and the *Summary Report of the Geological Survey of Canada*. Geographical society officers encouraged him to write articles as a means of enlisting interest in his forthcoming expedition to Victoria Island.

Stefansson wanted to leave for the Arctic in the spring of 1908, the American Museum of Natural History having agreed to back his journey. He originally planned to travel alone, but he changed his mind when Rudolph Martin Anderson, a friend and former classmate at Iowa State University, asked to go along. "This was a stroke of luck for the Musem and me," Stefansson recalled decades later in his autobiography. "Anderson was a Phi Beta Kappa, a Sigma Xi, an all-American athlete, a Ph.D. in ornithology, and the author of *The Birds of Iowa*. He was skilled in geology and botany as well as zoology, and had had considerable experience in field collection."[1] The expedition offered Anderson a fine opportunity to gain distinction in his own field, so the arrangement benefited everyone.

In May 1908 Stefansson and Anderson started out for the North, following the same route Stefansson had travelled two years earlier. From Winnipeg they journeyed to Edmonton and Athabaska Landing and then took, successively, a steamboat, scow, and whaleboat down the Mackenzie River, arriving at Fort McPherson in July.

Stefansson was astonished at the change in the delta and coastal Eskimos since he had first encountered them two years earlier. When they arrived, the Eskimos flocked to meet the sternwheeler because one of the passengers was a new missionary. Stefansson commented wryly, "Christianity and its exponents, which had aroused very little interest in 1906, now appeared to be the Eskimos' chief concern."[2] The Christian religion had spread rapidly through the influence of Eskimo converts, although few missionaries yet resided in the Arctic.

After a short stay at McPherson, Stefansson and Anderson voyaged with Eskimo companions down the Mackenzie River and west along the coast to Herschel Island. A storm kept the party at Shingle Point for several days, a delay that irritated Stefansson, who had hoped to reach Herschel to buy supplies and then push on east to Victoria Island. The weather cleared on Sunday but the Eskimos refused to travel. Breaking the Sabbath was proscribed by the missionaries, and Stefansson could not conceal his impatience.

It should be stressed here that for all its territorial vastness, the early twentieth-century Arctic could be a very small world for the traveller. There were few white men living there, but those who did dominated the Eskimos. It behooved Stefansson to get along well with the scattered traders, Mounties, and missionaries, and for the most part he succeeded. He wanted to be completely independent, yet this commendable aim was difficult to achieve. If a missionary or an influential trader were to criticize a traveller, there could be unpleasant repercussions. Society had stratified; the police and missionaries were in control and exerted a powerful influence over the natives.

Stefansson experienced delays because of his dependence on these Christian Eskimos and Mounties during the first stage of his journey. The delay at Shingle Point was not serious and ended when a good-natured Mountie drew the lightning of God's wrath away from the Eskimos by leading the Eskimo whaleboat convoy westwards on a Sunday evening. The second delay, however, set Stefansson's plans back many months, and all because of a trifling need for matches.

Mounties in the Arctic always felt a keen sense of responsibility for travellers, so when Stefansson and Anderson visited the police post on Herschel Island they were received by Inspector Fitzgerald with some concern. By that time Stefansson's party included nine Eskimos, all of whom were smokers, as was Rudolph Anderson. Stefansson asked Fitzgerald to either give or sell matches to him, but he was abruptly refused. In the Mountie's eyes the scientists were improvident and should not be in the North at all. Yet he assured Stefansson that if he would discharge his Eskimos, he would provide a hut for the white men next to the police quarters and keep them from starving. Stefansson's indignation raged; by this time he considered himself to be a veteran arctic hand and did not appreciate being talked down to or to being regarded as potentially destitute by a police officer. "It was in vain I explained to him that we had not come to the country for the purpose of spending the winter at Herschel Island."[3]

This was Stefansson's first dispute with someone else over his ability to live off the land. Such lack of confidence annoyed him whenever he encountered it, and it was at the heart of his subsequent quarrels with Anderson and others. Having lost in his dispute with the police over the matches, Stefansson had no choice but to journey west along the coast more than four hundred miles to Barrow to buy them from Charlie Brower. The few he had purchased at Herschel Island were insufficient because Anderson and the Eskimos smoked pipes and needed a huge supply to get through the winter. Stefansson marvelled that his expedition plans had to be altered radically just because Anderson was so dependent on tobacco. Whether or not he remonstrated with his companion is not known—but it is very likely.

Ironically, Fitzgerald lost his own life on a winter journey two years later while leading a patrol of four officers from Fort McPherson to Dawson. The Mounties liked to compete among themselves in demonstrating their travelling skills. In the hope of setting a time record, Fitzgerald had reduced his provisions to the minimum. When the patrol did not show up in Dawson on schedule, a search party combed their route. At several points they discovered gnawed dog bones, which indicated that the Mounties had killed their sled dogs for food. Eventually four bodies were found. Because of the incompetence of their guide and their limited provisions, the men had died of starvation.

Stefansson was stunned when he heard the news. He admired the courage of Fitzgerald and the two other Mounties whom he knew, yet he could not forget that "the last conversation I had had with Fitzgerald was one in which he told me his thorough disapprobation of my methods of travel."[4] The Mounties' starvation was the direct result of inadequate planning. Stefansson disapproved of their mode of travel because they carried all the food they thought they would need with them, without gathering more from the country in the event their stores became exhausted. In fairness, however, it should be noted that the interior did not provide as much game as the coastal region.

After their long trek was completed, Stefansson and Anderson decided to winter at Barrow with Brower, planning to go to Victoria Island the following spring.

In the course of their various excursions, Anderson and Stefansson were often separated. The two men got on well, although Anderson never came to share Stefansson's enthusiasm for living with the Eskimo people. Both explorers met all the white men who frequented the Arctic during that period: traders, whaling men, missionaries, and Mounted Police. Anderson spent much time with the trader Joe Bernard, whom he taught to preserve furs and other specimens. Some of the white men were singular characters. During the winter of 1909-10 Stefansson and Anderson spent some time on Great Bear Lake with John Hornby, an Englishman with whom they had voyaged the year before down the Mackenzie River from Fort Smith to Fort Norman. Hornby was something of a legend in the North, having lived most of his life in solitude in the country he loved, studying the animals and minerals. Many people thought him peculiar because he chose to live in the bush, although it was rumoured, somewhat inaccurately, that he had great wealth.

Over the winter Stefansson perfected his Eskimo with the help of Natkusiak, a Port Clarence, Alaska, Eskimo who commanded many dialects. Natkusiak later travelled with the explorer, earning from him the highest praise as the "best traveling companion...of any race."[5]

Stefansson deplored what he termed the "pernicious practice of building frame houses" that required expensive coal for heating. The Eskimo people tended to follow the fashion of white residents, and "active steps have been taken by various well-meaning persons to try to get the Eskimo to quit what the white men consider their 'native hovels.'" The U.S. Department of Education encouraged the natives to adopt the white style of housing, "presumably on the basis of their experience in the climate of Virginia and Maryland," he observed sardonically.[6]

A former teacher at Wainwright told Stefansson that Washington had instructed him to encourage the Eskimos to dig coal so that they might heat their houses and earn money to buy flour, rather than subsisting on seal and walrus meat. "It is hard for me personally," Stefansson commented acidly, "to get the point of view of a man who thinks that coal mining is a more desirable occupation than seal hunting. It is a safe bet that he himself has never either hunted seal or dug coal."[7]

The trend to impose the white man's lifestyle changed, however, "through the influence of Mr. Lopp and Mr. Evans, the present superintendent and assistant superintendent of the government schools of northern Alaska." These were experienced men, Stefansson said publicly, who realized "that the white-man style of frame house is one of the most serious evils which they have to fight."[8]

Stefansson was less optimistic in his diary: "The school situation on this coast is complicated by various things. Mr. Lopp is overears in his work, apparently, and has the best intentions, but looks upon the people as miserable wretches (of good natural qualities nevertheless) who need all *sorts* of help—which help seems to me to amount almost essentially to pauperication [*sic*]." At issue, as Stefansson saw it, was whether "people that have been independent for a thousand or so years are to be taught by all the subordinates of the department [of education] the essential superiority of white man's food, clothes, houses, etc. over the native variety."[9]

Stefansson disapproved of the influence of white men on the natives for other reasons. On one occasion, when one of his Eskimo companions refused to join a sled trip with him, Stefansson debated whether or not he would complain to the local missionary: "I am a little tired of his endless praying, face washing, and missionary-learnt insistence on his rights and their obligations to him without even a hint of his being supposed to render any return—a feature the missionary has apparently neglected." The change in the Eskimos he had known on his first expedition shocked him: "The whole people here are unrecognizable from what they were in 1906; this happens to be coincidental with their mass conversion."[10]

The opinion of the Eskimo people that Stefansson expressed not only at the time, but in later publications, was bound to rub the missionaries and their advocates the wrong way. Every white man who lives in the Arctic considers himself to be something of an expert on the Eskimo, so some took unkindly to Stefansson's then-controversial theories on proper housing and healthy diet.

The Rev. C. E. Whittaker, for example, established the first mission in 1895 at Fort McPherson. He worked among the Eskimo people for fifty years and wrote with satisfaction that he had observed an improvement in their diet during his stay in the Arctic. Whittaker observed that formerly "the Eskimo food supply consisted chiefly of one sort at a time, in each of several seasons. Fish only, seal only, caribou meat only, whale meat only." When white traders came to the Arctic, however, native eating habits changed dramatically, and Whittaker approved: "The fur trade has enabled them [the Eskimo] to procure a variety of food from world markets, to vary the local supplies; and cooking of all foods has almost altogether supplanted the raw fish or meat diet."[11]

Whittaker's assumption that the white man's varied diet must be superior to the Eskimo's traditional fare was typical. It reflected the bias of most white men, who did not like unfamiliar food such as seal meat, raw or cooked, and who were, in fact, somewhat contemptuous of native fare. Other observers were better informed, however, and realized that the new diet would have a detrimental effect on the natives. During the Alaska gold rush, missionaries and others warned Yukon Indians, who wanted to leave their village and resettle near a booming gold-mining community, that their health would suffer if their traditional diet were changed. It was obvious that town Indians had become sickly in just a few years because they were dependent on tinned foods, sugar, and flour.[12]

Stefansson fanatically defended the wisdom of the traditional diet. He observed that aboriginal people did not suffer from scurvy until they adopted the white man's diet and that "when natives ate European food it became evident promptly that no racial immunity was involved; for Eskimos who went along as guides on polar expeditions, or took employment with miners in Alaska, came down with scurvy like the whites, negroes, and South Sea Islanders who made up the rest of the parties."[13]

Stefansson first began studying the effects of the Eskimo diet among the Mackenzie River natives who formed Whittaker's congregation. "Some of them," he noted, "had been eating European foods in considerable amounts since 1889; toothache and tooth decay were appearing, but only in the mouths of those who affected the new foods secured from the Yankee whalers." The Eskimos told him that tooth decay was unknown in the youth of those who were now middle-aged. This evidence confirmed dental studies Stefansson had made in 1904 in Iceland. Those findings were later supported by scientists who studied skulls collected by Stefansson and Diamond Jenness. Altogether, Stefansson acquired one hundred skulls of Eskimos who had died before European food was introduced for the American Museum of Natural History, and he reported later in his book *Not By Bread Alone*: "These have been examined by many students, but no sign of tooth decay has yet been discovered."[14]

White men like Whittaker considered Stefansson to be a quack, but more recent specialists have recognized his pioneering scientific work. The renowned bacteriologist Dr. Rene Dubos commented in 1962 that "no one has been more perceptive, original, and constructive in establishing that the physiological study of the ways of life constitutes a legitimate field of anthropology and a very fruitful aspect of scientific medicine." Stefansson's critics like to accuse him of being a pseudo-scientist, a charge that leads one to wonder just what constitutes true scientific theory. Dubos praised Stefansson's studies of Eskimo adaptivity, which were based upon a precise application of the scientific method: "Through his gifts of observation and generalization he contributed new thoughts on subjects as varied as clothing, housing, nutritional regimen, or the causation of chronic diseases."[15]

Stefansson recorded his experiences living as a native in the account of his second sojourn in the North entitled *My Life with the Eskimo*. His training as an ethnologist and persistent study of the language sharpened his powers of observation, and although he was not the first white man to live with the Eskimo for a long time, no one else has ever interpreted their way of life with more enthusiasm and sympathetic understanding.

In his book Stefansson the ethnologist dismissed as false certain racial stereotypes attributed to the Eskimo. He argued that there is no truth to the belief that so-called primitive people have special mental aptitudes or instincts by which they can surpass white men in certain endeavours. Nor is the corollary accurate: that other mental qualities of natives render them in some respects inferior to whites. Stefansson argued that certain differences in *performance* between Eskimos and whites could be traced to environmental factors. "Of course an Eskimo can find his way about in the wilderness better than the city dweller or the sailor," reasoned Stefansson, "but he is likely to fall behind the white man of experience in just about the proportion you would expect from knowing the greater advantages of training in logical thinking which the white man has had."[16]

The key to Stefansson's mode of travel was his ability to adapt to Eskimo practices. He learned what to do when a blizzard caught him on the trail—a man had to keep his head. "The reason that so many white men freeze to death in the North is chiefly another one of their superstitions about cold which runs to this effect: that...you must keep moving continually, because if you stop and sit down, and especially if you go to sleep, you are sure to freeze to death."[17] The Eskimo practice is just the opposite—they halt until the blizzard stops. By resting they do not expend useless energy, and, most important, they do not perspire and freeze their clothing. Whites tend to walk until they are exhausted and, thus weakened, soon succumb to the cold.

Stefansson's success as an explorer, like that of Charles Francis Hall and John Rae, was owing to his ability and willingness to learn from the Eskimo. It was his conviction that hidebound observance of Royal Navy traditions had led to the loss of Franklin's men as well as to disasters on other expeditions. He experienced first-hand the conservative English attitude to exploration when he gave a lecture to the Royal Geographical Society in London. His praise of John Rae's adaptation to Eskimo methods of travel in the mid-nineteenth century met with a chilly response, for his audience did not look with favour on Rae's experiment in "going native." A gentleman would not adopt native habits. And, of course, Rae was a mere trader and not an officer of the Royal Navy.

Stefansson was at his iconoclastic best when discussing white attitudes to the Eskimo way of life. "Most travelers are a unit in characterizing the Eskimo's conditions of life as 'wretched,'" he observed. "What they really mean is that they suppose an Englishman would be wretched if he had to live as the Eskimo live."[18]

Stefansson knew that those who had actually lived with the Eskimo would not agree that their existence was "wretched." They also knew joy and comfort and had cultural amenities: music, dance, literature, and religion. Sometimes they suffered hard times, but is there any place in the world, he wondered, where this does not happen? Stefansson made a point of explaining an aspect of Eskimo life that was always noted with distaste—the uncleanliness of their dwellings and persons. Eskimos' huts, he said, smelled only because they stored food—usually seal flesh and oil—which were unfamiliar odours to most white travelers. When visitors become accustomed to the smell, they no longer think of Eskimo dwellings as being untidy, rank, and stuffy. As for cleanliness, he claimed that Eskimos enjoy bathing as much as anyone else when they are situated where it is available and convenient.

Stefansson conceded, however, that some Eskimo tastes would not be palatable to whites. For instance, "They roast their fish, stuck vertically near the fire on sticks run through their mouths, without removing the insides, which you merely leave in the dish when eating." He also observed that it was customary to allow dogs to lick plates after meals and for people to "dip their fingers deep into the seal oil and suck them with a smack."[19]

Other arctic veterans took exception to Stefansson's blithe dismissal of such cultural prejudices. Helmer Hanssen, a companion of Amundsen on the *Gjøa* voyage, disagreed with the explorer's assertion that Eskimo women would enjoy bathing ten times a day if they could. "That," he remarked tersely, "was not our experience."[20] According to Hanssen, the Eskimos would not wash at all, despite the urging of the Norwegians.

Such disputes, although they are tempests in teacups, nevertheless reveal differences in attitudes that are fundamental in determining relationships between cultures. Stefansson took delight in emphasizing the prejudices that white men had to overcome. What men like Hanssen and Amundsen could not understand was why Stefansson assumed the role of advocate for the Eskimo way of life. His motive was not just a pose, as his critics claimed, nor was it a means of ribbing those who were less capable of adaptation than he, but, rather, it was a plea for an end to ethnocentricity, for Stefansson believed that unless whites came to appreciate the Eskimo culture, they were not likely to take steps to preserve it. In fact, the degrading intrusions of white civilization into Eskimo life would be defended. Stefansson was one of a growing number of early anthropologists who were trying to break down cultural barriers, yet it was to be some time before more progressive attitudes were to prevail in governmental circles.

The practice among some Eskimos of exchanging wives aroused much interest in the South: "This is seldom more than one night at a time," Stefansson explained, "and seldom except upon the two families meeting after a protracted separation. After another separation this [ritual] may be repeated. This practice seems to be seldom indulged in except by close friends, partners, sort of blood brothers." Some Eskimo men had more than one wife: "O.'s two wives seem to get along well. The older is evidently boss, though she seldom uses her authority. Certain things, [such] as tea, she has in her charge and deals out to the other one. She seems as fond of the children as the mother is."[21]

Childbirth frequently seemed to come as a surprise to the natives, or so it seemed to him, judging by their rather casual preparation for the event: "Oaivuak's [Ovayuak's] daughter had child today, was planning to go East with father next Thursday, but now will stay until April. Sgt. F. [Fitzgerald] says that unless a birth is expected in a few hours the woman's abdomen is continually kneaded by other women. As today labour is seldom severe, the doctor said last spring half-whites were often born with difficulty." Childbirth often caused ruptures which were "due to the kneading of the abdomen."[23]

"'Modesty' in the exposure of the sex organs is said by Capt. L. [Louis Lane] to be far greater among men than women. In examining them for rupture, for instance, the women make no attempt to cover sexual organs, but the men almost always do."[23]

He went on to discuss the practice of infanticide, which missionaries and police were not yet able to stamp out. "Stein tells me of two cases last winter, a Point Barrow man and Nuntama wife; one Kogmollik woman who left her white husband. He has known of many other cases, usually girl babies."[24]

Stefansson knew that the Eskimo practice of infanticide horrified missionaries and most other white people, yet he understood the reasons for it. Unlike laymen, anthropologists consider the utility of the custom within native Eskimo life. Diamond Jenness, the famous anthropologist who had lived among the Eskimo for long periods of time, witnessed the abandonment of five girl babies during one winter he spent with the Copper Eskimo. Their crime may seem terrible, Jenness observed, but "they should not be condemned too hastily." All societies have devised some method of checking population growth, and infanticide, "the simplest of them all, was in past ages the most widely spread." Ancient Greeks and Romans condoned the practice, and even Christianity, with its emphasis on the value of the individual soul, still failed to eradicate the custom entirely, he said, "in civilized countries."[25]

Jenness emphasized the hard lot of the Eskimo mother, who received no medical care and no relief from her customary heavy work, either before or after giving birth. When her baby was born, and "until the child gained strength to walk alone she carried it everywhere on her back, from morning to night, except when a brief respite from work permitted her to lay it among the bed-skins." Even then she could not relax entirely: "The ravenous dogs would make short shrift of an infant left unguarded within the hut or tent."[26]

Feeding also posed a problem, for Eskimo larders contained neither cow's milk nor cereals. Babies could not eat fish or animal flesh, and so "for three years or even longer the mother furnished its nourishment from her own breast."[27] Jenness raised the obvious question: "Can we blame her if sometimes she shrank from the burden?" Often mothers had no choice: a woman could not raise twins nor children born within two years of each other. "Surely it was kinder," Jenness insisted, "to stifle the infant in its first hour of extra-uterine life, before it knew pain or hunger, or could awaken by its cries and smiles the tender love that as yet lay sleeping in the mother's heart!"[28] Of course, Christian theologians could not agree with Jenness, who had formed his own judgment from having observed the impact of unwanted births on Eskimo families.

Given the overwhelming stress of providing enough food for themselves, the Eskimo exhibited restraint and generosity in their social relationships. Stefansson marvelled at their honesty and natural concern: "People leave their household goods on a platform, or even on the ground, at any point where it is convenient to leave them. Although these articles are often of considerable importance and easily carried off, they are very seldom disturbed." Where food was concerned, however, it was different—visitors were expected to take food in case of hunger. "In the old days apparently no restitution was made, but in more recent times, since the Eskimo began to acquire ideas of private ownership from the whites, the custom is gradually growing up of making payment for food as it is taken from abandoned stores."[29]

Stefansson remained active during the winter, travelling after Christmas Day with medical missionary Dr. H.R. Marsh, southwest along the Alaskan coast to Wainwright. Neither the outgoing or return trips were difficult because of the scattering of Eskimo dwellings every twenty miles or so. Dr. Marsh was a well-educated man who tried to convince Eskimos that in certain circumstances, as in the whale hunting season, they could work on the Sabbath without violation of their Christian beliefs. Eskimos were suspicious of Marsh's liberalism in this and other respects and scandalized that the missionary, on Stefansson's misguided advice to show a good example, travelled on two Sundays. Later the Board of Home Missions dismissed Marsh, and the Barrow Eskimos accepted a more rigid replacement joyfully.

On 6 March Stefansson and Natkusiak set out to the east, hoping to meet Anderson who had spent the winter searching for a reportedly scientifically unknown variety of mountain sheep in the mountains south of Barter Island. After some days with the Colville River Eskimos, the travellers crossed the sea ice outside the delta, continuing east with sledge and dog team. Soon they reached Flaxman Island, and shortly beyond they met Anderson, who was returning to the coast with an impressive number of animal specimens.

In mid-April Stefansson, Storkersen, whom he encountered by chance, and an Eskimo family left Flaxman Island for Point Barrow and Cape Smythe, arriving after two weeks of hard work helping their dogs drag their sledges over soft snow. Stefansson was pleased to get mail on arrival, but there was also the bad news that a decline in whalebone prices meant that no ships would arrive from San Francisco. He had planned to board a ship for transport as far east as Cape Bathurst. Now he faced the arduous chore of hauling the gear and provisions he had stored at Barrow.

The imposing logistics of arctic travel explain why Stefansson became so zealous about living off the land—when possible. In order to haul his freight he needed plenty of dog food. Brower donated a whale recently killed on the coast, but even with the use of Dr. Marsh's dog team with his own it took five days to convey the meat to Brower's station. By 16 May he was ready to go. His gear included an Eskimo skin boat useful for river crossings.

Several weeks of hard travelling followed. Stefansson grumbled to himself about his lack of moral courage in not abandoning the flour and other store goods. Of course, he was not certain that enough game existed along Alaska's coast, where white hunters had depleted the animals in recent years. As it was later to turn out, the store provisions proved very useful.

On 30 May the travellers reached Cape Kellett, and within two weeks, as they moved on, the water and slush became too deep on the sea ice for further travel. They were still fifteen miles west of the western mouth of the Colville River, but they had to stop and wait for the break-up. Some days later they launched their umiak, paddling eastwards, skirting the inshore edge of the sea ice. In crossing the great Colville Delta they sometimes used arms of the river to aid their progress. Conditions were difficult until relief arrived with Eskimo boats from Barrow. The Eskimos took some of Stefansson's freight on to Flaxman Island. Stefansson arrived there on 5 August, and after meeting Captain C. T. Pedersen's schooner, the *Challenge*, he voyaged on to Herschel Island in comfort.

CHAPTER 5

Meeting a Stone Age People

IT WAS 18 AUGUST 1909 before Stefansson reached Herschel Island again, still determined to continue eastwards to Victoria Island accompanied by two Eskimos, Natkusiak and Pannigabluk. Anderson, who had been delayed to the west, had not arrived. The opportunity to make up for some lost time presented itself with the arrival of the *Karluk*. Its captain, Stephen Cottle, planned a whaling trip towards Banks Island and agreed to land Stefansson and his Eskimos on Cape Bathurst, a short distance southwest of Banks Island on the mainland. However, poor weather prevented the landing, so Stefansson transferred to the trading schooner, *Rosie H.*, at the Baillie Islands. Captain Fritz Wolki then took Stefansoon and his companions to Cape Parry where he had decided to winter. He established his base at Langton Bay, south of the Cape, and settled in to wait for Anderson and the other Eskimos of the expedition.

Since the caribou had already left the coast for the winter, Stefansson and Natkusiak made a hunting excursion to the Melville Mountains, three miles inland. Caribou were scarce, but Stefansson bagged a Barren Ground grizzly. On the hunt's second day the men killed seven caribou and found a better winter camp site in a ravine where a small thicket of trees provided a cheering relief to the monotonous, flat tundra.

Snow fell on 29 September to ease their travel movements to the new camp on the Horton River. Hunting was good in October and a considerable caribou meat cache was laid by.

Stefansson grew concerned over the delay of Anderson and his party in joining him and heeded the advice of the Eskimos. Their theory was that Anderson's men probably feared starvation in travelling eastwards beyond their usual range. The solution was for Stefansson to travel 150 miles to the Baillie Islands where local Eskimos could be told of plentiful caribou to the east. The word would reach Anderson's Eskimos who would then be willing to move on. Stefansson, as he realized later, made a serious mistake by travelling when he should have been hunting to store more food for winter. He did succeed in finding Anderson on the coast, but they then agreed on another separation because the large, combined party lacked tobacco and other necessities.

It was 23 November when Stefansson and Anderson and their Eskimo companions separated at the mouth of the Horton River. Each had about two days' supply of provisions, including 100 pounds of whale tongue. Finding the Bowhead whale had been fortuitous if not too appetizing. It was on the beach near the mouth of the Horton River where it had apparently died four years earlier. Three feet of snow covered the carcass, but tracks of Arctic foxes told the explorers where to dig. After a half day's work they uncovered the head and chopped meat from the tongue. While a freshly killed whale's tongue was fat, this one's consisted mainly of connective tissue. Their meat resembled chunks of felt, but it would sustain their always ravenous dogs for a time. Anderson, Natkusiak, and Pikaluk were to make a quick trip to Cape Parry for necessary stores, while Stefansson's party returned to the hunting camp. Anderson did not have to depend entirely on the food he carried as there was a meat cache at Langton Bay three days away.

Stefansson's party had to wait out a blizzard before leaving. The dogs refused to face the howling wind and snow, and in the two days' delay the party consumed much of their travel provisions. They started out on half rations, supplementing them with some boiled sealskins that had been intended for boots. In time they were down to the whale tongue which proved to be impregnated with sea salts and sickening to dogs and men. Their condition was not desperate because they had a whole sealskin bag of seal oil, but the oil was most satisfactory when taken with some bulk food. All they had to soak up the oil were tea leaves, ptarmigan feathers, and hairy caribou skin.

After ten days on the trail, the party reached the place where Stefansson had cached grizzly bear skins two months earlier. At that time he had laboured for hours to dig a hole in the frozen ground to preserve the specimens for scientific study; now the hungry travellers spent a day digging them out. They feasted on the bear heads and paws, a caribou ham, and five Canada jays that had also been cached. The next day they were back on an oil and skin diet, supplemented by snow shoe lashings and other fresh rawhide thongs. As the dogs were too weak for heavy hauling, the men had to help. Stefansson did not consider killing the dogs for food. They worked for men and were their best friends, sharing in good and ill fortunes. Finally, on 7 December the weary travellers staggered into camp where the Eskimo woman, Pannigabluk, was cooking over an open fire.

Stefansson's problems over provisioning went on. He had lost the lighter days for hunting. Winter days offered light enough for about three hours around noon—but only if there was no overcast. Stefansson's first hunting trips were unsuccessful. He returned to camp empty-handed with several Eskimos still suffering from the effects of the diet endured on their journey to camp from the Horton River mouth. On 22 December he recalled some dead-fall traps baited earlier with some blubber and recovered the bait still left. Other poor hunts followed and the camp's diet of lean caribou had left everyone sick except Stefansson—who felt none too vigorous himself. The experience did reinforce his theories about the pernicious effects of a lean meat diet. They had plenty of caribou and could gorge on it without satisfying their hunger. Diarrhoea afflicted the Eskimos severely. By 10 January the end of the lean caribou was in sight, and Stefansson was worried. He longed for Anderson's return. None of the Eskimos, even when healthy, were skilled enough for hunting under the unfavourable winter conditions. It did help when a visiting group of Eskimos arrived, carrying some nourishing seal oil.

The oil helped mend the camp people, so Stefansson, Palaiyah, and Tannaumirk started off for some distant caches of bear fat. At the first, thirty miles downstream, wolverines had beaten them to the food. They reached a second cache at Langton Bay a day later to find that a wolverine had gnawed its way through a two-inch pine plank, entered their storehouse, and eaten all but fifteen or twenty pounds of blubber. At least the well-fattened wolverine was still available to be killed and relished by the hungry men.

Anderson's long delay in returning from Cape Parry still worried Stefansson so he moved on there, arriving on 21 January. Anderson and Pikalik were convalescing from pneumonia—out of danger, but lacking fresh meat to supplement their store provisions. Stefansson remained with the sick men until they were fully recovered in March. Anderson then left for the Mackenzie Delta where mail and supplies from their sponsors were expected.

All in all it had been a tough winter, and Stefansson moved ten miles north of Langton Bay at Point Stevens for fishing. This was a renowned tomcod ground, and the party gathered a ton of fish in four days at the rate of forty per hour per man.

At a final conference before separating, Stefansson and Anderson considered prospects and accomplishments somewhat gloomily. They had experienced starvation, sickness, the reluctance of Eskimos to travel into unfamiliar regions, and the loss of many of their best dogs. After two years' work they had not yet reached the 300-mile stretch of coast to the east where they hoped to find Eskimos uncontaminated by civilization. Stefansson was sure that he could travel and survive anywhere that Eskimos did, although it was not known whether Eskimos lived between Cape Parry and Cape Krusenstern. Baillie Island Eskimos believed that the eastern coast was destitute of game, but Stefansson was determned to go on.

Finally, on 21 April 1910, accompanied by Natkusiak, Pannigabluk, and Tannaumirk, Stefansson began the journey east for Victoria Island and its strange Eskimos. "We were now two years out of New York," Stefansson complained, "and these mysterious people seemed as far away as ever. I knew that unless I took definite action they would remain far away." The hard winter taught him many lessons in the art of survival, and he had confidence in his ability to forage. So off the party went "with a sledgeload of two weeks' supplies and a brainload of theory about living off the land."[1] Because of the scarcity of game, Stefansson assumed that the coast between Cape Parry and his Coronation Gulf-Victoria Island destination was unpopulated.

As the party moved east, they managed to fare well on caribou and seal meat. They found traces of abandoned Eskimo dwellings, and then "we had a surprise that made me feel a little like Robinson Crusoe." At Point Wise, where the open sea begins to narrow into Dolphin and Union Strait, separating Victoria Island from the mainland, they discovered a piece of driftwood that "had been hacked at with a dull adz-like tool. This could only mean that men that were unknown to the western Eskimos, whalers, and explorers had been here looking for sledge-making material." Stefansson's Eskimos were alarmed. They had heard of "the People of the Caribou Antler," who captured their brides with a crook of horn, often killing them in the act, and who reputedly killed all strangers."[2] The next day, twenty days' travel from Cape Parry, they found a deserted village of over fifty snowhouses, the largest aggregation of such houses any of them had ever seen. A trail led from the dwellings across the ice of Dolphin and Union Strait.

Stefansson's excitement mounted as his long-sought goal seemed near. On 13 May the party followed the trail across the sea ice and came to another deserted village. Stefansson scrambled up on one of the snowhouses for a look and reported, "I could see, a long way off, a scattering of men sitting at seal holes, watching." The discovery aroused the travellers, and even their dogs sensed something alarming. Stefansson and his party hurried toward the distant men. "As we drew nearer, apparently unseen, we singled out one still figure and approached cautiously, Tannaumirk, fascinated though terrified, leading the way."[3]

The strange Eskimo jumped to his feet brandishing a long knife when he saw Stefansson and his men. After a few suspenseful moments, the seal hunter noticed the party's dogs and harnesses, which seemed to convince him that they were not evil spirits. Tannaumirk explained that they were unarmed, whereupon the seal hunter took him to meet the other villagers, while Stefansson and the other Eskimos stayed back, waiting until the alarm caused by their appearance was dispelled.

This remarkable discovery of a strange people reveals the isolation of the Arctic in the early years of this century. Needless to say, Stefansson and the strange Eskimos, when they overcame their fears, were intrigued by each other. The Eskimos asked a few questions; Stefansson, many more. "Their admirable reticence and good breeding made me feel more nearly ashamed of my calling than I had ever been before, for an ethnologist must make inquiries, and impertinent ones at times, but they answered with the greatest good humor."[4]

Few anthropologists had ever had an opportunity such as this encounter with the Copper Eskimo people provided Stefansson. Years later he would still look back to this meeting "with the warmest and most vivid of memories. It marked my introduction to men and women of a bygone age. Mark Twain's Connecticut Yankee went to sleep in the nineteenth century and woke up in King Arthur's time. I, without going to sleep at all, had walked out of the twentieth century into the intellectual and cultural world of men and women of an age far earlier than Arthur's."[5]

At first the Eskimos showed some apprehension at the sight of Stefansson and his companions, but after their fear subsided, their next impulse was to construct a snowhouse to house the visitors properly. While this was being done, the seal hunter who had been the first to see Stefansson insisted that the explorer share a meal in his dwelling. The man's wife asked Stefansson if she might dry his foot gear or mend his clothing. She boiled lean seal meat and wondered if he cared to eat the fat raw as they preferred it. "When I told her that my taste in seal meat coincided with theirs—as indeed it did—she was delighted."[6] Stefansson's preference convinced the Eskimos that people were much alike, even though they came from a long distance. Stefansson's command of their language also pleased them. The Eskimos had heard about a hostile forest-dwelling people to the south whose tongue was incomprehensible. Apparently, these were Barren Ground Indians who, in earlier times, had descended the Coppermine River to raid Eskimo villages.

Before eating, the Eskimos dispatched their child with a portion of seal meat for each of the four families in the village who had not been successful in the hunt. Other fortunate families also shared their kill so that there would be no hardship. Stefansson believed this communistic spirit was characteristic of a people who had known famine and who were essentially generous in spirit.

The Eskimos did have copper knives as reported, fashioned from local ore, and from this metal, the only one they had, their name was derived. They cooked and heated their dwellings with seal oil lamps. Unlike the western Eskimos, who lived in half-buried huts of sod and driftwood, the Copper Eskimos lived in tents during summer and in temporary snowhouses which they built as they moved about in the winter. Their hunting weapons consisted of bows and arrows and spears, and their dog sleds provided them with effective transport.

These Copper Eskimos had heard of white men and their eccentric behaviour—that they sometimes gave away valuable items for nothing and that at other times would demand exorbitant prices for useless articles. The white man's diet also puzzled them: "White people would not eat good, ordinary food, but subsisted on various things that a normal person could not think of forcing himself to swallow except in cases of starvation." This was strange because they could have better food if they wanted it: "seals, whales, fish, and even caribou abound in their country."[7]

After their first meal, the explorers were conducted to their snowhouse. Other villagers gathered inside to talk for a while. They were curious, but the natives did not press their questions. And since they were sensitive to the possible weariness of the travellers, they left soon. Stefansson and his Eskimo friends were too elated by their experiences to sleep. As he later recalled, "we sat up half the night discussing the strange things we had seen and heard." His companions were as excited as he was. "It was, they said, as if we were living through a story such as old people tell in the assembly house when the sun is away during the winter."[8]

The next morning the visitors were greeted once more by the Eskimos. It was the custom for callers to stand outside of the igloo singing loudly to announce their presence, identify themselves and their intention to enter, and to reassure the inhabitants that they were unarmed. Stefansson asked his callers if they did not find his blue-gray eyes and light brown beard unusual. They replied that "they are much like those of some of our neighbors of the north, whom you must visit." Naturally, Stefansson was eager to see the people Klengenberg had described earlier—the so-called blond Eskimos—and he set out the next day. But before he left, the Copper Eskimos built a large dance house out of blocks of snow, where they entertained the explorers with vivid dances, accompanied by drums—the only musical instruments they had. "Many of the dances," he recalled, "were performed without moving the feet at all, merely by swaying the body and gesticulating with the arms." Sometimes "the performer sang, recited, or uttered a series of exclamations. In others he was silent."[9]

Stefansson learned that the "blond" or Copper Eskimos of Victoria Island travelled to the mainland each fall to hunt seals. Their method of hunting differed from that of the natives of the Mackenzie Delta and Alaska, whose apprentice in hunting Stefansson had been. Copper Eskimos hunters stand with infinite patience over blowholes that seals use when they emerge to breathe, harpooning the mammals when they appear. The western arctic Eskimo moves on all fours across the ice to get within range of sleeping seals. Seals sleep only one half to two minutes at a stretch, then raise their heads to look around. As long as the hunter keeps still and looks like a seal, his quarry does not become alarmed.

After three days enjoying the hospitality of these Eskimos, Stefansson continued across Dolphin and Union Strait to Victoria Island. He reached another village where he found some unusual Eskimos. As had been related to him by Klengenberg and by the mainland Copper Eskimo, the people seemed to him to have definite white characteristics. "I knew I was standing face to face with an important scientific discovery. When I saw before me these men who looked like Europeans in spite of their garb of furs, I knew that I had come upon either the last chapter and solution of one of the historical tragedies of the past, or else that I had added a new mystery for the future to solve."[10] Why did these natives have European features? Could it be that they were descendents of the Viking colony that had been established in Greenland but had somehow disappeared in the Middle Ages?

Stefansson recorded his observations in his diary: "There are three men here whose beards are almost the color of mine, and who look like typical Scandinavians." His travelling companion, Natkusiak, also thought that these big men looked like the white men who manned whaling ships. The explorer noted in his diary: "I know over twenty half-bloods (in the Mackenzie district and Alaska), and none of them resemble a white man in particular—most of them could pass for Eskimo among either Eskimo or whites if no particular attention were drawn to them, but no one could fail to be struck by the European appearance of these people."[11]

Stefansson's description of these days shows his delight in the Copper Eskimo people. There was no question of the importance of his discovery, regardless of speculations as to their origin. The thought of returning outside to report his success does not seem to have crossed his mind, although general acclaim, and rewards in lecture fees and writing commissions could be anticipated. He could not entertain the notion of leaving the Arctic when the chance to study at leisure an intriguing Stone Age people presented itself. Furthermore, life in the Arctic attracted him far more than any other prospect. Each day offered challenges to his ingenuity. He bloomed with good health and enjoyed his hunting excursions and sled journeys. Stefansson was to remain there for more than another two years before he could bring himself to journey home.

By December 1910, Stefansson thought that his and Anderson's work of the previous six months compensated for the rather poor results of the first two years of the expedition. The following May, the American Museum of Natural History suggested that the men return to the south, leaving Stefansson uncertain as to whether further support would be forthcoming. He resolved to carry on, hoping that the museum would be satisfied when it received his reports on the Copper Eskimo. In his own mind their last months had been fruitful. They had studied a people who had had no previous contact with white men, becoming familiar with the dialect and their ways of living and thinking. Stefansson exulted, in a letter to a North Dakota friend, "This I believe to be the first time in North America" that an anthropologist had had such an opportunity. Furthermore, they had crossed "one of the largest unexplored areas in the Continental Western Hemisphere—from Dease River, [Great] Bear Lake to Cape Parry Peninsula," confirmed the nonexistence of two rivers, and traced four hundred miles of the Horton River.[12]

Stefansson warned his friend that if the museum withdrew help, he would appeal to friends for enough money to get back to New York, where he expected to earn money by writing articles for *Harpers,* giving previously arranged lectures at fifty dollars each, and lecturing two evenings a week for the New York Board of Education. Before he had left New York, the Board of Education had paid him ten dollars for each lecture, which he considered handsome remuneration because it only occupied him from seven to eleven in the evening. In January Stefansson added a postscript to the same letter announcing his departure for Coronation Gulf: "You see we don't let the midwinter worry us. That is all rot."[13] If one wore Eskimo-made clothing, the cold presented no problem, and they had not experienced temperatures nearly as low as the minus 55°F that had been registered near Stefansson's birthplace in Manitoba.

Stefansson thanked his correspondent for news about mutual friends, which interested him more, he said, than general information such as politics. He confessed that isolation affected his interest in all but the best of his old friends, yet a letter "wakes a memory almost dead—a blessed thing for there is too little sentiment in an existence such as mine." University news captured his interest, too. It galled him to see that he was not listed as an alumnus of the University of North Dakota. He was recorded by Harvard even though he had not received a degree there either. That North Dakota listed those earning a teaching certificate after only one year's residence added to his irritation. "I am sorry that is so, for the memories I value most center around the University. If I ever become prominent I shall value more than a degree from Oxford being reinstated on the rolls which include a half-dozen of my few friends—those of our little University."[14]

During his stay on Victoria Island, Stefansson planned his future movements. Anderson had remained at Langton Bay to carry on his zoological work, so Stefansson decided to explore the three-hundred miles over the unknown country between the Dease River and Anderson's camp. He then planned to return for the winter of 1910-11 to the forested region of the Dease River where caribou and fish were plentiful. Following this plan, he would be able to remain in close proximity to the Copper Eskimo without burdening them with the need to provide food for his party.

Stefansson and Natkusiak reached Langton Bay after a twenty-six day trek and there found Anderson and his party in good shape and well provided for, thanks to a whale that had drifted inshore near the camp. After a two-week rest, Anderson joined them on the return journey to the Dease River. This was a cold winter trip—the temperature hovering around 50° below zero—but otherwise the journey went well. They camped for the winter and kept busy hunting and stockpiling caribou meat in preparation for a spring trip across Coronation Gulf to visit other Eskimo villages.

Late in March, Anderson, Natkusiak, Tannaumirk, and Stefansson started out for Coronation Gulf. A nearly fatal incident disrupted this journey. The party had settled down one night in an abandoned snowhouse that was heated by a primus stove. Before they were aware of any peril, Tannaumirk and Anderson passed out. Natkusiak, who was also severely affected, staggered against the door and broke through the snow blocks to allow fresh air inside. Stefansson extinguished the primus stove, and the two men dragged themselves outside where the air revived them so they could haul Anderson and Tannaumirk to safety. "This narrow escape from carbon-monoxide poisoning, caused by civilized stupidity and civilized equipment, was the closest brush with death we had on that expedition," he observed, and he often referred to the incident when he lectured others on the superiority of Eskimo customs.[15] In this case, a seal oil lamp would have provided heat without the threat of asphyxiation.

When the party reached Coronation Gulf, they had the good luck to meet Joseph Bernard in his gasoline schooner, *Teddy Bear*. Bernard, a French Canadian, was one of the daring skippers of the Siberian and Alaskan arctic trade. In 1903 he and his uncle, Peter Bernard, quit mining in Nome and built a small schooner, the *Augusta*. Trade was not very brisk, perhaps because the men did not handle the rotgut whiskey favoured by Siberian and Chukchi Eskimos. Bernard found a means of supplementing his income, however, by robbing native burial sites of artifacts and peddling them to museums. This common white practice of grave robbery must have been resented by the natives, yet it never seemed to evoke violence.

In 1908 Bernard travelled to Seattle and commissioned a thirteen-ton schooner of his own, the *Teddy Bear,* which was launched at a Lake Washington shipyard. In his new ship, Bernard headed for the Alaskan arctic coast to gather more Eskimo artifacts and furs. The ship wintered on Barter Island in 1909-10. During his stay, Bernard visited Ernest Leffingwell's place on Flaxman Island and made a trip to Herschel Island for mail with another wide-ranging Alaskan traveller, the Rev. Hudson Stuck.

Bernard was also looking for Stefansson and Anderson while he was investigating the trading possibilities of Coronation Gulf. He took on Stefansson's heavy load of ethnological and other specimens for transshipment from the mouth of the Dease River to Great Bear Lake, Fort Norman, and, eventually, New York.

Stefansson left Anderson, Tannaumirk, and Pannigabluk at Coronation Gulf to collect zoological specimens while he and Natkusiak crossed the Wollaston Peninsula on Victoria Island to Prince Albert Sound. There they met more Copper Eskimos—the group described by Klengenberg in 1906. This tribe included more individuals with European features than any other they had yet seen.

Stefansson had originally planned to cross Prince of Wales Strait to Banks Island, study the Eskimos there, and then meet Bernard's *Teddy Bear* for the return voyage to Langton Bay, but when the Prince Albert Eskimos told him that Banks Island would be unoccupied that summer, he started south for Langton Bay directly, crossing a seventy-mile stretch of Amundsen Gulf and carrying a sledge laden with geological and ethnological specimens. Crossing this considerable distance safely increased Stefansson's confidence in his ability to cope with drifting ice, which seemed no more hazardous than jaywalking across Fifth Avenue in Manhattan.

During the summer months, he did archaeological work between Langton Bay and Cape Parry and was able to settle a controversy over whether the Eskimo used pottery by collecting a number of specimens of pottery utensils made by the natives. As usual, the iconoclastic Stefansson found pleasure in contradicting an established author, this time Dr. Franz Boas, who had contended that clay pottery was unknown to the Eskimo people. Boas was, he noted with satisfaction, "a somewhat intransigent theorist who was nevertheless the leading Eskimo authority of the day."[16]

During the winter of 1911-12 Stefansson hunted on the lower Horton River, improving his knowledge of Eskimo language and lore and "living entirely as the Eskimos did and, for my part, speaking Eskimo to all but one of the party."[17] He was unable to interest Anderson in the Eskimo language. Anderson's energies were directed to biology and zoology, and he saw no compelling reason to take up arduous language studies. For the sake of harmony it was probably just as well that the two men were often separated. No signs of a rift in this relationship had as yet emerged. On the contrary, they even discussed the prospect of making a new expedition together. Anderson would act as devil's advocate—the hard-to-convince potential funder—while Stefansson would rehearse a convincing justification of their proposed new venture.

By spring the partners agreed that they had accomplished their expedition goals. Having gathered a treasure trove of varied specimens for their museum sponsor, they decided it was high time to start for home. Anderson remained at Langton Bay to arrange shipment for their collections, while Stefansson and Natkusiak sledged for Barrow—a good nine hundred miles distant.

During his last weeks in the Arctic, Stefansson seriously considered his past work and future prospects. Writing in his diary in a depressed mood, Stefansson described his emotional state—a practice he usually did not indulge. His winter with the Copper Eskimos, though productive, left him vaguely unsatisfied, and although not as a rule given to self-pity, he depicted himself in his diary as a "dreamer thrown among the harshest realities of our earth, one who longs for sympathy but incapable of seeing the things he sees. To my unfortunate mind nothing seems worthwhile."[18]

As Stefansson then evaluated his work, his achievements did not seem to be overwhelming. What had he accomplished? he asked himself. Had he done enough to merit personal satisfaction, and, if so, would his work mean something to others as well? He cared deeply about both results. If he hoped to establish a successful career on the strength of the two terms of field work, his accomplishments must mean something to "the small circle of scientific men who are not always sympathetic or generous." And who, in fact, were "not even always scientific." How could he be sure "that the game would be considered worth even a small, cheap candle by those who knew of the game at all?"[19]

Stefansson knew what he wanted, and the goal was enough: "the interest shown by the giving of money [for exploration] and the lending of willing ears will keep me at work here twenty years," he decided. As long as support for his ethnological work and for geographical exploration was forthcoming, he would be satisfied to continue in the field. It would not even cost much because he could provide food for himself and his companions by hunting. Perhaps to clarify his thoughts, he summed up his position: "I have the education that colleges and books give, I have the education that experiences give, I know the land and I am learning the language of the people—and that learning is my work, together with telling what I have learned."[20]

Stefansson knew that telling what he had learned was important. He could foresee that his abilities as writer and lecturer would enable him to interpret the Arctic more effectively than other, less articulate explorers. And, unlike many others, he knew he did not need to depend upon a particular feat to capture public interest; rather, his strength and appeal would lie in the range and depth of his knowledge. In this way he differed from Peary and other explorers whose main contribution was to satisfy the public's craving for adventure and excitement. Not that he scorned Peary, but he knew that he could not find satisfaction in the goals that motivated most explorers. "Peary," he remarked, "was a 'man of one idea' and the best thing about him was that it always seemed to me that he was satisfied with that idea. If he [Peary] got to the Pole he would have something worthwhile—he could say to himself (as the world would say to him): 'You have a right to be satisfied'...and he would answer truthfully, 'I am satisfied.' "[21]

Thus Stefansson predicted his future course. With a little backing, such as he had so far enjoyed from scientific societies and museums, he could work in the Arctic for twenty years more—with interruptions from time to time to write about the land and its people. He intended to pursue writing in order to support his "play time," those periods between expeditions when he could "be with men who are not asleep." When he was in the field, he desperately hungered for other men's ideas. He confided his need to his diary: "Wherever, in Europe or America, there are men shaping the thought of our time, there I want to be (if they will tolerate me for the share I am trying to do) to spend my play hours with them."[22]

Some weeks later, in another diary entry, he returned to the theme of his "play time": "After the tent on the silent barrens I want Broadway by archlight and the Strand at five o'clock; after igloo I want the Century Club and the Criterion." Impatient now with monologues by the Eskimo on the wisdom of their forefathers, he demanded more: "I want scientific conventions where we learn things." As returning sailors must indulge in a glorious drunk, Stefansson needed "an intellectual orgy...till my next journey...calls me to the stagnant country where precedent is king."[23]

However, before he could enjoy such diversions, more work beckoned. Stefansson delayed his departure another two months to do archaeological work near Barrow before going on to Nome, and it was 13 August before he finally sailed for the Seward Peninsula gold town on the historic revenue cutter, *Bear*. After spending time in Nome visiting the Lomen family and other friends, he boarded a steamer for Seattle. Conversations with the Lomens and others cheered him and helped him see his field work and future in clearer perspective. Yet he was heading unawares towards a storm in Seattle, a controversy that was to become "the somewhat questionable beginning of a new phase of my career."[24]

Men do not necessarily achieve a public reputation simply by venturing into the Arctic, whatever their purpose may be. Two of Stefansson's contemporaries illustrate this point: Evelyn Baldwin only became known because of the ballyhoo created in the press prior to his attempt on the North Pole. His expedition seemed to be newsworthy because of the munificent financing that was provided by William Ziegler. It was evident that someone would soon reach the Pole, and because all the physical means were given to Baldwin, he seemed to have an excellent chance. Off he went, trumpeting to the world that he would be satisfied with nothing less than the Pole, but he failed. His patron removed him from command of the expedition and he quickly slipped into obscurity, denied even the glare of public scandal.

Baldwin's replacement, Anthony Fiala, similarly flirted with fame by taking over Ziegler's enterprise for a second attempt on the Pole, but he was just as unsuccessful. Fiala returned to New York and settled into a mundane job as proprietor of a sporting goods and field provisioning shop.

Stefansson had little in common with such adventurers, and he was on his way to lasting fame and notoriety.

CHAPTER 6

The Sensationalism of the "Blond Eskimo"

STEFANSSON met a number of friends in Seattle and enjoyed exchanging his experiences with other northern enthusiasts. Because Seattle dominated trade with Alaska, the city included a sizeable colony of Alaskan business people, retired sourdoughs, and others who maintained a lively interest in northern matters.

Newsmen usually met the ships from Alaska in order to interview any interesting passengers. Stefansson's travels in a little-known part of the Arctic caught the attention of John J. Underwood, formerly an Alaskan newspaper man, who was a reporter for the *Seattle Times*. Underwood interviewed the ethnologist and then used what he later described as "his ingenuity and imagination" to enhance Stefansson's account of his study of the Copper Eskimo. To his surprise, "I woke up the next morning to find myself famous, or rather, notorious," Stefansson recalled.[1] It was not that he objected to the publicity in itself. Indeed, it was encouraging to gain attention, which was by no means inevitable—ethnological discoveries seldom make news. The trouble was that Underwood's story made Stefansson look ridiculous by attributing to him assertions of fact that the evidence did not support. The *Seattle Times* reported:

Ranking next in importance from an ethnological standpoint to the discovery of the lost tribes of Israel is the discovery made by Prof. Vilhjalmur Stefansson of the American Museum of Natural History of a lost tribe of 1,000 white people, who are believed to be direct descendants from the followers of Leif Eriksson who came to Greenland from Iceland about the year 1000 and a few years later discovered the north coast of America....

The tribe of white people, which Stefansson declares are purely of Norwegian origin, never had seen other persons of their own color. Their number is about 1,000, and more than half of them have rusty-red hair, blue eyes, fair skins and two-colored eyebrows and beards. They live on both shores of Coronation Gulf, on the mainland of North America and Victoria Island, which formerly was known as Prince Edward Island.

It was for these people that Roald Amundsen, discoverer of the South Pole, searched while making his celebrated trip through the Northwest Passage. Amundsen, it will be remembered, stated that natives had told him of a race of white people living to the northward, but he was unable to find them. Amundsen sent an expedition along the shore of the island, but saw nothing of the tribe, nor did they see anything of him....

Professor Stefansson accounts for their existence by the fact that in the year 982, Greenland was discovered and settled by 5,000 Icelandic Norsemen. One thousand of these people sailed from Norway and missed Greenland but landed on the coast of New-foundland, where they established a colony, built fourteen churches, two monasteries, a nunnery and other structures, the ruins of which are still in existence....

The Norsemen settled in two colonies, one on the north and one on the south side of Newfoundland. In the fourteenth century Es-kimos came from the North and exterminated the people at the northern settlement.

Their record was complete till 1418, when the black plague scourged Europe, and for two centuries communication between Newfoundland and the old country was cut off. When communica-tion was restored, the people of the second settlement were missing. Their graveyards, buildings, and other adjuncts of their semi-civili-ation were found, and the theory was formed that the people had drifted to a settlement further to the west, across the narrow straits that divided them from the Arctic archipelago, where they inter-mingled with Eskimos, whom they took along with them to the islands on which their descendants now live.[2]

The story, Stefansson recalled, raised a chorus of ridicule "from Seattle readers who reprimanded me by telephone, and from foreign authorities who cabled their views through the news services." Stefansson insisted that all he had told Underwood and others aboard the ship "was merely that I had found Eskimos in and about Victoria Island, some of whom were in physiognomy and coloring quite unlike other Eskimos," and who still had never seen white men and manufactured articles.[3]

This controversy was important because the sensationalism surrounding the "blond Eskimo" story came to epitomize for Stefansson's critics all that they found vulgar and false in him. Stefansson insisted all his life that the exaggerations had originated with the press, but his enemies were never convinced that he had not deliberately provided a juicy item as a springboard to fame and fortune.

The first mention in the *New York Times* of Stefansson's encounter with the Stone Age Eskimos of Victoria Island appeared on 10 September 1912. The story had been wired from Seattle just after he arrived from Nome. According to the *Times,* Stefansson told Seattle newsmen that he had found a group of primitive Eskimos, some of whom had not had previous contact with whites. As Stefansson described them: "They were taller than the Greenland Eskimos, but not as tall as the Alaskan Eskimos. They spoke Eskimo, though I thought I detected some Norse words."[4] Obviously, Stefansson's remarks were intended to provoke interest in the controversy. Although he had refrained from making positive assertions respecting the origin of the Copper Eskimos, his remarks were quoted not as speculations but as fact.

On the following day the *Times* published a story datelined from Washington, D.C., carrying the headline, "New Race Solves Mystery of Ages." According to this story, "the discovery of the Eskimo descendants of the lost Scandinavian colonists of Greenland who disappeared before Columbus discovered America, is regarded by government scientists here as very important."[5] A photograph of the Copper Eskimos, taken by Stefansson, accompanied the article. Washington's press interviewed a "Dr. Walter Hough of the National Museum," who cautiously responded that he would await Stefansson's data with keen interest, adding that proof of the reported discovery would confirm the theories of some ethnologists regarding early Viking colonists.

Another item in the same issue of the *Times* reported an interview with Henry E. Rood, "former editor of *Harper's,*" who had worked with Stefansson prior to departure for the Arctic. Confronted with reports of the Stone Age Eskimos, and presumably the lost Vikings as well, Rood replied confidently that "if Stefansson says he has proof I'll believe him and so will anyone else who knows him."[6] Rood insisted that Stefansson was incapable of exaggeration.

The issue flared up on the following day, 12 September, when the European press began to check Stefansson's alleged discoveries with various ethnologists. The *New York Times* headlined its story: "Discredit Story of White Eskimos. Authorities in Europe Think Prof. Stefansson's Reported Discovery is Improbable. The Races Were Mixed." A correspondent in Christiana, Norway, interviewed a "Dr. Skattum, the ethnologist," who called for verification of Stefansson's claims. Skattum doubted the news report and informed the press that "Prof. Stefansson has not hitherto been regarded as an authority."[7]

The following day the *Times* published an article which endeavoured to set the record of Stefansson's statements straight. "Although the world was thrilled this week" with the excitement of the discovery of the Stone Age Eskimo and "possible descendants of Leif Eriksson's colonists," the article claimed that Stefansson had written about the Copper Eskimos more than a year earlier to Henry E. Rood. In this letter Stefansson described his long land trip to the Copper Eskimo country and his contact with Eskimos who had the "general appearance of north Europeans." Stefansson said that conjectures concerning the Eskimos' origins must be regarded as highly tentative. "It is possible (it is far too early to say 'probable')," he wrote Rood, "that we may have the beginning of the solution of one of the Arctic mysteries of large groups of white men."[8] This letter, under Stefansson's byline and accompanied by illustrations, was printed in full on 15 September in the Sunday edition of the *Times*.

The later *Times* stories, however, seemed to dispel the furore over the "Viking colony" story. Certainly it had not taken long to clarify the distorted reports from Seattle which repudiated the more sensational elements of his discovery. Stefansson's article managed to calm the storm—at least insofar as the *Times* was concerned. The *New York Sun* commissioned Stefansson to write a rebuttal of the sensational aspects of the story, and this account was published on 15 September.

Nevertheless, clarification of what Stefansson later described in his autobiography as "a hodgepodge of facts, half-truths, non-malicious fiction, and sheer nonsense" did not alleviate the damage that had been done to his reputation. He remarked ruefully that "the debate to which the telegram [to the *Sun*] was my first contribution is still continuing in 1961, unresolved after forty-nine years. The facts, as stated in this book [*Discovery*] speak for themselves and should have done so in 1912."[9]

During the uproar, Stefansson looked over his diary entries for "comfort...when European cables and American telegraphs clamored 'fake' so loudly that at times I almost doubted I had seen what I had seen." With some asperity he remarked, "there was scientific weight and reverent age behind the names of many of those who argued conclusively on the basis of a judicious confirmation of what they knew and did not know, to the conclusion that what is could not be." So convincing were the arguments of his critics, "that I who came from the place they theorized about felt...[like] an undergraduate in college when I listened to a philosophical demonstration of the non-existence of the matter, that I had to kick to convince myself that what must be wasn't so."[10] Stefansson's diary confirms that he had described the Copper Eskimos accurately and that his conjectures about their origin had been speculation only.

One unfortunate consequence of any exaggerated news report is its "snowballing" effect. For example, when in 1915 a reporter asked veteran skipper Joe Bernard to comment on the Blond Eskimo story, Bernard insisted that there was "no tribe of white Eskimos," but conceded that there might occasionally be an albino.[11] Bernard assumed that Stefansson had lied about the prevalence of white characteristics among these Eskimos, and he was indignant. Although Stefansson's book on the expedition had been published two years earlier in 1913, it was not able to dispel the false impression in the minds of men like Bernard. Setting the record straight probably would not have mattered to Bernard in an event, for by this time he had other reasons for disliking Stefansson, specifically, his friendship with Rudolph Anderson.

In *My Life with the Eskimo* Stefansson summarized his impressions after a year among these people: "Of something less than a thousand persons, ten or more have blue eyes," some had light-brown beards and rusty-red hair, "and perhaps half the entire population have eyebrows ranging from a dark brown to a light brown or nearly white. A few have curly hair." Stefansson then reviewed Viking history briefly and concluded that while "that is no reason for insisting now or ever that the 'Blond Eskimo' of Victoria Island are descended from the Scandinavian colonists of Greenland, looking at it historically or geographically there is no reason why they might not be."[12] Anthropologists, however, have generally rejected the Viking theory.

Some newspaper stories like the first embroidered the Copper Eskimo report by crediting Stefansson with the discovery of the lost tribes of Israel, but more responsible journals decried such fantastic claims. A British magazine entitled *This Week* protested that Stefansson's "serious work" on the blond Eskimo was being treated ridiculously by the press.[13]

Comments made during the uproar over the 'blond Eskimo' also embroiled Stefansson in another controversy over what seemed to be anti-missionary remarks. He had publicly questioned the wisdom of sending missionaries among the Eskimos, observing that "the coming of missionaries meant charity, and charity means the pauperization of the natives." In response, many good Christians, entirely missing his point, damned his wickedness in failing to understand the urgent necessity of spreading the Word. An editor of the *Detroit Free Press* tried to put the dispute into perspective for his readers:

Stefansson's opposition to the missionaries is not opposition to religion, though it must be confessed he does not show himself enthusiastic over the spread of Christian faith. But he maintains that missionaries would steadily wean the...Eskimo from the habits in which they have hitherto lived happily.

This was not the usual argument of those who warn of the dangers of civilization to natives, the article continued: "It is more usual to hold up the explorer, the merchant, and the adventurer as the germ cancer, and the missionary as the physical as well as the spiritual savior. And Stefansson did agree that missionaries provided a protective buffer between traders, whalers, and the Eskimo people. The Detroit newspaper tried to explain why Stefansson was critical of missionary activities and appealed for understanding of his warnings: "In the past, missionaries in many places have too much insisted upon changes in harmless customs. In preaching Christianity, they have often preached the necessity for adopting their national or family ideas of comfort and housing.[14]

Thus, Stefansson's hope that a newspaper publicity campaign might bring about some positive action to protect the Copper Eskimos from white intrusion was doomed to be misunderstood. The Boston *Transcript* barked: "This is one of the most extraordinary paradoxical propositions which could be advanced—this idea of using perhaps the most highly articulated machine of civilization, the press, to prevent the spread of civilization." How dare Stefansson question the values of our Christian culture? the article continued. He seems to be saying, "savagery is health and vigor; civilization, with all its blessings, means decay." And this, "coming from a former student in the Harvard Divinity School...is indeed astonishing."[15]

The editor thought Stefansson's proposition sounded "like one of Bernard Shaw's libels on society." In warning of the perils of commercial exploitation, Stefansson "has evidently shut his vision to the idea that commerce is the great binding tie between nations, and that organized religion, following the flag in the broad wake of commerce, cements the bond and is supposed to make it endurable and good as between man and man."[16] Such huffing and puffing amused the explorer, yet the paper's stance made him see even more clearly the impending doom of the Copper Eskimo.

Stefansson usually got a good press, but annoying righteous Christians in the United States and Canada did not do him any good. As the Boston editor quoted above trumpeted, "Doubtless when Dr. Stefansson has accustomed himself a little more to our civilized ways of living he will withdraw his propaganda, whose missionary object is to leave in heathen blindness the latest group of human beings discovered."[17]

Thanks to the Blond Eskimo Stefansson became a celebrity. He was now confident of his travel methods, hunting prowess, linguistic ability, and his theories of diet. His sponsors acknowledged the value of his ethnographic findings and evidently were not influenced by the sensationalism that had erupted in the press. After Clark Wissler edited his field notes for publication, the American Museum elected him an honorary fellow for contributions to the sciences of geography and ethnology. Only seven other men received such recognition. The American Geographical Society elected him to membership for his contributions to the literature of geography, and he received a similar citation from the Philadelphia Geographical Society. His future looked promising indeed. Two expeditions had only increased Stefansson's passion for the North and he was determined to return.

CHAPTER 7

The Canadian Arctic Expedition: Seeds of Dissension

THE ARCTIC held a firm grip on Stefansson, and he longed to return. Calculating that he could make it back to Bering Strait before the freeze-up, he had only eight months to find sponsorship for a new expedition, gather personnel, equipment, and provisions, and complete a few outstanding tasks (such as preparing his anthropological report on the complete Stefansson-Anderson expedition). He planned to write several magazine articles as well and a book for Macmillan on their first expedition. He was able to accomplish all these tasks with the help of Rudolph Anderson, who looked after expedition preparations while Stefansson went to England to solicit the patronage of Lord Strathcona (Canada's high commissioner in Britain) and recruit staff. Strathcona, formerly head of the Hudson's Bay Company, gave Stefansson substantial assistance that included a gift of a thousand pounds to cover incidental expenses.

Stefansson had originally sought the sponsorship of the American Museum of Natural History and the National Geographic Society, and while these institutions favoured backing his expedition, their contributions could not cover the purchase price of the ship required, so Stefansson was obliged to keep looking. He found his remedy in the Canadian government, which agreed to pay for the entire expedition. It was to prove a lavish commitment. Canadian officials felt it was time to undertake a comprehensive study of the central arctic coast that would embrace the topography, geology, zoology, botany, oceanography, and ethnography of the region and include exploring for as yet undiscovered territory. The idea of a major scientific expedition was a bold proposal, and Stefansson went along with it, but as time wore on he was to have reason to rue this expansion of his plans. He was, as Richard S. Finnie has pointed out, "really a lone wolf explorer...at his best when travelling by himself or with a few congenial followers." In his new venture, "he [was] heading a group of fifteen scientists on an expedition in which more than seventy persons, including Eskimos, took direct part, and entailing the use of a half-dozen vessels."[1]

Infighting among Ottawa bureaucrats over which department would control the Canadian Arctic Expedition began while it was still in the planning stages and caused the dissension that was to hamper the party's work later in the field. R. W. Brock, chief of the Geological Survey, objected to the decision to place the endeavour under the supervision of the Naval Service. Two of Brock's officials, O. E. LeRoy and W. H. Boyd, also objected to the appointment of Stefansson as commander of the expedition. "Stefansson is lacking in executive ability and is irresponsible," LeRoy complained. According to LeRoy, Stefansson allowed his men to buy whatever supplies they thought they needed, and the Naval Service did not coordinate provisioning of the expedition. Before the party left Ottawa, LeRoy asked Brock to allow John J. O'Neill, Kenneth Chipman, and J. R. Cox to resign from the expedition, but Brock refused. The expedition's orders were issued on the authority of the prime minister, so lower-ranking officials or members of the Geological Survey could not contest the status of the expedition's commander or the role of the Naval Service. George S. Malloch of the Geological Survey refused to resign from the expedition despite LeRoy's urging. LeRoy made sure that Chipman and Cox were "aware of our views regarding the apparent lack of necessary qualifications of their leader. They continually sought our advice which was freely given and it was to our regret that we could not withdraw them [from the expedition]."[2]

LeRoy employed other means to console himself for his inability to control the situation. He told the men of the Geological Survey to consider themselves independent of their commander, an irresponsible act of insubordination that encouraged petty squabbling and could have resulted in failure to achieve any worthwhile results.[3]

Geological Survey scientists objected to Stefansson's organization of the expedition from the beginning. Outfitting in Victoria in June 1913 was a hectic experience and left them disgruntled. They were upset even further by Captain Bob Bartlett's criticism of the *Karluk*'s shortcomings when they were steaming north. At the same time, Rudolph Anderson's confidence in his commander's leadership was eroding; his spirits were depressed at the thought of parting with his wife of a few months, who had sailed with him on the *Victoria* to see him off for the Arctic. The two problems came to a head when the expedition arrived at Nome.

Much of the confusion in preparing the expedition resulted from the organization of two separate parties. The Southern Party, led by Anderson, consisted mostly of men from the Geological Survey and was to be land-based in order to do coastal surveys and other similar work. The Northern Party was to be led by Stefansson personally. His exploratory activities were to be supported by the *Karluk,* and he was to engage at the same time in oceanographic and ethnographic studies. A proper allocation of stores and equipment could not be made until the two parties made their final arrangements in Nome.

In joining the Canadian Arctic Expedition, the men of the Geological Survey were availing themselves of a marvellous opportunity to advance their careers, but now that they were actually underway, they realized that they were also facing isolation and imminent danger. They did not refer to the discomfort and hazards, however; instead, they complained endlessly about Stefansson's mistakes and extravagances in outfitting and apportioning material among the several ships that were to convey them north.

Although only a month had passed by the time they reached Nome, it had been a period of intense strain. Apart from the scientists, conflict over writing for the popular press flared up between Anderson and Stefansson.

While the expedition was still outfitting in Esquimalt and Victoria, the two men signed a formal agreement in which Anderson promised not to write for newspapers except for reporting to the *London Chronicle* and *The New York Times* on the activities of the Southern Party, a restriction necessary because Stefansson was already under contract to those papers for reports on the expedition.

The pregnant Mrs. Anderson was miserable at the prospect of losing Rudolph for two years or more. But she was also ambitious— more so, perhaps, than her husband—and she was anxious for him to establish his name. To her the road to fame and fortune seemed clear: all Anderson had to do was write about his travels for popular books and magazines. This is what Stefansson had done, she reasoned, and it had worked for him. She took the matter up with Stefansson in Nome, and he promised to try to induce Rudolph to write about the expedition.

Unfortunately, when Stefansson told his partner that he need not be bound by the prohibition on writing popular articles that he had imposed on all other members of the expedition, Anderson misunderstood his motives. Apparently unaware that his wife had approached Stefansson, he interpreted his commander's generous release as a bribe to induce him to shoulder part of the responsibility for imposing restrictions on the other staff members. "Stefansson tried to get me to enforce his pet restriction on my own motion—offered me a share of newspaper profits, but I wouldn't have anything to do with his game. Told him he'd have to issue written orders on his own responsibility to cover details of correspondence."[4]

Worse yet—his wife's presence in Nome did not provide Anderson with the incentive to go on. Certainly he did not look forward to his scientific studies with the zest that characterized his bachelor days, and in this respect he was like several of the scientists who had not been in the Arctic before.

The low morale was documented by Kenneth Chipman. "While in Victoria," wrote the expedition's topographer, "I tried to find enthusiasm on the part of other members of the expedition and failed to find any." No one, it seemed, was very keen to venture into the Arctic. "Three of the best men expressed to me the opinion that it was impossible to withdraw at that day—the thing had gone so far that we could simply make the best of it," Chipman continued. There was no enthusiasm, "practically no confidence in the leader and little assurance of getting good work done."[5]

The scientists asked Stefansson to meet with them in Nome to discuss the equipment on the *Karluk*. Later, in *The Friendly Arctic,* Stefansson mentioned that the capacity of the *Karluk*'s water tanks was discussed at that meeting. The scientists were desperately afraid that they would run out of fresh water. Stefansson tried to allay their anxiety by explaining that ice floes lose their salinity in time and could be used for cooking or drinking water should the *Karluk*'s supplies ever become exhausted. Stefansson remarked later that he had been astonished to learn that the expedition oceanographer, James Murray, did not know that fresh water could be found on ice floes. Stefansson had to call in Bob Bartlett to confirm that fresh water could indeed be obtained from old ice, and the captain's verification seemed to mollify the worried scientists.

Other members of the expedition recorded quite a different version of the meeting. Chipman indicated that he and Murray had prepared an agenda on supplies and bases, and he summarized in his diary the discussion that took place at the meeting:

I referred especially to some twenty tons of provisions bought after June 17 in Seattle. We were anxious to know whether these were solid provisions, suitable for sledging work, of good quality, well packed, or if they were ordinary provisions. V. Stefansson intimated that we had no right to ask such questions as he had thought over the question of provisions, we should have confidence in him, and interpreted these as our kicking at a shortage of water. He has since told Captain Bartlett that we "kicked" because we couldn't have more water—He has informed Murray the question of sleeping bags was impertinent.

He assured us that Dr. A. [Anderson] is in charge of the Southern Party and any questions that came should be answered by him. Johansen [Frits Johansen, marine biologist] is worried over the lack of importance attached to his work and V. Stefansson told him he did not feel bound by his instructions and that he would reverse them if he chose.[6]

Statements in Chipman's diary are confirmed by the reports of others. For example, Diamond Jenness wrote a letter to his former tutor at Oxford one week after the Nome meeting, complaining of the situation:

There was great dissatisfaction amongst the party so we had a general meeting in which we requested Stefansson to answer several questions, relating to the supplies of food and clothing, the plans of each party, communications between them, etc.

The scientists were not satisfied by Stefansson's response. Jenness wrote, "Murray and Mackay afterwards wrote strong letters to Stefansson about the unsatisfactory arrangements for their party, but no reply had been received from him when the *Karluk* left Nome."[7]

Chipman's diary reflects his own dissatisfaction as well:

The general results of the meeting were not altogether satisfactory. General statements are not only very indefinite assurance, but they fail to convey any sense of assurance. I feel I have come so far and I'll go on but just as soon as I do not have facilities for my work I'll return.[8]

In a letter to his Geological Survey supervisor, W. H. Boyd, Chipman also reported on the conference that had caused Stefansson to "consider me a kicker." He wrote:

Murray and I were spokesmen and raised such questions as food supply, clothing, travel, equipment, where base is to be, coordination of work, etc., etc. There was nothing new!! I raised these questions twice in Ottawa and his answers are the same now as then. He however informed us that we had no business to ask these questions, that we should have confidence in him.[9]

And several of the men had indeed become infuriated in Victoria at being presented with a new contract supplementing the one they had signed in Ottawa, which was directed in part to the prohibition on publication.[10] Jenness's correspondence from Nome confirms Chipman's report of the hostile reaction of the scientists. "Stefansson, when he met us in Victoria, wished to make us send in our private diaries as well to the government, but we objected and apparently he has yielded."[11]

Members of the Northern Party were primarily concerned about having an alternative base to fall back on if the *Karluk* should get caught in the ice. Whether or not their wishes were reasonable, Stefansson could not easily satisfy them. It must have struck him as impractical to *assume* that the *Karluk* would be caught at a particular place in the ice and then plan to establish a base for operations near this unknown spot—no wonder he failed to ease their minds.

Responding to the questions of the Southern Party must have been much easier. What the scientists wanted was confirmation that adequate provisions, equipment, fuel, communication, and coordination of work would be forthcoming. Stefansson was able to relieve their apprehension about these details, and O'Neill, for one, was satisfied that their commander had provided everything that they might require. "Stefansson has paid a great deal more attention to details than I at first gave him credit for," O'Neill remarked in a letter to LeRoy, "I'm more enthusiastic about going now than earlier."[12] Anderson was still dissatisfied, but his anxieties were complicated by more than problems of logistics.

As in Victoria, Stefansson appears to have shown poor leadership in Nome. Probably he relied upon the representative of the Naval Service who had been specifically charged with provisioning the expedition. But he was annoyed by his men's anxiety, and no doubt he had communicated his irritation too sharply. Although he was an arctic veteran, he was inexperienced as a leader of large parties. In particular, Stefansson should have found a way to appease James Murray and Alister Mackay, the two Scots who were chosen by him because of their previous experience with Shackleton in Antarctica. These men considered themselves polar experts, too, and their anger with Stefansson over the publishing and provisioning issues undermined his authority over them. One cannot judge whether Stefansson's preparations were really as inadequate or careless as his men charged, but his treatment of them was arrogant. Yet the only man involved in the expedition preparations both at the Esquimault Navy Yard and in Nome whose position was independent of the factions took a severe view of the dissension of the scientists. George Phillips of the Naval Service warned Stefansson in Victoria that Anderson was impeding the expedition, and at Nome Phillips urged him to get rid of all the scientists who were baulking at his command.[13]

Certainly the Canadian Arctic Expedition started badly, but the initial discord did not necessarily determine the expedition's outcome since there was no fatal defect in the preparations themselves. The personal grievances against Stefansson might have been forgotten when the scientists had commenced their important work. By the time the expedition embarked from Nome in the *Karluk,* the *Alaska,* and the *Mary Sachs,* Stefansson was confident that things would go well and that once they were in the field, where his experience was superior, he would be able to exert his leadership more effectively.

A crowd of well-wishers saw the ships off from Nome in July 1913. The sailing was a gala festivity for townspeople and expedition members alike. There was no particular reason to fear that a catastrophe would occur, and, indeed, with a little luck all the ships could have reached their destination without mishap. Who could have foreseen that arctic conditions that year were to be far more severe than anyone could remember?

CHAPTER 8

The Karluk Disaster

THE *KARLUK* was fit for its purpose when the expedition left Nome. It was not a pretty ship, nor very powerful, nor specially designed for ice navigation, but it had been the best ship available when Stefansson had commissioned Captain C.T. Pedersen to find an expedition flagship. Pedersen, who then expected to be the ship's captain on the expedition, looked over the *Karluk* in San Francisco, recommended the purchase, then brought it north where the refitting was done. Stefansson was happy enough with Pedersen's choice, being familiar with the vessel from earlier experience.

The *Karluk*, a brigantine of 247 tons, 126 feet in length with a twenty-three-foot beam, drew sixteen and a half feet of water when loaded. It had originally been a fish tender, then was strengthened for ice work. For twenty years various mariners had guided the vessel into the Beaufort Sea seeking whales. Inspectors at the Esquimault drydock outside Victoria examined the ship before and after refitting and pronounced her sound. Captain Bob Bartlett, who replaced Pedersen, grumbled about the lack of power and recalled his glory days commanding Robert Peary's special ice ship, the *Roosevelt*. He knew the *Karluk* was not a battering ram but expected it would perform well enough as Stefansson's Prince Patrick Island base for geographic exploration. The smaller *Alaska* was to serve the scientists bound for Coronation Gulf, and the *Mary Sachs* would serve as a tender to both sections of the expedition.

As the *Karluk* moved through the Chukchi Sea north of Nome, a gale swept down. Neither the *Alaska* nor the *Mary Sachs* was in company when Captain Bartlett sheltered the *Karluk* off Cape

Thompson to avoid storm damage. At Point Hope, Stefansson went ashore where he bought a few dogs and a large quantity of walrus meat for dogfeed. He also engaged two Eskimos, Pauyurak and Asatsiak (Jimmy Kalignik).

The *Karluk* steamed north from Cape Thompson to Cape Lisburne, rounded the Cape, and proceeded to the east where, near Wainwright Inlet, the ship first met the ice pack, which halted them close to Point Barrow. Stefansson and Dr. Mackay left the ship and walked twenty-five miles to the Barrow village and the trading station of Charlie Brower, located at Cape Smythe ten miles southwest of Point Barrow. At Cape Smythe Stefansson engaged Kataktovik, Kwialuk, the latter's wife, Kiruk, and Jack Hadley, an Englishman. Including Hadley in the expedition pleased Stefansson, who respected Hadley's judgment and his extensive experience in the Arctic as trapper, trader, and whaler. Stefansson also bought an Eskimo skin-boat (*umiak*) as a precaution in case it should be necessary to abandon the *Karluk* later on. Hadley understood how to handle *umiaks,* so his presence and the boat provided some insurance in case of shipwreck.

On his second day at Cape Smythe, Stefansson saw the *Karluk* drifting by, less than a mile from shore. With the help of Brower and some local Eskimos, Stefansson got the *umiak* and the other expedition people safely aboard the ship. The ice carried the *Karluk* past the continent's northwest tip at Point Barrow before the pressure eased, allowing the ship to proceed under its own power.

Bartlett kept the *Karluk* moving along the inshore edge of the ice pack until the ice closed in near Cross Island. There he made his fateful decision: instead of following the practice of navigators in the western Arctic of watching for inshore leads that would allow the ship to progress further, Bartlett took the ship north, hoping to find a clear passage. Instead, the pack once again held the *Karluk* fast. No one realized it on 13 August, just two weeks out from Nome, but there would be no further escape from its deadly grip.

As the *Karluk* drifted eastward Stefansson tried to get Henry Beuchat and Jenness ashore at Camden Bay so they could pursue their ethnological work, but the ice proved too thin to support them, and the sledge party was forced to return to the ship.

In mid-September, after a full month of easterly drifting, fresh meat was needed, and Stefansson decided to take a hunting party ashore, including George Wilkins (later to become Sir Hubert Wilkins, the famed polar air explorer), Burt McConnell, Diamond Jen-

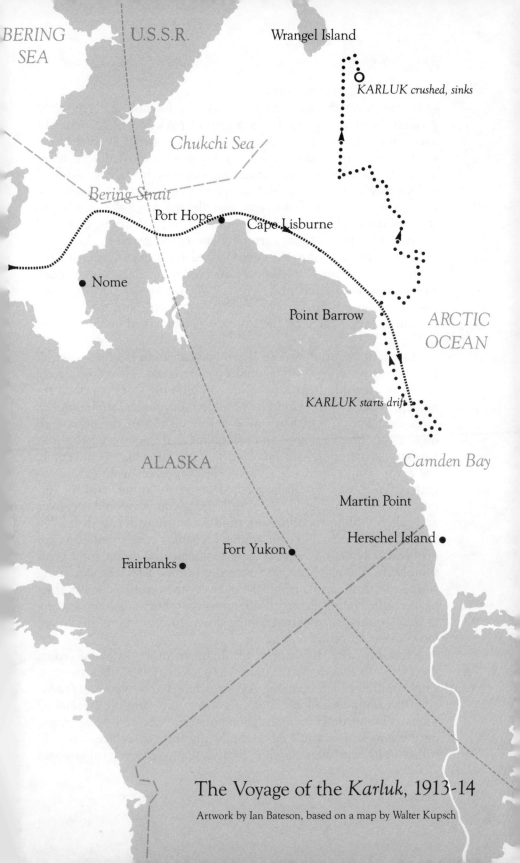

BERING SEA

U.S.S.R.

Wrangel Island

KARLUK crushed, sinks

Chukchi Sea

Bering Strait

Port Hope

Cape Lisburne

Nome

Point Barrow

ARCTIC OCEAN

KARLUK starts drift

Camden Bay

ALASKA

Martin Point

Herschel Island

Fort Yukon

Fairbanks

The Voyage of the *Karluk*, 1913-14

Artwork by Ian Bateson, based on a map by Walter Kupsch

ness, Asatsiak, and Pauyurak.

Shortly after the hunting party left the *Karluk,* a fierce storm pushed the ship, still in the firm grip of pack ice, off to sea. The men aboard were dismayed: "As the ice pack swept us further and further away from our leader, we felt not so much like soldiers sacrificing ourselves to a great cause, as lambs left to the slaughter," reflected William Laird McKinlay, magnetician and meteorologist.[1] There were twenty-five people aboard when the ship began its final drift. The succeeding months brought death to eleven of them and horror to those fortunate enough to survive.

Most of those aboard the vessel lacked arctic experience, and the knowledge of their helplessness unnerved them. "Darkness added to our worries," McKinlay wrote. "We no longer had our long days without any night. The nights lengthened, and the sense of insecurity, aggravated by the storm, was intensified by the eeriness of the dark."[2]

How tantalizing it was to be embedded in an ice floe when at times open water lay only a hundred yards away. How frightening to see the terrible force of the ice as adjoining floes smashed together. Weaker floes would be pounded into pieces, sometimes as large as a house, which would pile one on top of the other into huge ridges, then collapse and roll about as if they were as light as feathers. Sometimes, McKinlay wrote, "one large floe would crack, the crack would open a few yards, the two pieces would come together again, one would be pushed under the other, and the upper...heaved higher and higher until...large chunks would break off and roll, rumbling and tumbling amid the crashing devastation."[3]

In sensitive men like the young McKinlay, the thundering ice evoked excitement as well as fear: he imagined a theme for a great symphony, a Wagnerian orchestration formed from the deafening sound of "thunderous rumbles far away, then not so distant, then nearer still; coming from all directions; rending, crashing, tearing noises; grating, screeching; toning down to drumming, booming, murmuring, gurgling, twanging."[4]

A few days after this storm, a brilliant auroral display moved its spectators to wonderment and awe. McKinlay describes seeing a single streamer in the evening sky, stretching to the west and gradually spreading "until the sky was alive with similar streamers. Then...a small patch of light shone out near the zenith...growing until it was size of a full moon. Suddenly from its centre there unrolled a huge curtain extending right down to ice level, folding and unfolding with lightning rapidity. In seconds of time this was repeated until there were seven such curtains hanging in the sky, waving and dancing as if blown by a mighty wind...a large stretch of vivid blood-red hung in the west, slowly changing to salmon pink, then yellow and later to green....These colours were in vertical bands which chased one another across the curtains in quick succession."[5]

Descriptions such as McKinlay's of this magnificent spectacle intensify the human drama. The contest on the *Karluk* was essentially of men against the ice. Their situation called for a unity of purpose, but neither unity nor harmony existed on the *Karluk*. Personal differences created deep divisions between the men on the old whaling vessel. They were a mixed group:

Captain Bob Bartlett was a bull-necked, bull-headed mariner, much given to profanity, yet a hearty man of good will, an experienced Newfoundland sealer, and veteran of several winters in the Arctic. Unlike McKinlay and most of the others aboard the *Karluk*, he was accustomed to drifting ice. Bartlett was stubborn and self-confident—and although he proved an excellent leader to men who were willing to acknowledge his authority, he lacked subtlety and was not inclined to argue with recalcitrant men, particularly those who had the advantage of a formal education.

Dr. Alister Forbes Mackay was once a British naval physician and a former companion of the antarctic explorer Ernest Shackleton on his 1907-1909 expedition, during which Mackay repeatedly exhibited his daring, resourcefulness, and travel skills. Shackleton wished Mackay on Stefansson "to get him away from the evil influences of civilization," according to Rudolph Anderson. Apparently Mackay had a drinking problem.[6] Still there is no evidence that Mackay's problem determined his role as chief dissenter on the *Karluk*.

John Murray, biologist of Shackleton's 1907-1909 expedition and the Canadian Arctic Expedition's oceanographer, another Scot, was, according to R.M. Anderson, "too old and exceedingly overconfident because of his Shackleton experience."[7] Henri Beuchat, anthropologist from Paris and in Stefansson's eyes a writer of distinction, was an authority on American archaeology and ethnology; but, in Anderson's opinion, he was unsuited for the expedition because he lacked field experience.[8] By all accounts he was learned, gracious, and kindly—but he was not in physical condition for strenuous field work, particularly for sledge travel over sea ice.

William Laird McKinlay, 5 feet 4 inches and twenty-four years old, was a schoolmaster from Glasgow. Magnetician of the expedition, he was a sensitive, courageous man and the only survivor of the *Karluk* besides Bartlett to write a full account of events surrounding the disaster. George S. Malloch, American geologist, was a member of the Canadian Geological Survey as was Bjarne Mamen, a Norwegian. Mamen was also a veteran of the Norwegian-Spitsbergen Expedition.

John Hadley of Canterbury, England, was a born musician who could sing operatic and native songs from around the world and play a variety of wind and string instruments. A veteran of over twenty years in the Arctic, Hadley was a capable man and a true adventurer, but he resented slights and was too bluff to conceal his contempt for greenhorns.

The ship's complement included First Mate Alex Anderson, Second Mate Charles Barker, Chief Engineer John Munro, Second Engineer Robert Williamson, and crewmen John Brady, George Breddy, Ernest Chafe, A. King, Fred Maurer, S. Stanley Morris, Robert Templeman, and H. Williams. There were also two Eskimo men, Kataktovik and Kuraluk, a woman, Kiruk, and her two young children, Helen and Mugpi.

Except for the first mate, a twenty-year-old fellow Scot, McKinlay did not think much of the crew. As seamen they were fine, "but I had grave doubts in many cases about the other qualities which would be necessary for harmonious living in the kind of circumstances which might face us in the north."[9] One seaman who carried around syringes and drugs was a confirmed drug addict; another suffered from venereal disease, and two more had smuggled liquor aboard in Victoria.

The *Karluk* was not a happy ship. Of the scientists only James Murray, the oceanographer, had enough work, although George Malloch made the observations and calculations to determine the *Karluk*'s position. McKinlay kept regular and meteorological logs, but his magnetic work was a waste of time because the unceasing movement of the ice made it impossible to keep the instruments steady enough to make accurate readings. "Apart from all that, we were mere passengers on the *Karluk*," McKinlay complained, "and we were constantly reminded of the fact by a few croakers among the crew, who regarded us as a useless lot, enjoying privileges to which we were not entitled."[10]

A deep rift developed between Bartlett and Dr. Alistair Mackay and Murray. Had the consequences of their antipathy not been so tragic, the men might have argued good-naturedly about individual preferences in polar travel techniques and ranking of their respective exploration heroes. Some of the men thought Bartlett was obsessed with Robert Peary, and certainly he wanted everything done Peary's way, even to the type of cooking utensils and sledges they used. Of course, it was not only a matter of hero-worship, but also of Bartlett's faith and reliance on his earlier experience in the Arctic that dictated his decision. Mackay and Murray, the Shackleton men, remained unimpressed. They knew polar conditions from their own work—and they doubted Bartlett's judgment. On expeditions in the Antarctic the men had always discussed their plans and prospects. Peary kept more aloof from his companions and so did Bartlett, although by nature he was more gregarious than his mentor. How could the Scottish scientists retain confidence in a master who got the ship into a precarious position and who then refused to entertain questions or permit debate on the predicament in which they found themselves?

Another conflict existed between Bartlett and John Hadley. After Bartlett chose to ignore the western arctic tradition of shore-hugging navigation and instead took the *Karluk* out to open sea, Hadley lost confidence in the captain. He obeyed orders and put his skills to good use, but Bartlett kept his distance. Though both men were arctic experts, they were suspicious of each other's pretensions. Hadley recorded every instance in which he questioned Bartlett's competence and judgment in his diary.

After Stefansson left the ship, Bartlett was in undisputed command. Hoping their helplessness in the ice was temporary and that some scientific work could still go in, Bartlett praised Murray and other scientists for continuing to work. Murray's dredging brought up interesting specimens of sea life from the ocean floor, and Malloch's daily celestial observations relieved Bartlett of the need to fix the ship's position. Murray was "faithful and untiring in his dredging and his work, at which we all helped," Bartlett reported. He praised Hadley's care of the invaluable sled dogs: "No better man could have been found, for he understood not only how to feed them but also how important it was to have them well cared for."[11]

Bartlett's published description of the shipboard harmony and the efficiency of preparations for an emergency, however, are open to question. Robert Williamson recalled that after Stefansson left the ship, everything seemed to change on board. According to the second engineer, "there was practically no discipline. Bartlett avoided Mackay, Murray, and Beuchat; hardly spoke to them." Williamson thought he surmised the reason for Bartlett's cool attitude: "I guess they asked too many pointed questions. But Hadley, [John] Munro, and McKinlay were always around him, it was [considered] quite unsociable by the rest of the ship."[12]

McKinlay glowed in the captain's attention. Bartlett liked to tease the young schoolmaster whenever he found him working at what seemed to be an incongruous activity. With a hearty chuckle and a back-clap he would roar goodnaturedly: "This is better than teaching school, eh boy? Just think, you would never have known what a handy fellow you are if you hadn't come along." It pleased McKinlay to see Bartlett's attempts to appear light-hearted "when I knew the load of anxiety that lay on his shoulders."[13] But Bartlett did not feel at ease with the older, experienced men.

The disaffection of Mackay, Murray, and Beuchat became apparent, and it was evident they did not share Bartlett's feeling that the *Karluk* would eventually free herself from the ice. Murray's kit included a copy of a book describing the drift of the *Jeannette* off the coast of Siberia in 1879-81. After many months, the pressure of the ice smashed the ship, forcing her crew to abandon her. Why, Murray wondered, should the *Karluk* be spared her fate?

While Bartlett may have been tempted to order the scientists to stop discussing their fears so openly, he apparently did not do anything except avoid their questions. He was, after all, only the ship's captain, not the expedition commander, and his authority over the scientists had not been clearly established.

In his memoir Hadley notes that the scientists often talked of leaving the ship. "The captain used to lie in his bunk of nights and listen to them talking it over. The Dr. [Mackay] seemed to be the ringleader and seemed to be advising the rest to go as soon as possible."[14] Bartlett no doubt seethed over this threat to morale, particularly when the scientists communicated their fears to individual crewmen such as Williamson. The latter's shipboard duties kept him too busy to read the narrative of the *Jeannette*'s drift that Murray urged on him, but he noticed the effect fear had on the men: "Poor Beuchat...had to listen to all this talk for he said 'I leave my bones in the Arctic.' "[15]

Hadley sensed some undefined trouble between Bartlett and Mackay even though Mackay discharged his duties as expedition physician efficiently and never seemed to annoy the captain. But Hadley put forward an explanation for the antipathy: "It...appeared to me that the reason that the Captain disliked him [Mackay] was because Admiral Peary invariably had trouble with his Dr's that's why Captain Bartlett had to have trouble with his Dr's because everything that Peary did went with Bartlett."[16]

Whether Hadley's assessment has substance or not, it does seem that the captain was dangerously indifferent to the scientists. When Mackay and Murray talked of leaving the ship, Hadley offered to explain the hazards to them, but Bartlett ordered him "never to say a word about it but to let them go if they wanted to."[17]

Meanwhile the news of the *Karluk*'s disappearance reached the outside world through the efforts of two men who had been involved with the expedition: Olaf Swenson, a trader, and Captain C.T. Pedersen, the arctic skipper who had been Stefansson's first choice to command the *Karluk*.

Swenson had outfitted the newly purchased S.S. *Belvedere* in the spring of 1913 for a trading voyage from Seattle to Siberia and engaged a veteran whaling man, Stephen Cottle, as ship's master. After trading along the Siberian coast, Swenson called at Nome where he picked up freight for the Canadian Arctic Expedition and the R.C.M.P. station at Herschel Island.

Like the *Karluk,* the *Belvedere,* Pedersen's *Elvira,* and Louis Lane's *Polar Bear* were all caught in the ice in the western Arctic. News of the *Karluk*'s drift reached Swenson and other traders as they tried to ram their ships through the ice pack. They all assumed that the *Karluk* was drifting westwards. Swenson later explained what had happened. "It was known that while the *Mary Sachs* of the Stefansson expedition, commanded by Captain Peter Bernard (who had a great deal of local ice experience) had kept close to the shore, Captain Bartlett had taken the *Karluk* on an offshore lead, and no one saw how she could have escaped becoming fast in the ice and drifting towards the Siberian Arctic."[18]

Swenson and Pedersen decided to travel overland by dog sled to Fairbanks and return to the Outside rather than winter in the Arctic. They also wanted to carry news of the *Karluk*'s fate. The two men accomplished a remarkably swift twenty-six day journey from the coast near Herschel Island to Fairbanks. In setting local speed records, they were spurred on by a race with Louis Lane, who wanted to reach Fairbanks with the *Karluk* news first. Although Swenson and Pedersen did not foresee it then, both were to play important roles in the destiny of the personnel on the *Karluk*.

Aboard the *Karluk*, drifting to the west, life went on: "We celebrated Christmas Day, 1913, on board the *Karluk*," wrote Fred Maurer. "It was the last Christmas on earth for the larger portion of the company."[19] Captain Bob Bartlett ordered a festive Christmas dinner which included polar bear steaks, canned lobster, canned ox tongues, creamed peas, potatoes (which had been hoarded for the occasion), canned asparagus, plum pudding, cakes, nuts, and fruits. And, for the first time, the men were offered some liquor to wash down their holiday meal.

The morning after Christmas, a loud report alarmed everyone. As they dashed to the ship's rail they saw a crack in the ice running the length of the ship and fifty yards beyond. Until this cracking the *Karluk* had floated safely on its imprisoning floe, but now it looked as if the ice pressure might crush the ship.

Earlier the crew had unloaded coal, sledges, dogs, and provisions from the ship to the floe as a precaution against sudden disaster. Now Bartlett ordered further preparations, this time for abandoning the ship. All necessary sledging rations were unloaded onto the ice, and the men were occupied in helping Kiruk, the Eskimo seamstress, prepare skins for clothing. At least they knew where they were. On 29 December they sighted either Herald Island or nearby Wrangel Island. In their plight the sight of land was a comforting prospect.

The men celebrated the New Year by having a football match on the ice, drinking the last of the whiskey, and singing a heart-rending "Auld Lang Syne," followed by recitations from Robert Burns by the Scots.

As the days passed, they became increasingly apprehensive as they listened uneasily to the noise of surrounding ice twanging and drumming ominously. At 6:45 P.M. on 11 January Bartlett found water pouring through a ten-foot gash on the port side. It was a terrible sight that spelled doom for the *Karluk*. Bartlett ordered all hands to abandon ship at once.

There was time to put all the necessary stores on the ice before the end. Bartlett stayed on board that night, playing Chopin's Funeral March over and over on the gramophone, drinking coffee and tea, and brooding. Late the next day, with her flag flying, the *Karluk* went down. Her bow settled and sank gradually. A puff of steam rose as the galley stove was immersed in sea water, and then the masts disappeared into the depths. Everyone watched the sinking vessel while Bartlett played Chopin's Funeral March one last time.

"So there we were," McKinlay wrote, "perched on an ice floe in the Arctic Ocean, twenty-two men, one woman, two children, sixteen dogs and a cat."[20] Fortunately, the snow house that had been erected on the ice floe provided shelter, and they had plenty of provisions. They named their new abode Shipwreck Camp.

What the survivors lacked most was experience—only Bartlett, Hadley, and Kuraluk had traveled over sea ice before. However, all the men were aware of the dangers ahead, and, with a few exceptions, they were content to stay on the floe until the sun disappeared.

Bartlett put McKinlay in charge of stores. These included almost 10,000 pounds of pemmican, tea, sugar, butter, tinned milk, and chocolate and an ample supply of skin clothing, underwear, mitts, blankets, ammunition, coal oil, and other equipment. One thing McKinlay failed to locate was a box of shotgun shells, and, McKinlay wrote, "there came a day when we bitterly regretted its loss."[21]

Before the *Karluk* sank, Hadley told Bartlett that he wanted to take a shotgun. If Hadley's version of the encounter can be believed, Bartlett almost committed a monumental act of folly. According to Hadley, "he said 'no,' explorers don't use shotguns these days. But I told him that he wasn't going ashore to explore but to live." Hadley knew that Wrangel Island held bird rookeries so he thought a shotgun "would be of more service to us than a rifle."[22] Hadley got his way, but he learned later that the shells that were put ashore were the wrong size.

Bartlett's strategy was to send out an advance party consisting of First Mate Alex Anderson, Second Mate Charles Barker, John Brady, and A. King to establish a base on Wrangel Island. Bjarne Mamen and two Eskimos were to help the advance party to reach the island and then return to Shipwreck Camp. Meanwhile, parties of two or three men would cache stores along the advance party's trail. Bartlett knew that some caches might be lost on the moving ice before they could be taken on to Wrangel Island, but stores were plentiful.

The mate's advance party got close to Herald Island before an open lead stopped their progress. Anderson decided to wait for the chance to get ashore, even though he realized that the land was not Wrangel Island, because his stores were limited. Mamen, who was apparently in charge until the advance party established a base, decided to return with the dogs and Eskimos to Shipwreck Camp. When Mamen returned, Bartlett made no complaint, but McKinlay, Anderson's good friend, was dismayed. "Mamen," McKinlay reported, "had decided to go back, leaving the four men thirty-eight miles from their real objective. Herald Island, if they ever managed to land there, was absolutely devoid of resources, and they had no dogs to get them to Wrangel Island."[23] Thus, four men, none of whom had any arctic experience, were missing—and would never be seen alive again.

At this point, Mackay announced his intention of trying to reach land. He decided to aim for the coast rather than adopting Bartlett's strategy of establishing a base on Wrangel Island. Mackay and Murray believed that their exploration experience with Shackleton in the Antarctic armed them for the journey. The inexperienced Beuchat and Stanley Morris, a sailor from the *Karluk,* formed the rest of the party. Even the ominous report that Anderson's men appeared to be stranded by open water near Herald Island did not deter them. According to Hadley, Bartlett tried to keep this bad news from Mackay. Hadley recalled that he "took no notice of [this order] for I considered that as far as he [Bartlett] took no pains to stop them from going, that he had no right to withhold any information from them which might help them on their road."[24]

In his published account of the events, Bartlett described the split-up of the expedition tersely: "The evening of the fourth Murray came to me and said that the doctor's party planned to leave the next day. The fifth opened clear and calm and the doctor, Murray, Beuchat, and Morris got away about nine o'clock hauling their sledgeload of supplies along the trail."[25] Before they left, Mackay's party gave Bartlett a letter absolving him of any responsibility for their journey. Bartlett gave them the necessary provisions but, according to Hadley, refused to give them sled dogs. As Hadley put it, "When the Dr. asked for dogs the Capt. said not one dog, if you go you play dog yourself."[26] Hadley warned Murray that the trip would not be easy without dogs.

Bartlett's version contradicts Hadley's on the subject of dogs: "I offered the doctor's party their proportional share of dogs, as soon as the dogs returned with Mamen, but they declined the offer, saying that they preferred to haul the sledge themselves."[27] If Bartlett had refused to give up the dogs, he was justified in being concerned for the safety of the main party. But it is not unlikely that Mackay and Murray placed little importance on the dogs, since they had constructed man-harnesses for sledge-hauling while the *Karluk* was still drifting. They were, after all, heirs of the Royal Navy tradition of sledge travel which believed in the superiority of men in harness. This bias cost Robert Scott and his companions their lives on their return from the South Pole and may have doomed Mackay's men as well.

It seems odd that Bartlett should have accepted Mackay's decision to leave with such equanimity unless he considered that their chances were good or, on the contrary, that the scientists were no longer his responsibility and he was washing his hands of them. Some member of the *Karluk*'s crew told Hadley that Bartlett expressed the hope that "he'd never see them sons of bitches again."[28] If Bartlett actually expressed such a wish, it was soon granted: like the mate's party, Mackay and his men perished. Within a few weeks of the shipwreck, the death toll of the *Karluk* had reached eight.

Shipwreck Camp was three hundred miles off the Siberian coast and eighty miles north of Wrangel Island. The only hope left of survival lay in the same ice that had crushed the *Karluk*. "We knew not how many miles of open water might be between us and the nearest land," wrote Maurer. It was a fearful situation, yet the survivors were reassured by the Eskimos' calm, particularly that of Kiruk, or "Auntie" as she was called. The Eskimo woman tended her children while she worked on skin clothes for the men. Her help was never forgotten by those who survived the experience. "Though crude and uncultured, she was still a woman, and exerted a woman's influence among us. We looked upon her as a mother," remembered Maurer. "The presence of her little children created a sort of domestic influence in our frigid quarters."[29]

Although they had planned to stay only three days on the ice, their wait was extended to a month. They provided themselves with improved quarters from boxes which formerly had held provisions. Although the temperature was often forty to fifty degrees below zero, the heat from primus stoves kept their huts warm. But the darkness was oppressive—for sixty days they did not see the sun at all. Their dogs huddled close by the huts, sleeping when they were not howling or fighting. "At night we could hear the booming sound of immense ice floes grinding against each other, or the sharper crash of an opening lead," Maurer recalled.[30] Then all would hurry out into the darkness, terror in their hearts, to see whether a lead had opened near camp. Life was not quiet on the arctic ice floe, and it was far from serene.

The party finally set out on the hazardous journey for Wrangel Island in two separate groups. Soon a blizzard caught them on the trail, and they huddled in snow houses until it passed. Although the trail was marked by the advance parties, the movement of ice sometimes eradicated the tracks. Pressure ridges also slowed their pace, for men and dogs either had to pass or scramble over them. Each night they camped, listening to the sound of the shifting ice. Maurer recalled the scene vividly, "We could hear the ominous grinding and creaking of the ice; then a loud boom would break upon our ears."[31] As they had done earlier at Shipwreck Camp, they would jump, startled, from their blankets to investigate the proximity of the opening lead.

After ten days on the trail, the travellers encountered an obstacle that seemed insurmountable: an enormous pressure ridge seventy-five to one hundred feet high loomed, blocking the way. They lost two days while they searched east and west for the end of the ridge, without success. There was no solution except to cut a passage through the barrier. "With picks, axes and shovels, " Maurer recorded, "we toiled like beavers against huge walls that were holding us prisoners [in] a world of ice and snow."[32] It took the party six days to chop a three-mile passage across the mountainous pressure ridge.

The rest of the way was easy. Wrangel Island was only forty miles distant, and the ice in between was firmly bound to the coast of the island. Six more days of travel brought them at last to land; it was 12 March 1914. When the seventeen men landed on the desolate, snow-covered shore of Wrangel Island, they were wild with delight. "In their gladness the men dug through the snow so they might touch the earth with their hands, or pick from the frozen ground a pebble, a real pebble to feel of it."[33]

Wrangel Island did not offer many amenities, but the ship-wrecked survivors of the *Karluk* thought it was wonderful in at least one respect—as Maurer put it, the island "was securely anchored to the bottom of the sea."[34]

With the help of Kataktovik and Kuraluk the men quickly built snow houses for temporary shelter, and Bartlett announced his new plan to cross the ice to the Siberian mainland. None of the *Karluk* survivors questioned Bartlett's judgment concerning the journey, although Malloch and Mamen who wanted to accompany him were deeply disappointed at being left behind. The others had had enough of ice travel. Now they were willing to put their hopes in the man who had helped Robert Peary reach the North Pole.

Bartlett hoped to make a rapid journey across Siberia with the help of one Eskimo, Kataktovick. "To attempt to get such a large number as the entire party over to Siberia at the speed that was absolutely necessary for crossing before the ice broke up," he reasoned, "was obviously out of the question." Since the Wrangel Island party had enough food for eighty days, they would be sustained until June. Then "the birds would be back again, and always the polar bear and the seal were reliable sources of supply."[35]

The captain appointed Munro, the chief engineer, to command the party left on Wrangel Island. Hadley, the only white man with arctic experience, and Kuraluk were charged with the responsibility of hunting.[36]

Following Bartlett's instructions, three men under Munro started out with sledges and dogs for Shipwreck Camp to bring in more of the food that had been left there. About half way to the camp, a wide lead stopped their progress. After waiting for three days for ice conditions to improve, the men had no choice but to return to Wrangel Island. By good fortune and hard pushing for forty hours, without rest, they made it back to camp. Their feet were badly frozen, and had to be held against their mates' chests to thaw. H. "Clam" William's big toe needed to be amputated. Williamson, the engineer, performed the surgery successfully. "We had neither anaesthetic nor antiseptic. Our surgical instruments were a pocket knife, a piece of a broken hack saw, and a pair of tin shears."[37]

Before leaving for the mainland, Bartlett urged the survivors to try to live in harmony. To help ensure good relations and to provide better hunting opportunities, he ordered two separate camps set up. According to McKinlay, quarrelling over the distribution of biscuits started soon after the failure to reach Shipwreck Camp for more stores. After "much strong and obscene language...Munro's arrangement was accepted with very bad grace." Although "there was a feeling of every-man-for-himself in the air," McKinlay noted, the Eskimo children never suffered. "Even when the food situation was at its grimmest we always saw to it that they had sufficient to eat," he wrote.[38]

Several of the men fell sick soon after landing on the island, and the healthier survivors took turns caring for them. Malloch did not appear to be sick, but he lacked vitality and had little interest in what went on around him. Robert Templeman, the ship's cook, "was another problem, a potential source of real trouble with his unbridled tongue and capacity for lying."[39]

Munro and McKinlay followed Bartlett's orders to continue the search for Anderson's party, but they could not reach Herald Island through the impenetrable barrier of pressure ridges. In April, Munro tried again to reach Shipwreck Camp. He and two other men failed to reach their destination, incurring the wrath of the entire group because they were forced to abandon a sledge, dogs, two rifles, ammunition, food, and other equipment; the rifles and ammunition in particular were needed desperately.[40]

A crisis occurred when Hadley wanted to set up a separate camp with Kuraluk and his family. Some of the men insisted this was a trick by which Hadley intended to keep all the hunting spoils since he and Kuraluk had been the only effective hunters. Threats of violence were voiced, but the trouble finally subsided with McKinlay helping Munro smooth things over. If the survivors had had a strong leader, their discomfort probably would have been considerably reduced. Munro did his best, but he lacked experience, force of personality, and the men's respect.

On May first, Malloch died and then Mamen, probably as a result of nephritis. Most of the survivors suffered some illness or other because the pemmican that provided most of their food contained too little fat. Hadley and the Eskimos ate more fresh meat, including seal blubber and bear fat, and it kept them in better health. The others, however, refused to adopt their diet.

Kuraluk, who came from Barrow, provided most of the fresh meat, mostly by hunting seals and birds. For want of a shotgun, the men could not kill birds very successfully although countless thousands flocked to the island in the spring. Gathering eggs on the cliffs also proved frustrating because the men could not build a long enough ladder that would still be portable so they could reach the higher places where most of the eggs were deposited.

On 25 June another death occurred. G. Breddy was found in his tent shot through the head, a Mauser revolver lying beside him. Hadley and McKinlay were sleeping in the tent next to him when the shot sounded. Hadley wondered at the circumstances. Breddy's right hand lay open—"not like a hand that held a gun that shot himself. There is something very peculiar about this and that his eye was shut when the shot was fired."[41] Five days later the men finished digging a grave, and there they buried Breddy. Hadley reported his suspicions in his diary: "I...think that it's nothing but murder."[42]

Hadley's account in his memoir differs from his diary in one important respect. In the narrative he claims, "I told McKinlay and the Indian [Kuraluk] to view the body before we moved it and they were both of the same opinion as myself, that the man was killed in his sleep." Hadley suspected that Williamson had shot Breddy, and in his narrative (but not in the diary), he recalled that "for several days after this the Second [Engineer] acted like an insane man, and told us that there was one good thing about it, there was one mouth less to eat the grub."[43] Williamson was referring to a couple of occasions when Breddy had angered his companions by taking more than his share of food.

Hadley disliked Williamson and blamed the engineer for instigating an attack on him during an earlier episode that had involved the sharing of food. His antipathy may have encouraged suspicions arising from the circumstances of Breddy's death. It is also curious that Hadley described events in his narrative that were not recorded in his diary.

McKinlay's account of Breddy's death made no mention of examining the body nor of agreeing with Hadley's conclusion that the man had been murdered. Probably McKinlay avoided raising the issue in print to avoid a scandal although he had spoken of it earlier to others. A journalist reporting McKinlay's story wrote that "one man shot himself—or was murdered."[44]

As the summer advanced, the dwindling supply of food continued to preoccupy the colony. Kuraluk made a bolo-like device which he threw at birds with some success, and they had several polar bears that Hadley had killed on their trek from Shipwreck Camp. The bears on Wrangel Island, however, were wary of hunters. The men finished the last of their pemmican, a food that McKinlay always found so objectionable that he could hardly choke it down. Afterwards, eider ducks and their eggs became their principal fare until August, when the birds began migrating to the south. It was not a cheerful sight to see fowl on the wing as the season advanced.

In mid-August the survivors buried the men who had died on the island. A cross was placed at the head of each grave and a flag, flying at half mast, was mounted as well. "The presence of the graves was a constant reminder of what might be in store for us," wrote Maurer. "We often talked of the possibility of our own bodies left a prey to the foxes that inhabited that land."[45] Time after time they speculated on Bartlett's fate. Had he managed to make it to the mainland, or did his body lie at the bottom of the

Arctic Ocean? All their hopes for rescue rested with the captain of the *Karluk*.

In September the prospect looked grim. If a rescue expedition did not arrive soon, they faced another winter, and chances for survival would be slim because of their weakened condition and the precarious food supply. When they chopped driftwood for their fires, they found themselves exhausted after only three strokes of the axe. Most of the time they lay in their beds, half dozing. When foxes began coming into their camp, the men shot them without much effort. They killed enough to provide every man with two of the skimpy animals every week. Their supply of ammunition was soon to run out.

On the morning of 7 September 1914 the men were awakened by an unusual noise. This time it was not a scrambling fox or a lumbering polar bear—but a steam whistle! Bartlett had made it! Lying about a quarter of a mile offshore was a little trading schooner, the *King and Winge,* owned by Olaf Swenson. No ship had ever looked so lovely. "We yelled at the top of our voices in a delirium of delight," Maurer recalled. "We staggered down toward the shore attempting to run, weakly and unsteadily, and swinging our arms and shouting."[46]

The *Karluk* survivors owed their lives to Bartlett and Kataktovik. These two men travelled two hundred miles over the sea ice, climbing over pressure ridges and skirting leads until they finally reached the Siberian coast. The journey only took seventeen days, partly because they were skilled travellers and partly because they had good luck. Their landfall near a Siberian village was fortunate, too. Natives there guided them along the coast to Emma Harbor on Bering Strait, a thirty-seven day journey of seven hundred miles. From Emma Harbor the problem was to get to Alaska for help. When the navigation season opened in May, Captain C.T. Pedersen's ship *Herman* arrived to trade, and Bartlett sailed with her as far as St. Michael, Alaska, where he telegraphed the news and arranged for a rescue ship. Pedersen's timely appearance was an interesting coincidence, since he had been Stefansson's first choice for captain of the *Karluk* and also had sent out the first news of the *Karluk*'s drift.

In response to Bartlett's telegraph, the U.S. revenue cutter *Bear* tried to reach Wrangel Island, but it failed because of heavy ice. Two Russian icebreakers also made the unsuccessful attempt before Swenson finally reached the island.

CHAPTER 9

Defiance

MEANWHILE, Stefansson and the other C.A.E. men knew nothing of the fate of their comrades on the *Karluk* until months after the rescue. Stefansson's hunting party, after leaving the ship in mid-September 1913, faced their own immediate problems. Crossing the sea ice to shore was a novel experience for everyone but the leader, and he took pains on their first night out in showing them how to fold their sleeping bags and how to be comfortable while lying naked in them. The men did not know how to lie still so that warm air remained in their sleeping bags, and consequently they shivered all night. As Wilkins recalled, "we made martyrs of ourselves and endured the cold but we were not very enthusiastic in the morning."[1]

That morning the men faced more urgent problems for the ice was moving and splitting. Wilkins described the scene: "Soon the whole pack shuddered violently and the ice split up about us. The mist rose from the newly exposed water like smoke from a smouldering fire; it hid everything beyond a few yards from us."[2] They waited for hours until the ice closed and the fog cleared and then set out for land.

The party reached one of the Jones Islands, a short distance from the mainland, where a storm broke up the inshore ice, marooning them for several days and preventing further travel. During the gale Stefansson had his last view of the *Karluk*, which appeared to be moving against the wind and current in an easterly direction.

When the ice thickened, the hunting party crossed to the mainland. The *Karluk* could not be seen at all from shore, so Stefansson abandoned the hunt to lead his men west toward Barrow, some 175 miles away. Wilkins was worried. He summed up their situation in a terse sentence: "We were about four hundred miles from any known source of civilization and we had lost our ship." Their prepared food was almost exhausted, and their dress was inadequate for winter conditions. Living off the country had to begin at once. The men followed the coastline, subsisting on seals, foxes, ravens and snowy owls, hoping as they journeyed to come upon the *Karluk* or another of the expedition ships. Game was not abundant in the area, and for that reason no Eskimo villages were to be found. "Those were sad days for us," Wilkins wrote, "and they must have been heartbreaking for Stefansson."[3]

Eventually, the men reached Barrow where they learned that the *Karluk* had last been seen drifting along the coast. Brower reported that the expedition's two other ships had already passed Barrow sailing east. How far they got no one could say, but if Stefansson pushed on, his party knew they would eventually encounter the ships. With winter closing in, there was no reason to hurry. In late November they went on, covering six hundred miles before finally reaching Collinson Point, Alaska, where the men of the *Mary Sachs* and the *Alaska* were in winter quarters. The scientists of the Southern Party had hoped to begin work in Coronation Gulf that season, but their easterly passage had been held up by the ice.

Before leaving Barrow, Stefansson wrote to G. J. Desbarats, informing him of the *Karluk*'s drift and outlining his revised plans that included leaving Jenness with the Eskimos of the Colville River region so that the anthropologist would not have to travel further overland. "Jenness," he explained, "suffered in fall from tropical fever contracted in New Guinea and the trip would be an undertaking for him."[4] Observing the Alaskan Eskimo and studying their language would be just as useful to Jenness as working among natives of the Mackenzie Delta. The other scientists, however, could make the trek and establish themselves in the Delta. Topographical work there would be very valuable in view of an anticipated increase in ship traffic on the river. Stefansson's own object of searching for new land to the north—the first priority of the expedition— would go forward despite the fate of the *Karluk,* which was to have been his exploration base.

When Stefansson reached Collinson Point, Anderson had just left for Herschel Island to get mail. In his absence, Chipman was in charge, and the expedition scientists were idle. In Chipman's opinion, it was impossible to do any worthwhile work in the winter. Anderson had agreed, not only because he realized that the Survey men lacked arctic experience, but also because he was not inclined to push other professionals. "It was easy for me," wrote Stefansson later, "to convince him that a far wider program was open to us." Chipman moved immediately at Stefansson's urging because "like any good workman he [Chipman] was anxious to do as much work and to have as much to show for his time as possible."[5]

The expedition suffered another loss during that winter: Andrew Norem, the *Mary Sachs*'s steward, had asked to talk privately to Stefansson when he arrived at Collinson Point. Norem confided that he was despondent and feared for his sanity. Because of his queer behaviour, Anderson had lightened Norem's work load, a decision that Stefansson supported, although some members of the party argued that the steward was malingering. However, several months later the unfortunate man shot himself.

Stefansson stayed only a few days at Collinson Point; he was anxious to meet Anderson and settle arrangements for the coming spring activities. The two men met about twenty miles east of Collinson Point, and there the trouble that had been brewing for so long erupted. Anderson opposed Stefansson's plan to survey the Mackenzie Delta, arguing that the government had ordered an investigation of Coronation Gulf. Stefansson replied that it made no sense to remain idle—instead, why not make a useful survey of the Delta? Anderson offered to resign so that Stefansson could direct the Southern Section personally. Stefansson rejected Anderson's manoeuvre, reminding him that the expedition's first priority was geographic exploration off the coast. He refused to abandon his exploration plans. Anderson, he said, must stay because neither Chipman nor any of the other scientists had enough arctic experience to replace him. Having registered his protest, Anderson agreed to carry on.

However, Anderson argued that Stefansson had no right to divert either supplies or men from the Southern Section in order to compensate for the loss of the *Karluk*. Stefansson asserted that he had been charged with leadership of the expedition and added, "I could not escape the blame if the expedition failed; it was for me therefore to insist on the carrying out of the plan I thought most likely to bring success."[6]

From this point on, the breach between the two erstwhile friends was never to close although Stefansson explained in his book that he felt "sure that Dr. Anderson on mature consideration would see the advisability of following instructions, protecting himself as I had suggested by putting his disapproval on record and assuming the position that he considered it his duty to carry out orders, irrespective of his opinion of their wisdom."[7]

In this conflict one can see the contrasting attitudes of the two men. Stefansson was not daunted by the absence of the *Karluk* and was determined to find the means of accomplishing his mission by redistributing resources and extending the government's credit. Compared to Stefansson's indomitable optimism, his antagonist revealed an abiding pessimism that was aggravated by hostility toward his commander. Expedition resources would not support exploration of the Beaufort Sea, Anderson declared. He insisted that the effort would only waste money, and perhaps lives, and would not produce worthwhile results. As he had not been too satisfied with his own work on the previous expedition, he may have felt a heavy responsibility for the Southern Party's success and a deep fear that Stefansson's demands would saddle him with a failure in the government's view.

To avoid tension, Stefansson remained away from the Southern Party's Collinson Point base during the 1913-14 winter. He was busy enough arranging for stores to replace some of those lost with the *Karluk,* in drawing up a plan for the scientists' work in the McKenzie Delta, and in making preparations at Martin Point for his 1914 ice trip. He also travelled to Fort Macpherson to send dispatches to Ottawa. With the spring he had to return to Collinson Point to confront the scientists bearing the unhappy news that Anderson's wife had lost her newborn baby.

By the time Stefansson reached Collinson Point, he was not in a comfortable state of mind. He had sent Storkerson to Anderson with orders directing him to prepare equipment and provisions for the ice journey that was to start from Martin Point, about forty miles east. Anderson, however, refused to provide any assistance and wrote Stefansson that the scientists would protest if he used any of the expedition supplies that were carried on the *Belvedere.* Stefansson was outraged, but in writing about the letter later on he was able to be facetious. "They [the scientists] were no stage villains bent themselves on being criminal. In their own esteem they were acting in the public interest in trying to forestall misuse of public property." In the "interests of science" they were preventing a foray...which in their opinion could yield no knowledge."[8]

When Stefansson confronted Anderson at Collinson Point, he asked the chief of the Southern Party whether it was his view that he had independent command of the southern section. Fritz Johansen volunteered to reply to Stefansson's question, defiantly informing him that Anderson was commander of the Southern Party and that Stefansson "had better go home to Ottawa" to report his failure.[9] Anderson expressed himself, too, pointedly accusing Stefansson of planning an ice journey out of his desire for notoriety. No amount of rational discussion could sway Anderson. "I've wasted three years of my life on your fool errands," he snapped.[10]

Stefansson finally gave up the argument and called for volunteers for his proposed ice party. He immediately got the willing support of Captain Joe Bernard, Wilkins, Captain Nahmens (of the *Alaska*), J.R. Crawford, and finally even Johansen. These volunteers, and several Eskimos, provided an ample support party. Stefansson purchased provisions from Captain S.F. Cottle's whaler, *Belvedere*, and, in addition, he received offers of help from several sportsmen who had chartered the *Polar Bear* for an arctic cruise. (The *Belvedere* and the *Polar Bear* were also caught in the ice that season.) Stefansson had been given a pocket chronometer, an essential piece of equipment, by J. J. O'Neill, the geologist of the expedition. This instrument was extremely important for his ice journey; without it he might have been forced to cancel his plans. When he was given the chronometer, Stefansson was ready to go, but not without some natural forebodings. He directed Anderson to dispatch the *North Star* to Banks Island in the event he did not return to Alaska by late summer. The ship would be used as a base for further northern explorations the following season, assuming the drift of the ice did not prevent the exploration party from reaching Banks Island, thereby forcing her to return to the Alaskan coast. If Anderson disobeyed orders and refused to send the *North Star,* Stefansson knew he would be stranded, but he had to take the chance, relying heavily on the sympathy and integrity of George Wilkins to ensure that the *Star* would be sent.

Final preparations for the ice journey were impeded to some extent by the mischief-making of some expedition members. Rumours and slanders fly thick and fast in the sparsely populated Arctic and some of the scientists had warned white traders and Eskimos that the Canadian government would surely refuse to acknowledge any obligations incurred by the expedition commander. While these innuendos were annoying to Stefansson, they were not fatal to his preparations, although he was forced to pay higher prices and wages because of the supposed risk.

CHAPTER 10

First Ice Journey

O N 22 MARCH, 1914, after delays caused by a heavy gale, the exploration party started out from Martin Point. The party consisted of four sledges, twenty-five dogs, and seven men, carrying 3,500 pounds of equipment and provisions. Stefansson, Storkerson, and Ole Andreasen were to be supported at first by a party of four men—Peter Bernard, Aarnout Castel, Burt McConnell, and George Wilkins—to help them get through the ice hummocks near shore. Pulling sleds over such obstacles was exhausting, and sometimes a trail had to be carved out by hand. They were less likely to encounter hummocks a few miles out to sea, and the support party could then be sent back to shore.

The journey got off to a bad start. On the second day out, Pete Bernard smashed his forehead against the handle-bars of his sled and tore his scalp open. McConnell closed the gash with a fourteen-stitch operation, and the party returned to shore with the injured mariner. The next day they set out once more. Unfortunately, the temperatures were much higher than usual, so in places the ice was not frozen solidly and they were forced to cross from floe to floe where the corners touched, sometimes having to leap across narrow openings.

The ice was in constant motion, throwing hummocks where sea ice ground against the shorefast ice and where one ice floe ground into another. The first time McConnell saw a lead [a channel of open water between ice floes] where this action was taking place, he was impressed: "A magnificent and awe-inspiring sight...met our eyes. The whole field on the other side was in motion to the eastward and often would come in contact with the floe on which we stood. Then the rending and tearing and crushing of the floes was almost deafening, and pieces of ice larger than an ordinary house would be tumbled about like corks in the water. The opposite floe would come tearing along at a speed of over a mile an hour." Where the floes collided, ridges up to thirty feet high and more were thrown up. "It was a weird and impressive sight," McConnell observed. "I was a little sobered by it."[1]

McConnell made a good addition to the ice party. Earlier he had impressed Stefansson as "an exception to the general rule of my men," one willing to assume that if Eskimos could hunt game on the ice, he could also hunt successfully. McConnell had been away from Collinson Point when the ice party left for the ice journey, but, eager to go along, he caught up with the explorers on the ice just before Bernard's accident. Although Stefansson instructed Anderson to have McConnell bring along a badly needed heavy sledge McConnell was using, Anderson had advised the young man to take a light one.[2]

Their run of bad luck was not over yet, however; they were compelled to give up an attempt to travel directly out to sea because the ice remained too mushy. A raging gale struck as they camped along the shore-fast ice about six miles offshore. Winds up to 86 miles per hour were recorded. When the storm abated, Stefansson was amazed to find that they were now twenty miles offshore, having drifted forty miles to the east. Worse still, Wilkins and Castel had left the main party before the storm in order to put their movie equipment safely ashore. Now their services as part of the support party and the valuable supplies they carried with them could not be utilized.

The men felt uneasy when they pitched their tent and bedded down at night. New to sea-ice travel, they could never be sure that a storm might not split the floe and dump them into the frigid sea. If the floe looked safe, the men would undress before crawling into their sleeping bags. However, they had to be alert for other noises as well as cracking ice. Dog fights had to be halted immediately in case these indispensable animals injured each other, and it was also dangerous if a polar bear approached unheard. On shore, polar bears were timid, but on the ice they were unafraid of men. All the bears expected to encounter at sea were seals—and seals were their natural prey. In such instances the men dashed out naked from their sleeping bags. As long as they could either stop the fight or kill the bear within two minutes, they suffered no ill effects from exposure.

Sea ice travel could intimidate the dogs at times. This occurred when the travellers moved across a floe that was being ground at its perimeter by heavier, surrounding floes, creating pressure that built up ridges. The newly formed ridges would sometimes march slowly towards the travellers from all sides causing a startling, noisy roar. The movement made all the ice shiver and paralyzed the dogs. Then the men had to drag dogs and sledges to a more stable area. The dogs became even more terrified when forced to cross water moats formed on the flow as it sunk a bit against the pressure of an adjacent one. The dogs resisted movement and had to be man-handled to cross to the safer floe.

The first polar bear they encountered almost got Stefansson, who had to turn his back on the animal (which was standing a mere five yards from him across a lead) in order to unstrap his rifle from his sledge. Storkerson got to his rifle first, and it took several shots to dispatch the retreating bear. Stefansson did not approve of all the hullabaloo of the chase. He believed that excitement on a hunt indicated a poor hunt. Hungry professionals should kill what food they required calmly and efficiently.

As the men moved beyond the shallow waters of the outer continental shelf, they were cheered to discover that seals could be found in leads where the water was deep. Stefansson had counted on shooting them for food despite the opinions of Eskimos and whaling men who insisted that seals did not live far out on the sea ice. Stefansson did not heed Eskimo lore on this occasion because the natives did not hunt far off shore, and in his eyes whalemen were not authorities on seal habits. Nor had he been influenced by Robert Peary or other explorers like Fridtjof Nansen on this point. Peary had made no attempt to look for seals on his great ice trips to the pole as he was not dependent upon hunting. This was also true of Nansen.

Stefansson and Storkerson had learned earlier from Eskimos about hunting seals on ice near shore. The technique for hunting far out on the alleged "lifeless" sea was the same. Hunters could approach seals as they lay napping near their surfacing hole on the ice. Seals slept warily, frequently raising their heads to look for enemies before slumbering again. Approaching hunters had to crawl on all fours. They would thus appear to be other seals. When the hunter got within fifty yards, he could readily dispatch his quarry before the mammal could dive to safety.

In letters to Wilkins and Anderson which he sent back with the returning support party of Crawford, Johansen, and McConnell on 7 April, Stefansson informed them that he might have to return to land at Banks Island or Prince Patrick Island, rather than Alaska as he had planned originally. The easterly drift on the first portion of the journey had made it unlikely that they would be near Alaska when they decided to head for shore. If it seemed feasible to travel east on the ice and land on Banks Island, they could spend the summer hunting caribou for food and clothing and then set out for the north the following spring. For this contingency Stefansson wanted Wilkins to take command of the *North Star* and bring it to Banks Island as soon as it was possible to navigate. As it turned out, to Stefansson's great annoyance, Anderson claimed to have misunderstood these directions and gave Wilkins the *Mary Sachs* instead. Stefansson was later sure that this was a deliberate attempt on Anderson's part to hinder his work, because the *Star* was a superior ice vessel and would have provided much better support.

By 26 April the party was some two hundred miles off the coast and still they had not discovered any new land. Storkerson and Andreasen wanted to turn back, but Stefansson proposed his plan of establishing a base on Banks Island. Which course was better? Stefansson feared that the westward current might well sweep them north of the Bering Strait if they attempted to reach the Alaskan coast. He appreciated his companions' preference for the known hazards they faced on the ice to the south to the unknown conditions of the ice to the east, but an ice journey along the great circle course to Banks Island would take them through an uncharted region, and exploration of the unknown was their chief purpose. Stefansson's companions feared that seals would be scarce to the east since they had noticed a decline in their numbers as the party travelled farther out to sea. They also feared that Banks Island, which was unpopulated, would have no game. Eventually, Stefansson prevailed by giving in to his companions' demands for a pay raise.

Stefansson complained in his diary that the two men "wanted to soak the government."[3] Apparently they had threatened midway on the journey to return to shore unless their pay was raised to twenty-five dollars a day—a handsome wage for those days, even though few men would travel over sea ice at any price.

Stefansson was never free from apprehension about the activities and malice of the Southern Party. He also worried about the scarcity of game as the travellers started eastwards for Banks Island. Although his provisions were running low, he felt sure game would turn up, and he resolved not to kill the dogs except in case of dire necessity. His anxieties seemed to fuel his resolve to get back after a successful journey: "If I fail to reach the Alaska shore many things that should be done will remain undone and many others, even of those I have given instructions about, will be done badly in order to prove that they should not have been done at all."[4]

During the first week of May, it appeared that Storkerson's and Andreasen's fears were to be confirmed. They did not see any seals, and both men and dogs were reduced to half rations. Stefansson professed to believe that there actually were seals nearby, but that the necessity of travelling fast in order to reach land before break-up left them no leisure time for watching leads. In fact, he was worried too, but he confined his fears to his diary, while he assured his companions that all would go well: "It is difficult and dangerous to be traveling out on the sea ice in this latitude of the Beaufort Sea after May first. If we should get strong easterly winds now, for instance, our chances of reaching Banks Island would be small." He attributed most of the hazards they faced to the two weeks' delay in making preparations caused by "silly jealousies." Had Storkerson received "proper assistance" from Anderson, he continued, they could have started off while the midwinter frosts still held. He concluded, "One thinks back to the perversities of human nature which can, if one keeps that point of view, be seen as the source of all one's evil fortune."[5]

On 15 May Stefansson shot a seal at a distance of 3,100 feet. The men were immediately cheered by the feast this occasioned. From this point on seals abounded, and the men enjoyed their journey. Stefansson was delighted: "We are taking solid comfort, with no worries for the morrow. If it takes us a month to get ashore, we shall feed well the whole time as we have done today—a feast on boiled seal liver, tripe, flippers and blubber."[6] Living off the country was, he felt sure, superior to the traditional mode of provisioning with pemmican. "It is a game as well as work...the incentive of pure sport...[It was] no sordid desire to best a rival but merely to show what you and your method can do."[7] The weather was not agreeable, so they took a day's rest and then marched on.

The journey was slow going because the party encountered leads more frequently and also because the drifting ice was carrying them westwards while they were trying to travel east. For several days they were marooned on an ice floe, surrounded by extensive stretches of open water. It looked as though they might have to spend the summer on the ice island, and so the question of provisioning arose once again. This time their dilemma was suddenly resolved. A polar bear wandered into camp, and they immediately killed it. In the next few days four more bears fell before their rifles, providing them with a well-stocked larder.

On 5 June the lead that separated the ice on which they were stranded from a neighbouring floe narrowed, and they were able to cross by sled boat, made by fastening a tarpaulin around their sledges. This useful device ferried them from one floe to the next when leads opened up; otherwise, they would wait until the wind pushed the floes together and closed the lead. Finally, on 23 June, they landed on Norway Island just off the northwest coast of Banks Island. Thus, the expedition's first extensive ice journey was crowned with success, and Stefansson's theories about living off the land were brilliantly vindicated. He had not yet discovered new land, but he had demonstrated command of the means by which new lands, if they existed, could be discovered.

Stefansson had two excellent men in Storkerson and Andreasen. Storkerson's earlier experience in ice travel with Leffingwell and Mikkelsen had given him confidence, and Andreasen adapted satisfactorily: "They are as well suited for this work as it is easy to imagine," Stefansson confided to his diary. "Neither of them worries or whines and both are optimistic about the prospects. This last is important. Traveling with an empty sled and living off the country is no work for a pessimist." Stefansson added a retrospective endorsement of his companions in *The Friendly Arctic.* "The longer the time that intervenes the more my feeling of gratitude to these men and my appreciation of them has grown. Those who have gone through a difficult experience anywhere will know that nothing more could be said, after all, than this: that if I had a similar trip to make over again I could not imagine any companions I should prefer to Storkerson and Ole."[8]

Stefansson had first met Ole Andreasen in the spring of 1912, and Andreasen's good nature charmed him at once: "He had at least the admirable quality of cheerfulness under all circumstances and an absolute inability to see how anybody could be lonesome anywhere, no matter how isolated or remote from various things that ordinary people enjoy....Those who philosophize on such things would say he had 'resources within himself' which are lacking in most of us."[9] Andreasen was well fitted for the expedition work because of his northern experience. In 1900, as a seventeen-year-old seaman, he had emigrated from Norway. He landed in San Francisco, learned to speak English, and shipped aboard Alaskan fishing boats for a number of years. In 1909 he voyaged to Nome, but he could not find work in gold mining or in anything else. When one of the Nome mosquito boat skippers engaged in the Siberian trade offered him a job as a deck hand, Andreasen eagerly accepted. Nome-based traders generally exchanged contraband liquor for Siberian products and were anxious to avoid Russian authorities. Although Andreason's schooner, the *Edna*, narrowly escaped a Russian gunboat patrolling the coast in 1909, the Scandinavian sailor did not hesitate to make a return voyage the next year.

By coincidence, Andreasen met his elder brother Martin, whom he had not seen for twenty years, in Nome. Martin had gone to sea at the age of thirteen, eventually enlisting in the U.S. Navy and serving as gunner on a ship that took part in the Manila Bay battle during the Spanish-American War. He left the navy, built the schooner *North Star*, and entered the Nome-Siberian trade. In 1910 the two brothers ventured on the *North Star* into the western Arctic for trading, whaling, and trapping.

When Stefansson met Martin at Atkinson Point, he appreciated the navigational qualities of the little *North Star*. The schooner drew only four feet two inches of water when loaded, and it could skirt the shallow water between ice pack and shore along the arctic coast, where large whaling ships, working far offshore in the heavy ice pack, were unable to force their way through. Andreasen described another feature of the *Star*'s ability to navigate sea ice which impressed Stefansson—when the ice closed in and threatened to imprison the schooner, Andreasen would steam at a large floe and slide partially up on it. Then the crew would use ice anchors, blocks, and tackle to haul the boat up on the floe to avoid the ice pressure. When conditions improved, Andreasen would blast the harbouring floe apart with dynamite and free the *North Star*. Such stratagems fascinated Stefansson, whose preferred method of dealing with such difficulties was by adaptation and avoidance rather than by force. He resolved to buy the *North Star* if the opportunity were ever offered, and later on he had the chance.

Both of the Andreasen brothers thus were to give Stefansson's endeavours useful support: Martin, by teaching him the value of inshore navigation in small, unreinforced vessels, and Ole, by agreeing to travel on the sea ice. Ole's reasons for joining the ice exploration venture were the result, in part, of his respect for Stefansson. When others would refuse to participate in such "folly," Andreasen did not want the explorer to be held up for want of "a man." Perhaps he also remembered that it was Stefansson who had hauled wood to his camp the previous year when he lacked dogs for the purpose.[10]

While the travellers journeyed across the ice, Wilkins had made a memorable voyage in the *Mary Sachs*. He did not have a blue-ribbon crew—"Three of [them] were confessed murderers and they had killed more than once."[11] Aboard the ship, in order to placate the reluctant crew, Wilkins broke out a case of whiskey. The men drank themselves to stupification while Wilkins, Captain Peter Bernard, and Natkusiak got the *Sachs* moving.

By the time the drunks revived, the schooner was eighty miles from shore, and they were not to happy. They were sure they had been shanghaied, which was partially true. Bernard was a tough skipper, as he had to be. Even later, when a seaman's life had become by comparison somewhat decorous, arctic masters were forced to coerce and brutalize their seamen. Neither captain nor crew had much opportunity to appeal their grievances to an authority. When one of the drunks jumped overboard into the ice-littered sea in hopes of swimming to an Eskimo village, "he was hauled back, keel-hauled, and shackled until he was submissive."[12] Another malcontent tried to brain Wilkins with an eight-pound hammer, but, just in time, the cook felled him with a gridiron. Although physically subdued, the crewmen still refused to work until Wilkins promised them pay at extortionate rates.

Settling things with the rebellious crew did not end the travails of the voyage. The *Sachs* was not effective in ice navigation. One of her propellers was lost in an encounter with the pack. The vessel then was nipped by the ice, the rudder unshipped, and a hole stove in the bow. Leakage was constant. At one point the piling ice shoved the *Sachs* high and dry on the beach, but the crew kedged it off. Later they were caught in the pack and drifted helplessly for miles. It began to seem to Wilkins that the Southern Party men who had warned him against making a suicidal voyage had been right. Eventually, however, in late August 1914 they landed safely on Banks Island.

Wilkins immediately set out on a hunting expedition. He found no signs of game near the coast and reflected morosely that even if the ice party had reached land, they had probably starved to death. However, he speculated that it was more likely that they had not been able to make any headway against the wind and drift of ice floes and had probably died of starvation on the ice. For months in fact they had believed Stefansson dead, and news of his loss had long since been flashed around the world. As Wilkins put it later, their enterprise had been dismissed by "Eskimos and whalers" as " 'one crazy and two deluded men going north over the sea ice to commit suicide.' "[13]

After a couple of days of unsuccessful hunting Wilkins discovered a mound that seemed to have built by human hands. Could Stefansson have erected it? "I found myself running wildly and reached the mound breathless and exhausted," Wilkins recalled later. He tore a clod of earth from the top of the mound and found a note left by Stefansson. "I was wild with joy. Never before or since have I been stirred with such emotion. To this day I do not know what capers I cut, alone on that lonely hilltop: any observer might have thought I was mad."[14]

Wilkins relied on his experience as a youth in the Australian bush as he followed the tracks left by the three explorers. In the early hours of the morning he reached the coast and found the missing men fast asleep in the *Sachs* camp. He burned to hear their experiences, but could not bring himself to waken them. "They looked well-nourished," he reported. "Their dogs were fat and well and all of them were there. It seemed a miracle. But even this did not prepare me for the healthy and well-fed appearance of the men."[15]

When the eager Wilkins heard how they had lived for five months with an ample larder of bear and seal meat, he was amazed. "They told no tale of hardship, hunger, or adventure. We were almost disappointed," he remarked.[16] In travelling over a thousand miles, they had never missed a meal.

Stefansson was disturbed that Wilkins had not insisted upon bringing the *North Star*. Wilkins explained that he had accepted Anderson's decision to switch vessels because he assumed that Stefansson was dead. Had this been true, Anderson would have been in charge of the entire expedition. As much as Stefansson appreciated Wilkin's loyalty in volunteering for the ice journey earlier, and in coming to Banks Island even though there was little hope of finding them, he could not quite forgive him for assuming that he might not be able to accomplish what he had set out to do.

The sight of the *Mary Sachs,* hauled up on the beach for repairs to leaks and her damaged screw, was not pleasing, nor was the absence of essential equipment. Anderson kept a large tarpaulin, sounding wire, and a sledge, as well as the ship Stefansson had wanted, at Coronation Gulf because, presumably, Stefansson would not need them. The tarpaulin was needed to replace the worn one used to convert sledges into boats in crossing leads; the wire for water depth measurements; and the sledge to replace those worn out in service. "Here I was," recalled Stefansson later, "with two companions, ready to continue with the plans of which everyone was aware. Instead of having supplies and equipment necessary, I had a land-fast ship that had lost one of her propellers and leaked so badly that she could not be refloated. And I had an unseaworthy launch that could not be made ready for use before the freeze-up."[17]

Wilkins did have some good news that relieved Stefansson's mind considerably. The men on the *Karluk* had been rescued from Wrangel Island. It was not until later that Stefansson learned that many of the *Karluk* people had not survived.

Although the *Mary Sachs* carried provisions for a year, fresh meat was needed to avoid scurvy. Now there were thirteen people to feed, and Stefansson was amused that the leader who had been written off as dead now had to provide for his rescuers.

From their camp at Cape Kellett, Stefansson, Wilkins, and Natkusiak took advantage of the long summer days to make hunting excursions. As the season advanced, the pressure to find game mounted: "We were working against time in a strange and difficult land," Stefansson wrote, "no longer beautiful with sparkling brooks and golden flowers but frostbitten and rocky, the ponds freezing and cracking like artillery, the caribou growing leaner and more scarce, the light becoming briefer and thinner."[18]

Dark days ended the hunting season, but all hands kept busy over the 1914-15 winter preparing for the next year's explorations. The Eskimo women sewed clothing and boats, Peter Bernard made sledges, and the others trapped and made caribou pemmican.

The diary Stefansson maintained on the expedition sometimes reflected his daily mood. On Thanksgiving Day, 1914, as the explorers feasted on Banks Island caribou, Stefansson mused on his luck. "In a way, many things have been going wrong the past year, but still there is much to be thankful for." Prospects for future work seemed good, in comparison to a year earlier, "for all the men here are harmonious and well-disposed toward the expedition.

So far as I know there is no intrigue, no jealousy, no double dealing—a pleasant contrast with last year."[19]

He was particularly pleased with Wilkin's performance. "Wilkins is as efficient and reliable as ever and co-operates with me
better than he could have last year for he is coming to realize that
the things he disapproved of...were mostly dictated by experience
and my familiarity with local conditions and prospects." Peter Bernard's work pleased him too. Bernard laboured long hours to repair
sledges and otherwise behaved as if his "sole concern was the success of the expedition."[20]

Stefansson often thought about Anderson's mutiny. In January
1915, everything was going well, "unlike last year" when all but
Bernard were "half-hearted or the reverse of interested and offered
little encouragement in any way." He thought he understood the
reasons for the improved atmosphere: "There is now no ring leader
to foment discontent, and they seem to have been impressed by
what we accomplished on last year's trip in spite of all the accidental
and malicious handicaps we were under."[21]

While Stefansson had been exploring the northern seas, the
Southern Party continued surveying and other scientific work. Anderson established a base in May 1915 at Bernard Harbour on the
south shore of Dolphin and Union Strait. Wilkins arrived to take
over the North Star, and with great reluctance, Anderson complied
with Stefansson's request for the ship. Before Wilkins could take
the ship north, however, he was ordered to convey Anderson and
other men to Bathurst Inlet. Anderson sent with Wilkins a report
to Stefansson on the Southern Party's activities, and its tone indicated that he was still hostile.

CHAPTER 11

Mail Call

STEFANSSON'S correspondence reveals much about himself and his aspirations. Although he was selective in the information he chose to divulge, he was not secretive or particularly circumspect. He was candid with his friends. Once he was asked if he had read H.G. Wells. "Of course I read H.G. Wells," he retorted, "and everything that falls to hand. I am omnivorous." His ambition was to cover as wide a range as possible. "I don't want to be merely an explorer or merely an ethnologist or merely anything—I want to be what a friendly critic would call an 'all around' man and what a hostile one would refer to as a 'jack-of-all-trades, master of none.' " He was not above noting with some pride that "it seems that some people see in my book that I am what I want to be."[1]

The reviews of *My Life with the Eskimo,* published after he had returned to the Arctic with the Canadian Arctic Expedition, did not reach him until 1915, and he relished them. It relieved him to see that his earlier work had won approval. One reviewer pointed out, "it is not often that an explorer combines the philosopher, the scientist, the man of action, and the writer....Through its quiet, nervous, lucid English shines the light of a strange and engaging personality."[2] This handsome tribute appeared in the *London Star* in December 1914. Like any author, Stefansson glowed in the light of the praise. All of his reviews at the time seem to have been favourable, but Stefansson could not resist singling out the most discerning. In a letter to Mrs. Anderson he wrote: "One of the American reviews says that there are but a book or two in a decade that belong both to the domain of literature and of science, but that this book does. Modest, am I not, to quote you these things? But, you see, I trust others better than myself to judge not me but what I have done." And how should one react to adverse criticism? "When one damns you, it sort of saves your face to set against him another that blesses. And then, as a good debater might argue, we will have to assume that if he who praises is not wholly wrong, the one who damns must err in part."[3]

Mail reached the expedition infrequently, and so, although the news was old, it was devoured greedily. Stefansson's correspondents tried to cheer him on and pass along information of mutual interest. Cyrus C. Adams of the American Geographical Society wrote that all the explorer's friends were gratified that he was ashore when the *Karluk* moved off with the ice pack. "[We] all realize you could do nothing if you were on the ship, and believe that you will be able to carry on and do all a mortal man can." In geographical circles, people were still upset about the deaths of Robert Scott and his party on their return from the South Pole. "I think Scott made a mistake," wrote Adams. "To die of scurvy today is 'inexcusable' and it was wrong to travel without dogs."[4]

An English geographer wrote in praise of Stefansson's *My Life with the Eskimo* and indicated that he was reviewing Hudson Stuck's account of his Mount McKinley climb. Stuck, Stefansson replied, is a "good missionary...a real man who *helps* natives, and travels in the cold to do it."[5] Later, Stuck was to travel many miles to aid Stefansson when the explorer was stricken with typhoid.

Close friends wrote Stefansson that they were confident he would overcome the loss of the *Karluk*. "We know what you are and have been to science and to your friends. Your past is safe, your future is assured, for you will do all that a man can do."[6] Such messages were a tonic. Stefansson sometimes experienced depression and self-doubt, and it was good to be reminded that firm friends retained their faith in him and his work.

Other letters were less cheering. An editor of Macmillan's wrote that Stefansson could expect virtually no royalties. Newspaper reports claiming that the Canadian Arctic Expedition had practically failed at the outset had hurt sales. Yet, the editor assured him, the book is good, and the haste in preparation caused by his departure was not too apparent.

Stefansson's reflections on arctic missionaries in *My Life with the Eskimo* were not calculated to win him popularity, yet he felt his honest criticisms were worthy of respect even if his readers disagreed with him. However, a clipping from Toronto's *Catholic Register* savaging both his present and past work angered him because he felt its criticism hit "below the belt." The editor predicted the Canadian Arctic Expedition would fail. "We have no faith in this expedition," he wrote, "especially now that Captain Bartlett, the only really experienced explorer, is separated from it." Even more stinging was the editor's assertion that "Stefansson is a blowhard, anyway. His claim of discovery of the White Eskimos put him in the Cook category of [polar] explorers."[7]

For Stefansson, it was one thing to be criticized, but to be rated with Cook, whose fraudulent claims to reaching the summit of Mt. McKinley and later, the North Pole, had made him northern exploration's surpassing liar, was too much. Stefansson wrote to the *Register,* sturdily denying that he had ever claimed to have *discovered* white Eskimos, insisting that he had only *reported* in 1910 what Franklin had seen in 1826, Simpson in 1837, and Klengenberg in 1906. He added that had the editor consulted Eskimo authorities or noted the scientific organizations which had honoured him and contributed to his expeditions, he would hardly have placed Stefansson with Cook. Stefansson added that a church paper should maintain a higher level of journalism than the average newspaper, and he reminded the editor that Christ spoke favourably of charity. Perhaps, Stefansson speculated, the editor thought Stefansson had misrepresented missionaries in the North and therefore that "you consider me an incompetent ice traveler on the ground that I am hostile." In fact, Stefansson pointed out, the lay press found his views "untinged by hostility" and impartial, although some Protestant missionaries complained that he praised Catholics too highly. "Comments of that sort are 'all to the good' from my point of view [because] they will raise up...defenders who might not otherwise take interest, for gratuitous insolence always does. So, my dear sir, dip your pen in gall and write with a flourish—and may my clipping bureau not miss a paragraph of it."[8]

Abuse from the press was uncommon in Canada. Only the Toronto publications *Saturday Night* and the *Catholic Register* showed personal hostility toward Stefansson. *Saturday Night* published news of the explorer's supposed death as a good thing and cautioned the government to avoid risking other lives in search of him.[9]

Press criticism notwithstanding, Stefansson's ethnographic studies among the Copper Eskimo were extremely important. Diamond Jenness, who followed up Stefansson's work in 1909-10, admitted that "the main sources of information for all that relates to the ethnology of the Copper Eskimos are the works of Mr. V. Stefansson, the commander of the Canadian Arctic Expedition. Mr. Stefansson obtained an astonishing amount of very valuable information in a comparatively short space of time, and while it was inevitable that a certain number of errors should have crept into his accounts, yet his works will always stand as the basis on which future investigations will have to build."[10]

Great explorers wrote to him as well. Adolphus W. Greely, who led a U.S. Army expedition to the Arctic in 1881-84, assured Stefansson that the *Karluk* survivors would be rescued soon. He had heard that two Russian icebreakers had departed Nome for Wrangel Island to rescue them. As it turned out, the ice-breakers were unable to penetrate the sea-ice, and the ship that eventually reached the island was a small trading schooner.

Stefansson told his side of the *Karluk* story to Robert Peary. He knew that Peary and the *Karluk* skipper, Bob Bartlett, were old friends and comrades, but he wanted to clarify the situation. "Bartlett went against my judgement while I slept, after I gave the local knowledge of whalers to him." Stefansson confessed to Peary that he had written a letter earlier about Bartlett's ice navigation but had decided not to send it. In his first letter, he said, there had been "too much telling tales out of school," and he had "no desire to upbraid Bartlett, but just wanted to make things clear."[11]

Stefansson wrote to Desbarats in January 1914 sharply criticizing Bartlett's attitude and seamanship. He hoped his remarks could be kept "personal and confidential," but he felt that the facts should be recorded in case there might be an official inquiry if the *Karluk* went down. Bartlett was no quitter and managed the ship well and cheerfully when things went badly, Stefansson wrote, "but he has a Big Head in Arctic matters. Peary, Shackleton, and Amundsen listened attentively to information about districts new to them, but Bartlett is diametrically the opposite." Bartlett was not inclined to heed others and even "declined the assistance of Nome dog drivers, Leffingwell (who has made the only map of the north coast of Alaska that can be relied upon for soundings and passages inside islands and who offered it) and Hadley, who has been sailing the north coast continuously since 1889." Both men advised Bartlett that it would be better to work the ship as near shore as possible. When Stefansson directed Bartlett to assign a seaman to test the depth of the water as they rounded Point Barrow, the rumour on ship was that "this was done in deference to Stefansson's 'landsman's whim!' "[12]

Stefansson reiterated in this letter, as he did elsewhere, that he accepted the responsibility for what happened and that Bartlett had not been insubordinate. Stefansson conferred that he had "lacked assertiveness or moral courage to carry his opinion in the face of the ship's company."[13] Certainly, by deferring to the ship's captain Stefansson made by far his greatest mistake of the expedition.

The sharpest letter that Stefansson wrote from the field was addressed to R.W. Brock, chief of the Geological Survey. Brock had responded to the complaints from the Southern Party that Stefansson, after losing the *Karluk*, was demanding provisions and equipment that the Southern Party could not afford to give up. Desbarats had instructed Stefansson not to interfere with the work of the Southern Party, and Brock, although he had no direct authority over the expedition leader, cautioned him in the same manner. Stefansson was angry—Brock had given him the same advice that his "juniors and subordinates" had already given, and it had never been his intention to impede the work of the scientists. He fumed, "the fact that made me sore was that everybody should assume that I alone had no sane idea in regard to the conduct of the expedition. Don't try to lord it over me," he warned, "Your scientific position does not give you that right."[14]

On the lighter side, Stefansson received a letter from Arthur Conan Doyle, the English author, who confessed that he felt in addressing Stefansson in care of the Royal North West Mounted Police at Herschel Island as if he were sending a letter to the man in the moon. Doyle had heard about the *Karluk*'s plight and was sympathetic, but he advised his adventurous friend to come to England when he returned from the Arctic. "Marry and settle down," he wrote. "You'll get more out of life forty miles or so from London than anywhere else."[15]

Mrs. Anderson made a teasing reference to her talents as matchmaker for Stefansson when he returned from the North, if he would ever care to have a close relationship with a woman. The explorer was somewhat irked: "As for my ever meaning very much to any woman—that is rather a flight of your imagination," was his spirited reply. "There are many women who are my close friends, and surely you have never seen signs of any of them being more? Old people are my best friends of both sexes, and especially women

with white hair. And I would not have it otherwise though I could."
And he explained further, "When you combine such work as mine
with such a temperament as mine you get a person of whom any
woman might well beware—and most of them do."[16]

A review of the correspondence between Stefansson and Anderson's wife during the first two years of the expedition, reveals
deeper sources of Anderson's disgruntlement. The germ of the discord, which very nearly destroyed the purpose of the Canadian Arctic Expedition, owed something to Anderson's wife. The former
Mae Belle Allstrand had known both Anderson and Stefansson
when they were students at the University of Iowa where she had
earned a Master of Arts degree shortly after the two-man expedition
returned in 1912. In 1913 she married Anderson. During preparation for the C.A.E., the newly married couple saw a good deal of
Stefansson, yet their relationship with him was somewhat inhibited
by Mrs. Anderson's obvious ambitions for Rudolph. Stefansson
was aware of the difficulty, but he wanted to avoid any personal
conflict with Anderson on the eve of their important work.

If Stefansson believed that his relationship with Rudolph would
improve once they reached the field, their initial meeting at Collinson Point taught him otherwise. Nevertheless, he did not fail to
treat Mrs. Anderson with consideration and respect.

Early in 1914 Stefansson learned from Mrs. Anderson's letters
that she was apprehensive about Rudolph's involvement in the ice
journey. He wired Ottawa immediately to assure her that her husband would not participate in any dangerous work and then confirmed his promise in a letter to her.

Stefansson showed his concern for Mrs. Anderson's worry and
loneliness by treating lightly her obvious digs at him, such as her
reference to the "great and famous explorer" (his publisher's description). Stefansson treated it all as a joke. "Don't blame me for
being great, seeing that 'greatness' had been 'thrust upon me' in
my absence—behind my back, as it were." After all, he explained,
it was to the financial advantage of his publishers if "they can hoodwink the public" this way. "You and I know it is rot—we both
know the great explorer too intimately—but you and I will both
profit if Macmillan's can get away with it."[17] Her share of the profits, he teased, would be the ice cream soda he promised to buy her
from book royalties.

Both were concerned about Anderson's reluctance to issue press
releases. Mrs. Anderson had complained that her Sioux City news-

paper did not carry expedition news. "One gets no credit from any-body—not even from oneself—for going out of his way to hide his light under a bushel, as Dr. Anderson will persist in doing," wrote Stefansson. "Had he telegraphed the *Times* as well as the government his [Anderson's] name would have been cabled all over the world and would have appeared in papers in much smaller towns than Sioux City—incidentally informing you of his safety and situation." This was the advantage of being in command of a separate section of the expedition, "but he [Anderson] seems unwilling to use it." Stefansson was depending upon Anderson's dispatches to fulfil his own contract with the newspapers when he was unable to communicate information to them himself. Anderson refused to comply because it would be doing a service to Stefansson and because of his "professional disinclination to engage in newspaper correspondence."[18]

Anderson's refusal to deal with newspapers puzzled the expedition leader. "[Anderson] seems to admire Amundsen," he observed, "and Amundsen is the most unblushing advertiser of the lot." Amundsen, he went on, had his own press agents "and deliberately laid plans that out-Herod Herod." In comparison, Stefansson considered himself modest. "The worst I have had the stomach to do so far is to take what comes my way accidentally and to prod up a missionary now and then when things get too quiet."[19]

Stefansson made some pertinent remarks concerning his own character and talents as well as those of some of his unnamed colleagues. Probably he had the loss of the *Karluk* in mind when he remarked that things usually went better when he did not allow the judgments of others to prevail over his own. After all, he reasoned, he had more experience. And, he added pointedly, "more important still, I am able generally to keep my feelings from influencing my judgments." He insisted that there was not a single person he disliked, nor did he "have any interest in proving anyone wrong." He was not stressing his virtues so much as the advantage his attitude gave him "over those who hate, feel fear or envy...and especially over those who are jealous."[20]

In September 1914, Stefansson received letters from his good friends the Ed Deming family, and he replied with a lengthy account of his plans. He reported being in better spirits than in October 1913, when he had written about the *Karluk*'s drift and was facing the failure of the entire expedition. The situation did not appear much brighter in February 1914 when he wrote again. "It is hard

writing while everything is so unsettled and uncertain that we ourselves don't know what to think or hope for, nor what to do tomorrow."[21] It was some relief to be able to express his forebodings in
a letter since he dared not reveal any such doubts to expedition
members. From his Banks Island camp in September 1914, he
wanted the Demings to know what letters from his friends meant
to him. "Please tell them for me that to me such a letter written in
a time of adversity has more value than the coveted medals in the
hour of success."[22]

The few long personal letters which he wrote from the Arctic to
distant friends are more revealing of his moods and ambitions than
anything he wrote after he left the North behind. Among the best
were those he wrote in 1914 and 1915 to Charlotte Rudyard, who
had been working for *Harper's* magazine as an editor when Stefansson met her. She had taken particular care with one of his first
articles and later edited *My Life with the Eskimo*, his first book.
Since he had to leave for the Arctic before it was ready, he was
particularly dependent on her skill. In the fall of 1914 Stefansson
expressed his gratitude from Banks Island. He also chided her for
asking that he "try to think kindly of her. What nonsense—and to
say it to me of all persons, who admire you for what you are and
who am grateful to you for what you have done and wanted to
do."[23]

From his university days Stefansson had always communicated
more freely with women than men on personal topics. And he told
Miss Rudyard events from his Dakota college days to try to explain
what he valued in his relationships. Only co-educational schools
met with his approval, and he knew three girls and many boys there
"from whom I could have borrowed money and who could have
borrowed from me (had I not always been broke)." These girls were
friends, not lovers, and everyone was amused when he made up an
alphabetical list of every girl in the college, sending an unsigned
love sonnet to each one. "I was proud then, and am still, of the
fact that nobody who saw the verses thought that anyone but I had
written them."[24] This meant that they accepted him as an individual
rather than as a type—and such approval mattered very much to
him.

He described the making of his favorite youthful composition,
"A Philosopher at Twenty" to Miss Rudyard, explaining "it was
not so much that I meant it as that I thought the idea 'poetic'."
Only the last four lines were significant, he said, and what he meant

was that men are moved to perform great deeds because they lack a great love and are unable to live the life of a common man. Stefansson had derived the idea from Ibsen, and he still liked it twenty years later.

He was reading Ibsen again in his winter quarters on Victoria Island, and he compared the author's feelings with his own in the letter to Charlotte. Ibsen's later plays, he suggested, reflected the dramatist's tendency to look back, the effect of an unrealized youth. He felt himself drifting that way too and remarked, "I don't doubt it is a symptom of growing old." He would soon be 36![25]

In the years since his teens, he continued, one of his childhood beliefs was further fortified: he had discovered early in life that although he found the commonplace unendurable, common things could lead him to happiness more surely than the unusual. So, he reflected, he could not rationally expect to be happy: "I must always cry for the star because of its very distance; I should less than most know what to do with it if I had it." His case was distressing, he felt, but common, as illustrated in the "hackneyed epithets" others used to describe a similar malaise.[26]

The young man who wrote "The Philosopher at Twenty" had achieved something in the intervening sixteen years: his clipping bureau charged him $500 (at five cents per clipping) for articles mentioning his name in the past year, so at least he had achieved some fame. He had longed for recognition, not so much for its positive value, but rather because he "could not well brook the negative side of not being a specially noticed figure in the crowd."

Stefansson was pleased to reaffirm another youthful conviction: "I always thought that friends and friendships are the best things in life. The real friends of my younger days I keep still." The real value of "my little greatness," as he put it, "is chiefly in the opportunity it gives me for the friendship of the men and women whom I already admire at a distance, or those who have the same qualities as they."[27] Stefansson did not very often express his creed about friendship, although he acted on it throughout his life. It explains why he always found time, no matter how busy he was, to write letters, to arrange meetings, and do favours for his friends.

CHAPTER 12

Gossip

THE SOUTHERN PARTY

THE REPORT from Anderson on the southern party's work given to Wilkins in spring 1915 reached Stefansson in August. Anderson summed up the work in progress and included some complaints. It was "disagreeable and unfortunate that Stefansson's personal unpopularity has prevented [them] from getting Eskimos and has forced [them] to go short handed."[1] The reasons for their supposed animosity bear consideration. Possibly, some Eskimos were disinclined to work for the scientists because they had been warned earlier by them that obligations arising from the expedition would be ignored by the government. Even more likely is that Anderson and Chipman, second-in-command of the Southern Party, were themselves unpopular with their Eskimo companions. The natives had been treated contemptuously in the past by arrogant whaling men and traders and could perceive a disdainful attitude even when it was not overtly expressed.

Over the years Stefansson had established an intimacy with his Eskimos that contrasted sharply with Chipman's fastidiousness. Chipman once complained to his supervisor in Ottawa that he found the company of Eskimos offensive. At first, when he was surveying the Mackenzie Delta, he refused even to consider using Eskimo whaleboats and oarsmen, even though the lack of any other means of transport delayed his work. Stefansson urged Chipman to use the whaleboats, explaining that he believed in using whatever was available to attain results. The only effect this pragmatic advice had on Chipman was to make him "wonder what was behind" the explorer's remarks. Chipman wanted to maintain his "self-respect," as he put it, and in an obvious slap at Stefansson, he huffed: "It may be heroic to sacrifice dignity and efficiency to accomplish in four years what might be done in one—but we are not here for heroism."[2] Needless to say, neither Chipman nor any other of the expedition scientists except Diamond Jenness made any effort to learn the Eskimo language, and they considered it beneath their dignity to adopt the Eskimo diet.

Anderson's diary reveals one cause of misunderstanding that affected Stefansson's relationship with the police, Leffingwell, and some scientists of the expedition. The commander of the police post at Herschel, Inspector J.W. Phillips, evidently complained to Anderson about Stefansson's solicitude for his Eskimo companions. Anderson reported in his diary: "Phillips offended Stefansson very much by suggesting (or ordering) Talliak to cut a share of the camp firewood instead of going along as a gentleman of leisure. Results! fiddle-sticks! I wouldn't hire the Talliak stripe for their 'society.'"[3]

Anderson's and Phillips's grumbling had significance beyond simply their differing tastes and attitudes—the complaints reflected their unconscious racial prejudice. No doubt they could not comprehend the pleasure Stefansson took in Eskimos—particularly those who had had little previous contact with whites. For Stefansson, the opportunity to study their culture represented a scholarly feast, but to the other members of the expedition, the Eskimos were a nuisance, except when they were needed to help with work. Anderson groused in his diary: "He [Stefansson] had no Eskimos (uncivilized) to study last year, and expects the whole Prince Albert Sound population to come to Banks Island next and enjoy open house. They'll get it all right if they come there."[4]

Anderson's annoyance over the presence of Eskimos was longstanding. Stefansson's efforts to communicate his enthusiasm during their 1908-12 expedition failed completely. As early as 1908, Anderson had complained, "Stefansson says I do not properly appreciate the beauties of the communist life and is surprised that after all he has told me that I should...'adapt the point of view taken by missionaries, travelers, and *other* illiterate people.'"[5] For Anderson the missionaries and other whites in the Arctic were clearly superior to the Eskimo, yet Stefansson insisted on placing the uncivilized, untidy aborigines on a sort of pedestal and then arrogantly presumed to lecture him on his lack of understanding.

Half a century afterwards, during the McCarthy era, Anderson recalled Stefansson's approval of the "communist life," convinced that the explorer himself was a communist!

When Stefansson received the report, he commented only mildly, advising Anderson that he should discuss the matter of hiring Eskimos with the Mounties at Herschel Island, where he would learn that Stefansson "had no difficulty in getting all the Eskimos he wanted."[6] This had been true even when the missionary Whittaker had interfered with Stefansson's recruiting, warning the Eskimos that their women would be debauched if they joined the expedition, but they went anyway. Indeed, Stefansson had even heard that another missionary had explained the severe ice conditions of 1913 as caused by God in order to keep the *Karluk* out of the area.[7]

Letters of the expedition's young topographer, Kenneth Chipman, best illustrate the disaffection of the Geological Survey men. "I have, since the Expedition started, grouched so much about certain characteristics of Mr. Stefansson that I am sure you are thoroughly familiar with him," Chipman wrote to his division head in June 1915. "I know I am more or less ashamed of the pettiness of some of the incidents. But one or two more have now crystallized and they may interest you." Stefansson, he said, had spent the summer "ostensibly" hunting inland after his ice journey. "His loss of public attention in connection with the *Karluk* was so great that he now has to play for big stakes." Chipman thought he had his commander's motivation figured out: "Up to a certain point the longer the public hears nothing of him, and the greater the story when they do hear, the greater is his chance of regaining popular attention."[8]

Chipman considered Stefansson a sort of outlaw, who disregarded his responsibility to the government and expended public monies recklessly. Stefansson was able to justify all of his spending to himself, but he was not so successful with his critical colleagues. He was determined to accomplish his mission, and his critics were equally bent on indicting him for the manner in which he discharged his duties. Chipman continued: "He has said that he would disregard any Government orders of which he did not approve, and in other ways has essentially said that the Government has no authority over him." Chipman professed to be startled by this "information." It would be one thing if "some definite public purposes" were involved, he said. "But even he [Stefansson] himself makes no secret of the fact that his object is personal publicity and what it brings, to him."[9]

Other members of the Southern Party had also been viewing their commander's actions with dismay. During the two years they were in the field, interminable discussions and private ruminations of the scientists over Stefansson's audacious behaviour only intensified the suspicions they had brought with them from Ottawa. "Mr. Stefansson," Chipman reported, "has been an interesting study. I am now pretty well convinced that personal publicity is the prime object for which he works. He professes to be interested in the scientific work of the expedition but his interest is limited to the prominence that work will bring to him. Everything is considered in the light of the public attention attracted by it. His experience with the public has been an unfortunate one," the young scientist continued, "for it has, to his mind, shown that the public is both an easy mark and keenly interested in him personally (he doesn't seem to see the humor of his belief in both of these things)."[10]

Stefansson sometimes bragged that he had always lived by his wits—a confession that shocked the young scientists, whose university training was immediately followed by secure civil service jobs. Stefansson must have made these thoroughly conventional men uneasy when he told them that he could earn $600 for a magazine article or that he would enjoy lecturing and writing after the expedition returned.

Chipman's grievances affected his view of Stefansson, as did his lack of sophistication. In the same letter to Ottawa he did try to strike a balance in his assessment: "Possibly I have been unjust to him in some things," he wrote, "Stefansson is a good hunter and one can learn much from his experience in travel and hunting. From the personal equation there is also much to learn. Of some of his personal characteristics I don't approve, but in many ways he has my sincere admiration." He remarked that his commander was "a mighty good companion" in camp, except that he avoided the menial work of cooking, campbreaking, and the like because "it apparently hurts his prestige."[11]

Although Chipman's obsession with his commander was almost overwhelming, his brooding was healthier than Rudolph Anderson's resentment, which was more closely related to his own measure of himself, aggravated by his wife's incessant questions. Anderson could not bring himself to give Stefansson credit for anything. Even his commander's effectiveness in sea-ice travel and in geographic discovery became distorted in his mind, unleavened as it was by any appreciation, wit, or a sense of humility. Anderson insisted later that he had not disbelieved in Stefansson's ability to live off the land. What had bothered him was the apparent vagueness of his plans. If he were really interested in geographic or mapping work, Anderson wondered, why did he not carry surveying instruments in order to locate himself accurately? "He couldn't use them if he had them, for want of knowledge of scientific geographical methods," he sneered in his diary. "He has to depend on Storkerson for what is done in that line, and Storkerson is only a little less ignorant than his leader....Their method of rushing blindly ahead from one seal to the next seal they can kill does not allow the stops that must be made to get suitable weather for observations." Anderson never failed to uncover what he considered to be "evidence" of fraudulence—"Anything such parties can add to the map (if he can persuade Geographical Societies with sufficient eloquence to hoodwink them) will be as misleading as the old charts," he wrote. The observations of earlier navigators depended upon dead reckoning and rule-of-thumb, and Stefansson's methods resembled theirs. "I can give V.S. credit [for] marked ability when he sticks to his trade, but when he decided he could be a geographer and oceanographer with absolutely no training except as a dog-musher and pedestrian with literary leanings, he got way beyond his depth."[12]

Although no one ever alluded to it after the Geological Survey men returned from the Arctic in 1916, Chipman's correspondence reveals their lack of commitment to the expedition. How could men in the field perform their scientific work enthusiastically, knowing their superiors in Ottawa did not want them to be involved in the work of the Canadian Arctic Expedition at all? One can imagine Chipman's state of mind when he wrote to LeRoy in April 1914. At this time he had not yet had an opportunity to do much field work. He was hoping to earn some recognition in Ottawa, and yet his superiors hinted that he might have an excuse to desert the expedition and return home. "Both you and Mr. Boyd speak of your hope that lack of supplies will force us to return," Chipman wrote. "It is perhaps unfortunate that our G.S.C. outfit was packed and listed in such a way that we checked it in Victoria and Nome and took care to see that it was complete and all together on the *Alaska*."[13] Morale must have been on a low plane if the rest of the Southern Party shared Chipman's sentiment that it was "unfortunate" that their equipment had not been on the *Karluk* so they could justify scurrying home. Although Anderson liked to insist that the Southern Party never had any disagreements, some of them shared certain fears. Would Stefansson find some means of ridiculing men who had been unwilling and defiant? Would he be able to convince the government that they had been rebellious?

Their fear of Stefansson's genius for publicity may also account for their gossip about Stefansson fathering an Eskimo child. Chipman was not the kind of man who would spread a slander for simple enjoyment. He was, on the contrary, respectable and rational, yet his diary and letters reveal a man looking for weapons to defend himself. "With the people at Herschel Island and among ourselves," Chipman wrote, "we are ready to bet any money that if occasion ever demands, Stefansson will produce a statement from a man named Storkerson to the effect that the kid is his and not Stefansson's."[14]

The story that Pannigabluk, the seamstress on the Stefansson-Anderson expedition, had conceived Stefansson's child was widespread. In *My Life with the Eskimo* Stefansson refers to her only in passing: "I took with me my favorite companion, Natkusiak, and an elderly country-woman of his named Pannigabluk, whose husband had died the year before."[15]

It would hardly be remarkable if Stefansson, like Robert Peary and other arctic voyagers, had indeed shared a native woman's bed, but he never alluded to it, nor did he reply to the C.E. Whittaker's charges that he had neglected his Eskimo family. It was the missionary who reported the gossip to the Ottawa press, perhaps in retaliation for Stefansson's belittling of the missionaries in his book. Chipman regarded Stefansson's supposed philandering as an understandable occurrence, but he professed to find his failure to acknowledge his native child shocking. "I don't know or haven't heard of a man in this country, white or native," he wrote, "who doubts that the kid is Stefansson's although he himself refuses to recognize openly the woman and child and to make provision for them," adding, "people up here would accept the whole thing as a matter of course and pay no attention, but his failure to recognize them and make provision (which is the usual thing and common among whalers and others) is arousing...comment."[16]

Chipman's analysis of how permanent arctic residents would regard the matter was probably correct, although it is unlikely that the Southern Party would ever have accepted the affair merely "as a matter of course." The paternity gossip was an effective weapon in their campaign to disparage Stefansson, though they apparently never aired the story for the press.

Thus, Chipman's gossip about Stefansson ranged from the momentous to the trivial. One last example demonstrates the range of his attention:

It may interest you that Stefansson is known in this delta country as the only man who ever packed a life preserver down the Macken-zie on the steamer. He did this in 1906 and when he reached Fort McPherson said he came down the river because he was afraid to come around on the Duchess of Bedford. *That reputation stuck.*[17]

Such grumblings would have gone unnoticed had they ended when the men left the Arctic. But, unfortunately, the multitude of grievances that accumulated during the Canadian Arctic Expedition persisted, and later on they were the cause of much damage to Stefansson's reputation.

MRS. ANDERSON

By early 1915 Stefansson had gained some additional insight into the unfortunate division within his expedition. His friends conveyed gossip and speculations as readily as his enemies, and he wrote a long letter to Mrs. Anderson, thanking her for several "good letters," and explaining his side of the dispute with Rudolph. "I never liked anyone so well, in the long run—[and then] to find when I came 'home' off the *Karluk* that he [Anderson] not only was clearly not glad to see me, but told me in the hearing of men of the expedition that he was 'through fetching and carrying for me,' that I had probably come to make a farce of his section of the expedition as I had made...of the previous expedition...also that I was untrustworthy, untruthful, without scientific ability or the scientific spirit, a 'bull-con artist,' and so on." Anderson also warned him "that if I continued the ice exploration I would be deliberately misappropriating government property just to get myself into the newspapers again."[18]

Stefansson was badly stung by Anderson's defiance and the accusations that he made in front of the other men. Chipman's papers disclose that he had done his part in bringing Anderson to this stage of exasperation, but perhaps Anderson did not require any encouragement. Stefansson was unaware of Chipman's animosity and so assumed that it was principally Anderson's open rebellion that undermined his command. The others did not know him well, and so, he reasoned, they would naturally think that "if Anderson, who knows him does not trust him, why should we?" He realized that Anderson's "deserved personal popularity" encouraged the dissension that hurt the expedition. The bad feeling between Stefansson and Anderson generated all kinds of rumours. Stefansson was extremely annoyed by "the story I had run away from the *Karluk* because I was afraid of the ice." Among the small white population in the Arctic this slander had become widespread. "The story," Stefansson fumed, "is all over the coast."[19]

Ever anxious about the squabbling, Mrs. Anderson tried to reassure Stefansson that things would be better in the future and told him that Rudolph "wants to do the square thing." "I think that is true," replied Stefansson. "He does not mean to be unjust but I think that he is, but I admit freely that he thinks he is not....He seems to be in a frame of mind which says of my seemingly bad actions: 'The Scoundrel'; and of my seemingly good deeds he says: 'The Hypocrite.' "[20]

In several earlier letters to Stefansson, Mrs. Anderson expressed her opinion that Anderson ought to earn more money from the expedition. Stefansson agreed, "You are right about everything you say as to your husband's duty to make as much out of the expedition in money and prestige as he can. He has had his chance, and has it still, though not quite so good as formerly, because by reducing my chance of success he has reduced that of all of us." Stefansson had no reservation about expressing his own ambitions. He regretted that he had not discovered any new land on his first ice journey. "Had luck favored us with 'land' or some other spectacular triumph we would all have ridden on a tidal wave of success," he told Mrs. Anderson while admitting that he himself would receive "the lion's share." Anderson would also receive a portion, for "even the most ultra-scientific are influenced by the paper they read at breakfast as much as by their technical journals."[21] Stefansson cited a monograph on freshwater mollusks that would have found more readers had the study been done on a well-publicized expedition.

Another sore spot raised by Mrs. Anderson concerned the credit due to Anderson for writing part of *My Life with the Eskimo*, Stefansson's popular narrative of their expedition of 1908-12. Anderson's actual contribution to the book consisted of a "Report on the

Natural History Collection of the Expedition," which appeared as a ninety-page appendix to the 538-page volume.

The Andersons were certainly furious when the book appeared because, although Anderson's authorship of the scientific appendix was acknowledged, his name did not appear on the title page. Stefansson gave Mrs. Anderson his explanation: "It is a regrettable oversight that [Rudolph's] name does not appear on the title page. That is hardly my fault, however—I am afraid I never thought about it one way or another, but if I had I should have taken it for granted they would put both our names there—we were joint authors and had separate contracts with Macmillans."[22] Anderson's contract stipulated that he was to receive 20 per cent of the royalties. Neither man read the proofs, and the Andersons, who were rather naive about the world of publication and its capacity for committing such errors, believed that they had been duped by Stefansson.

Stefansson sympathized with Mrs. Anderson's anxieties even though he was aware of her trouble-making. He made allowances because she was alone and worried about the future. She assured Stefansson that she was not mercenary, "but expected more from the expedition than a tiny salary and baby's grave."[23] By 1915, however, he could no longer forbear mentioning that her animosity had influenced relations between himself and Rudolph. "Your heart, as you say of mine, is in the right place. But you have been indiscreet and have hurt me more than you will ever believe." He said he thought he could see the reasons better than she could. "You had or have, for one thing, a low opinion of my ability, especially my scientific ability and standing. Probably you were influenced by the fact that I was 'such small fry' in Iowa and Anderson must have allowed you to believe that my scientific work on the Museum expedition was of a low grade."[24]

Stefansson introduced the Andersons to several of his friends in New York, who later had tales to tell of the couple's attitude. "It was not long before first one and then another of those people began to tell me that you said unkind things about me," he wrote.[25] His friends, growing alarmed because Anderson listened to his wife's remarks without apparent disapproval, suggested that Anderson ought to have dropped from the expedition. Stefansson, however, made light of the matter.

Their academic careers make Stefansson's analysis of Mrs. Anderson's comments seem plausible. As an undergraduate, Anderson had had a distinguished record. He earned a Ph.D. in ornithology afterwards, and by the time he asked to join Stefansson on their first expedition together, he had already written a scholarly monograph entitled *The Birds of Iowa*. Stefansson's academic career, on the other hand, was checkered. His only degree was his B.A. from Iowa. He did graduate work at Harvard, but he had not completed his degree requirements. Could Mrs. Anderson be blamed for believing that the fame Stefansson achieved by 1913 was more the result of clever publicity than solid accomplishment? Perhaps, she may have thought, Stefansson was using Anderson, climbing over the back of his friend and field companion, deliberately trying to keep true scientific genius in the shadows while he scrambled for success.

Stefansson tried to convince Mrs. Anderson that he had achieved something on the museum expedition besides reaping worldwide publicity as the "discoverer" of the blond Eskimo. He enumerated the awards he received and quoted his sponsor's praise of the 1908-12 expedition as "one of the best" ever sent out by the American Museum of Natural History.[26] "This will show at least that these organizations consider my results of good quality. I believe you were sincere in thinking that I was a 'four-flusher,' especially in scientific things," Stefansson wrote, "and I am willing to remain friends. Quarreling is pointless. But certain things have to be said. The members of our scientific staff gathered from you the idea in Victoria and Nome that my scientific work was a joke among those who know. That idea was the basis for much of the dissatisfaction which has so hindered team play among us."[27]

CHAPTER 13

New Lands

IN PREPARATION for his second sea ice journey Stefansson sent out an advance party under Wilkins from Cape Kellett on 9 February 1915. The plan was to follow the west coast of Banks Island north 150 miles, then cross McClure Strait to Prince Patrick Island, then move northwest on the ocean from that island's southwest corner. Stefansson and his party set out after Wilkins but the crusty snow cut their dogs' feet badly. On the northwest corner of Banks Island the travellers rested while the dogs' feet healed and waited for Storkerson and Thomsen to travel back to Kellett to replace kerosene lost from leaky containers. It was 5 April when the party left the shore, too late to cross over to Prince Patrick Island, so Stefansson, Storkerson, Andreasen, and Thomsen with two sledges struck northwest from Cape Alfred.

Stefansson would have liked to have Wilkins along, but he needed him more for a mission to Coronation Gulf. Wilkins carried Stefansson's orders to Anderson that the *North Star* be turned over to him so it could be used as a base for the coming season.

The weather was cold, temperatures down to 42 degrees below zero, yet care had to be taken that the melting ice remained thick enouygh to bear the weight of the sledges. Initially, too, the ice was sticky with surface ice crystals that slowed their average hourly speed to three miles from the normal five to six miles.

They sounded the sea bottom at intervals as they moved over the ocean. The uneven bottom was found at varying depths from 100 to 200 fathoms for the first two weeks, then reached depths their 4,500 feet of wire could not reach. Daily astronomical observations were also made to compare with their dead reckoning of their location. The ice moved steadily to the southwest, which was inconvenient to men trying to travel northwest. They had to take more chances crossing leads on thin ice because delays could be too costly with the drift running counter to their course. When they encountered open water they quickly converted sledges to boats with tarpaulin wrappings.

On 25 April a near disaster occurred on a strip of young ice only ten yards wide. The first sledge, built by Bernard to Stefansson's plans modifying the standard Nome sledge design, crossed safely. The second, a standard Alaskan design, did not distribute its weight over as great an extent of its runners as did the modified design and broke through the ice. Luckily, the dogs were on firm ice, and the men swiftly helped them pull the submerging sledge to the surface safely. Necessary articles like rifles, ammunition, and foot gear had been divided between the two sledges so that the loss of one might be tolerated, but obviously the loss of any food or gear could have caused them trouble eventually.

Stefansson found the ice movement peculiar as they moved on. Wind from the south or southeast, no matter how hard, would stop the ice's movement. With calm or wind from the northwest, north, or east the ice moved steadily southwest. Thus their gains in marching northwest were neutralized by the prevailing southwest drift when they camped for the night. Consequently, Stefansson headed towards shore, barely making the southwest corner of Prince Patrick Island because of the drift and landing on 4 June.

Prince Patrick Island, explored in 1853 by Captain Leopold McClintock's expedition was a barren land of gravel and snow that seemed to support no game. The explorers followed the coast northeastward improving on the mapping that had been done by the Royal Navy men and confirmed the absence of game, then they went offshore ten or twelve miles to where the landfast ice met the moving pack and killed several seals in the lead. The party of three men and six dogs only required two seals a week for sustenance.

On 15 June they reached the north end of the island and found a cairn left by McClintock. It was a thrill to uncover and read a message left on the same day so many decades before by the British explorers who had achieved travel records with their man-hauled sledges. Stefansson appreciated McClintock because the naval of-

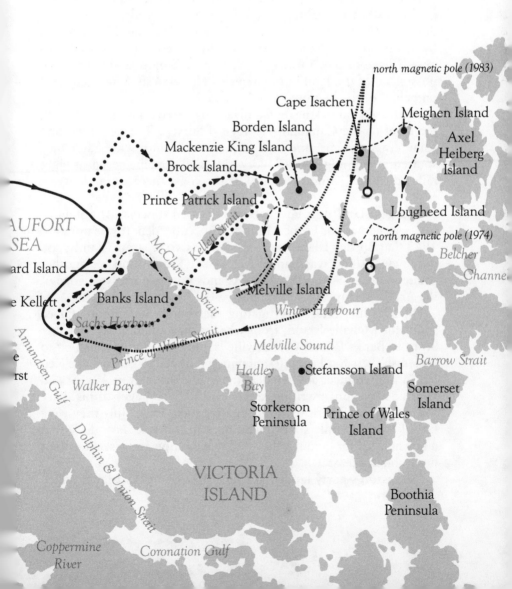

Stefansson's Journeys, 1914-17

1917 . . . . ▪▪▪▪▪▪▪▪▪▪▪▪▪▪▪▪▪▪▪▪▪▪▪

1916 . . . . ----------------------

1915 . . . . ●●●●●●●●●●●●●●●

1914 . . . . ─────────────────

Artwork by Ian Bateson, based on a map by Walter Kupsch

north magnetic pole (1983)

Cape Isachen

Meighen Island

Borden Island

Mackenzie King Island

Axel
Heiberg
Island

Brock Island

Prince Patrick Island

Lougheed Island

ΛUFORT
SEA

north magnetic pole (1974)

ard Island

Belcher

Channe

e Kellett   Banks Island

McClure   Kellett Strait

Strait

Melville Island

Winter Harbour

Sachs Harbour

Prince of Wales Strait

Melville Sound

Barrow Strait

e
rst

Amundsen Gulf

Walker Bay

Hadley
Bay

●Stefansson Island

Somerset
Island

Storkerson
Peninsula

Prince of Wales
Island

Dolphin & Union Strait

VICTORIA
ISLAND

Boothia
Peninsula

Coppermine
River

Coronation Gulf

ficer had been the first arctic explorer to realize the possibilities of living off the land through hunting and thereby lengthening his journey.

The C.A.E. explorers moved out on the ocean from the island, and on 18 June Storkerson spotted the first new land. Stefansson was five miles south of the camp when the discovery was made, but he hurried forward when he noted the excitement of the Norwegians. By the time Stefansson arrived a celebration had commenced, and some hoarded malted milk and biscuit crumbs were being prepared.

On the following morning, the explorers landed and raised a discovery mound holding a memo of the particulars. Stefansson gave credit for the first sighting to Storkerson while Andreasen was credited with first setting foot on Brock Island. The island was claimed by Stefansson: "By authority especially vested in me for that purpose, I have to-day hoisted the flag of the Empire and have taken possession of the land in the name of His Majesty King George V on behalf of the Dominion of Canada."[1]

Stefansson named the first land he discovered for Reginald Brock, the chief of the Canadian Geological Survey. The new land had some grass, lichens, and a great many caribou tracks. Later they spotted a lemming and an ivory gull, and at some seven or eight miles distance, some caribou. Off the coast there were plenty of seals.

A larger island, only later recognized as a distinct land by Stefansson, was named for Prime Minister Robert Borden. It was not until 1947 that Borden Island was found to be two separate islands, and the "new" island was named Mackenzie King Island for another prime minister. Altogether these islands on the northwest edge of the Arctic Archipelago encompassed 3,120 square miles.

On 22 June, after investigating the island, Stefansson started south for Melville Island, from whence they could cross McClure Strait to Banks Island. On Melville Island they hunted musk-ox to replenish their food supplies. Stefansson hoped to get to Cape Kellett in time to meet any whalers that came through in August and kept busy evenings writing letters on the back pages of his diary for possible shipment with the whaling men. By 13 July they were out of food but only six or eight miles from Banks Island. Within a few hours after landing, they had two caribou and a seal for their homecoming feast.

Stefansson's party landed at Mercy Bay on Banks Island, which had been discovered in 1851 by Captain R.J. McClure who had been forced to spend two winters there on his Northwest Passage discovery voyage. The Canadian explorers found some articles left by the Royal Navy men and did some mapping to correct the charts made by McClure. Eskimos had long since visited Mercy Bay to salvage what they could use from the *Investigator,* the vessel McClure abandoned to walk out for rescue by another ship. On 20 July, after completing their observations and making packs for the dogs, the C.A.E. party started across the island for Kellett.

Two days out Stefansson killed three caribou bulls, happy to get their ample fat because his seal blubber had run out. Lean caribou were plentiful along the way, but salt and tobacco gave out. Stefansson had probably long since wearied anyone who ever travelled with him on the perfidity of salt and tobacco habits. He, Storkerson, and Andreasen had learned on the previous ice trip to prefer meat without salt, and earlier on the current trip Storkerson quit smoking to provide more tobacco for Thomsen. Stefansson had learned from Peary to discourage tobacco use among his men, but he had allowed it this time. It is possible that the three non-smokers watched with some satisfaction as poor Thomsen chewed pieces of tobacco pouches and then his and Storkerson's pipes.

The party moved across Banks Island at night for the advantage of the cold and firmer snow. "This was one of our most delightful summer journeys," Stefansson noted.[2] There were no mosquitoes in the late season and they were far enough inland to be free of the fogs along the west coast. They arrived at their camp on 9 August, having completed the first recorded crossing of Banks Island: "All has gone well in general," Stefansson recorded, "Nine Eskimos were around for several days...and gave us several hundred geese. Levi [W. J. "Levi" Baur] and Bernard together killed one caribou and Bernard two caribou and a bear. They have also secured numbers of hares, ducks and ptarmigan....A new sod house has been built....A considerable ethnological collection has been made by purchase from the Eskimos. All of our provisions are in good order and there is enough, except of condensed sled rations, for our real needs if no whaling ship comes. If one comes, I shall have to buy vegetables, milk, coffee and butter to keep the men in good humor."[3]

His discoveries demonstrated the practicality of Stefansson's methods of travel and his theories about sustenance, and he had found new lands and compiled important data on ocean depths, ice movements, winds, and other natural phenomena. It had been a satisfactory journey, as Stefansson had written to his friend Ed Deming while still en route on 4 July, after the travellers had feasted on "rather tough muskox meat." Since they started out on the ice the previous spring, they had travelled 134 days, and it would take another month to get back to Cape Kellett. In all they had used 10,000 pounds of meat, much of it fat for fuel. Stefansson bragged a little in a letter to Deming: "There are few who consider themselves 'sportsmen' who are not better shots than I, but there are not many who have made the rifle more useful. Bears, seals, caribou, muskoxen, all have contributed, each in the appropriate environment." Whether on land or on the sea ice, they had shown the ability to live "indefinitely" on the country. "And as for me," he added, "I enjoy it." It was good to be able to tell Deming that "luck has not been entirely unkind. We seem in a fair way to accomplish a considerable part of the *Karluk*'s original program and most of what I hoped since she went adrift."[4]

In December Stefansson told Deming that although prospects were good for the next year's work, they were not good enough to allow him to return in 1916, but that nothing would prevent his returning in the fall of 1917. "I'd like to be with you in September, 1916, but we'll have to finish our work if we can, even if it keeps us away from our friends a little longer."[5]

At Cape Kellett on Banks Island Stefansson was "rescued" once more. When Wilkins reached the same place the year before, he was astonished to find his leader alive. In August 1915, Captain Louis Lane arrived with his ship, the *Polar Bear*. When one of the *Polar Bear*'s seamen thought he recognized Stefansson at a distance, Lane replied, "Don't you think it: The fishes ate him long ago."[6]

Lane brought news of the outbreak of World War I and a somewhat confused account of what had happened to the *Karluk* and its crew. Stefansson did not hear the full story of the disaster until he met John Hadley on Herschel Island a little later. As for the war, magazines and newspapers aboard the *Polar Bear* predicted an early end to the fighting, and Stefansson had no reason to expect otherwise.

When the news of Stefansson's meeting with Lane reached the outside world, the press reported the event variously. Some editors insisted that on hearing the news of war, the explorer wept. Just as inaccurately, others described Lane's "rescue" of the explorers from starvation, although Lane had truthfully reported that he had found Stefansson and his men in robust health.

A rescue effort promoted by Burt McConnell, who had returned "outside" in 1914, did not get government support. McConnell proposed that a ship ought to carry airplanes north for reconnaissance flights in search of both the missing *Karluk* men and Stefansson's party. Bartlett had advised the government that the eight men who sledged away from the *Karluk* had been badly outfitted and were probably dead. And Stefansson had advised against any rescue attempt of his party unless their position was accurately reported.

Stefansson praised G.J. Desbarats, deputy minister of Naval Service, for taking for granted that he could walk out to safety as planned. But actually Desbarats was not all that sure, and he did suggest to R.C. McConnell, acting deputy minister of the Geological Survey that a Southern Party vessel under Chipman might conduct a search. McConnell argued that a special ship was needed for a search as he would not risk the lives of any more Southern Party members for Stefansson's sake. The Survey's hostility to Stefansson and to the Naval Service for purchasing a "condemned" ship, the *Karluk,* was obvious.[7]

Based on Captain Lane's opinion that Wilkins had probably failed to get the *North Star* away from Anderson in 1915 as he had failed in 1914, Stefansson worked out other plans. Lane told him that the government had sent supplies to Herschel Island on the *Ruby*. In order to establish a base north of Kellett in the absence of the *North Star,* Stefansson needed transport to Herschel and a ship. Lane's *Polar Bear* was available for both purposes, so Stefansson chartered it and left for Herschel on 12 August 1915.

Four days' passage brought them to Herschel even with some hours delay killing a bowhead whale for future dog feed needs. At Herschel Stefansson found the *Ruby* and other vessels, including the Hudson's Bay Company's *Macpherson,* on which Jack Hadley now served as ice pilot. Hadley, of course, had been one of the *Karluk* men, and now Stefansson hired him again for C.A.E. work.

The arrival of Stefansson surprised those who thought that he had perished on the ice. Martin Andreasen, skipper of the *Olga,* and Inspector J.W. Phillips of the R.C.M.P. had been the only old arctic hands who believed that Stefansson would be back—and their delight was heartwarming.

While waiting for his gear to be unloaded from the *Ruby,* Stefansson hired several Eskimo families. The women's skills at making clothing and boots were indispensable, and to get their services Stefansson would put up with their children and "comparatively useless husbands." He also answered his letters, a smaller bundle than usual because many friends believed the reports of his death. Even the government had addressed all its 1915 communications to Anderson, not because G.J. Desbarats assumed Stefansson's death but because Anderson informed him that no means existed of communicating with Banks Island. The government ordered the termination of the Southern Party's work in the summer of 1916 and made an attempt to determine the C.A.E. commander's fate by sending a ship to Banks Island. Stefansson figured that if he could telegraph news of his survival and discoveries to Ottawa the authorities would approve his continued explorations—and proceeded accordingly.

There were arrangements to be made for the Southern Party. Stefansson had heard that the *Alaska* needed repairs, and he found an engineer willing to voyage to Anderson's headquarters for the work. Stefansson also arranged to send stores to Anderson on the motor schooner *El Sueno*. Since the charter fees on the *Polar Bear* were mounting during the days at Herschel, Stefansson bought the ship from Lane and made the first mate, Henry Gonzales, the new skipper.

In late August the *Bear* was ready to go, and after an irritating delay at Cape Bathurst for other arrangements, the party pushed on to Kellett. At Bathurst Stefansson got the cheerful news that Wilkins did have the *North Star* and was proceeding up the west coast of Banks Island. The *Bear* reached Kellett and picked up Storkerson, and Stefansson left Peter Bernard in charge of the reserve base with Errol Lorne Knight, Charles Thomsen and his family, and a number of Eskimos to help out.

It was 3 September before the *Bear* could leave Kellett, and the season was too far advanced for successful navigation to the north. When the ice stopped the ship before it could reach Melville Island, winter quarters were set up at Armstrong Point on Victoria Island in Prince of Wales Strait. Now the explorers had three bases since Wilkins had pushed the *North Star* to the north side of Banks Island, twenty miles beyond Cape Alfred.

By late September Hadley had supervised the construction of a house at Armstrong Point, Stefansson was preparing to survey the north coast of Victoria Island, and the hunters were busy laying in meat. In October Stefansson led a hunt for seals along the coast, combining the hunt with ethnological studies of his Eskimo com-

panions and Copper Island Eskimos he visited. The Victoria Island
Copper Eskimos were those he had encountered on his previous
expedition, and his fascination with their still uncontaminated culture remained strong. A couple of the Eskimos later visited Stefansson at Armstrong Point and were returned to their Minto Inlet village by Gonzales while Stefansson travelled to Kellett to get the
sledges Bernard had constructed.

Gonzales had trouble on his trip with the Copper Eskimos because he, like other whalers, customarily made Eskimos understand
their inferior status. Stefansson had warned him to treat the Eskimos as equals, pointing out that unlike the Herschel Island people
they were unused to the ways of whites and might well resist if they
were treated unfairly. Gonzales, a crude type, ignored his leader's
admonition. He took his ease sitting on one of the two sledges that
carried the party; when the Eskimos sat down as well, they were
ordered off. Unfortunately for him, Gonzales only spoke the trade
jargon with which these Eskimos were not familiar. When he found
he could not communicate his displeasure, Gonzales angrily tipped
over the sledge, tossing the hapless passengers into a snow bank.
The cheerful Eskimos thought this was great fun and laughingly
clambered aboard again. Gonzales dumped them off the sledge once
more, scowled, shook his fist, and raged. Utterly perplexed, the
natives left Gonzales and his party on the trail and travelled on to
their village alone.

When Gonzales finally reached the village to buy artifacts for
Stefansson, the Copper Eskimos ran off with his trade goods. The
two expedition Eskimos who were travelling with Gonzales managed to prevent violence by calming him and convincing the Copper
Eskimos that Gonzales had peculiar ways. After long discussion,
the trade goods were returned.

This attitude of white superiority also caused the murder of two
Roman Catholic missionaries in 1915. Fathers Rouvier and
LeRoux were killed and robbed by Coronation Gulf Eskimos at
the mouth of the Coppermine River. The Eskimos were arrested in
1916 by Mounted Police who voyaged east from Herschel on the
Mary Sachs, and they stood trial in Edmonton the following year.
To the dismay of some authorities, the defendants were convicted
but not executed, their defence attorney having successfully argued
that Stone Age people should be treated leniently. Eventually, the
Eskimos were taken back to Herschel Island and served their sentences by acting as interpreters for the police, who realized that

such crimes were often caused by misunderstanding or fear when natives were confronted with a strange situation.

1916 EVENTS

In November, Stefansson started for Cape Kellett on Banks Island. He sent a message to the *North Star,* and Wilkins arrived at Kellett for a meeting on New Year's Day in 1916. Spring plans were formulated. Stefansson sent a party back to the *Bear* with instructions for Storkerson to meet him in February on the north coast of Banks Island after making a survey of Victoria Island and for Gonzales to assist in the preparations.

Stefansson left for Cape Alfred and the *North Star* on 23 January with four Eskimos and reached Wilkins with no difficulty. While waiting for Storkerson, he pursued ethnological studies with his Eskimo friends and read among the books that he had received since his library had been lost with the *Karluk.* Some books were serious studies of mathematical astronomy and other sciences, but he found time for lighter reading too, including his perennial favourite, Rider Haggard's *King Solomon's Mines.*

Storkerson was delayed when Gonzales froze his feet and he sent a message that he would abandon the effort and prepare to explore the new land in the spring. Stefansson therefore set out across McClure Strait to catch Storkerson at Liddon Gulf, travelling with Harold Noice and Errol Lorne Knight, Charlie Thomsen, and Emiu. Shortly after leaving Banks Island Stefansson sprained an ankle and was forced to ride on a sledge. On 3 May the parties met at Cape Murray, the original landfall on Brock Island.

The expedition's most serious setback during the 1916 explorations was a disease that killed several of the dogs, including the two best ones that they had used on ice trips in 1914 and 1915. With the death of his favourite dog, Stefansson reported that he had "lost a considerable part of the pleasure in this work and of my confidence in the future." He had never seen the like of Isuk for grit and willingness to work. "His place was next to the sled to keep it moving in difficult places, and it never struck hard enough to make him quit trying to start it; he was never too hungry or so tired that anyone ever saw his traces slack, and when the rest of the team were tired out or so discouraged they no longer would try to pull, we would move him to the head of the team and he would infect them with a little more courage by his optimistic way of tackling the job." Stefansson could not make use of his dogs as some explorers did, thinking probably of Amundsen's methods on his South Pole drive: "I suppose I am too soft and sentimental. A real explorer would have fed him to the other dogs and commented on the amount of pemmican saved."[8] Stefansson was not given to relating humorous anecdotes about his dogs, as were many travel writers, but his grief was strong enough to keep him from making diary entries for some time.

Stefansson changed his plans at Cape Murray. He sent Storkerson to the *Bear,* ordering Gonzales to try to bring the ship to Liddon Gulf, but, failing that, not to retreat south of his present position. Storkerson was also to select a winter quarters for 1916-17 at Liddon Gulf and supervise a hunt for meat. While Stefansson rested his ankle Noice, Aarnout Castel, and Emiu began a survey of the new land. Later Castel and Emiu were sent back to Melville Island with instructions for Storkerson.

On 4 June Stefansson, Charlie Andersen, and Noice headed north into the unknown region between Cape Isachsen and Axel Heiberg Island. On 12 June, twenty miles out, Noice saw land. They landed on 14 June on what Stefansson called Meighen Island after Sir Arthur Meighen, Borden's successor as prime minister. Further explorations led to the last of the lands discovered, Lougheed Island, "an arctic paradise, full of game and certainly capable of sustaining human life."[9] After exploring the island they set out for Borden and Brock islands on 9 September. On Borden Island there was no sign of the *Bear,* and without the supplies they expected, the plan for a winter base at Cape Murray had to be abandoned. The party returned to Melville Island, landing on 2 October.

The trip had gone well, although there had been causes of annoyance that provoked some sharp entries in Stefansson's diary, as when Castel left some vital sledge equipment behind on the march, and they had to send a party back to retrieve it: "It seems they are after all a helpless lot when left to themselves. Such foolishness seems fitly commented on only by tears of regret."

A few days later he was provoked when one of the party claimed that previously Wilkins had argued that exploration was a useless activity. Stefansson considered this remark poor form. Why did he always have to fight with companions who were unsympathetic to his objectives? He needed men who were willing to see the job through, "but I must do everything with wage-workers."[11]

A month later, when he was laid up with his sprained ankle, he admitted that he was depressed. Only Storkerson and Peter Bernard were good men. The Eskimo members of the expedition were complaining all the time. However, on further reflection, he cheered up. "Certainly commanding such an Arctic expedition as this is not an unmixed pleasure—but then all the other explorers seem to have had the same sort of experiences, insofar as I have learnt their 'inside histories.'"[12] His observation is accurate. The entire history of exploration is a pageant of acrimony, slander, backbiting, and mutiny, a chronicle as amazing in its way as are the glorious accomplishments of the same men.

Men have always worked against their commanders, Stefansson reflected, "human nature hasn't altered." He remembered some poetic celebrations of men's aspirations, but, he said, "Tennyson is in a small minority when he sees that men may rise on stepping stones of their dead selves to higher things; it is far more commonly accepted that the way to rise is on stepping stones of dead or discredited fellows."[13]

However, Stefansson did not grumble about his men all the time. He had words of praise for two new members of the expedition who joined in 1916. Karsten Anderson and Harold Noice had readily accepted his strictures on the necessity of a fresh meat diet, and they were willing to provide bulk to their meals by making watery soups, but the other men insisted upon having biscuits, refusing to eat what they called "slops." Anderson and Noice were better men: "This shows how a more enlightened mind is of value in our work," Stefansson observed. He was tired of hearing that his system of dining was a hardship for those whose "self respect won't allow them to experiment."[14]

Harold Noice, a sailor on the *Polar Bear* when he met Stefansson on Banks Island in 1915, had some interesting observations to make about his leader. Prior to becoming a member of the expedition, he had listened to whaling men at Herschel contemptuously describing Stefansson as "a college professor who carries books in his sledge where a sensible man carries grub." Even worse, "Did you ever shake hands with him? He's got a hand soft as a woman's!" Obviously, he had never done a real day's work in his life! "What do you know about a man that doesn't drink, doesn't smoke, doesn't dance?" Noice marveled. He did not even hum or sing a tune. "He detested athletics, loathed cards, never made a bet for money, and had never been heard using any stronger ejaculation than 'gee-whiz'!" Noice decided that he was not going to like a man with so "few 'human' traits and no human weaknesses. He was so entirely different from what I thought an explorer should be. His features fit the stereotype alright—high cheekbones, blond hair, and blue eyes characteristic of Scandinavians, but his voice was soft like a woman's, his manners were almost, but not quite, effeminate, his hands were long, white, and delicate like an artist's. Rather than being broad and massive, he was tall and slim. His arms were just arms—not muscular and brawny as an explorer's arms ought to be."[15]

Finally meeting Stefansson did not improve Noice's opinion. But when the expedition's little schooner was caught by ice well short of the place where winter quarters were to be established, Noice was impressed by Stefansson's calm. While the *Bear* tried fruitlessly to push through the ice, their commander read a novel, and when it became apparent that further progress would be impossible, Stefansson faced the situation with equanimity.

Having established the party's winter camp, Stefansson prepared to hunt caribou. Noice considered it unlikely that there would be many caribou steaks for the men to set their teeth into. How could a scientist with "lily-white hands," who so far had done nothing but read novels or pound away on his little typewriter, "carry out long hunting journeys and risk getting those hands of his all bloody butchering the skin."[16] Of course, Stefansson soon demonstrated that he was an excellent hunter.

1917 EVENTS

The 1916-17 winter passed with plenty of work for the men ferrying meat from a cache at Winter Harbour on the south coast to Cape Grassy, their winter camp. The Eskimo women worked on clothing. Gonzales showed up in February offering an unsatisfactory explanation of his movements. Disobeying his instructions to avoid retreating south, he had moved the *Bear* south to Walker Bay on the east coast of Victoria Island. The ship was of no use to Stefansson at that location.

On his birthday in November Stefansson reflected gloomily: "Thirty-seven years of small accomplishments, tho part of the time, and especially the last two years, I have done my best." But what really bothered him was an ailment of many months duration, a painful, embarrassing one that he had to keep to himself:

*I have had more than wind and weather to fight since March, 1914,
and now my health seems giving way. My ankle is a little weak tho
rather untrustworthy than weak; a more serious thing, which I have
hitherto kept out of my diary, is that I suffer from hemmorrhoids.*[17]

His ailment caused Stefansson more than physical pain, and he
was to remain sensitive on the subject for many years. His diary
makes clear why the temporary disability disturbed him so much:
"I knew it first on the Martin Point ice trip the day before that on
which we built the first (and only) snowhouse used on that trip.
That was the reason of the delay then, and of many delays since,
which I have excused on various grounds, for I feared to let my
companions know that there was any serious trouble."[18] A leader
of such men as the tough and independent Storkerson, August
Masik, and Herman and Martin Kilian could not appear frail.

On 12 April Stefansson set out for the exploration of Victoria
Island—a goal for the previous year that had had to be postponed.
The party including Noice, Knight, and Emiu had not proceeded
far when Noice and Knight became ill with scurvy. Both young
men suffered because in winter quarters they had feasted on canned
groceries and well-done meat, ignoring Stefansson's advice on a
proper diet. They could not go on, and because ice conditions were
so bad they had to head for Cape Isachsen rather than Borden Island. They set up camp on 11 May, and the sick men soon recovered
their health eating the caribou Stefansson provided. They were able
to move out again for a closer investigation of Lougheed Island.

In mid-August the explorers returned to Cape Kellett and to disappointment. Stefansson expected to find the *Mary Sachs* repaired
and ready for service and Gonzales awaiting him with the *Bear*.
Instead, Gonzales had been there and left, after ordering the Eskimos to scuttle the *Sachs*. Apparently his scheme was to maroon
his commander for another year while he applied to Ottawa for
his full pay. Luckily the *Challenger*, a trading schooner, happened
along. Stefansson purchased her and sailed west for Herschel Island. En route, they encountered Gonzales and listened to some
lame excuses. Stefansson did not press charges against Gonzales,
but he reported the matter to Ottawa.

Stefansson's hardest loss of the summer came with news of the
death of Peter Bernard, a travel companion he ranked just below

Wilkins and Storkerson in skills and loyalty. The two Nome men, Peter Bernard and Charles Thomsen, had not survived their sledge trip across Banks Island during the winter of 1916-17, probably because Bernard overloaded his sledges with Stefansson's mail and freight. "I lack the words now, and may always do so, to express my feelings," wrote Stefansson in his diary. "Through much experience...I have come to worship fidelity to your trust and thoughtfulness of others." He was conscious that two men died trying to assist him. "I cannot approve Bernard's carrying news magazines for me to read, but I love him for it. As I think Ovid says, he at least fell in a noble attempt."[19]

His thoughts then turned to certain other men on the expedition. "If I lack words for Bernard, I equally lack them for the men who, by inexcusable shirking and direct disobedience of orders, produced the conditions, before and after November 6, 1916, which resulted in the death of those two men."[20] He believed that if he had received more support from the members of his party, the sacrificial trip would not have been necessary.

When Stefansson reached Herschel Island in the summer of 1917, he received orders to return home. War was still raging in Europe, and it did not seem advisable to continue scientific work. Accordingly, the expedition men boarded the *Polar Bear* and started out for Nome. What actually occurred on this voyage has been disputed. In his account in *The Friendly Arctic* Stefansson said that during their visit to the trading station under the charge of Thomas Gordon just west of the International Boundary, Gordon told him that the ice was heavy and close to shore, and he was of the opinion that the *Polar Bear* would not be able to make it. Captain C.T. Pedersen had passed through a week earlier on the *Herman*, and he had been afraid he would not be able to get through.

In spite of these misgivings, Stefansson continued his voyage. Ice conditions improved, and on 13 September the *Polar Bear* reached a harbour at the east end of Barter Island. During the stormy night, the anchored ship was grounded. Stefansson wrote: "there was so little water around us that we could not have floated the ship off, even if we had removed her entire cargo."[21] It was not Stefansson's habit to complain about such incidents, and, indeed, it may be that he was not entirely displeased because the delay provided an opportunity for making the ice journey he had planned.

Others aboard the *Polar Bear* were not so happy. Peter Donahue, who had been ship's carpenter aboard the *Challenge*, had only

taken passage in the *Polar Bear* because the *Challenge* was to remain in the Arctic. By the time the *Polar Bear* reached Barter Island,
Donahue was "convinced that it was their intention to winter
there." He did not believe that ice conditions were the reason for
the halt. Donahue insisted that after an hour's work the grounded
ship was once again afloat, and there was no reason why it could
not have proceeded. Instead, they stayed in harbour for a week,
and when the weather turned frosty, Stefansson ordered the construction of winter quarters. Donahue observed acidly, "it seems
it was all that the commander was waiting for."[22]

Another critic was Captain Joseph Bernard of the *Teddy Bear*,
who secured Donahue's affidavit containing the charges discussed
here. Bernard argued that the *Polar Bear* had taken several days to
make a run from Herschel to Barter Island that could easily been
made in one day. Bernard had other hearsay evidence of Stefansson's intent. When Bernard was at Herschel in 1920, an RCMP
officer told him that he had warned the commander not to linger
because freeze-up was pending. According to the policeman, Stefansson calmly replied: "Nelson ignored an order and made history."[23]

1918 EVENTS

Now that they were icebound, Stefansson decided in the spring
of 1918 to make good use of the winter by preparing for a novel
journey. He would lead a party out on the ice and float east in
order to make scientific observations. However, after they reached
Herschel Island to gather their equipment, Stefansson was struck
first by typhoid fever and then by pneumonia. A missionary
stationed at Herschel nursed him for a few weeks until he felt
stronger, and then he decided to strike out for the nearest hospital
at Fort Yukon, Alaska. Storkerson agreed to lead the ice drift party
in his place.

Five volunteers accompanied Storkerson: August Masik, Adel-
bert Gumaer, E. Lorne Knight, Martin Kilian, and Fred Volki, all
of whom except Masik and Volki (son of the whaling skipper, Fritz
Volki) had had some experience on previous ice trips. Masik had
first sailed into the Arctic from Nome in 1916 with the *Challenge*,
one of the little schooners that often participated in the Bering Strait
trade with Siberians. He and a partner had established a camp on

the southeast coast of Banks Island where they hunted white fox. After one season, he signed on with Stefansson and proved to be a valuable member of the Expedition. He helped navigate the *Polar Bear* from Banks Island to Demarcation Point in 1917 after Gonzales wrecked the *Mary Sachs*.

Masik, a robust character, seemed a good choice. He was strong and reliable, and he spoke Russian, which would be helpful if they should drift to the Siberian coast. Masik, however, was wary. "I had heard enough from other parties about ice trips and 'living off the country' " he wrote later. He wanted to go outside for a spell to sell his furs and take his pleasures. But Stefansson was a "smooth talker" who managed to persuade him to go along, although Masik claimed his feet were in poor condition and his stomach worse. Stefansson offered mukluks to save his feet and raw seal meat to improve his digestion. "He said I looked healthy and physically fit," Masik reported. "I saw that he was after me and that there was no way out."[24]

Storkerson's party started off in March. After a couple of weeks' travel, their provisions were almost gone. "We only had white man's grub on Sunday," grumbled Masik. "The rest of the days we ate seal meat till I thought flippers would grow under my armpits." Polar bears that wandered onto their ice floe also provided sustenance. The men did their cooking over blubber lamps, the soot of which gave them a dark hue. "We had no soap, no tobacco, no tea, no coffee! A hell of a life!" Masik complained.[25]

The party did not accomplish as much as they hoped, but they sounded the depth of a good portion of the Beaufort Sea and proved the nonexistence of some imaginary islands. The party returned to land when Storkerson's asthma weakened him. Altogether they had spent eight months drifting on the sea ice, and even if Masik and the others missed their coffee and tobacco, they did not lack for food. The hunting was excellent. They killed ninety-six seals and six polar bears in all—enough to supply all their needs. After they returned to shore, Storkerson wintered at Herschel, and Masik, who had been in the North for nine years, eventually started for the South. Eager by this time to get out, it took Masik only seventeen days by dog sledge to reach Fort Yukon from the coast. By this time Stefansson had recovered from his illness and made his way down to Seattle. Masik caught up with Stefansson in Seattle and received part of the pay due him.

Later he was to get something that was just as important to him—

his formal discharge from the Canadian Arctic Expedition. He treasured the document and showed it with pride for the rest of his life. Stefansson praised his work: "In every capacity he has proved himself competent and faithful. There is no man who has been with me in Arctic work in a non-scientific capacity whom I would rather have with me again."[26]

Hudson Stuck, an Episcopal minister stationed in Alaska, was making a six-month journey along the arctic coast when he heard of Stefansson's illness. He and his travelling companion, Walter Harper, grandson of one of the pioneer prospectors of the Yukon Valley, dashed for Herschel Island intending to take Stefansson to the Fort Yukon hospital. (Fort Yukon lies just above the Arctic Circle on the Yukon River some four hundred miles from Herschel.)

Stuck and Harper reached Herschel Island only to find that Stefansson had already left, conveyed by dog sled on which was erected a comfortable spring bed. Stuck mushed south himself, catching up with Stefansson's party at Rampart House, a trading post just within the Canadian border, midway between the coast and Fort Yukon.

The trip agreed with Stefansson. Once they were under way, he lost his fever and regained his appetite. He ate raw fish and meat and over the twenty-seven-day journey, he gained thirty pounds. Stuck "was not surprised to find him mended" despite the fears that had been expressed at Herschel by the Mounted Police, who thought the explorer would die on the trail. Stefansson quotes Stuck in *The Friendly Arctic:* "I think that had he stayed in the little cabin where he lay so long sick, with several zealous amateur practitioners doing their rival best for him, he would very likely have died."[27] Stuck, a hearty and experienced musher, believed travelling was more healthful than idleness under any conditions.

Stuck's charity toward the stricken explorer was not prejudiced by Stefansson's comments in press interviews and in *My Life with the Eskimo* about the ill effects of white contact on natives. However, he was well aware of the issue. While Stefansson was still hospitalized, Stuck wrote to a friend: "I find him a very interesting man, quite willing to have his brain picked." When someone raised the missionary controversy, Stefansson was tactful. "He attributes nearly all, indeed *all,* the anti-missionary utterances with which he is credited to misrepresentation by newspaper reporters," Stuck explained. He did not accept Stefansson's explanation unreservedly, however. "There is certainly an animus in his book which

ilhjalmur Stefansson as a student at the University of North Dakota, 1900. **2.** The University of North Dakota campus
:fansson's time. **3.** Stefansson (centre) at Point Barrow, 1912. Trader Charles Brower is at his right, and John Hadley,
among the survivors of the *Karluk* disaster, is at his left.

4. Vilhjalmur Stefansson, in the Arctic, spring 1914. **5.** Copper Eskimo igloos. Stefansson's encounter with the "blond Eskimos led to the first negative publicity about him and his work. **6.** Copper Eskimo umiak drawn on sledge. The lac this kind of craft was in part responsible for the Wrangel Island disaster. **7.** The "lost" Sir John Franklin. The disappearance of his ship and crew in 1847 altered the public conception of the Arctic forever. **8.** C.F. Hall, the Amer

rer who learned the fate of the Franklin Expedition from Eskimos. **9.** Norwegian explorer Roald Amundsen, who made rst Northwest Passage journey in the *Gjoa*, 1903-6. **10.** Norwegian Fridtjof Nansen, whom Stefansson regarded as the est of all polar explorers. **11.** British explorer, Sir Ernest Shackleton, who recommended his press agent to Stefansson. Robert E. Peary with a dog sled. Stefansson was one of Peary's major defenders in the North Pole controversy.

13. Stefansson on board the *Karluk* at the beginning of the Canadian Arctic Expedition. **14.** The *Karluk* at Esquimalt harbour. Dissension among the men and criticism of Stefansson began even before she sailed. **15.** The Canadian Arctic Expedition at Nome, Alaska, 13 July 1913. Front row, l. to r., F. MacKay, surgeon; Capt. Robert Bartlett, skipper of the *Karluk*; Vilhjalmur Stefansson; R.M. Anderson, leader of the Southern Party, who became Stefansson's most bitter antagonist; James Murray, marine biologist; Frits Johansen, marine biologist. Back row, l. to r., B. Mamen, meteorologist; B.M. McConnell, secretary; K.G. Chipman, topographer; (behind Chipman), G.H. Wilkins, photographer; George Malloch, geologist; Henri Beuchat, anthropologist; J.J. O'Neill, geologist; D. Jenness, anthropologist; J.R. Cox, topographer

McKinlay, magnetician and meteorologist. MacKay, Murray, and Beuchat died on the ice in the Chukchi Sea, and
en and Malloch died on Wrangel Island. **16.** G.H. Wilkins and "Billy" Natkusiak, spring 1914. Later that year, these
en and Captain Peter Bernard brought the *Mary Sachs* to Banks Island. **17.** R.M. Anderson at Collinson Point, 1913.
Coppermine River, Northwest Territories, an area explored by the Southern Party. **19.** The Southern Party's head-
ers at Bernard Harbour in July 1916. **20.** While reindeer herds survived in Alaska, attempts made to establish them
Arctic on Stefansson's advice failed.

21. Anderson ignored Stefansson's 1915 order to send this schooner, *North Star*, to him. 22. The *Mary Sachs* on the 1914. It was not effective in ice navigation. 23. Diamond Jenness, ethnologist, left, and W.L. McKinlay, magnetician meteorologist. 24. Members of the Canadian Arctic Expedition on board the *Karluk*.

e snowhouse on Wrangel Island, where Williamson, Breddy, and Maurer were living. Breddy, who died of a t wound later in June, is seen in foreground. **26.** The last picture taken of the *Karluk* before she sank. **27.** Mugpie, Barrow Eskimo girl, youngest person aboard and one of the survivors of the SS *Karluk*. **28.** The survivors of the uk rescued from Wrangel Island by the schooner *King and Winge*.

29. Portrait photographer Yousuf Karsh of Ottawa with Stefansson in May 1947. 30. Vilhjalmur and Evelyn Stefan at their Vermont farm shortly after their marriage in 1941. 31. 1937 portrait of Rudolph M. Anderson. 32. Stefans at the far left in the front row in this group picture taken at the Explorers Club.

is hard for him to explain away, though he tries his best."²⁸

While Stefansson remained in the Arctic, his scientific colleagues had a good chance to tell their stories. One rather sly attempt to discredit Stefansson appeared in a Vancouver newspaper's interview with H.V. D'Ardier, who had arrived from the Arctic in 1915. D'Ardier told a newsman of a rumour in the North that Stefansson was neither dead, lost, nor in jeopardy, but that he just did not care to have his present whereabouts known. The inference was that Stefansson was really in hiding, intending to appear at some future date and describe a hazardous journey that he had not made, after the pattern established by Dr. Frederick Cook.²⁹ D'Ardier's motives are not clear, and he may have been reporting the suspicions of members of the Southern Party, for whom he had worked briefly under Kenneth Chipman.

Chipman may have been the "informant" whom the *Ottawa Citizen* quoted in a 1916 news story that attacked Stefansson for ignoring the government's order to end the expedition in 1915. Inspector Phillips of the RCMP was alleged to have told the "informant" this fact.³⁰

Although such orders were issued, they never reached Stefansson. For different reasons Phillips and Chipman were annoyed that Stefansson stayed in the Arctic, Phillips probably wishing that there were no expeditions in the Arctic to worry about, and Chipman, who left the field with great relief, always imagining wrongdoing in anything Stefansson did.

The *Citizen* story drew a sharp contrast between the work of the northern and southern parties, claiming that Stefansson had procured the *Polar Bear* at an extravagant rent of $1,000 a day to make the voyage from Herschel to Banks Island and then dawdled along the way. The paper reported that he had spent seven days in port doing absolutely nothing, and then he paid $28,000 to purchase the *Polar Bear* as well as an "exorbitant" price for its provisions. The Southern Party, on the other hand, was "doing splendid work." They had resisted Stefansson's insistence that they live like the Eskimo and had separated from him two years earlier "because it was impossible to remain on good terms with the Norwegian [*sic*] explorer."³¹

How Stefansson became a "Norwegian" is uncertain, but the informant knew that he had "sold body and soul to American newspapers and magazines." The paper charged that Stefansson thinks "he can flip his fingers at the Dominion government—because of the distance."[32]

These two newspaper attacks were to be followed by others, the most vehement of which followed publication of *The Friendly Arctic* in 1921. Later, Stefansson's enemies were to insist that they had said nothing against him prior to their outrage after publication of his book. Probably they had forgotten about the articles of 1915 and 1916 cited here, although Chipman preserved them carefully in his scrapbook.

CHAPTER 14

From Field to Platform

THE SUMMER OF 1918 was a watershed in Stefansson's life. Although he did not know it then, his days of arctic field work were over. While convalescing from the wasting effects of typhoid in St. Stephen's Hospital at Fort Yukon, Alaska, he had ample leisure to plan his future and catch up on correspondence. He arrived at the hospital in May, weak and needing rest, but out of danger. For the first time in five years he had access to the telegraph system and the relatively efficient Alaskan mail service. Until he arrived at Fort Yukon, he had received virtually no mail for three years.

Fort Yukon, a trading centre of some three hundred people, mostly Athapaskan Indians, was established in 1864 by the Hudson's Bay Company. The Bay moved the community downstream a couple of miles from the original site founded by Alexander Murray in 1847. The British traders were forced to move again in 1869 when an American army officer pointed out that the post (at the junction of the Porcupine and Yukon rivers) was within the Alaskan border; the Alaska Commercial Company subsequently took it over.

Wires and letters from many friends greeted Stefansson at Fort Yukon. The messages cheered him, especially those where the writers indicated that they had discounted the reports of his death. Alexander Graham Bell, for instance, assured him that knowing his "pertinacity and adaptability to Arctic conditions of living, I was one of those who never gave you up for dead."[1]

Cheering, too, was a wire from H.L. Bridgman, the publisher and patron of exploration, who, knowing Stefansson must be broke, made a generous and timely offer of an unrestricted loan. But most of all Stefansson thirsted for news. His friends gave him the latest word on Amundsen's *Maud* expedition, Donald MacMillan's report on his recent "Crocker Land" journey, and Bob Bartlett's plans for future exploration. His editor at Macmillan also wrote, assuring Stefansson that there was no need to hurry in preparing his account of the expedition. Exploration could not compete with war bulletins, and the book would go better after the war was over.

Stefansson received several urgent messages from Jafet Lindeberg, a Nome gold-mining proprietor who was a partner with the Lomen brothers in the reindeer industry. Lindeberg hoped to enlist Stefansson's help in selling reindeer stock to the Canadian government. In response to another appeal, possibly from Hudson Stuck, Stefansson either wrote or wired everyone he knew in government and conservation circles protesting the establishment of a commercial salmon cannery on the lower Yukon River, arguing that it would have a detrimental effect on Indian subsistence fishing. Later, he asked Desbarats to appoint him as an unpaid investigator of the fishery situation, but Canada's jurisdiction did not extend to the sea.

Stefansson left in August for Dawson, Skagway, and Seattle, then for a visit with his mother in North Dakota, and, finally, he reported to Ottawa. In the months following his return, he was still occupied with expedition matters. Every request for salary or expenses had to be approved by him, and in some cases, disputes over money owing caused extensive correspondence, as did the disposition of expedition ships and stores.

When Stefansson met Ernest Shackleton on his pre-expedition trip to England in 1912, Shackleton convinced him of the importance of lecturing about his explorations. Shackleton explained how the platform would help: lectures sold books, books sold lectures, and the newspapers sold both, "particularly when you come home from an expedition with a big hurrah."[2] Shackleton knew much more about promotion than Stefansson did, and he had already demonstrated his ability to raise money from the public. Stefansson had never had to do this, but he respected Shackleton's personality and drive, particularly since he knew that the Irishman did not have the kind of influence Robert Scott had with Britain's exploration establishment and that he was compelled to live by his wits. Shackleton recommended lecture manager Lee Keedick to Stefansson, who signed a contract in 1913 for series of speaking engagements following the return of the Canadian Arctic Expedition. Unfortunately, the "big hurrah," so necessary for a successful lecture tour was proclaimed in 1918 over the end of World War One—not over polar exploration.

Stefansson's continuing obligation to the Canadian government prevented him from embarking immediately on his lecture tour. G.J. Desbarats, deputy minister of naval services, took exception to the proposed tour because it threatened to delay completion of the report. "Your plan," Desbarats wrote, "would defeat the objects of the Government in manning, equipping, and financing the Canadian Arctic Expedition." The object of the expedition "was to obtain information for the benefit of the people of Canada and unless a report is made setting forth this information in proper shape, so that it can be published and laid before the public, the object of the Department would be entirely defeated and Canada would obtain no return for its expedition."[3]

Desbarats pointed out that the Southern Party was working diligently on its reports. "If the report of the Northern Branch is lacking...the inference will be clear that there is nothing to say on the subject." Desbarats believed that he "would be the first to regret such a result, and it would, undoubtedly, lead to a severe attack on the Government and on yourself."[4]

Stefansson replied at length. He argued that he had asked for permission to lecture for the benefit of the Red Cross not for his own profit. Furthermore, he thought it would be a good idea to tell Canadians about the expedition while it was still news. The scientific reports could wait, he said; there was no reason why a delay would cause people to think nothing had been accomplished. He correctly pointed out that "some of the great expeditions have had volumes of scientific results appearing many years after the return home."[5] Moreover, he claimed the government must have misunderstood his patriotic purpose. While he had served without salary for about six years, other expedition members enjoyed full salaries and have given press releases contrary to their contracts, yet he was prepared to forego writing articles and a popular book to help the wartime efforts of the Red Cross.

Stefansson was obviously annoyed at being pressed. He did not yet have his diaries and other papers, which were being shipped from Nome. However, he told Desbarats he was cutting short his convalescence so that he could get to Ottawa sooner and clarify the situation. Desbarats's reply was sharp. He reminded Stefansson that if he had not considered the war effort important, he would not have "sent instructions not to continue your explorations" about two years before, and that Stefansson had never acknowledged receipt of such orders. Desbarats insisted that Stefansson prepare an official report "as soon as possible."[6]

It is easy to understand the positions of both men. Desbarats was responsible for the orderly conclusion and reporting of a major government project, and he knew that scientists and other project managers often found it easy to postpone writing reports. Both knew that lecturing—even without a fee—would undoubtedly benefit Stefansson personally. Such appearances would keep his name in the limelight, guaranteeing that his future publications would gain in popularity.

Desbarats was annoyed about Stefansson's decision to extend his explorations beyond the Beaufort Sea, and particularly about the ice floe drift which Stefansson planned before he became ill and in which Storkerson was still engaged. Stefansson replied that Desbarats's orders recalling him must have been among letters lost when Peter Bernard and Charles Thomsen died in a blizzard while trying to carry the mail from Banks Island to Melville Island. He noted too that at the time Desbarats had concurred with his decision to explore the interior of newly discovered lands.

As far as the ice drift was concerned, it would cost the government virtually nothing: Storkerson served without any salary, and the other men drew only small wages. Nor was provisioning an added burden. The expense of the drift, thus, was minimal, and the scientific gain was potentially immense—so he had taken the chance that Desbarats would approve his plan.[7]

When Stefansson got to New York on 1 November he wrote Desbarats that he had cancelled all lectures except for the first five that were scheduled for New York, Brooklyn, Philadelphia, Washington, and Toronto. Seats had already been sold for them, he explained, and it was too late to cancel the tour. After he had delivered his lectures, Stefansson devoted more attention to expedition matters. Although he was willing to forgive Anderson's disobedience, he wanted the government to acknowledge that he had indeed been the expedition commander:

So long as you are satisfied with the good faith of my management of the expedition, and seeing that its scientific success seems as-

sured, I feel satisfied with the six years of the organization and field work of the expedition. The nervous strain of the continual fear of failure consequent on the disobedience of orders by Anderson and Gonzales is now happily over and I would rather forget them, I think, than receive a public vindication on any point that may seem doubtful or discreditable to those not fully informed.[8]

Stefansson's willingness to forgive was one of his finest qualities. In this case, forbearance was also prudent. Explorers generally try to keep their field bickerings out of the public eye. As Roald Amundsen once put it, "When success has crowned one's efforts," it is far better to bury bad feelings "in the agreeable oblivion of mutual felicitation."[9] It would be foolish to risk sullying one's own reputation by attacking others. After having expressed this wise advice, however, Amundsen recognized the exception of particular circumstances and issued a savage attack on an expedition comrade.

Later in November, from the Harvard Club on West 44th Street in New York where he was residing, Stefansson wrote Desbarats specifically about Anderson, enclosing a letter Anderson had written to Isaiah Bowman, secretary of the Explorers Club. In it Anderson threatened to resign if Stefansson were elected president for the year 1919. Stefansson nevertheless was elected, and Anderson's resignation was duly accepted. Anderson also wrote to Bowman as head of the American Geographical Society, but in spite of his urgings, the society granted Stefansson its highest award. Although Stefansson said he regarded the actions of the society as "sufficient refutations of Dr. Anderson's contention," he was not one to take chances on having his record blemished. He asked Bowman to write a letter for Desbarats's files giving a concise statement of his opinion as to the geographical value of the expedition's work.[10]

The Explorers Club was founded in New York City in 1905 to provide a common meeting ground for explorers and travellers from all parts of the world. Many members already belonged to professional societies relating to their fields of expertise such as biology, geology, archaeology, and geography, but the Explorers Club provided common ground. At its best, the club functioned as an informal, interdisciplinary, scientific and geographic seminar—a moveable feast for scholarly exchange.

The organizers of the club hoped to promote professionalism in exploration, to bring favourable public attention to successful discoveries, and to provide a forum for the exposure of fraud. In 1909 the Explorers Club heard evidence disputing Frederick Cook's alleged climb of Mt. McKinley and eventually rejected his claim. Such action served an important public purpose, for there was no other medium for formally declaring against a fraud. Because of friendships, loyalties, and gentlemanly reluctance, such actions required courage. After all, Cook had been elected president of the club for the year 1907, and so the rejection of his claim had embarrassing implications for the membership.

Apart from the annual formal dinners, the club offered a drop-in centre for good talk and chance meetings with friends. The famous Long Table quickly became an institution. In the afternoons, tea and coffee were served to any who might gather around the big oak table to describe their adventures. Informal letters from travellers to the membership-at-large were often simply addressed to "The Long Table," where they were publicly read. The club also provided a sanctuary, and was a fraternal headquarters for many world wanderers.

For a bachelor like Stefansson, the club assumed more importance than it might have for many family men, and he went there often. Stefansson enjoyed the amenities of the club, which he repaid by serving as president in 1919, 1932 and 1937, and by otherwise taking an active part in its affairs. The presidency was no sinecure, judging from Stefansson's correspondence for the period.

Stefansson was to live at the Explorers Club for a time before he moved to Greenwich Village, and afterwards he spent many evenings there. In the 1920's the club was housed in a three-storey Victorian house at 47 West 76th Street, just west of Central Park and close to the American Museum of Natural History. Later, the club moved into a new building (on 110th Street east of upper Broadway) that had a sizeable auditorium for lectures, a library, and some guest rooms.

In the meantime, while Stefansson was establishing himself on the Outside, Storkerson's party ended the C.A.E.'s field activity. They set up camp on dry land on 8 November 1918, after an arduous journey over sea ice that took, in all, 238 days.[11] In the summer of 1919 Stefansson invited Storkerson to join him at Banff, the Rocky Mountain resort where he had been given accommodations so that he could prepare his expedition report.

With the help of his secretary, Olive Rathburn, Stefansson recorded Storkerson's account of his drift, and he also dictated an account of his own activities. As he recalled many years later, this dictation "turned out to be, though probably neither of us dreamed it, the first of more than twenty book-length manuscripts of mine transcribed and edited for publication by Olive Rathburn."[12] In 1956 he dedicated *Not by Bread Alone* to "Olive Rathburn Wilcox, collaborator on fourteen previous books and on this one."[13] His rate of publication, as he generously acknowledged in his preface, owed much to his assistant.

Stefansson wrote Desbarats from Banff requesting that he ask Anderson both to write a narrative report for the Southern Party and to provide a copy of the letter he had written to Stefansson explaining why he had disobeyed instructions. This defiant missive had disappeared from a locked box, and Stefansson, supported by Wilkins, believed that Anderson had stolen it so that it could not be used against him.

Anderson, however, denied having any knowledge of the letter after he had given it to O'Neill and claimed that his report for the year 1914 had covered the matter fully. To this rebuttal, Stefansson replied: "If this is so, this part of his report has not been published, for it is not contained in the published report which I have read."[14]

In November and December 1919 Desbarats urged Stefansson to finish his report and wind up other expedition matters. Stefansson replied that he was working steadily on the preparation of a book which "is essentially the same work as the preparation of a report."[15] Obviously, Stefansson intended Desbarats to accept *The Friendly Arctic* as his report. Eventually, Desbarats was forced to accept a short summary which could be supplemented by reports Stefansson had sent from the field. As it turned out, no general narrative of the expedition (as distinguished from particular scientific reports like Jenness's on the Copper Eskimo) was ever published by the government. Anderson balked at writing an account of the Southern Party's work. Had he done so, he would have had to explain why he defied instructions. Also, Stefansson, who would have had the task of putting the reports together, would have had the final word.

Stefansson had some distractions at Banff and elsewhere arising out of his romance with Betty Brainerd that dated from the time of his return to Seattle from Fort Yukon in the fall of 1918. Betty's father, Erastus Brainerd, was the well-known promoter of Seattle during the Klondike gold rush. Brainerd's publicity campaign for the Chamber of Commerce established the Puget Sound city as the gateway to Yukon and Alaska. Betty poured out her love for Stefansson in her letters to him: "I love you with every atom of my being....If you were indifferent it would kill me....I am absolutely at your command." She discussed marriage with him both when she thought herself pregnant and afterwards. She was also tormented in 1918 by a fear of hurting another man in her life, as well as by a physical ailment. After these crises passed, Stefansson told her that the "only thing I care to know about you is that you love me...past is past...I love you."[16]

In December 1918, Betty disclosed other health problems to him, and then she did not write for a time. At last Stefansson telegraphed her mother asking for word of her, and after receiving her reply, he telegraphed $500 to Betty for doctor's bills.

He urged her to move to New York, but she was reluctant to give up writing society news for a Seattle paper and reporting for the King County Juvenile Court. Her next crisis concerned her need for dental work. Stefansson offered to pay for that, too. He exchanged telegrams from Banff with Betty's dentist, who assured him that she had withstood the pain of an extraction satisfactorily. In September, Betty Brainerd wrote Stefansson, "many people in Seattle have asked if I would marry you." Seattle would not be a good place to marry, she continued, because "our friends would push for a big wedding." Banff, too, was unsuitable. "Probably it would be better if I came to New York...if you still desire so undesirable a person as me."[17]

What happened after that is not clear, nor is it even certain that Betty moved to New York. In 1920 she was arrested in Tacoma, Washington, for helping a friend kidnap his two-year-old son from the mother. Charges against her were dropped, and judging from press clippings of the incident, it was a popular decision.

In December, 1923, the relationship between Stefansson and Betty reached the breaking point. Betty was in New York, but she wrote a letter to Stefansson complaining that toothache and other troubles precluded her from talking to him; she confessed to being "stunned" by a "confession" he had made at breakfast and by his indifference to answering letters. "Silence," she fretted, "is not an alarm—but a rebuff. Remember I have always been *sought*. When it is a concession to make any advance, the blow of a refusal falls heavily. Pride recognizes change without understanding it." Betty could not find the right words to describe her mood; "On top of your change and my hunger...I thought I was going to have a child."

Thus, his impersonal manner, although "uniformly kind," really hurt. " 'Little Stef' would have been a darling."[18]

His decision to become a professional lecturer in 1918 was also an important turning point in Stefansson's life, which, as he put it, "economically had till then been a scheme for getting someone else to pay my way."[19] Stefansson felt for the first time that he had abandoned his dependency on sponsors: "Like a tennis player renouncing his amateur standing, I was joining the ranks of the professionals."[20]

He made his first lecture tour in 1919. His earnings (at $300 per engagement) were satisfactory, supplemented as they were by the occasional appearances that brought between $800 and $1,100. He found the idleness that was forced on him along the lecture route a drawback, despite the time he spent pounding out letters and other writings on his portable typewriter. He brooded over remarks by his agent, who had rubbed him the wrong way in his attempt to explain what he considered to be the "proper" platform manner for an explorer. Eventually, Keedick approved of Stefansson's undramatic performances, not because he had heard any lectures himself, but because good reports of the lectures had come back to him. Adding fuel to Stefansson's discontent was an offer that came to him from the Affiliated Lyceum and Chautauqua Association. This agency guaranteed him an income of $2,000 a week for six to ten lectures, plus all expenses and a travelling companion to handle routine matters. Such an arrangement, Stefansson realized, would enable him to earn more over a short period. He would be free to devote much more time to writing, which always appealed to him as the most satisfying and rewarding work he could undertake. Like all fledgling authors, he imagined that the making of books would only occupy him part time, while answering all of his spiritual and physical needs. When he was an old man, he reflected on the appeal of that offer and the possibilities it opened up, and he marvelled that the prospect of having nothing to do for several months each year had so excited him.

For a time Stefansson lectured for both Keedick and the Affiliated Lyceum, an arrangement that worked out satisfactorily for both. Keedick's stationery and brochures enhanced Stefansson's reputation by giving him equal billing with Shackleton among the "World's Greatest Heroes," and ranking him before some other clients, including Roald Amundsen, Sir Douglas Mawson, General Robert Baden-Powell, and Dr. Maria Montessori. "Swell-headed as I was getting to be," he wrote, "it was no mean thrill to see this display." He was delighted even though the substance of his lectures stressed his conviction that survival in the Arctic did not depend on acts of heroism.

When Robert Peary and Frederick Cook had returned to America, each claiming to have reached the North Pole, there was a frenzied competition among lecture agents for their services. For a time they could expect to have spectacular success as lecturers and command lucrative fees. Cook made a fortune for himself in a short period of time while Peary, who had other sources of income, declined to lecture except to large audiences, and then only when the engagement was preceded by lavish promotion that would ensure a substantial fee. Book and magazine publishers also pursued them, eagerly offering generous advances: *Hampton's Magazine*, for instance, paid Peary $50,000 for a series of articles on his exploits.

Stefansson's place in the public eye was far less prominent. The success of his lectures depended upon the care with which each one was promoted, and conditions varied greatly from city to city. Some of his 1919 appearances on the Pacific Coast were so disappointing that he was tempted to give up lecturing altogether. Later, under better management, conditions improved.

Stefansson could not have continued to fascinate audiences in the 1920's and 1930's merely by recounting his 1913-18 achievements. He could go back year after year to Iowa City or Seattle because he offered genuinely fresh insights on the Arctic and because his writings kept him in the spotlight.

In those early years Stefansson's greatest difficulty was in ridding himself of an agent in whom he had lost confidence. After working under another agent who proved to be much more satisfactory, Stefansson tried to break his contract with Keedick. Keedick resisted and Stefansson quit. His attorney advised him that Keedick's cavalier handling of advance publicity provided a good defence to a suit for breach of contract. Furthermore, Keedick had ignored Stefansson's protests concerning the agent's misrepresentations in news releases and publicity handouts. In his view a bit of exaggeration did no harm. But Stefansson, who was aware of the damage that had been done to Peary and other explorers because of irresponsible reporting and who had been ridiculed himself over the "blond Eskimo" publicity, knew that such misstatements constituted a grave risk. Often enough he had been called a sensationalist and charlatan. What defence could he offer if his own agent planted stories that made him appear dishonest or ridiculous?

Keedick's wild releases even linked Stefansson with Christopher Columbus, asserting confidently that the explorer had concluded the task begun by Columbus by writing the last chapter in the history of exploration. According to Keedick, Stefansson had found the "long sought Arctic Continent"—an area of some one million square miles.[21]

Finally, Stefansson broke his contract in 1922, and Keedick sued him for damages. The press observed Stefansson's defence of "over-exploitation" with a mixture of glee and amused disbelief. Stories captioned "PRESS AGENT TOO GOOD," "PRESS AGENT OVER ZEALOUS," and "STEFANSSON SUES HIS PRESS AGENT FOR OVERDOING" appeared in New York papers. One story's lead article noted that Stefansson "dislikes publicity" and explained the circumstances of what it archly termed "this startling fact." Another story sarcastically referred to Stefansson, "the Norwegian [*sic*] explorer," who "once had a notion that a press agent is a pretty good thing for an explorer to have, but now...has altered his views," because his agent had made "exaggerated and untruthful statements, instead of sticking to the plain undignified truth. Overexploitation is something that Stefansson cannot forgive."[22] The dispute was eventually settled and Stefansson gained his freedom, but his counter-claim for damages did not prevail.

Stefansson enjoyed lecturing, particularly when he had an attentive audience, and in this he was more fortunate than such others as Charles Francis Hall, Roald Amundsen, and Ernest Shackleton, for whom the lecture platform was only a means of raising funds. Lecturing provided a significant portion of Stefansson's income, but it was also a means of disseminating his ideas about the North. He was no "nine days' wonder," but rather a serious teacher and proselytizer whose consistently argued theories conjured up a new conception of the Arctic in the minds of his audiences.

Stefansson liked to poke fun at so-called "polar heroes." It pays to be a hero, he once told some college students, explaining, "If I want to be a hero I have to go to the far North. Then, if I do not brag too much about it I'll be admired for my modesty as well."[23] Having established a rapport, Stefansson could plunge with confidence into the substance of his "friendly Arctic" theory.

The press sometimes ridiculed Stefansson's theories. After he gave a lecture in London in 1929, a reporter admitted that he was "shattered" to learn that Eskimos do not live in ice houses. Equally disappointing was Stefansson's insistence that future air traffic between Europe, North America, and Asia would be routed over the Arctic. "The vision of the North Pole as a sort of international Charing Cross," he remarked, "is decidedly novel."[24]

Two years later, lecturing in Camden, New Jersey, Stefansson took teachers to task for perpetuating myths about the Eskimo. The Eskimo people, he argued, know more about white society than the latter know of theirs. Stefansson went on to predict great things for the future development of the North. A *New York Herald Tribune* reporter, however, thought that the lecturer went too far: "If the Arctic explorer and author can be depended upon, real estate developers have been overlooking a sure thing in not cutting the north polar region into building lots, laying out a beach, installing a cafeteria and a filling station, and advertising them as an ideal summer resort."[25]

"Another tradition smashed," was the facetious comment of a Montreal newspaper on the same lecture. "Now this is most distressing. Here for long years we have been sedulously cultivating among our children a sympathy for the poor benighted Eskimo in his igloo...and now this picture must be rudely shattered. All this sympathy has gone to waste just because Mr. Stefansson must tell the world the results of his investigations. It seems so unfortunate. We might just as well have gone on believing. It is a hard world when we are robbed of all our pet traditions and deprived of all our pet beliefs about Eskimo and suchlike folk."[26] Prophets can be such a bore!

In his book, *The Standardization of Error,* a philosophically minded Stefansson wrote that a fact may be only a fact until one asks *why* it is so. "What's the good, again, of learning that most Eskimos live in snow houses when you may discover later than most of them have never seen a snow house?"[27] Stefansson understood his role as teacher as well as the dilemma that confronted students. It was inconvenient, if not perhaps just too much to expect them to learn, then unlearn, re-examine, and learn anew.

Sometimes the debate over his "friendly Arctic" theory grew acrimonious, as happened when Amundsen launched his famous attack; more often the only public reaction was simply good-humored disbelief. One auditor of his lectures at the University of Washington expressed his reaction in verse:

Though Stefansson may think it nice
to lay him down on cakes of ice
Which often crack and drop one smack
among the icy billows,
And though he loves to lie awake
and hear the floes around him break,
I know I sleep more sound and deep
on mattresses and pillows.
Though Stefansson is fond of meals
composed exclusively of seals
And says to eat that kind of meat
At least becomes a passion,
The more I read his Arctic book
The more I find I'm fond of cooks,
And realize my love for pies
That mother used to fashion.[28]

Bad verse but good fun—and a reaction that was probably the response of most of Stefansson's auditors. Even if they were not tempted to tramp through the Arctic themselves, they were still getting his chief message.

Lecturing is not the easiest way to earn a living unless one finds one night stands, short sleeps, long rides, and frequent contact with strangers enjoyable. During his first season, the routine affected Stefansson's "nerves, or whatever side of one's nature it is through which all the rest suffers."[29] Why, he wondered, could people feel pity for his suffering the so-called hardships of an ice journey and envy his life as a lecturer? Over the years he travelled to most parts of the United States and Canada, usually during the fall and spring seasons. From 20 May to 12 June 1921, for example, he delivered lectures in eighteen towns in California, four in Nevada, and one in Utah. His list of engagements reads almost like a railroad time-table: Turlock, Modesto, Lode, Stockton, Los Gatos, Richmond, Petaluma, Eureka, Willits, Ft. Bragg, Ukiah, Lakeport, Healdsburg, Sebastapol, Santa Rosa, Sacramento, Grass Valley, Reno, Lovelock, Winnemucca, Elko, and Ogden. During those twenty-three days, he slept in twenty-three different hotels, and this was just part of his season's itinerary!

Besides giving him a forum, lecturing also allowed Stefansson to renew acquaintances with his friends. His pace slowed down in the 1930's, and even more in later years, yet the lecture platform continued to be an important means of communication with the public throughout most of his life. It may be that more people learned of his theories through his lectures than read his books; and certainly what these audiences heard or read from Stefansson constituted a substantial portion of the American public's knowledge of the Arctic.

Friends of Stefansson during this period included the aviators Orville and Wilbur Wright and their sister, Katherine, Theodore Roosevelt, Jr., Charles Lindbergh, and many other individuals associated with exploratory, literary, and scientific endeavours in New York and elsewhere.

On his lecture tours Stefansson often stayed with friends, although when he was in Ottawa he preferred to stay at the Chateau Laurier—the grand old hotel that dominates the downtown—because of its proximity to government offices. He thoroughly enjoyed being entertained, so he did not share a fellow lecturer's aversion to social life, although he could appreciate his point of view. Elbert Hubbard, a well-known writer, at one point teamed up with Stefansson on the same program. On Hubbard's business card, according to Stefansson, were prominently displayed his terms for lecturing: "$100 IF I STAY AT A HOTEL, $250 IF I AM ENTERTAINED."[30]

Aside from his affair with Betty Brainerd, Stefansson's relationships with women in the early 1920's appear, in most cases, to have been platonic, although not lacking in passion. Constance Lindsay Skinner met Stefansson after one of his 1919 lectures, but she had been thinking about him for years and had always followed his arctic adventures. The reports of his death had not dismayed her; she knew he would come through: "You are the man my spirit met in those white nights...something of me went with you during those five years."[31]

Constance Skinner was a good writer, and she offered to help Stefansson on a manuscript "out of love rather than money." She was a friend of Harold Noice as well: "You can trust him," she insisted—wrongly, as it turned out. Constance felt comfortable enough in her friendship with Stefansson to chide him about his "Icelandic suspiciousness" and his vanity ("that blond wig you are so vain about") and would see him off for lecture tours with the facetious wish "that you were as virtuous as you are dear."[32]

Stefansson gave Constance money to pay her rent when she was in financial difficulties, and he encouraged her not to marry out of desperation a particular man whom she did not love. Constance assured Stefansson, "You know I would shoot myself six months after marrying him." Later she affirmed that Harold Noice had spread unfounded gossip about their alleged intimacy, and she hastened to set the record straight for Stefansson: "There is no such intimacy, as he knows, but he also knows that because you exist, there is no other man for me and that my long illness last spring was due to shock and grief."[33]

His women friends tended to express their affections warmly. "I am longing for you; please love me," wrote one southern beauty to Stefansson in 1921. The famous novelist, Fanny Hurst, was just as forthright; "I'm sorry I can't give a return for your light, wisdom, vision, sweetness...this high plane of our friendship—before it I am...a little humble."[34] Another woman wrote; "If you write a line to every page of mine I'll be more than happy. I *do* love you."[35]

In 1922, as he was negotiating with Canadian officials for the leadership of a new expedition, Peggy Fletcher, another of his woman friends, cautioned him gravely: "I hope you never go North again. It couldn't add to your stature as an explorer and none could take your place here in the work that should be done in the development of the land—and the resources." She was writing a novel and had a clear conception of the principal character she wanted to create: "I would like to make a living man step out of the pages—a man as arresting and *full of mystery* as you are."[36] Many of Stefansson's female admirers found him mysterious, but perhaps the term they used was really a polite euphemism for his adroit evasiveness. Stefansson was capable of returning as much love as he received, but he was constantly on the move and disinclined to settle into domesticity.

Occasionally a woman took a sterner line. Peggy Fletcher once shrewdly observed that she had come to realize that "the foundation of our friendship is based upon what you want—not upon what I want. No matter what my inclinations are," she complained, "I must do the thing most pleasing to you." She added that she "thought of him constantly." Like many another who was uncertain of her grasp on her man, she found herself often "sinking in the slough of despair."[37]

Two years later these two friends were discussing an autobiography that Stefansson was planning to write. Peggy thought such a work could not sufficiently represent his many sides: the man of science, the explorer, the dreamer, and the man himself. "Many people who know you see something different in you. None see what I see or don't mention it." "I know your generosity," she wrote, "your impatience with falseness of any kind, [your] humor, and caustic wit." Sometimes, she continued, "you are kind, other times harsh...because you hate mediocrity." She appreciated his "clear, quick thinking, and interest in other people and problems. There is much greatness in this not belonging to the power of your mind. It is the quality of your imagination that is unique."[38]

When Stefansson was interviewed in his Greenwich Village apartment by a journalist who described him as "hulking" and "too big for his four walls," Constance Skinner suggested that he might not appreciate the description. "You like to pose as a small, slender man who doesn't look like an Arctic explorer but to those who look with their mind's eye you'll always look very big, massive and powerful. You *are* 'mountainous' and your efforts to appear effete and delicate go for nothing." The journalist in question was probably V.S. Pritchett, who later wrote that he had detected an element of masochism in Stefansson and other explorers.[39]

Other friends also enjoyed teasing Stefansson about his physical characteristics. "I have seen you shiver [from] chill walking Fifth Avenue on a windy day," wrote Fanny Hurst in 1924. "I know you can't cook coffee or sew anything at all—much less mend tents...and that a mildly rough sea makes you feel squeamish and that your hands haven't ever, I am sure, had a rough place."[40]

Fanny Hurst was Stefansson's lover for seventeen years. Immensely successful, she became a best-selling novelist in her twenties and made more money from the sale of her books and magazine stories than any other American woman. It seems unlikely that Stefansson would have been attracted to her because of her writing, but he was indeed smitten. When she died in 1968 at the age of seventy-eight, the *New York Times* recalled that some critics had called her the "sob sister" of American letters: "A generation of students made fun of her clichés and awkward words even while millions of readers, especially women, enjoyed everything she wrote."[41]

Fanny Hurst was married and later separated from her husband. She dreaded adverse publicity, and so, like Stefansson, she tried to be discreet about their relationship. Still in 1939, when he published his book, *Unsolved Mysteries of the Arctic,* she complained that he did not acknowledge fully "17 years of human relationship" by writing a dedication to her.[42] Yet in her own autobiography, *Anatomy of Me: A Wanderer in Search of Herself*, which she published in 1958, Hurst made only fleeting reference to the explorer.

And then there were books—the other enduring passion of his life. All dedicated book collectors flirt with insolvency when tempted by the latest great "bargain" whose acquisition seems essential to the collection. Usually the opportunity to buy a rare book takes precedence over practical considerations. So it was with Stefansson, who was smitten by the collecting bug during the 1920's. Stefansson's talent for rationalizing his expenditures increased as his library grew. He would explain that his library was a monumental resource, a collection of the world's accumulated knowledge on every facet of the polar regions. The uniqueness of his library gave him satisfaction, but perhaps it could not equal the joys of opening a newly arrived parcel of books—the fruit of some discovery found in a Chicago shop on his last lecture tour or in a dealer's catalogue that he may have pored over on a train.

Ordinary people cannot really understand or appreciate the intensity of a bibliophile's secret life, even though collectors are not usually reticent in calling the attention of their acquaintances to a fresh acquisition. And Stefansson was typical. He was pleased to be acknowledged as a discerning collector in a bookseller's published memoir—Charles Everitt's *Adventures of a Treasure Hunter*. Everitt wrote humorously of his professional life, buying, selling, and appraising books. Among the low and the high points of the memoir are his recollections of dividing a set of books by the same author among seven jealous legatees who insisted on an equal division of their inheritance and his appraisal of Stefansson's collection, which he called "the longest and most interesting appraisal I ever made." Booksellers know the dark secrets of enthralled customers, and Everitt cheerfully admitted that "Stef has kept himself poor for most of his lifetime by unremitting devotion to those books."[43]

Building his arctic library was a pleasant obsession of Stefansson's that occupied much of his time in New York, and a considerable amount of travel time as well. On his visits to Britain in the 1920's he made extensive purchases over the protests of his secretary, Olive Wilcox, who contended that if money seemed to be rolling in, it rolled out just as quickly because of his expenditures on books. Stefansson regarded his journeys to Britain and elsewhere as good opportunities to add to his library, although the ostensible purposes were government negotiations or lecturing. In an early, unpublished section of his autobiography, he imagined that his biographer, "if there were one," would be duped into associating trips to England with meetings concerning northern development, neglecting the activity that actually occupied most of his time—poring over racks of books for two-shilling bargains.[44]

Stefansson made his headquarters for two summers in the early 1920's at the Savoy Hotel in London, and later a friend offered him the use of a flat in New Court, Middle Temple, for the summer. After London, Stefansson knew Cambridge best. In the spring of 1928 he occupied rooms at Clare College while lecturing at the University twice a week for a term. He felt at home in Cambridge because the Scott Polar Research Institute there was (and still is) the centre of polar studies in Britain, and because he was visited by many of his friends—J.M. Wordie, Raymond Priestly, and Frank Debenham.

Stefansson continued to lecture in Britain on the "friendly Arctic." Once he suffered some embarrassment when the *London Telegraph* reported some startling new "truths:" "Every midsummer, according to the lecturer, there is more snow in Great Britain than in Greenland!" What Stefannson actually said, as he teased his way through his familiar theme, is that those areas of Greenland that are free of snow in August are larger than Britain. Until this slip appeared, Stefansson was pleased that the *London Telegraph* had assigned a special writer to his lectures. As he ruefully remarked later, "Thus would I have learned, if I had not known it already, that the misrepresentations of your friends can be as damaging as the misrepresentations of your foes."[45]

CHAPTER 15

Canadian Prospects

IN 1919 Canada's claims to the arctic islands received a jolt. A.P. Low had taken formal possession of Ellesmere Island for Canada on a 1903-1904 expedition, and Joseph Bernier asserted Canada's rights over the several islands in voyages from 1904-11. In 1907 Bernier made a formal claim to Axel Heiberg Island in a cairn set up on southeastern Ellesmere Island. Bernier, an early exponent of the sector theory of territorial sovereignty, believed that Canada had rights to all land within the longitudinal pie-slice based on the Canadian arctic coast and ending in a point at the North Pole.

But other claims antedated those of Low and Bernier. The Norwegian explorer, Otto Sverdrup, after taking over Nansen's famous *Fram,* explored some ten thousand square miles among the islands from 1898 to 1902, claiming the Sverdrup Islands, including Axel Heiberg Island, the Ringnes, and Ellesmere Island for Norway.

Norway did not react to the Canadian claims, but in 1919 the Danish explorer Knud Rasmussen took Eskimos from Greenland to Ellesmere Island for a large-scale musk-ox hunt. When the Canadian government protested that he had not asked permission, Rasmussen argued that the entire region north of Parry Channel was a no-man's-land. The Danish government endorsed this view, and Sverdrup urged Norway to send police out to protect his discoveries.[1]

Canada's officials thought it advisable to follow-up on the claims made by Stefansson and his predecessors to take a firmer grip on the disputed areas. The situation seemed particularly threatening because Rasmussen was planning a major expedition across the

arctic mainland. Rasmussen's journey, the renowned Fifth Thule
Expedition (1923-24), was to be a scientific landmark for ethnolog-
ical and other studies, but in 1919 Canadians suspected that the
Danish government also harboured territorial ambitions.

For several years Stefansson had already been advocating that
the government increase its activities in the North. He had written
Sir Robert Borden in 1916. "I presented the polar ocean as an arctic
Mediterranean, a hub from which the other oceans and the conti-
nents of the world radiated like the spokes of a wheel, with the
powerful and populous lands of the North Temperate Zone form-
ing the wheel's rim."[2] By October 1920, it appeared that Stefansson's recommendations had sufficiently impressed the government,
and they discussed mounting an expedition for 1920-23. Borden
was keen, and his secretary, Loring Christie, after visiting Washington and finding that scientists there held Stefansson and his work
in high esteem, supported Stefansson's advice.[3] In October 1920,
Stefansson met with the minister of the interior, Arthur Meighen,
and other departmental leaders and was asked to submit a plan for
affirming Canadian sovereignty in the Arctic. He proposed extensive exploration of the north, including establishing police posts
on Baffin Island and elsewhere and creating a patrol boat organization along the lines of the United States Revenue Cutter Service
that patrolled Alaskan waters. He also urged the Canadian government to proclaim sovereignty over Wrangel and Ellesmere Islands
because of their strategic importance.

The government was slow in getting its plans in motion. The
delay forced Stefansson to explain his personal predicament to them
in January 1921. He pointed out that he had served the government
for years without a salary, so it was necessary to organize a lecture
tour for the coming summer if the expedition were not to be carried
through. He asked for a firm decision by February. At this point,
J.B. Harkin, the commissioner of dominion parks, was designated
to represent the government in the exploration plans. He offered
strong encouragement to Stefansson: "You are the man," he said,
adding that Stefansson was Canadian and that the venture would
be "a natural extension of your earlier work. Let me know your
terms and we will be glad to enter into an agreement."[4] Harkin
assured him that he would try to meet the February deadline. He
also impressed Stefansson with the importance of keeping their
plans secret because of possible international rivalry.

In February, Harkin seemed to have full authority to ask Stefansson to carry out the proposed expedition, and Stefansson immediately wired his acceptance.[5] He began to make preparations and line up other men to accompany him. He met Harkin at the Chateau Laurier to go over a proposed list of equipment. Harkin approved the engagement of E. Lorne Knight, who had worked for Stefansson on the Canadian Arctic Expedition and on his lecture circuit, and agreed to sign a letter to university presidents that was to be drafted by Stefansson, asking them to suggest names of promising students who might wish to volunteer for arctic work.

Canada, however, did not maintain her "good faith." In April, Stefansson was told that the expedition, planned for the summer of 1921, had been set aside. An impending national election was given as the reason. Having long since cancelled his lecture tour, Stefansson now found himself out on a limb. He wired Harkin angrily: "I assume absolute good faith on the part of officials now in power and am willing to take chances on change of administration."[6] Harkin made two more efforts that April to get clearer direction from W. W. Cory, but to no avail. Stefansson was left dangling until May, when the expedition was formally cancelled.[7]

When Harkin informed Stefansson of the cancellation, he offered neither apology nor explanation. He claimed that there had always been "a great deal of uncertainty" about the project and that he could not have answered any sooner Stefansson's repeated requests for authority to go ahead. Harkin assured the explorer, "I personally thought that in the end the decision would be favorable."[8]

Stefansson's failure to reply worried Harkin. He became even more alarmed when Stefansson announced to the press that he was planning another expedition, to explore the islands north of Canada. "Presumably he is not feeling very friendly towards Canada," Harkin wrote Cory, adding pointedly, "From this one would infer that he has distinctly in mind that Canadian sovereignty does not extend to these islands."[9]

Harkin suspected that Stefansson intended to seek American backing, probably because Stefansson had earlier warned the Canadian government that the United States was interested in the arctic islands. Stefansson had sent a news clipping to Harkin telling about a proposed U.S. Navy expedition to the North and advised that "the Americans are at last after the lands north of Canada because they want them as territorial possessions." He thought Bob Bartlett (who by then had become a naturalized American citizen) might head the expedition. But Stefansson remained confident: "I can beat them to it if Canada wants me to. It is optional with us whether it is our territory or theirs."[10]

Stefansson had clearly been trying to apply pressure to the Canadian government for a favourable decision concerning both the expedition to the Arctic Islands and his earlier request that Canada should sponsor the colony he was organizing on Wrangel Island. There is no record that he ever contemplated leading an American expedition for the purpose of establishing territorial claims to the islands north of the Canadian mainland or that the U.S. government had any interest in so doing. Harkin, however, continued to be suspicious. "Stefansson knows the weaknesses of Canada's claims as well as we do. He is generally regarded as being more of an American than a Canadian." Should he decide "to throw in his lot" with the United States, Harkin reasoned, any information he might gather on his expedition would be disastrous to Canadian interests. The United States was on friendly terms with Canada, but Harkin considered it would "not be good policy to presume much on that." Irish- and German-Americans were traditionally anti-British, Harkin argued, and as for Ellesmere Island, he reckoned that the "U.S. has now an inchoate title probably at least as good as Canada's."[11]

The involvement of Ernest Shackleton was another aspect of these curious dealings with the Canadian government over a possible expedition. When Shackleton wanted an expedition, he was enterprising, to say the least. Shackleton's eminence and his good connections in Ottawa among the anti-Stefansson faction enabled him to arrange a private conference with Prime Minister Meighen in February 1921. He made a spirited bid to command the same expedition Stefansson hoped to lead. Apparently the antarctic veteran told the prime minister that Stefansson had decided to give up further exploration, but Meighen knew very well that this was not so. He wrote later to Sir James Lougheed, "I told Sir Ernest that I did not understand Mr. Stefansson's attitude in the same way that he did and I was of the opinion Mr. Stefansson was anxious himself to take charge of such work in the North as the government decided to have done."[12] In his meeting with Meighen, Shackleton claimed to have a letter from Stefansson disavowing any interest in exploring, although he did not produce it.

Meighen let Stefansson know about Shackleton's gambit. Stefansson immediately fired off a memorandum to the prime minister's secretary explaining a meeting he had had with Shackleton in

London in March 1920 and his subsequent letters. In London, Shackleton expressed an interest in getting information on the Canadian North. Others had told him, he said, that Stefansson probably would not help another explorer. Not so, Stefansson replied. He told Shackleton that if he wanted to go North, he would advise him to the best of his ability. He reminded Shackleton that conditions are quite different in the Arctic and Antarctic and that Shackleton's southern experience could actually be a handicap to him in exploring Canada's North. Shackleton asked Stefansson for a letter that would verify his offer of advice. Fortunately, Stefansson retained the correspondence, and, at Meighen's request, he was able to send copies of the letters.[13]

Shackleton kept on pushing for either leadership of the proposed expedition or support from Canada for an independent expedition. He was not a timid man, and he was well accustomed to raising private funds. In April he wrote to Meighen after "having assurances of government's sympathetic attitude to my request." He had already raised half of the $250,000 needed for his expedition. Canada would only have to give $125,000 to get him into the Beaufort Sea with fifteen men, nine of whom were antarctic veterans. He proposed to undertake both geographical discovery and scientific work. Canada would not have to send a relief expedition, he added, because he was insured with Lloyds. And, as for his reliability: "I alone among polar explorers am known never to have lost a life under my direct command."[14]

Once again, Shackleton insisted that Stefansson had told him he would not go north again. And, he continued, "even if he does, the shores and seas are wide, and there is room for all. The expedition which makes the most active movements will make the greatest discoveries."[15] In encouraging the prime minister to support rival expeditions, Shackleton seemed to have misunderstood the situation: money was tight, and government officials were reluctant to finance one expedition, much less two, with the same general purpose.

Shackleton besieged Meighen by telephone and letter until the prime minister finally had to remind him that the Canadian government had made "no commitment" to him, adding that its "promise of consideration was upon conditions that at no time to date have been complied with." (Apparently Meighen had heard that Shackleton had neither engaged a ship nor otherwise made serious efforts to prepare for his expedition.) Meighen concluded sharply, "The government does not need your assistance this year."[16]

During the summer of 1921, Canada decided to act on two of Stefansson's proposals: to send a patrol vessel to the Arctic and to establish police posts on Baffin Island and elsewhere. There would be no expedition. The main thing was to establish visible signs of sovereignty so that other nations would not encroach on the arctic islands. As Joseph Bernier, Canada's veteran arctic navigator, warned Meighen, "Alaska was taken away from us, and to our everlasting shame. The Americans must not be allowed to get another foothold in the East as they have in the West."[17] Bernier presumably held the common Canadian view that Canada had been badly treated in the settlement of the boundary dispute in 1903. Bernier was particularly alarmed by the announcement that an American expedition under veteran explorer Donald MacMillan was planning to go to Baffin Island.

Canada, after negotiations in 1929-30, paid Sverdrup for his work after Norway relinquished territorial claims.[18]

Stefansson made clear in his autobiography that he felt Shackleton had double-crossed him, but he did not censure the Canadian government. He understood that the government could not always be expected to go along with his projects and was amused at the failure of Shackleton's backers, who had aspired to replace "a faker and charlatan" with a better choice. "Many prominent Canadians," Stefansson remarked, "felt that a second-rater like me should not be supported by the government when it was possible to get an authentically great man in my place."[19]

Stefansson believed that his government detractors had deliberately arranged to have him blackballed in an election to the prestigious Rideau Club in order to embarrass him and give Shackleton an advantage. Whatever he felt, Stefansson was pursuing other projects with the government, and he did not scold officials either privately or publicly. In the winter of 1922 Meighen was out of office, but Stefansson was quick to write a "note of good wishes" in which he assured him that he took "a personal interest in your success, and because I think your leadership is good for Canada."[20]

Stefansson always believed that the expedition had been cancelled because the Cabinet could not agree on whether he or Shackleton should be sponsored. While it is true that James White and others were pushing for Shackleton because of their antipathy towards Stefansson, it is likely that the rivalry had little to do with the cancellation. There is no evidence that Meighen or his successor,

Mackenzie King, shared Harkin's suspicions of Stefansson's loyalty. Expeditions were expensive, and Harkin's schemes to buy Stefansson off by dispatching him to the North may have struck them both as absurd. Indeed, there is no evidence in Harkin's papers to substantiate his hysteria. But the Shackleton intrigue is interesting on its own. The events reveal what kind of tactics even a famous explorer would resort to in order to gain backing.

Stefansson hoped, however, that the whole story could be clarified. In 1949, after Harkin's retirement, Stefansson wrote to Hugh Keenleyside, the deputy minister of mines and resources, requesting that the complete account of the squabble over the proposed expedition be recorded. It would be a disservice to history and to Canada, he argued, if all the facts could not be known. Stefansson suggested that the details could be declared classified information and kept in the Public Archives for the lifetime of the people involved. Harkin dismissed what he termed a "fishing expedition" and thought it "absurd to think I have anything not in state files."[21] What he told Stefansson, however, was that the matter was secret and ought to remain so until all those involved were dead, at which time the information could go into the Archives.

Stefansson had other irons in the fire. One of them, the reindeer project, also involved the Canadian government. Stefansson was successful in interesting the Canadian government in reindeer husbandry. As early as 1918 he was urging the federal government to support a reindeer industry in the North, pointing to the example of the American government, importing herds from Siberia to Alaska. Prime Minister Arthur Meighen agreed that this might be worthwhile, but he preferred not to involve a government agency directly in the project, offering instead a leasing arrangement to any sound commercial company that would undertake the enterprise. Stefansson tried to raise capital both in Canada and in the United States, but he was unsuccessful. Finally, in 1921, he convinced officers of the Hudson's Bay Company in England that the reindeer project had potential value, and as a result, the company dispatched 550 Norwegian reindeer to Baffin Island.

Stefansson served as an unpaid adviser to the Hudson's Bay Company. He did not go to Baffin Island himself, recommending instead his old travelling companion, Storker Storkerson, as field supervisor. Storkerson reported that the region could support a sizeable herd without difficulty. But, a few months later, before any animals were shipped to the North, Storkerson resigned because he had not been given full control of purchase and shipping arrangements.

Storkerson was replaced by W. T. Lopp. Lopp had had an interesting career in Alaska, where he was first a missionary to the Eskimos. Later he was a successful teacher in villages where no whites had ever lived. Lopp's report to the Bay doomed the reindeer project. He noted that the herd had been mismanaged on its arrival. "On landing [the reindeer] commenced to scatter in all directions in search of food" and so could not be controlled, Lopp reported, but he believed this was not the chief problem. According to him, "the cause of the failure of the enterprise is attributable entirely to the lack of feeding grounds." Also, he continued, "Storkerson, not being conversant in the herding of reindeer," had assumed that all of the lichens he observed would be suitable food for the herd, which was not the case.[22]

Stefansson tried to resist the impact of Lopp's report. In a letter send in 1923 to Prime Minister King, he summarized the situation as he understood it. The herders who had first brought the reindeer to Baffin Island were Laplanders, hired under the assumption that they were accustomed to herding the animals in their native country, but in fact they were fishermen. The Lapps allowed the reindeer to stray, and most of the herd were lost the first year. These Lapland "herders" were eventually fired and replaced by native Eskimos and whites, who managed the herd so successfully that it began to increase in size. "It seems, therefore, to be established that Baffin Island is suitable for reindeer," Stefansson declared optimistically.[23]

Stefansson believed that Storkerson, who "was himself in part brought up among herders in Lapland," could have handled the job.[24] Stefansson argued that Storkerson had travelled one hundred miles into the interior of Baffin Island where he found ample forage for the animals, while Lopp insisted that Baffin Island lichen was not plentiful enough to support the herd.

Lopp, later commissioned by the Hudson's Bay Company to look for more suitable pasturage, recommended the region east and west of Hudson Bay. He was confident that the company had been, as he put it, a "good loser" and would try again despite the "costly and cruel failure" of the original effort. Lopp's opinion that Baffin Island is unsuitable for grazing reindeer has been confirmed by experts, whose findings indicate that the island's severe weather prevents the adequate growth of lichen.[25]

The Baffin Island experiment with reindeer was the end of Stefansson's involvement with animal husbandry, although the H.B.C. tried again some years later after purchasing an Alaskan herd. Driving the herd from Alaska to Canada caused heavy losses among the animals and ended the efforts. Indirectly, Lopp had a hand in the later reindeer operation. As supervisor of all reindeer activity in Alaska and a recognized authority on the Eskimo people, he persuaded the American government to restrict ownership of reindeer to natives. This put Stefansson's friends, the Lomen family of Nome, out of the reindeer business.

The end of the Baffin Island reindeer experiment was a setback for Stefansson's advocacy of northern development just as the cancellation of the proposed exploration expedition had been, but neither incident reduced his optimism or adversely affected his good relationships with government officials.

CHAPTER 16

The Friendly Arctic

STEFANSSON'S account of the Canadian Arctic Expedition, *The Friendly Arctic,* was published in 1921. It is a large volume, comprising 784 pages of text, numerous photographs, most of them taken by Wilkens, and well-drawn maps, and it is a tribute to Stefansson's boundless energy that he was able to bring the book out so soon after his return. He had his diaries, his correspondence, and the field notes of other expedition members—but compiling all this material required a prodigious effort. Stefansson's work was complicated by personal hostilities between him and the expedition scientists, and he agonized over the presentation of his side of the dispute. Knowing there would certainly be an adverse reaction from some Ottawa bureaucrats, he had to ponder his version of the expedition with care.

To ward off as much criticism as possible, Stefansson prefaced his book with testimonials written by the biggest names he could summon. Gilbert Grosvenor, for instance, then president of the National Geographic Society, praised Stefansson's achievements, and he included in his foreward tributes that Robert E. Peary and General Adophus Greely made when the society presented him with its Hubbard Gold Medal. Peary, in particular, was very generous in his salute to the explorer:

What Stefansson stands for is this: he has grasped the meaning of polar work and has pursued his tasks in the Arctic regions section by section. He has profited by experience piled upon experience until he knows how to face and overcome every problem of the North. His method of work is to take the white man's brains and intelligence and the white man's persistence and will-power into the Arctic and supplement these forces with the woodcraft, or, I should say, polar-craft, of the Eskimo—the ability to live off the land itself, the ability to use every one of the few possibilities of those frozen regions—and concentrate on his work.

Peary pointed out that Stefansson had shown "he could have lived in the Arctic fifteen and a half years just as easily as five and a half years. By combining great natural, physical and mental ability with hard, practical common sense, he has made an absolute record."[1] With Greely's admiring comments, Stefansson had America's two greatest living explorers running interference for him. Greely praised Stefansson's "several unique Arctic records," including five-and-a-half years of continuous polar service, during which time he had pioneered living on game, both on land and sea, while making long journeys over sea ice. "The contributions of his expeditions," Greely continued, "are important and extensive. Besides the natural history and geologic knowledge, he has made inroads into the million square miles of unknown Arctic regions, the largest for many years. His hydrographic work is especially important, in surveys, and in magnetic declinations. His numerous soundings not only outline the continental shelf from Alaska to Prince Patrick Island, but also disclose the submarine mountains and valleys of the bed of Beaufort Sea." Stefansson had discovered approximately 100,000 square miles of arctic land and sea that were previously unknown regions, including "about 65,000 square miles of Beaufort Sea to the north of the Mackenzie Basin, 10,000 square miles of the Arctic Ocean west of Prince Patrick Island, over 3,000 square miles along the northeast coast of Victoria Island, and over 15,000 square miles of land and sea to the northeast of Prince Patrick Island."[2]

Even better as a lightning rod, Canada's prime minister, the Right Honourable Sir Robert Laird Borden, wrote the introduction and stressed both the importance of Stefansson's scientific work and his predictions concerning the potential wealth of northern resources. Borden praised Stefansson's accomplishment in adding "many thousands of square miles...to the territory of Canada," while gathering material of great scientific value. At the same time, Borden continued, Stefansson dissipated many illusions with respect to arctic conditions. Borden thought "Stefansson's anticipations as to settlement and development in these northern regions

[are] interesting. Who would venture to declare that they may not be justified as fully as his confidence in the Beaufort Sea?"[3] Borden also recommended that Stefansson's proposal for domesticating muskoxen should be explored.[4]

The explorer's star seemed to be on the rise in Canada. Borden noted that "honors have been showered" upon Stefansson by scientific societies as well as tributes from other polar explorers and that "great universities have recognized by their highest degrees his contributions to scholarhsip and science." The prime minister concluded with an evaluation of the Canadian Arctic Expedition: "The results accomplished would have been impossible if Stefansson had been a man of less resource and courage. His commanding intellectual powers, remarkable faculty of observation, capacity for keen analysis of facts and conditions, splendid poise and balance, and immense physical strength and endurance made great results possible."[5]

In *The Friendly Arctic* Stefansson set the framework for his travels with two introductory chapters defining the problems that his experiences would elucidate. The opening chapter, "The Four Stages in Polar Exploration," provided a summary history of explorers' notions about the Arctic. In the first stage the winter was considered by explorers too dreadful to be endured; in the second, they believed it could be endured but no work could be done until it was nearly over; in the third, winter was preferable to summer because work could be done most easily. Robert Peary had achieved the breakthrough of the third stage. It remained for Stefansson to demonstrate the fourth, one in which travel in any season and for any distance became feasible because explorers need not be dependent upon what provisions they could carry.

In chapter two, "The North That Never Was," Stefansson contrasted the popular conceptions of the Arctic with the reality he and others before him had experienced. "The literary north is barren, dismal and desolate," he noted.[6] Even the stars in the North were frequently referred to as cruel. Yet Eskimos did not see their land as desolate and were not depressed by the long winter nights so why should stereotypes prevail?

Some shifts in the popular ideas about the Arctic were the direct consequences of exploration ventures from Elizabethan times to the mid-nineteenth century, and Stefansson intended that his own work should expose the fallacies of the past and stimulate a benevolent attitude towards the region. Thus his thesis and his explorations struck hard at attitudes and raised the hackles of some who resisted his ideas.

Stefansson had cautioned the members of the Canadian Arctic Expedition that they must remain active in winter as the best means of avoiding melancholy and sickness. His travelling companions soon learned that his advice was good, but it was harder to convince those who had had no actual experience. "Despoiling the Arctic of its heroism," he complained in *The Friendly Arctic*, "is likely to be about as popular as taking candy from a child."[7]

Stefansson had some support too in Ernest de Koven Leffingwell, who had made Flaxman Island, off the coast of Alaska, his base for charting the coast of the Beaufort Sea in 1907-09. Leffingwell did not publicize his views and refused, on several occasions, to encourage inquiring journalists: "Most of it [arctic exploration] doesn't seem worth telling after you've been there and know the facts." He believed that the hardships of the Arctic are no greater than those of outdoor life anywhere else. He acknowledged that there were discomforts and difficulties to be faced, "but you aren't dying every minute of the day."[8] He had made it a point to be comfortable in the North, and he claimed never to have encountered any difficulty dramatic enough to make him want to write a book.

Even the formidable Robert Peary made public statements about the Arctic that were intended to sweep away some popular misconceptions about the North, and he was rewarded for his efforts with ridicule. In a newspaper interview in 1902, Peary had the audacity to claim that consumptive members of his expedition had been restored to health in the Arctic. "Well," puffed an English editorial, "that the Arctic air is splendidly bracing there can be no doubt, and when properly provided with anti-scorbutics the members of various expeditions have generally enjoyed rude health in their task," but, the writer added sarcastically, according to Peary, the Arctic Circle will shortly become a recognized retreat for convalescents. "We see in fancy a chain of sanatoria from Siberia to Greenland," he jibed.[9]

Stefansson was a zealot, devoted to correcting misapprehensions about the North by recounting his own experiences there—he *must* change people's minds. Stefansson tried to explain his feeling: "Since I began to know the North, its beauty, freedom and friendliness have continually grown upon me." These characteristics of the land had always been there, he insisted, but at first he "could not see them, for even in that clear air I walked wrapped in the haze of my bringing up." It was his "southern feelings," that is, "an assumption of the inferiority of that which is different," which had blinded him "to the resources and values [that] lay before me."[10] When he made these observations, Stefansson and Ole Andreasen were wandering about the interior of Banks Island, the first white men ever to do so. They were travelling light: a team of three dogs pulled their sledge and equipment with ease. Fat caribou were plentiful, the novelty was thrilling, and the scenery was grand. In good health and at the peak of physical endurance, they were in a position to enjoy their journey to the utmost. Reading Stefansson's account reveals how thoroughly he had abandoned the traditions of polar exploration—traditions that called for grim suffering in the cause of knowledge and fierce tenacity of purpose in the achievement of a specific goal. Stefansson, too, intended to break records, prove his thesis, and discover new lands—but *he* would do so without suffering physical hardship. He knew the land would yield its bounty to those who approached it with a sensitive awareness of its potential dangers. Stefansson was convinced that it was not necessary to wage war against nature or to *subdue* it in order to survive in the North. This truth was Stefansson's most important discovery, and he devoted his lifetime in an attempt to explain its significance. Those who had not roamed the tundra in comfort could not absorb the point of his argument. And even some of those who had had arctic experience were resentful of what he seemed to be saying, perhaps simply because his experience conflicted so dramatically with their own.

The essential tenets of polar exploration had been set down often enough before Stefansson's time. Anthony Fiala, for example, an American who had led an expedition in quest of the North Pole in 1903-1905, wrote that the polar explorer has a "hard, cold, and lonely way," and so needs endless patience..."and the highest qualities of Christian character." The explorer, he said, "operates in a decidedly hostile and uncultivated territory, where there are no cornfields or hen roosts along the line of march, but instead an active enemy in every wind that blows from the north, and opposition to his advance in every pressure ridge and water lane that crosses his path."[11]

Adolphus W. Greely also provides a good example of this "heroic" school of arctic exploration in his foreword to Miller's *World's Greatest Adventure,* published in 1930. Greely describes men at work:

In the field, exhausted humanity struggled at the drag ropes; strength-bereft sledgemen fell helpless on the ice. Often eyes blinded by dazzling light made safe travel difficult. Enfeebled bodies were half starved by repellent or insufficient field rations, while limbs and bodies were frostbitten or frozen solid. In camp many suffered from unaccustomed conditions; darkness was long continued; prolonged absence of the sun was depressing; entire absence of forms of life caused an uncanny sense of isolation; monotonous surroundings oppressed many; unbroken silence became awful and overwhelmed one with the feeling of utter abandonment by the world.[12]

The scientists of the expedition, eager to scale the ladder of bureaucratic success in Ottawa, awaited publication of Stefansson's book with dread, fearing that he would indulge in the "sensationalism" they had so long accused him of at their expense. Although the scientists were dismayed by what Stefansson actually wrote, he dealt with them far more gently in *The Friendly Arctic* than he had in his diary and field correspondence. He believed that some of his men had treated him very badly in the Arctic, and with the passage of time this conviction did not change. Stefansson observed that the dispute had to be discussed fully because failure to mention the conflicts would raise doubts about his credibility. However, he tried to be magnanimous in his explanation of the scientists' behaviour: they had "felt no doubt of the substantial insanity of my project, and no doubt were justified in taking steps to prevent me from carrying it out."[13] Stefansson did not label the Collinson Point defiance as mutiny in *The Friendly Arctic*, but he did so in letters to Ottawa and elsewhere. In the book he explained mildly that the scientists "were quite sincere in their opinion that the government of Ottawa and public opinion in general would sustain them in that position."[14]

In his discussion of the conflict with Anderson over his decision to equip himself from the Southern Party's supplies for his northern journeys, Stefansson did not elaborate on his subordinate's defiance, preferring instead to treat the affair as a mere divergence of views. "I had full faith in that method [living off the land]," he remarked, "and my colleague had none."[15] Stefansson's references to Anderson's performance were carefully phrased and unlikely to arouse curiosity in the minds of readers lacking inside knowledge.

Other members of the expedition were treated with the same consideration. Stefansson was only sarcastic when he complained of their insistence on having a familiar southern diet and their reluctance during the first winter to embark on a program of work—both topics on which Stefansson had obsessive views. In particular, the need to adopt a healthy, convenient *local* diet was central to his theory of survival in the North. Almost as important to him was his conviction that continued activity during the winter was essential; keeping busy made it easier to resist the twin threats of scurvy and melancholy. His men had winced often enough in the field when he lectured them as if they were rebellious schoolboys. Now they suspected that readers all over Canada would be amused at their timidity and stuffiness.

Stefansson had staked his life on the validity of his theory concerning the prevalence of arctic game, and he had been vindicated. "Few men are able so completely to triumph, to vindicate a theory, by such absolute success," wrote a reviewer of *The Friendly Arctic*. Once more it was the mastery of mind over matter as well as over the inertia of fellow-men; the kind of initiative based on clear calculation which step by step through the ages has brought man to his present security from the threatening elements and made known to the world."[16]

Another reviewer, geologist William H. Hobbs, praised the "ultra-modest" explorer whose narrative sought to convince readers that "his achievements were commonplace rather than heroic." He extolled the scientific values of the book as well as Stefansson's personal achievements. Explorers are rarely men of scientific training, he added, but "Stefansson is an exception."[17] The Icelander's observations on diet, shelter, clothing, methods of travel, and the Eskimo people show his effective application of the discoveries of modern science unhampered by cumbersome conventions. In the prestigious *Geographical Review,* another writer remarked that Stefansson was not out to make himself a hero in *The Friendly Arctic.* "He is studying a problem, and he reports on it."[18]

Such good press was sweet praise indeed, and Stefansson revelled in it. There were, of course, mutterings in the background that sometimes flared into print, but for the most part Stefansson's standard was waving high. Yet he remained somewhat discontented because certain honours were not forthcoming, nor had there been any formal recognition of his work by a Canadian university or scientific organization. Why this reluctance to recognize his accomplishments? he wondered. Certainly he had not been too shy to point out to several Canadian officials that he felt he was being overlooked, and he even voiced his complaint in a lecture in Ottawa. It was obvious to him that the enmity of the Geological Survey was having some effect.

An editorial appearing in the *Montreal Standard* viciously attacked Stefansson, charging that his expedition "cost ten times more than the estimate" and urging the government to look into his direction of it. The writer did not think arctic expeditions ever accomplished much, but he felt that "our Canadian scientists...are entitled to a square deal from the imported adventurer who makes the Arctic his stock-in-trade." Fairness, he argued, is particularly important when "Mr. Stefansson goes out of his way to write a book and insult [the Expedition scientists] to our faces." To the *Standard* writer it was clear that when Stefansson returned, he "seemed...more anxious to discover a rich magazine or an opulent newspaper to cache his copy...than to spill the fruits of his search freely and copiously to the general public."[19]

When they denounced him, editors were in the habit of pointing out that Stefansson was not a Canadian citizen. However, they ignored the fact that only five of the fifteen members of the Canadian Arctic Expedition were. The editor insisted that Stefansson behaved "more like an exploiter than an explorer....[He] did not represent the pure scientific spirit."[20] This devastating editorial was typical of many criticisms made in the Canadian press, all of which apparently emanated from the same source—Anderson and his colleagues in the Geological Survey.

Stefansson responded with his usual vigour. A contemporary Canadian historian who has strong sympathies with the Geological Survey claims that the scientists found *The Friendly Arctic* "misleading beyond endurance" and argues that "as civil servants...[they] had to content themselves with trying to set the record straight in scientific journals and keeping the general public from taking too seriously the exaggerated, dangerous conclusions propounded by the very title."[21] But their status as civil servants did not keep them from responding to Stefansson's arguments. They complained about Stefansson to their superiors in Ottawa for several years before they were ordered to refrain from a public discussion that might prove embarrassing to the government. Anderson and others presented their side of the controversy to the press when *The Friendly Arctic* was published, and they took full advantage of the opportunity to vent their spleen. Later, they continued to launch private attacks, in government offices and on social occasions. They gave little attention to setting the record straight by writing in scientific journals. Rudolph Anderson was given ample opportunity to write, but he declined to do so. In fact, his refusal to record the official narrative of the Southern Party is one of the minor scandals of the expedition's aftermath.

Aside from these press interviews, members of the anti-Stefansson faction were not inclined to air their views publicly. They expressed their anger by gossiping and exchanging letters—devices which exposed them to fewer risks of counterattack. As they often reminded each other, Stefansson had a talent for rebuttal that always made him appear to be in the right. One exception to their self-imposed restriction on publication was a long article in the magazine *Science* written in 1922 by Diamond Jenness. He purported to be attacking Professor Raymond Pearl (whose favourable review of *The Friendly Arctic* had appeared in a previous issue), but he managed to get in some digs at Stefansson and a bold denial that Stefansson had authority over the Southern Party. Pearl had asserted that Anderson and others, assuming that Stefansson was "not merely silly but probably also insane," felt justified in disobeying his orders. Jenness, however, conveyed the impression that the government orders gave Anderson independent command of the Southern Party. To do so, he quoted several widely separated portions of the original instructions that had been issued to Stefansson. The gist of these orders was clear, explained Jenness—the Geological Survey had attached the Southern Party to the expedition solely for the purpose of doing work in Coronation Gulf and had issued precise and detailed instructions to their scientists concerning that part of it. Jenness argued that Anderson was not disobedient in 1914 when he did not follow Stefansson's instructions to send the *North Star* to Banks Island. Jenness offered several defences of Anderson's action, including the pert remark that Stefansson's orders were "contradictory," adding, "it was considered more ethical to follow out the carefully considered plans of the government."[22]

Stefansson replied to Jenness's article in a later issue of *Science,* as did two other members of the Northern Party. Stefansson's rebuttal focused on the garbled quotations Jenness used to dispute the command situation.[23] Burt M. McConnell and Harold Noice, on the other hand, directly asserted that the "mutiny" of the Southern Party was "fully, fairly, and (we think) too leniently described in *The Friendly Arctic.*[24] Jenness, they pointed out, had not been present at the critical time (he was studying the Alaskan Eskimo at Point Barrow in 1913-14) and had to depend on the statements of others concerning the events.

Stefansson's defenders did not try to trace "all the adroit misquotations" employed by Jenness, but they came down hard on "one part of the Jenness paper that astounded us," his use of the government's instructions.[25] Stefansson asked the author of the instructions, G.J. Desbarats, to comment on Jenness's interpretation of his orders. Desbarats's reply was a devastating indictment of Jenness's effort to justify the actions of the Southern Party. The complete text of his letter follows:

DEPUTY MINISTER'S OFFICE
OTTAWA

1st August, 1922

I am in receipt of your letter of the 29th enclosing a clipping from *Science* which contains a letter from Mr. Jenness regarding your book, *"The Friendly Arctic."*

On reading the quotations from the official orders beginning at foot of page 9, I was extremely surprised at the idea of my having written anything of the kind. On comparing the quotation with the text of the instructions I find, however, that the quotation is correct, *only it is made up of three different paragraphs which in the original are separated by pages of instructions. The sentences quoted, when gathered together, as they are in Jenness's letter, give a different impression to that which they were intended to convey, or did convey when read together with the rest of the instructions.* [These are Desbarats's italics.]

There can be no doubt of the government's intention to appoint you in command of the Canadian Arctic Expedition. The order in council authorizing the expedition states "Mr. Stefansson to have full responsibility, and to have the choice of the men going on the expedition and of the ship, provisions and outfit needed for the trip."

The instructions which I issued to you and from which Mr. Jenness takes his quotations are equally clear. They state, "The expedition will be under your personal direction and control, and you will give general directions to the various leaders of the parties, as may be required."

The instructions which I sent were always addressed to you. Instructions to Dr. Anderson were given to him only in your absence on your long exploring trip.

(Signed) G.J. Desbarats
Deputy Ministry of Naval Service[26]

McConnell and Noice explained why, in their opinion, the mutineers were eager to justify their disobedience: in exploration, as in war, men's lives depend upon loyalty and discipline, and the mutineers had shown neither. "It is difficult to see, however, why they keep nagging until they drive into breaking silence us who know disagreeable things about them which Stefansson has left untold."[27]

The two writers argued that it was time to recognize that Stefansson's methods were successful and that the Southern Party's disobedience could not be justified. They added, pointedly, "Would it not be better both for those who supported Stefansson and those who opposed him to stop squabbling and turn to more constructive things?"[28]

This article might have clarified the dispute for the impartial reader. Certainly, Desbarats's letter must have been a great embarrassment to Jenness, who had clearly overstepped the line between accurate reporting and advocacy. However, McConnell's and Noice's admonitions to "stop squabbling" were destined to go unheeded. The Southern Party members may have lost the debate in *Science,* just as they failed to discredit Stefansson with the government; nevertheless, in their minds they had to be right. As Stefansson explained later in a letter to a friend: "My men were in the psychological condition of Columbus' men—believing that it [the sea ice journey] amounted to suicide." And, of course, the men under Columbus and Henry Hudson also had spent the rest of their lives justifying *their* actions. "No more is it strange," Stefansson mused, "that my mutineers should now and in the future try to justify themselves."[29]

Deputy Minister Charles Camsell of the Geological Survey tried to end the squabble by writing a letter to *Science.* He declared that mutiny was too strong a term to apply to the decision made by the scientists "to adhere to instructions originally given them by the Geological Survey." Both Stefansson and members of the Southern Party had asked for an investigation but, Camsell claimed that the minister's only motive in refusing to have a review was that "no good comes of such an inquiry and much harm might be done." Camsell wanted to do justice to the scientists, but he hoped that no more would be said of a controversy that "can do no one any good."[30]

R.W. Brock, head of the Canadian Geological Society until 1914, did not share the animus towards Stefansson that prevailed in his department. By 1923 he had left the government and taken a university post in Vancouver, but even there much of the controversy over *The Friendly Arctic* reached his ears. Brock thought that the squabbling and backbiting ought to end and blamed the scientists for prolonging the dispute. "There may be something to be said against Stefansson—but I can vouch for this in his favour, when he got back he wished to make up with Dr. Anderson and to be fair with him and let bygones be bygones." Commenting on *The Friendly Arctic,* Brock said Stefansson's references to the scientists were "unfortunate," yet he believed that Stefansson had been "goaded to the explosion point...[but] still desired to be fair."[31]

Charles Camsell disagreed with Brock. He believed that the scientists wanted to have peace, but that "Mr. Stefansson is not inclined the same way. It is regrettable that these differences will continue to rise, but we have no control over Mr. Stefansson's actions."[32]

Anderson's charges against Stefansson and call for a government investigation made at this time did not attract as much attention in the United States. The *New York Times* devoted about four inches of a back page in its 14 January 1922, issue to Anderson's charges and gave equal treatment to a rejoinder by Stefansson that appeared in the paper the following day. Stefansson declared that he would welcome a government investigation and reminded his readers that he had asked for an official inquiry into the expedition on his return in 1918. To Anderson's complaint that the expedition members had been forbidden to telegraph or write home except by way of Ottawa, Stefansson replied that if he had given such orders, no one had paid any attention to them.[33]

Professor J.J. O'Neill's blasts at Stefansson were reported in the *Times* on 16 January and repeated two days later. O'Neill, who was the geologist with the Southern Party, informed newsmen that he understood why Anderson had felt compelled to answer the "unjust accusations" of *The Friendly Arctic* and recalled the alleged mistreatment of the expedition scientists. The unseaworthy condition of the *Alaska* (the schooner assigned to the Southern Party) had upset the scientists. Residents of Nome, said O'Neill, had even placed bets on the probable time the ship would remain afloat, adding that the *Karluk*, by way of contrast, was the "finest fitted out ship that ever left for polar work." The scientists wanted to quit the expedition in Nome and return home, but, they complained, "what could we do if we had returned. [W]e would undoubtedly be accused of cowardice."[34]

O'Neill deplored the extravagance of the expedition, and his accusations drew some space in the *Times* of 18 January. The expedition cost $500,000, a sum which, in O'Neill's opinion, was more than was necessary. According to him, the government officials had lumped the expenditures under war costs to obscure Stefansson's extravagance, knowing the expedition leader's propensity for spending. Burt McConnell (probably at Stefansson's suggestion) responded to Anderson at length in the 17 January *Times*. He answered the charges point by point and accused Anderson of trying to obscure the fact that Stefansson was in command of the entire expedition—*including* the Southern Party.[35]

On 19 January, under the headline "Charges That Answer Themselves," the *Times* ran an editorial on the controversy. The writer observed, "to anyone at all well read in the literature of arctic exploration there is nothing unfamiliar and there is nothing surprising in the quarrel between Mr. Stefansson and some members" of his expedition. "Just such bickering has taken place in the course of almost all such invasions of the world's dead ends, and not infrequently it has been much fiercer than in this instance." Such disputes, the editorial continued, were understandable taking into consideration the conditions of arctic travel, problems with food, and the tensions created by long confinement. As for the questions raised by Anderson and O'Neill, the editorial stoutly insisted that "nobody who has met and talked with Mr. Stefansson, and hardly anybody who has read his books, can have any more doubt of his honesty than of his courage and competence." In appearance, bearing and blood Stefansson was cast in the Viking mold. "Presumably he has some of the defects of his qualities, and his execution of authority would be likely to seem stern, or even harsh, to men with the characteristic American distaste for discipline....But that, apparently, is all there is to the present 'scandal.' " To the writer, the matter at issue was leadership of the expedition. He reminded his readers, "the responsibility was his [Stefansson's], not theirs, and his critics in effect admit that they were mutinous and hard to manage, or unmanageable." The editor concluded by summing up the controversy: "the case as it stands is against *them*."[36]

CHAPTER 17

The Karluk Blame

THE CANADIAN government did not launch an inquiry into the *Karluk*'s loss at the time, nor after the expedition ended in 1918; neither did the newspapers speculate on the cause of the disaster. The survivors had little to say, except for Maurer, who wrote an innocuous account of the adventure for a magazine, and Bartlett, who published a book that did not raise any controversial matters.

It was Rudolph Anderson, reacting to the publication of *The Friendly Arctic* in 1922 with a lengthy press release and interviews, who opened discussion of some of the vexing questions.[1] Anderson, of course, had not been with the *Karluk,* and he was not interested in questioning Bartlett's conduct or that of the survivors on Wrangel Island. His thrust was at Stefansson, resting on charges that the commander had provided an unsound ship and that he had deserted it.

Stefansson believed that the best man to refute charges that the ship had been unsound was Captain C.T. Pedersen, who had chosen the *Karluk,* and he wrote to Pedersen after Anderson's accusations were published, reminding him that both he and independent inspectors had verified that the ship was fit for navigation in arctic waters. Pedersen replied at once to confirm his original opinion of the *Karluk:* "Would I choose an unsound ship that I was booked to spend four years on?" he asked.[2] Given the unusually severe winter, any ship could have suffered the *Karluk*'s fate, Pedersen believed.

Earlier Stefansson had been annoyed by some press clippings that he received at Banks Island in 1916 quoting Pedersen as having said that what Stefansson had "required" of Bob Bartlett was unreasonable. He protested in a letter to Pedersen that he had *not* interfered with Bartlett's ice navigation—and that his silence was precisely the reason why the *Karluk* had become caught in the ice. Stefansson insisted that if he had been in command, the *Karluk* would still be afloat. During the same period Stefansson wrote the experienced whaling skipper Ben Tilton, who had also been interviewed about the loss of the *Karluk*. Tilton told a newsman that Bartlett was a poor choice as captain because he had had no navigating experience in the western Arctic. Stefansson agreed with Tilton's opinion and thanked him for acknowledging that Stefansson was the only man on the expedition who knew anything about ice conditions. Stefansson admitted that his knowledge of winter navigation was gathered by hearsay, but he believed it to be accurate because it had come from veterans like Tilton and Pedersen.[3]

It was unfortunate that Pedersen decided against joining the expedition. Apparently someone had advised him that as a naturalized American he would lose his citizenship if he took part in a Canadian-sponsored venture. This was nonsense, of course, but Pedersen believed it and asked to be discharged. His skills in ice navigation, which were so noteworthy in 1913 did not diminish, and as late as the 1940's he was still voyaging in the Arctic, still mostly to trade.

Stefansson's opinions in 1914 and 1916 were expressed only in his correspondence. In *The Friendly Arctic*, he made no reference to his reservations about Bartlett; rather, he gave the skipper unstinting praise: "When Bartlett took charge of the *Karluk* I found him everything that Peary had said," he wrote. "With the reputation he brought with him and his efficiency in managing the affairs of the ship, he won the admiration and confidence of everybody. And he obeyed every order effectively and without quibbling."[4]

In a letter written in January 1914 to a friend, Stefansson complained that the *Karluk*'s skipper had referred to the ship as a "museum piece." On the same date, he wrote in a similar vein to Robert Peary—but then he decided not to send the letter and risk upsetting the aging, ailing polar hero. In his letter to Peary, he described Bartlett as a garrulous character, "the worse case of Big Head possible in all matters concerning the North." Stefansson fancied that Bartlett had changed from the man who had been Peary's staunch navigator and travelling companion.[5]

Bartlett had complained vociferously about the *Karluk*'s performance in the presence of the expedition scientists. His tactlessness amounted almost to malfeasance and damaged the morale of the ship's company, most of whom were in unfamiliar circumstances. And it also undermined Stefansson's leadership—little wonder that he lashed out in his correspondence. As a professional, Bartlett should have refused command if he considered the *Karluk* unfit.

Bartlett's strictures against the ship did not appear in his published narrative, either. He observed that she had neither the strength nor the engine power to force her way through loose ice, and he knew that the *Karluk* was no *Roosevelt* or *Fram* (the ship designed by Fridtjof Nansen for his famous ice drift). He also knew that such specially constructed ships were not available for the Canadian Arctic Expedition. Even the *Roosevelt*, he said, could not have broken out of the ice into which he drove the *Karluk*.

Bartlett's decision to take the *Karluk* away from shore in search of open water has already been thoroughly discussed. It was a bad decision, and Stefansson publicly blamed himself for allowing it to stand.

Anderson's second charge, accusing Stefansson of having deserted the *Karluk*, was not as easy to refute. Anderson believed that when Stefansson left the ship with his hunting party, he was providing himself with an alibi for deliberately deserting his men, and he cited Diamond Jenness's claim that "[Stefansson] made only a very perfunctory hunt for part of one day after coming ashore and then struck [off] to Point Barrow to send out dispatches."[6] But Anderson was straining; if Jenness actually did concur, he did not record it in his diary. Furthermore, Jenness gave no hint that he entertained doubts about Stefansson's motives. In *Dawn in Arctic Alaska*, he observed: "It seemed quite certain that the *Karluk* would remain there all winter. South of us, only fifteen miles away, was the delta of the Colville River where Stefansson had hunted caribou four years before. Why not hunt there again, and procure the fresh meat that would be so welcome after weeks of canned food?"[7]

Nor did Bartlett express any suspicion about Stefansson's reasons for his hunting trip, "the problem of laying in an adequate supply of fresh meat for the winter, for our dogs and ourselves, was...beginning to be a serious one." A year's delay because of the ice "meant, too, the unforeseen question of a winter's supply of fresh meat for the thirty-one human beings...now on board the *Karluk*. Without fresh meat there was always danger of scurvy, that blight of so many earlier Arctic explorers."[8] Indeed, though Bartlett himself volunteered to lead a hunting party ashore, as he said, "Stefansson was the only one on board who not only knew how to hunt caribou but was also fully acquainted with the country." Bartlett would hardly have volunteered to leave the *Karluk* had he considered such an excursion a desertion. "Stefansson," Bartlett noted, "expected to be back in about ten days and there seemed no reason to suppose that the ship would not remain where she was until the next summer brought a genuine smashing-up of the ice and freed her."[9]

Stefansson needed the *Karluk* and its supplies for his exploration base. When he lost the ship, he improvised brilliantly. Surely, he would not have given up carefully formulated plans for what appeared to be only a temporary inconvenience.

It is surprising that William Laird McKinlay should question Stefansson's reasons for his departure from the ship. Writing after years of consideration, McKinlay declared that it was "inconceivable" to him that Stefansson should have left the *Karluk,* and blamed all the subsequent woes on Stefansson's departure.[10] In trying to fix the responsibility on Stefansson, McKinlay reveals that in his view Bartlett could do no wrong.

The Andersons urged Bartlett to reply after *The Friendly Arctic* was published, hoping that he would blame Stefansson for the *Karluk*'s misfortunes. Mrs. Anderson assured Bartlett that in the governmental inquiry Rudolph was demanding, "you have nothing to fear...I wrote McKinlay what V. Stefansson had done to you—the worst thing in the book I think."[11] Bartlett, however, remained silent. Stefansson, too, knew the value of discretion, as he acknowledged in *Discovery,* published so many years after the events took place. "I had sometimes questioned Bartlett's handling of the *Karluk* in the Beaufort Sea ice and had been puzzled by his decision to leave the *Karluk*'s people on Wrangel Island after the ship was lost while he went ashore for help. I had not, however, criticized Bartlett publicly."[12]

Stefansson's private criticism of the *Karluk*'s captain, after he compared Hadley's version of the events with newspaper interviews given by Bartlett, were written from Banks Island to Desbarats in January 1916. He ruled out, as unworthy of discussion, various charges that Breddy had been murdered, that Bartlett's preparations for the sinking of the *Karluk* were inadequate, or that the captain failed to make a sincere effort to dissuade Mackay's party from leaving. But Stefansson felt compelled to comment on Hadley's fourth charge—that the mate's party were not properly equipped to survive if they happened to be prevented from rejoining the main party.[13]

Bartlett dispatched Alex Anderson's advance party on 20 January with three sledges, six men, eighteen dogs, and provisions for three months. When the party reached Wrangel Island, Mamen and the two Eskimos were instructed to return to Shipwreck Camp with two of the sledges. (Mamen returned to Bartlett after leaving the mate's party stranded by open water three miles from Herald Island.) Bartlett hoped Anderson would try to make Wrangel Island as ordered because Herald Island was inaccessible to rescuers, and, furthermore, it had no driftwood that could be used for fire. Bartlett also feared an attempt by inexperienced men to travel over young ice.

One press story quoted Bartlett as having said he believed the mate's party was dead because they did not have a suitable outfit. Stefansson agreed that the travellers required some means of getting across open water, and he blamed Bartlett for dividing the party and not providing Anderson with the necessary equipment.

Stefansson also criticized Bartlett for leaving caches along shifting ice between Shipwreck Camp and Wrangel Island and thought it almost a miracle that half of the caches were recovered. He wondered that Bartlett could not see the resemblance between the treacherous ice on this journey with that which he had experienced north of Ellesmere Island when he sailed with Peary: "A mere book knowledge of the expeditions of Baron Wrangel, DeLong, and Leffingwell-Mikkelsen shows the recklessness of what was done; besides that, Bartlett had with him Hadley who knew the ice of this region."[14] In his memoir, Hadley says he warned Bartlett that the caches might not be found, "seeing that the ice was on the move all the time."[15]

Stefansson conceded that leaving the mate's party in a dangerous situation and caching food on moving ice were examples of Bartlett's ignorance—"culpable ignorance, but nevertheless genuine," but he condemned Bartlett's rescue journey as a "grandstand play." Stefansson believed that all of the *Karluk* personnel could have reached the Siberian shore with Bartlett, and the captain, in his view, had risked many lives in order to obtain for himself a "little extra news prominence."[16]

So serious a charge deserves analysis, particularly because the explorer himself was often accused of "grandstanding." Stefansson tempered his criticism of the disaster by admitting that Bartlett might have had reasons "which I cannot see now" for leaving his men on Wrangel Island. Had it really been necessary to leave the party behind, however, Bartlett should at least have given them instructions to build log cabins, provided enough ammunition to last two years, and left one of the skin boats from the *Karluk* for their use. Had they been properly provided for, the survivors could have waited for rescue almost indefinitely. Stefansson noted grimly, "How nearly they failed to be picked up in 1914 is shown only too clearly by the actual story of the rescue."[17]

In 1925, when Stefansson wrote *The Adventure of Wrangel Island,* concerning the colonization disaster discussed in the next chapter, he made only passing reference to the *Karluk.* Bartlett and the others had already given their versions of the disaster, and Stefansson avoided any direct mention of Bartlett's fault, although he did rely on Hadley's opinion. "The entire party from the *Karluk* could have 'had a picnic' on Wrangel Island for one or several years," he argued, if the *umiak* had been brought ashore and if proper use had been made of the ammunition.[18] In substance, when all reports were in, Stefansson supported Hadley's judgment over Bartlett's.

William McKinlay, however, had complete faith in Bartlett, "and nothing that Hadley has written, nor anything that Stefansson has written or said, or may write or say, has, or will, affect that." "In some matters," McKinlay conceded, "my inexperience renders me unfit to pronounce a verdict; if [Bartlett] made mistakes, they were merely errors of judgment, and would hardly have affected the course of events."[19]

Having shared the *Karluk*'s misfortunes with the captain, McKinlay dismissed Hadley's strictures as his failure to appreciate the dilemma that confronted Bartlett. But Hadley was better equipped to make sound criticisms of Bartlett's actions, as McKinlay seems to admit.

In one of the memoranda which he issued to the press after publication of *The Friendly Arctic,* Rudolph Anderson complained of Stefansson's decision to include the Hadley memoir in his book. "Hadley being dead, Stefansson has cleverly put Bartlett in the difficult position of discrediting the evidence and character of a dead man." Moreover, he evidently had as low an opinion of Hadley as he did of Stefansson: "the statements of the irresponsible Hadley do not add any information of value, their inclusion in *The Friendly Arctic* is one of the most dastardly things Mr. Stefansson had done."

Anderson hinted darkly that Bartlett could expose Stefansson and that the captain would "be glad to be called as a witness, and has plenty of evidence on the *Karluk* which will be of value" if there were a government investigation.[20]

Publishing his book in 1921, five years after Bartlett's, *Last Voyage of the "Karluk"* had appeared, Stefansson naturally thought it more useful to summarize Hadley's story, "for the interest that is given by a different point of view."[21] Hadley, after all, had remained on Wrangel Island until the rescue ship arrived. Stefansson carefully deleted some of Hadley's more inflammatory charges against Bartlett, the most devastating of which was that the captain prohibited the use of aluminum cooking pots in favour of utensils made from coal oil cans, thereby causing the deaths on Wrangel Island. Stefansson also omitted Hadley's suspicion that some members of the party had planned to kill him and had murdered young Breddy.

Writing in 1959 to Williamson, the second engineer, Stefansson explained that he did not want to hurt Bartlett's feelings "beyond the minimum needed to get the approximate truth before the public." Stefansson also explained the circumstances under which Hadley wrote his memoir at Barter Island. Having reason to believe that Stefansson would die of typhoid, "Hadley may have been expecting never to see me again—which would give his writing both a certain impartiality and a certain bias."[22]

Williamson's letters, written so many years after the tragic *Karluk* disaster, uphold Stefansson's prudent decision to edit the Hadley material carefully. While preparing his autobiography, Stefansson asked Williamson to read and comment on Hadley's story as it appeared in *The Friendly Arctic* and later on Hadley's original memoir. With respect to Hadley's published account Williamson admitted that "he has made a pretty fair job of it." But after reading the original Hadley memoir, Williamson's blood pressure rose. He marvelled at Hadley's "silly, stupid charges against me," which included an almost open accusation of murder.[23]

Finally, in 1976, William Laird McKinlay, the last white survivor of the adventure, published *Karluk,* his account of the experience. The book itself and the published interviews attending its publication are fascinating documents. Their interest, however, does not lie in any new revelations concerning events surrounding the disaster, for McKinlay, then ninety years old, did not bring forward any new facts or interpretations. What he graphically described is the haunting, lingering effect such an experience has on a man who has suffered through it. When asked why he finally decided to write about the *Karluk,* he replied: "I wanted to forget about it because thinking about it made me ill. I thought if I went on talking about it, the thing might blur and gradually die out. But no...now I'm hoping that if I calmly accept the situation and go on discussing it until I finish the job, that I might completely wash the thing out."[24]

McKinlay brooded for decades over the *Karluk* catastrophe, comparing it to his impressions of men caught in crisis during his combat experience in World War One. The war, for him, was far less terrible than Wrangel Island: "Not all the horrors of the Western Front, nor the rubble of Arras, nor the hell of Ypres, nor all the mud of Flanders leading to Passchendale, could blot out the memories of that year in the Arctic." The contrast was glaring; he compared the expedition with the army where men had loyalties and exhibit an *esprit de corps* which "enables them to survive the horrors of war." He realized that it was this spirit that had been missing in the North: "It was the lack of real comradeship that left the scars, not the physical rigours and hazards of the ice pack, nor the deprivations of Wrangel Island."[25]

McKinlay's deep faith in God sustained him on Wrangel Island, and he met the challenge with courage and dignity. Other men did not. McKinlay's memories of selfish, brutal conduct overwhelmed other accounts of the event, and so it is not difficult to understand his feelings—these memories must have left a bitter taste in his mouth. Perhaps if the blame could have been fixed, once and for all, he might rest more easily.

All accounts agree that McKinlay performed heroically over the period of the *Karluk*'s drift and the seven-month-long travail on desolate Wrangel Island. But he survived only to be nagged for the rest of his life by recollections of the tragic loss of eleven good men—eleven lives that were squandered so long ago. The memory of his dead companions tormented McKinlay throughout his World War One service, his years of teaching, and his otherwise happy retirement in Scotland. During all this time his resentment of Stefansson mounted: Stefansson had become a hero because of the expedition, but when medals were awarded no mention was made of the eleven dead. Adding to his bitterness over their neglect was McKinlay's belief that *The Friendly Arctic* gave "an inaccurate account of the Karluk affair, subtly putting blame for all the mistakes and disasters on everyone but Vilhjalmur Stefansson."[26] McKinlay was also incensed by Stefansson's criticism of Bartlett, who in his estimation was the true hero of the affair. The expedition leader's accusations of mutiny, insubordination, and disobedience levelled against Anderson and the other Southern Party members infuriated him. He denounced the expedition as "ill-conceived, carelessly planned, badly organized, haphazardly manned and almost totally lacking in leadership." As a consequence, McKinlay believed the deaths were needless and that those who were fortunate enough to survive were put to unnecessarily severe tests of endurance and character. None of the men on the *Karluk* had been trained in arctic survival, so that when the ship drifted towards doom the "inexperienced scientists and crew members were deprived of their leader and all the knowledge and experience of survival on which the whole enterprise was based."[27]

McKinlay's charges in his emotional indictment of Stefansson extend far beyond his own involvement with the expedition. Because his knowledge of expedition events that did not directly concern the *Karluk* was derived from other sources, many of his criticisms lose force when examined.[28] Complaints about the calibre of the *Karluk* crew, for example, are unfair, since it was impossible at the time the expedition was formed to find well-trained men of fine character to man the ship. Stefansson was compelled to take on those who were available. Difficulties in the field, moreover, can only be anticipated within limits, and the overall plan of the expedition was carried through despite the misfortunes. Perhaps the expedition would have been more successful had more time been spent on preparations. Today it would be unthinkable for a government-sponsored venture of the same magnitude to be launched as quickly as was the Canadian Arctic Expedition of 1913-18. Red tape alone would tie up preparations. Stefansson indeed made mistakes—in misjudging the spirit of his men, for instance, and, more importantly, in allowing Bartlett to leave the shoreline. Still, the planning, organization, and leadership must be judged in view of the achievements of the entire expedition—not just the tragic episode of the *Karluk*. And, of course, history *has* judged the expedition successful. It was not perfectly executed, but it did achieve its primary goals.

CHAPTER 18

The Wrangel Island Disaster

IN 1923 four men died in an effort to colonize an island off the coast of northeastern Siberia. Were these men sacrificed to the mad ambition of Stefansson, who sponsored the expedition that claimed the island in the name of Britain? Some critics of the venture at the time thought this was the case, and attacks on Stefansson's project have not abated over the years.

The colonization scheme originated while Stefansson was lecturing on the Chautauqua circuit. At the time, Stefansson was being assisted by two young American veterans of the Canadian Arctic Expedition, Errol Lorne Knight and Fred Maurer. Both men were eager to get back to the Arctic. Despite his near-fatal involvement in the *Karluk* disaster, Maurer had been captivated by the "friendly Arctic" theme, as were Knight and a personable Texan named Milton Galle, who also travelled on the Chautauqua circuit. In the idle hours between performances there was much talk of a new expedition, and Wrangel Island came to be the favoured choice. Stefansson had never been to Wrangel himself, but he had heard much about it from Jack Hadley, a twenty-five year arctic veteran and another survivor of the *Karluk* party's sojourn there. He was an authority on Wrangel Island's natural resources—its polar bears, its myriads of birds, and the numerous walrus that could be found along the edge of the ice pack. To Stefansson, the island seemed to be a land of plenty that was designed by nature to illustrate his theories.

The enthusiasm of the Chautauqua travellers to mount an expedition grew, and they decided to put their eagerness into practical operation. Stefansson was to assume responsibility for raising funds for the expedition if he failed to convince the Canadian government to sponsor it. It was also deemed necessary to appoint a Canadian to command the expedition, and so a twenty-year-old science student at the University of Toronto, Allan R. Crawford, was chosen. Stefansson made clear to the young man that he would have to depend on Knight and Maurer for advice, since Crawford himself had no experience in the region, though he had done some field work with the Geological Survey. Crawford had written Stefansson earlier about joining him in an expedition and seemed fit and capable.

Stefansson needed Ottawa's approval before he could claim the island for Canada in the name of King George V, and he thought he had permission to do so in a letter from Prime Minister Meighen dated 19 February 1921:

I have discussed the matters which you laid before me today and desire to advise you that this government proposes to assert the right of Canada to Wrangel Island, based upon the discoveries and explorations of your expedition. I believe this is all that is necessary for your purposes now.[1]

Stefansson took for granted that this message constituted a clear signal to go ahead but on 1 March, to his dismay, he received a countermanding letter, instructing him to make no use of the previous letter "pending further advice."[2] Later he was told informally that because of the objections of some officials, the expedition could not be approved for 1921, but that he could look forward to a favourable decision the following year. He resolved not to wait but to go ahead with his plans, "believing that once the expedition was underway I could win government support."[3] He was, of course, free to act as a private citizen using his own resources, but his decision was to cause him grief.

The young members of what came to be called "The Stefansson Arctic Exploration and Development Company, Limited," incorporated in Vancouver, B.C., voyaged from Seattle to Nome, Alaska, in the famous old Cunard ship *Victoria*. Like their sponsor, they kept close-mouthed concerning their plans—it would not do to let word of their destination get abroad before they could accomplish their purpose.

People in Nome were curious about the expedition. It was

rumoured that they were seeking gold. They had to tell Jack Hammer, whose *Silver Wave* they were chartering, their destination, but enjoined him to secrecy.

Provisioning for the expedition included traps, weapons, hardware, tents, but only five thousand pounds of provisions, which were considered emergency rations only. Knight had made two long ice trips with Stefansson and knew how to live off the land. Maurer knew that Wrangel Island had a rich meat supply. The men expected to be on the island for two years and planned to subsist primarily by hunting.

Stefansson advised his men to acquire two necessities, Eskimo families and an *umiak* (skin boat), but Knight and Maurer did not follow his instructions. The price of an *umiak* at Nome and later at East Cape, Siberia, seemed too high, so they did not buy one. And Ada Blackjack, hired to sew skins, was the only Eskimo to accompany the colonists. These initial mistakes were to destroy them.

These ebullient, confident young men sailed on 9 September 1921 from Nome on the little *Silver Wave*. Their optimism seemed well founded. It was not every year that a schooner could run through open water to Wrangel Island, yet the *Silver Wave* encountered no ice on the trip. Once ashore with their provisions, the party ran up the Union Jack and claimed the territory for Britain. Less impetuous men would have waited. Hammer and his crewmen, good Americans, had unknowingly helped Britain seize another colony, and they felt duped. There were mutterings in Nome among businessmen and Front Street saloon loungers, followed by a wire dispatched to Washington, D.C., to protest such buccaneering. The citizens of Nome, after all, were possessive about the Arctic and Bering Sea regions. Stefansson explained how these people regarded the British claim: "Here had been this valuable island lying right under the nose of Alaskans these many years, and now some Britishers had come and run off with it."[4]

When word reached the outside world, the Canadian press reacted adversely. Why, editorial writers asked, should Canada interest herself in a remote island when so much of her contiguous North was undeveloped? The American press was also aroused, but for a different reason. Stefansson gave his version of the colony to the *New York Times* on 20 March 1922.[5] Some American newspapers suggested that the right of the United States was greater than that of Britain. English newspapers condemned the colonization of Wrangel Island on different grounds, emphasizing the threat which Stefansson's claim posed to the British-American accord.

While the world's press was debating the question of sovereignty, the adventurers on Wrangel Island were preparing for winter. The diary of Lorne Knight is the chief source of information for what occurred. According to his journal, the colonists built a sound hut and successfully hunted a polar bear on 21 September, just six days after they landed. Other bears were sighted on the following days, but they were not pursued. The colonists could not foresee that there might be a scarcity of meat in the future. They were sure the bears would still be there when snow fell, and then they could haul the meat by dog team. No need to be anxious about stockpiling food so early in the season!

Snow was late in coming, so the men continued to subsist on the groceries they had brought from Nome. Even their dogs were fed from the store provisions. Fall passed, and with it the best season for hunting bears. In the first weeks they saw very few, and, unaccountably, they did not even shoot the two that were bold enough to come into their camp.

The party's fox-trapping was not very successful either, but then foxes were not the food they were hoping to rely on—seals, walruses, and polar bears were much more important to them. They often saw seals as spring approached, yet even of these they killed few.

In August they spotted walruses off-shore. The men launched their clumsy dory and managed to kill two of the giant beasts. However, if they had bought a *umiak* or constructed one, as Stefansson advised, navigating through the drifting ice would have been easy. They realized their mistake too late, yet according to Stefansson, after their first year on the island they were still not worried about the future; they were all healthy and well. Knight did not know that Captain Joseph Bernard's schooner, *Teddy Bear,* had been trying unsuccessfully for three weeks to reach the icebound island. On 18 September Knight wrote without apparent alarm that they had given up on a rescue ship for that season and planned to move camp because they had used all the wood in the vicinity. He also wrote that they would follow a plan discussed earlier with Stefansson to make a spring ice journey to Siberia to relay their news and to telegraph Stefansson of their progress either from Anadyr Bay or Nome, if Anadyr had no telegraph.

Knight and Crawford started out for the telegraph in January

1923. Their sledge was overloaded, and they had only five dogs to pull seven hundred pounds of food and equipment. Before long they discovered how ill-prepared they were for the arduous journey. Knight had scurvy and both men suffered frostbite. Travelling was slow. Eventually they had no choice but to return to camp.

Galle, Maurer, and Crawford were the next to try. Leaving Knight in the care of Ada Blackjack, they departed on 29 January. The three men mushed off on a journey that was to end in their deaths, leaving Knight to the same sad fate.

Knight died slowly of scurvy, or perhaps nephritis. He kept to his sleeping bag from January until his death on 23 June, 1923, yet he kept his diary, recording his symptoms, changes of mood, and camp activities almost to the end. Blubber and hard bread were his chief fare, except for the rare times when Ada Blackjack was successful in trapping a fox. Each time he was fed a meal of fox—especially the fatty meat which Ada undercooked to preserve its best qualities—he recovered his health and spirits. Acute mental depression is one symptom of scurvy, and Knight's diary reveals that he suffered episodes of despondency. yet, remarkably, his natural optimism survived just below the surface even on his darkest days. Knight was well-named—he was a gallant man. Ada Blackjack, although she, too, suffered the symptoms of scurvy, did all of the camp work—trapping, wood-cutting, firemaking, and cooking. Knight knew what he needed to restore his health: fresh meat and plenty of it. A typical diary entry for that time was made on 6 March:

Feeling the same today. The woman cut a little wood and broke the spade handle. She saw one fresh fox track. Nothing of importance to note except that this existence is extremely monotonous for me stuck here in my sleeping bag all day.

The entry ends with his heartfelt cry: "All I want is to get a crack at a bear."[6]

Meanwhile, during the summer of 1923, Stefansson sought backing in London for a rescue operation. He had had enough experience with government officials to know that it took some time for them to arrive at decisions, so he schooled himself to be patient. He went to London at the suggestion of Prime Minister King, hoping to present his case within two weeks. This period, added to his travel time, would allow him to complete the transaction in a month. But there were delays. He wrote King: "About ten days ago, when I had already been absent from Canada six weeks, I was informed over the telephone by the Foreign Office that I must not expect a decision within a week or two from that time." Later he was told that the Foreign Office could not come to a decision and were passing the matter on to Cabinet. He was then informed that the discussion in Cabinet had been scheduled for "the comparatively near future."[7]

Three weeks later Stefansson was still waiting, and his mission was becoming increasingly urgent. The 1922 attempt to reprovision the men on Wrangel Island had failed, so it was imperative to get a relief ship through to them by 1923. Because Stefansson did not have the money to back the rescue operation himself, he tried to exert pressure on the government so that he could wire the Lomen brothers in Nome that the expenses of a relief ship were guaranteed. Raising an alarm went against his grain, and he was convinced that the five members of the colony would be able to provide for themselves by hunting indefinitely. Actually, although he could not know it, the men who were still alive at that time were slowly starving to death.

On 30 July Stefansson wrote the Colonial Office, quoting a telegraph he had just received from Toronto:

NOME WIRED MUST LOAD IMMEDIATELY OR JEOPARDIZE SUCCESS STOP UNLESS RECEIVE CREDIT AUGUST FIRST (FRIENDS HERE) INTEND BROADCAST WORLDWIDE APPEAL FOR HELP STOP SIBERIANS SENDING SHIP FROM VLADIVOSTOK TO CAPTURE WRANGEL ISLAND MUST PREVENT CAPTURE BY LEAVING IMMEDIATELY.[8]

In the same letter he cited a second telegram from Toronto that had been sent by the parents of Crawford, the colony's leader:

UNLESS TEN THOUSAND (DOLLAR) CREDIT ESTABLISHED IMMEDIATELY AT NOME BY GOVERNMENT OR YOU IRREPARABLE DAMAGE MAY RESULT FROM PUBLIC APPEAL WHAT CAN WE DO.[9]

Stefansson asked that the gist of the British Cabinet discussion be conveyed to officials in Ottawa. "What I fear," he wrote, "is that if the Government does nothing and if I am unable to raise the money personally there will be a sensational appeal made in Canada and the United States for the 'rescue' of the four men on Wrangel Island." He saw a parallel in the situation a few years earlier when some of Shackleton's men were left on an antarctic island after their shipwreck. They had been in no particular danger, but still, "you will remember the excitement there over that case, even with war at its height." He was afraid that the same kind of public hysteria could be aroused over the Wrangel Island colony. "Sensational handling is exactly what we have to fear. The appeal to the public will have two parts—first, there will be a demand for a rescue and second, there will be a demand that we give up the folly of any Arctic enterprise." Such a public appeal "will be handled by my personal enemies in Canada and by those others who, although they have no personal feeling in the matter, are very old-fashioned in their attitude towards the Polar Regions and very certain of the folly of everything we are trying to do."[10]

Finally, an English friend offered to provide money for a relief ship on condition that Stefansson would call for a subscription in England. Stefansson agreed, and an appeal was duly published in the *London Times*. The British public—receptive as ever to the cause of exploration—responded generously.

Meanwhile, Harold Noice, a veteran of the Canadian Arctic Expedition, left for Nome to supervise the relief ship. The trading schooner, *Donaldson,* under Captain Alexander Allan, was engaged to make the voyage. As it turned out, the charter cost far more than the original estimates obtained by the Lomen brothers. The skippers of Nome's mosquito fleet were not unaccustomed to dodging Russian gunboats while engaging in illegal trade along the coast of Siberia, but they were reluctant to make the run for Wrangel Island after the Soviet government alerted the world to intrusions on Russian sovereignty. The Soviet press announced the government's intention to protect Russian territory, and the governor of northeastern Siberia sent a message to Nome demanding that any relief ship bound for Wrangel first call at East Cape, Siberia, and take on a contingent of Red Guards. Certainly, Siberia was the last port of call any of the freebooting schooner operators of Nome were likely to make! Stefansson was convinced that the Soviets did not have a legal claim "and that the nationality of Wrangel Island would not in any case be determined by the results of any predatory expedition such as the Soviets threatened, but rather according to international tribunal or committee of arbitration."[11] In this expression of sanguine hope, he was exhibiting a promoter's optimism.

Stefansson was still in London when the *Donaldson* returned to Nome on 1 September with Noice and the astounding news that the four colonists were dead and that only Ada Blackjack had been carried back to safety. "It seemed to me, at first," he wrote, "as if I had lost at one blow four dear friends and a cherished cause." But he summoned up his courage and reasserted his credo: "The men who were dead had been fighting for two things, their faith in the coming development of arctic lands and their hope that the English-speaking countries might become the leaders in that development and chief gainers by it."[12]

Harold Noice, who led the rescue party, broke the news to the press in sensational fashion. He told of the party's youth and inexperience and alleged that the attempt by Crawford, Galle, and Maurer to cross the ice to the mainland was motivated by a scarcity of food, whereas the party's documents, at least as Stefansson interpreted them, suggested that starvation was not the reason for the fatal trek. Even more titillating to newsmen was his story of Ada Blackjack's demand that the dying Knight marry her, and her refusal to hunt when he declined.

Something had snapped in Noice when he saw the colony's camp at Wrangel Island. He found Ada Blackjack beside the body of Lorne Knight, heard her account of their sufferings, and read Knight's diaries. Then, or sometime later, he apparently erased some entries in Knight's diary and tore out some of the pages. Perhaps the pages he removed referred to Ada's ostensible courtship, although there is no tangible evidence to confirm it. The mystery is why Noice should have taken such precautions to be discreet with Knight's notebooks and then disclose scandalous details to newsmen. Sensational news stories invented by the press even went beyond Noice's interviews. The *New York World* printed a garbled version of an interview with Noice, charging that Ada killed Galle after he spurned her.[13]

The *Montreal Standard* mounted an editorial attack on Stefansson. According to the writer, Stefansson's "ambition to keep in the limelight was hardly worth risking the lives of three young men on a desolate Arctic Island." These three men starved to death, the editorial asserted, because of Stefansson's efforts to prove his "friendly Arctic" theory. The editorial charged that first Stefansson had tried to push Wrangel Island on Canada and then on England.

Such pressure would not do: "After this it would be advisable for Mr. Stefansson to hold down his own islands."[14]

A Toronto newspaper published a long article entitled "The Unfriendly Arctic" that referred to the "erratic Canadian explorer" who had invented a catchy phrase, "friendly Arctic," in order to sell his book, "but at the same time...promulgated a grotesque fallacy that has wrought tragic mischief." The men were deluded, and "they paid the penalty of this mistake with their brave young lives." It was clear where the fault lay:

Noice, without openly censuring anybody, makes it clear that the lives of all these victims would probably have been saved had there been any clear plan or adequate preparations in connection with Stefansson's Wrangel expedition. The lads he took with him were for the most part novices who went in a spirit of adventure and knew little or nothing of what they had to face. Elementary precautions against the prospect of starvation appear to have been overlooked. The neglect to provide a proper craft that could be used to hunt walrus in northern waters was a contributory cause of the ultimate tragedy. Again the lack of means and precautions to protect food against marauding animals made the maintenance problem still more serious. It is quite possible that a body of experienced Arctic voyagers, provided with sufficient ammunition might have been able to maintain life for an indefinite period on Wrangel, but Crawford and his companions were novices led away by a false lure and with little real knowledge of the problems with which they had to deal. Thus they perished while the author of the wild enterprise was far away talking nonsense about the supposed strategical importance of Wrangel. That adventurous lads of so fine a type as Crawford and his companions should needlessly perish is something difficult to forgive.[15]

Most Canadian newspapers expressed their views in similar fashion although the Toronto *Morning Post* blamed the government for first having sanctioned the project then withdrawing its support.

Stefansson met with Noice and questioned the more sensational details of his interviews. Noice admitted that he had overreacted to the tragedy and provided Stefansson with a written explanation. "These stories were given out verbally in interviews at a time when I was in a serious nervous condition," he said. "They were based on a hasty reading of the documents." Before going to Nome, Noice had undergone a serious operation and had not yet fully recovered. The strain of chartering a relief ship and directing the rescue had unnerved him. In Nome he met with suspicion and antagonism— Alaskans were still annoyed that the Wrangel Island party had claimed possession of the island for Britain, and they treated Noice's relief efforts as a further usurpation of Nome's sovereignty in arctic seas.

What particularly galled Stefansson were Noice's references to the "youth and inexperience" of the colonists. In his confession Noice admitted that he had given the wrong impression: Maurer and Knight were 28 and 29 years old when they started on the Wrangel Island expedition, and were experienced men in the North."[16] Noice's retraction was published but it was too late for it to have any effect. As far away as Paris, a journal editor felt inclined to ridicule the "friendly Arctic" theory, and the stinging rebukes, encouraging Canadians to hold Stefansson in contempt, did irretrievable damage to his cause in Canada.[17]

Stefansson's sturdiest support during this trying period came from the father of Lorne Knight. John Irvine Knight grieved deeply over the loss of his son, but he had been in constant communication with Stefansson throughout the life of the expedition, and he knew what preparations had been made for it and for the rescue operation. He believed in Stefansson and felt that his son's trust had been justified. Stefansson's *Adventure of Wrangel Island* was based on Lorne Knight's diary, and the young man's father wrote the introduction. The elder Knight condemned Noice's "reprehensible conduct" and accepted Stefansson's explanation of the misfortune.[18]

In reviewing Knight's journal in his book, Stefansson defended his men and himself against charges of ignorance and incompetence. He was sensitive to the feelings of their families and about his own judgment in having selected them as members of the expedition. The newspapers had all but charged him with murder. Stefansson took pains to point out that Knight and Maurer were experienced arctic travellers, yet he admitted his bewilderment at some of the expedition's more glaring mistakes.

It was more politic for government officials to heap all the blame for the affair on Stefansson rather than to remind the public of their temporary infatuation with the Wrangel Island project. Obviously, if the government had insisted upon claiming the territory, and had prevailed, the episode would now be viewed in a different light. But Canada and Britain bowed to Soviet pressure and renounced their interests in Wrangel Island.

The Russians did not appreciate Stefansson's attitude towards their claim to sovereignty. When Noice took the *Donaldson* there in 1923, he landed a party of Eskimos led by Charles Wells, a white trapper. The well-equipped party expected to trap enough furs to make the enterprise profitable, but the Soviets moved to thwart this commercial scheme. An armed ship, the *Red October,* reached the island, ran up the Russian flag, and took Wells and the Eskimos captive. Several of the colonists, including Wells, died before they could be released.

Before the *Red October* steamed to Wrangel Island, Stefansson offered his interest in the island to his friends, the Lomen brothers, for the sum of $3,000. The Lomens had several business enterprises on the Seward Peninsula and were willing to take the chance that the American government would insist that it had a stronger claim to the territory (by virtue of discovery in 1881 by Captain Calvin L. Hooper in the U.S. Revenue Cutter *Corwin*). Carl Lomen apparently received assurances from the State Department because, although no formal claim was ever actually made, the American government years later was prepared to reimburse the Lomens rather generously for the value of stores left on the islands: the award amounted to $30,000 plus $61,630 in interest.[19]

CHAPTER 19

Northward Course of Empire

THE WRANGEL ISLAND tragedy was hard to live down. The sad parting of the ways with the Canadian government weighed heavily on the Manitoba-born exponent of northern development, and it affected the course of Canadian history. The breach that caused the decline of Stefansson's influence in Ottawa, aside from the Wrangel Island affair, has been variously explained. In an interview with the National Film Board of Canada that he gave in the last months of his life, Stefansson did not refer to any of his personal adversaries—although he had made ample note elsewhere of the effects of their savage sniping. Instead, he explained the causes of the split in more general terms—that the government had mistrusted the northern frontier theories that he had advanced in the book he published in 1922, *The Northward Course of Empire*, certain that he was trying to deceive them. As the filmed interview progressed, other topics were discussed that compared the current pace of Canada's northern development with earlier predictions Stefansson had made. There was no need to belabour the obvious— Canada had not listened to its Prophet of the North.

What were the startling proposals made in *The Northward Course of Empire*? The chapter titles indicate the arguments: "The Northward Course of Empire," "The North That Never Was," "The Fruitful Arctic," "The Liveable North," "The Established Arctic Industries," "The Domestication of Ovibos," "Transpolar Commerce by Air."

In "The North That Never Was," Stefansson explored some commonly held fallacies concerning northern weather, especially snow and ice conditions. He remarked that if the average American or European university graduate had ten ideas about the North, nine of them would be wrong, and he discussed some principal misconceptions: that the North Pole is the coldest place in the northern hemisphere; that the North is cold in summer; that the ground is snow-covered in all seasons; and that snowfall is heavier in the North. After disposing of these myths, he went on to describe the potential of the North, but in 1922 his forecasts seemed farfetched. The Canadian public was largely indifferent; fewer than two hundred copies of the book were sold in Canada. Elsewhere, however, Stefansson's views were understood. In 1923 the *Times Literary Supplement* reviewed the book approvingly: "This is a remarkable book, for it teaches us correctly so many things which we knew wrongly." The reviewer was persuaded by the author's contention that people had remained ignorant of the North for so long that they would be forced to unlearn certain misconceptions. "He says that we are northward bound, and that the north polar sea will presently be as familiar to a large part of the human race as the Mediterranean is now. He says that we have, during the course of history, always been northward bound; and so far from there being any reason why we should now stop or reverse our direction of travel, all the reasons are just the other way, especially that of food supply. He says that those who feel attracted to the tropics are the loafers of the race, doomed to disappear in favour of the active and enterprising. He says that none of us really minds cold, whatever we may think." Stefansson was always arguing, and the reviewer imagined that he could hear the explorer discussing views with others on a railroad journey, "offering a gentle correction of some misstatement, but so as to secure a moment's startled attention; seizing his opportunity to emphasize his point, albeit without aggressiveness, but betraying the experience which secures respect; following up his advantage by a development of his theme, until he holds his audience enthralled by the vision of a new world which they had regarded as condemned at the outset."[1]

From time to time other Canadians called for northern development. An editorial appearing in the *Ottawa Citizen* in 1929, for instance, poked fun at the "old notion of desolation." Winston Churchill, the writer reminded his readers, had recently made a speech in London in which he predicted that Canada's development would have a northern emphasis. "Not even the little Canadians who have tiresomely smirked at Stefansson's 'friendly Arctic' idea and his gospel of the northward course of empire can ignore [such] statements." The *Winnipeg Tribune* published a similar opinion, asserting that "a prophet is seldom without honor, except at home." The article pointed to Stefansson's books as proof that he "had in mind the interests of Canada." Stefansson dealt with the possibilities ("hitherto unexpected") which lay in the North and had made some practical suggestions for opening up the region. "All he had hoped was that intelligent Canadians would be interested enough to look into his statements, study them and see what truth was in them." The writer perceived what "seems almost to have been a conspiracy of silence in Canada regarding the matter." The Ottawa paper commented that "The book, in fact, seems to have won its way everywhere except Canada." Men could flourish in the North, "but for some unexplained reason this idea of Northward flow has failed to impress itself upon the Canadian mind."[2]

In 1931 Stefansson persuaded himself to try once more to find favour for his ideas in Canada. He accepted an offer to make a lecture sweep through Ontario, western Quebec, and the Maritime Provinces. His reception was not encouraging. He tried to explain Canadian indifference to him in his autobiography: "My 'message' about the inevitable greatness of northern Canada was growing stale; the Canadians had heard it from me so often before. If greatness was inevitable, why not just wait for it?"[3]

Neither Stefansson's message nor his presence in Canada pleased Canadian government officials. Efforts to establish rapport with Prime Minister King, to whom he referred in *Discovery* as "my old Harvard friend" (it does not appear from the records that the two men had ever been close) came to nothing. King scrupulously avoided him and lesser officials followed his example: "Others were palpably bored and made signs and grimaces as they got out of my way." The Liberals held power in Ottawa and snidely referred to the islands discovered on the Canadian Arctic Expedition as "the *Conservative* Archipelago," since the islands bore the names of their political rivals.[4]

But the disfavour that Stefansson found in Canada went beyond a mere shift in political power. The interest that had resulted in government support for him during the early twenties was dead, and nothing could be done about it. Stefansson resolved to keep away from Canada "for a decade or so, until the value of their northern resources became apparent even to them."[5]

But for all his protestations and declarations of intention to keep away from Canada, he could not accept this indifference to his ideas, and he never gave up trying to vindicate himself. To Stefansson, this parting of the ways *must* be temporary.

Why was Stefansson still a controversial figure in Canada while in the United States he was either wholeheartedly admired or ignored? The difference in attitude was perhaps partly owing to the geography of the two countries. Canada had huge, undeveloped northern regions and most of its small population resided in the South. The United States had its north, too: Alaska was also a huge territory and comparatively undeveloped, but its destiny did not weigh heavily on the national consciousness, and the few advocates of Alaskan causes did not concern American government officials to any extent. But in Ottawa it was otherwise. Financial resources in Canada were limited, and competition for government funding was keen. Imagine the indignation of Ottawa bureaucrats when a brash "outsider" like Stefansson traded on his reputation as an explorer to insist relentlessly on a massive shift in the direction of national effort towards what they regarded as the unproductive and unpromising Arctic. Little wonder that officials listened avidly to rumours spread by members of the Geological Survey, unsavoury stories that were calculated to show that Stefansson was unscrupulous. Stefansson was personable and persuasive, and to those public officials who were sympathetic to his pleas, he seemed to be concerned solely with the well-being of Canada. His supporters, however, were too few and he had formidable enemies.

The zeal of those who were dedicated to "exposing" Stefansson sometimes led them to commit silly blunders. James White, a former chief geographer to the Canadian government, embarrassed himself by contending that what Stefansson termed "discoveries" had in fact appeared on older charts and that his statements about the charting of Banks Island were incorrect. White's arguments, published in the *Geographical Journal* in June 1924 and April 1925 were disputed by *Journal* editors at the time. Finally, in 1946, aerial surveys made by Keith Greenaway corroborated Stefansson's claims.[6]

The Wrangel Island disaster in 1923 and the subsequent failures of the reindeer domestication experiment on Baffin Island soured Canadian officialdom further, at the same time strengthening the case of Stefansson's opponents. According to Calvin White in 1952, Stefansson then "spent the next 30 years sniping at Ottawa." White added that Stefansson was "probably right in most of what he says, but that hardly endears him to Anderson or other officials."[7] White also observed that Stefansson's criticism of the Canadian government for failing to promote northern enterprises was a mistake since the government was merely responding to the prevailing public attitude.

A suggestion made by Stefansson in *The Northward Course of Empire* provides a good example of his pragmatism and of how he could be thwarted. As has been observed, Stefansson was a fanatic on the topic of food prejudices, mainly because failure to overcome certain aversions was a serious detriment to successful polar exploration. But they were also partly responsible for delaying acceptance of several of his favourite projects, such as his scheme for domesticating musk-oxen in an effort to develop a meat industry in the North. Part of public resistance to musk-ox meat when it appeared in the markets, he thought, came from the animal's name. There was nothing "musky" in its flavour and Stefansson's expedient recommendation was simply to change the animal's name to ovibos.

Stefansson had suggested the change earlier, and from the reaction he received in Ottawa he saw that there were prejudices other than nomenclature to be dealt with. In 1920, Rudolph Anderson was acting chief of the Biological Sciences Division of the Geological Survey of Canada. The commissioner of dominion parks asked his opinion of Stefansson's proposal. Anderson swiftly perceived a shady scheme to cheat the public and insisted that Canada could not let Stefansson change the name of the musk-ox. According to Anderson, Stefansson was following the "identical tactics" of his tenth-century compatriot, Eric the Red. "That worthy outlaw found the inhospitable shores of Greenland but named it so that people would sooner be induced to go thither in case it had a good name.' "[8]

While Stefansson's theories concerning the prospective value of resources in the North were shared by others in Canada over the years, his supporters were very much in the minority. Today, of course, no one questions the importance of northern development, since the discovery of petroleum resources and other events of recent years have been momentous.

Richard Finnie, the Yukon-born northern traveller, writer, and documentary film-maker, notes in his book, *Canada Moves North* (1942), the "curious fact that Canadians know almost nothing about one third of their country." Like Stefansson, who was his good friend, Finnie observed that whatever information Canadians were able to pick up was usually at least partly incorrect. This, Finnie explains, "is due to the tradition of the Frozen North that has been handed down through many generations, a tradition that began with the hardships endured by ill-equipped explorers."[9]

In *The Political Economy of the Canadian North*, Kenneth Rea, a Canadian economist, makes no mention of Stefansson's prophesies and promotions, but he criticizes the Canadian government for having neglected the North. "It was not until a private company discovered commercial quantities of petroleum near Fort Norman on the Mackenzie River that any official enthusiasm, or even interest, developed in connection with the Northwest Territories." The discovery at Norman Wells to which Rea refers was made in 1920, and it certainly helped Stefansson push his cause in Ottawa. Yet federal interest still tended to follow a "boom and bust" pattern. The extent to which the government ignored the North was admitted in a speech by the deputy minister of northern affairs and national resources in 1957. He observed that "the North was left to the missionary, the fur trader, the Eskimos, and the Indians." He identified a succession of factors that account for what he called the "obliteration of the North from the national mind." These were a national preoccupation with western settlement, the First World War, the Great Depression, and lastly, the Second World War. Neglect of the North was not limited to the indifference of the public to economic development, but also extended to the welfare of northern peoples. The Canadian public's attitude only began to change when Prime Minister John Diefenbaker disclosed his now famous "vision of the North" during his 1957-58 election campaign.[10]

Stefansson constantly urged the American and Canadian governments to follow the Soviet example of development in Siberia. Ironically, it seems that the only result of his advice was that he convinced some people that he was a Communist sympathizer. An even more ironic footnote is that in 1971 Canada's Prime Minister Pierre Trudeau visited Siberia for the purpose of examining Soviet techniques in arctic development, particularly with respect to pipeline construction.

By the 1970's the periodical *North*, published by the Department of Indian Affairs and Northern Development, was praising Stefansson. The writer remarked that because of Stefansson's "friendly

Arctic" notions he had been "roundly condemned by all and sundry as a fraud, guilty of gross distortion and extreme exaggeration." Had critics delved deeply enough, the writer contended, they would have found that Stefansson was "the only explorer of note who really understood the Arctic" and would have realized that his "friendly Arctic" concept referred to learning to live in harmony with the Arctic rather than fighting nature.[11]

Writing in 1971, Richard Finnie described how Stefansson urged Canadians and Americans to recognize the value of the North, but neither government was ready for his innovative projects. "They were tired of his wild ideas," Finnie concluded. "By the time some of...them had become realities his efforts to promote them were all but forgotten."[12]

In his introduction to *Pathfinders of the North* (1970) John Diefenbaker scolded Canadians for failing to recognize Stefansson's achievements. "The great Canadian explorer, Vilhjalmur Stefansson," he wrote, "between 1906 and 1918 endeavoured to turn the eyes of Canadians northward by his successive expeditions into the North to prove by personal example that the North was livable." Diefenbaker realized that Stefansson's message was difficult to convey. "He experienced many discouragements in his efforts to make the North live in the hearts and imaginations of Canadians." Diefenbaker himself claimed credit for having initiated the first major economic thrust into the North in 1958. His threefold program called for the compilation of a continuing inventory of northern resources, development of energy resources, and a policy of conservation that would allow the most effective utilization of resources.[13]

In attempting to review the history of Canada's northern policy, David Judd, a former administrator of the Yukon Territory, explained that the government looked north only when the gold rush of 1897-90 attracted attention to the Klondike. Even then, it took the discovery of gold and the fear of an American land grab to stimulate the Canadian government into action. However, Judd claims, from 1900 to the 1930's, "almost all Canada's scanty northern policy was devoted to the task of fending off claims and incursions of American, Danish, and Norwegian explorers."[14] Later, the Second World War and the postwar Distant Early Warning Line sparked new interest, promoting construction of roads and other facilities.

The Second World War also brought American military men into the North, outnumbering Canadian residents by at least three to one. Judd observes that the presence of American soldiers seemed to threaten Canada's claim to sovereignty in the Arctic. Ottawa at the time "was concerned about the casual United States attitude, particularly of the armed services, toward Canadian ownership of the Arctic mainland and islands." Something had to be done to prevent the Americans from pre-empting Canadian territory. "It was this uneasiness in Ottawa," Judd concludes, "which prompted the design of a new policy for Canada's North."[15]

In 1946 the Royal Canadian Air Force was ordered to photograph and maintain air reconnaissance over the Arctic; Royal Canadian Mounted Police posts that had been closed during the war were reopened. The Canadian Army took over operation of the Alaska Highway in Canada and began to hold manoeuvres in the Arctic. Some administrative reorganizations were also made to secure a firm control on the North. In spite of these activities, Judd argues, the "major preoccupation" of the government up to 1953 was its aversion to the presence of the American military, and its "extreme sensitivity" to possible derogation of Canadian sovereignty.[16]

New social policies were devised following construction of the Distant Early Warning Line in the mid-1950's. Before that time, a study by Diamond Jenness on Eskimo administration recommended a policy that, had it been implemented, would effectively have depopulated the Arctic of its aboriginal people. One of Jenness's recommendations held that the best means of ending poverty and reducing the costs of social services was to encourage migration of certain elements in the population to the South, in order to provide vocational education for these aboriginals. Fortunately, Jenness's advice was rejected. Between 1954 and 1961 there was a fourfold increase in government expenditures. More schools were constructed, co-operative stores were established, and health services were improved.

David Judd concluded his review of Canada's northern policy by emphasizing current Canadian preoccupation with "a moral and political concern for the welfare of northern people" rather than sovereignty, which he believed was no longer an issue except, perhaps, for "future definitions of territorial waters." It was not, in 1969, apparent to Judd that the British Colonial Office official who advised Canadians in 1879 that they should annex the Arctic Islands for the sole purpose of preventing the United States from taking them, "and not from the likelihood of their proving of any value to Canada" was clearly wrong. Judd summed up the situation in the North as it was in 1969: "The North today means subsidy," adding almost as an afterthought, "it is probable...that, in the future, the economic motive will become more important."[17]

New concerns and older ones have emerged since the Arctic's petroleum development. In 1970 oil companies exploiting Alaska's north slope resources sent the huge tanker *Manhattan* to Prudhoe Bay from Canada's east coast. More recently, luxury cruise ships have made the Northwest Passage. But the August 1985 departure of the U.S. Coast Guard's *Polar Sea* to Barrow from Greenland raised questions of Canada's sovereignty, defence strategies, and environmental impact. The U.S. and Canada are concerned about reports of U.S.S.R. submarines operating near Canada's communications and research station on Ellesmere Island. Canadian officials asserted the nation's sovereignty over the Northwest Passage and expressed concern over the effect of pollution on Inuit villages in the Arctic. The Inuit themselves have been more vocal on this issue than the government.[18]

CHAPTER 20

"Friendly? Like Hell!"

" **O** F ALL the fantastic rot I have ever heard of, this comes close to the top," said Roald Amundsen of Stefansson's *The Friendly Arctic*.[1] Amundsen's savage attack during an Ottawa press interview in 1926 and later in his autobiography jolted Stefansson. By this time he was used to controversy and criticism that had started with the "blond Eskimos" story in 1912, continued with skirmishes over the Canadian Arctic Expedition, the Wrangel Island colony, the sniping of American explorer Donald MacMillan, the defenders of Nansen, and the vitriolic partisans of the Cook-Peary North Pole dispute. He avoided public disputes when it appeared that the damage to his or a friend's reputation was minor, but did not hesitate to counterattack when circumstances demanded it.

With most explorers Stefansson's only contact was professional and cordial, and in dealing with their partisans he tried to be open and to play down grounds for further aggravation of the issues. There were exceptions, as with his persistent championship of George Wilkins and his responses to Amundsen's ridicule.

Some of Amundsen's grounds for antagonism were easy to understand. The very title of *The Friendly Arctic*, as Stefansson was pleased to note when the second edition appeared, "irritates and antagonizes most people," who recall all the heroic tales and horror stories they had ever read or heard about the Arctic. Their usual reaction was: "Friendly? Like hell! But, even if they have not read the book, they remember it and argue about it with readers."[2] Such controversy kept interest in his book alive.

Stefansson defined and redefined his theory of the "friendly Arctic" in virtually every book he wrote, in hundreds of articles, and from the lecture platform. He attributed his own experiences with arctic survival to successful adaptation to the true characteristics of the North. On occasion, he would make fun of the expectations of readers of other polar narratives. Perhaps the law of supply and demand accounted for narratives "about suffering, heroic perseverance against formidable odds, and tragedy, either actual or narrowly averted," but Stefansson's thesis demanded a total rejection of this view.[3]

Stefansson noted that the conventional depiction of the Arctic underwent a change in the mid-nineteenth century, after the loss of the Franklin expedition. The earlier seekers of the Northwest Passage, with sanguine expectations of finding a new route to lands of wealth, were inclined to report that seas were calm, ice was scarce, breezes were gentle, and summers were warm. "The explorer was an advance agent of commerce and development, a herald of empire."[4]

But the Franklin tragedy changed the image of the North forever. "Thereafter the explorers tended to become pioneers of science if not martyrs of science, daring souls who, with a modesty equal to their fortune and their self-sacrifice, risked their lives to expand the horizon of man's knowledge." The spirit of the runner of marathons and the scaler of mountain peaks had also slipped in. It suddenly became important to make the longest sledge journey or the longest ocean voyage. Perhaps this change of emphasis was in response to popular demand. After Franklin, no one believed a navigable Northwest Passage existed; therefore, explorers no longer were expected to make discoveries for commercial purposes. Rather, "what the public now wanted from explorers was a record which they could admire for perseverance in the face of difficulties, courage in the face of danger. Triumph over obstacles was the goal—which made it desirable that their difficulties should be many and the dangers great."[5] The purpose of exploration had changed from a quest for wealth to a quest for honour; and there was no longer any motive for emphasizing the favourable features of the North. Stefansson cited references in early narratives to the extreme summer heat as an illustration, pointing out that few such references were to be found later.

Post-Franklin expedition explorers like Elisha Kent Kane, the first American hero of polar exploration, stressed Arctic terrors.

Kane even asserted that the arctic night tended to age men at an accelerated rate. Nansen, to Stefansson's satisfaction, directly contradicted this bit of Kane's lore: "For my own part," Nansen said in *Farthest North*, "I can say that the Arctic night has had no aging, no weakening influence of any kind upon me; I seem, on the contrary, to grow younger. This quiet, regular life suits me remarkably well." He wrote ironically: "I am almost ashamed of the life we lead, with none of those darkly painted sufferings of the long winter night which are indispensable to a properly exciting Arctic expedition. We shall have nothing to write about when we get home."[6] Nansen's men were comfortable and secure. They dined well on fresh bread, beer, tinned tongue, corned beef, coffee, and marmalade; they enjoyed their pipes, reading, and conversation.

Nansen's feeling for the Arctic was one reason why Stefansson rated him so highly among explorers. Stefansson was unstinting in his praise of explorers whom he admired. He ranked Fridtjof Nansen "with Pytheas and Eric the Red" and saluted him as the greatest of all polar explorers.[7] Obviously, he did not make reciprocal arrangements for approval: Nansen did not usually indulge in public controversies over exploration and paid no attention to Stefansson beyond a terse reflection to newsmen, when the "blond Eskimo" furore broke, that the United States had produced another Dr. Cook. Later, someone told Stefansson that Nansen stopped criticizing him when he realized that no Icelander could be as ignorant of Scandinavian-Greenlandic history as the newspapers suggested.[8]

The two men never met. Since Nansen was close to his countryman Roald Amundsen, Stefansson's severest critic, he really did not expect to find much praise in Norwegian circles. Stefansson once became upset when he heard that Storker Storkerson, his loyal ice trek comrade, had been abused by other Norwegians because of his association with him, but usually he was not concerned by muted undercurrents in Scandinavia.

As much as Stefansson respected Nansen's skill as an explorer and statesman, on several occasions he refuted Nansen's theory of a lifeless polar sea. His own experience had been to the contrary, and so he was gratified when the first scientific station established by the Soviets on ice islands demonstrated that plankton and other marine life flourished under the ice in polar seas.

On one occasion a British writer and clergyman, J. Gordon Hayes, accused Stefansson of belittling Nansen because he had criticized Nansen's method of polar sea observation. This kind of

stupid charge provoked Stefansson, and he responded irritably—
could not his critic distinguish between justifiable criticism and dis-
paragement? "Scientific etiquette would demand that the object of
the criticism and everybody else should behave as if no hard feelings
could possibly result on either side."[9]

The problem, as Stefansson saw it, is that explorers both expect
recognition as scientists and emoluments appropriate to the level
of their scientific achievements, "yet call for that immunity from
criticism by our peers that belongs to sport."[10] If exploration is
truly a science and not a sport, then Stefansson reasoned that critics
should stop trying to apply the ethics of one to the other.

It is obvious from Roald Amundsen's writings that he did not
share the sensitivity of Nansen or Stefansson to Arctic life. But
Amundsen's attacks on Stefansson should be placed in the context
of the Norwegian's woes in the mid-1920's. From 1918 to 1925,
he had been involved in an attempt to drift across the Pole with
the polar ice pack in the *Maud*. That unfortunate ship was delayed
in the Bering Strait and off the coast of northeastern Siberia by ice
and achieved nothing. The failure hurt a man accustomed to spectacular successes. Worried and frustrated, Amundsen finally left
the ship in charge of his second-in-command, probably so that he
could raise more money. During this period, he visited Frederick
Cook, who was then serving a jail term for a business fraud.
Amundsen liked Cook, and the two men had been together on an
Antarctic expedition in 1898 and 1899. Officers of the National
Geographic Society interpreted Amundsen's visit to Cook as evidence that he supported Cook's claim to have discovered the North
Pole before the society's hero, Robert Peary. The Society cancelled
forthwith a lecture that Amundsen had been engaged to give under
its auspices in Washington. Such petty conduct by Society officers
was disgraceful, and, understandably, it embittered Amundsen. In
1926 Amundsen suffered further indignities after the successful
Arctic flight of the airship *Norge* when ship commander, Umberto
Nobile, claimed too much of the credit for Amundsen's taste.
Amundsen's subsequent attacks on Nobile even exceeded those on
Stefansson.

Personal antagonisms did not cause the feud between Amundsen
and Stefansson, and the two men had met only once, quite briefly,
when Stefansson was making his first sojourn in the Arctic and
Amundsen was wintering over during the course of his voyage
through the Northwest Passage. Amundsen was not known as a

prima donna. In correspondence with others, Stefansson sometimes made passing references to Amundsen's public taciturnity, once comparing him to the silent Calvin Coolidge. Unlike most men, however, Amundsen grew more controversial and prone to dispute as the years passed. Amundsen had been quiet on the "blond Eskimo" dispute after its initial eruption in 1912, and Stefansson had no intimation that Amundsen was gunning for him until the interview appeared in the Ottawa *Journal*. The *Journal* had sided with the Canadian Arctic Expedition scientists against Stefansson earlier, and presumably the paper's reporter threw bait to Amundsen during the interview. When asked his opinion of Stefansson, Amundsen replied: "I have never concealed my opinion of Stefansson. He knows perfectly well what I think of him, and he never comes near me." The reporter then asked if Amundsen did not think Stefansson was a clever writer. "Yes, Stefansson writes well," admitted the Norwegian. "His book about the blond Eskimo was entertaining reading—but was it true?"[11]

When he was then asked his opinion on Stefansson's "friendly Arctic" theory, Amundsen exploded: the book is "entertaining, and highly plausible to one who has not been 'up there,' but it is fantastic rot."[12]

More criticism came when the Norwegian edition of Amundsen's *My Life as an Explorer* was published in 1927. Amundsen described *The Friendly Arctic*, which he called *The Hospitable North*, as "a dangerous distortion of the real conditions." Men in search of adventure in the North would be led astray "by this prattle about the 'hospitality' there," and he charged, if anyone attempted to do what Stefansson declared he had done and dared to venture into those regions equipped only with a rifle and a little ammunition, he would meet certain death. "A more unreasonable distortion of conditions in the North has never been set forth than that a skillful marksman 'can live off the land,' " declared Amundsen. Then he launched into a heavy blast: "Stefansson has never done it, although he says he has. Furthermore, I am willing to stake my reputation as a polar explorer, and will wager everything I own, that if Stefansson were to attempt it, he would be dead within eight days, counted from the start, provided that this test takes place on the Polar ice, which is constantly adrift over the open sea."[13]

What makes Stefansson's theory seem plausible, Amundsen continued, was his claim that there was "a trifle of game" on the mainland and on the large islands. A skilful hunter might survive along the coastal strip; however, in Amundsen's opinion, out on the sea ice, chances of living off the land are "just as good as they would be to find a gold mine on the top of an iceberg."[14] He admitted that a few seals might come up on the ice, but fishing would be impossible. What really irked Amundsen, apparently, was the threat the "friendly Arctic" theory posed to fund-raising: "Stefansson has done the cause of really serious exploration an infinitely great injury by this fantastic tale."[15]

Amundsen had been rebuffed by potential donors who advised him that he ought to live off the land. It is easy to see why he was aggrieved, but his case did not gain strength from his ill-natured and unsubstantiated general condemnation of Stefansson's expeditions: "They have always been marked by the same lack of valuable results, and in many instances also by terrifyingly poor power of judgment. Many of Stefansson's companions have returned to civilization as his bitter enemies." Amundsen admitted that neither lack of success nor dissension was unusual, "but when one man combines all these common faults with an ungovernable imagination, then it is...the duty of one who can speak with the authority of experience...to point out...nonsense."[16]

Stefansson believed that Amundsen's wrong-headed views about *The Friendly Arctic* and *My Life with the Eskimo* were the result of his not having read either book, relying instead on garbled newspaper reports of Stefansson's claims and theories. Stefansson was told that Amundsen rarely read a book in his last years, and he cited as evidence that Amundsen had given the wrong titles for both works. Perhaps Carl Lomen came closest to the mark when he suggested to Stefansson that "one little quip" of his in *The Friendly Arctic,* that had been passed on to Amundsen, was the basis of all the excitement." The reference in question was probably to Stefansson's discussion of Franklin's discovery of the Northwest Passage, which was followed by the parenthetical comment: "(some think it was found by Amundsen in 1905)."[17] Stefansson denied he had been trying to insult Amundsen.

Besides the obvious differences in exploration theories and goals of the two explorers, it is probable that Amundsen's spleen owed more to his pressing financial difficulties than to anything else. His autobiography describes the harassment he suffered at the hands of his creditors, his subsequent bankruptcy, and the ingratitude of his fellow Norwegians. Slandered, he felt by his countrymen, he was a beleaguered man whose spirit must have snapped during those months of torment.

Reviewers of Amundsen's book shared something of Stefansson's distaste, although they noticed the attack on Nobile more than that on Stefansson. The *New York Evening Post* noted a "regrettable pettiness" in Amundsen's discussion of Nobile and the *Norge* flight. Another reviewer commented on Amundsen's "considerable invective," but he went on to remark that all famous explorers have their detractors: "He has been vehemently abused, doubted, distrusted," the writer explained, "So, like the old lion that he is, he can and does roar, for being an explorer he is pugnacious. A man of authority cannot be expected to adopt the martyr pose."[18]

A third reviewer was less charitable, and he doubted that Amundsen would let *My Life* stand as his autobiography. "The book is so laden with controversy, with bitterness, even with rage, that the Amundsen of 30 years' experience in the Arctic and Antarctic is an indistinct figure, all but lost in the storm of the battle that has arisen between the explorer and Col. Nobile."[19]

Stefansson's friends offered advice. University of Michigan geologist, W. H. Hobbs reacted with some discernment to Amundsen's attack on Stefansson. He wisely advised Stefansson to ignore Amundsen's statements, "in which case the personal side of the man will disappear." Amundsen's state of mind almost deserved compassion: "I feel confident that he has really in a measure gone off his head."[20]

Isaiah Bowman, President of the American Geographical Society, was a man whose advice Stefansson took seriously. After the Canadian Arctic Expedition, he had warned both Stefansson and Bartlett that they should ignore any efforts to stir up a controversy between them. Now Bowman made an effort to smooth over the Amundsen-Stefansson quarrel "because any direct answer to his [Amundsen's] statements seems to lead to controversy and this is always to be deplored, even when it becomes a necessity."[21]

The officers of various geographical societies had considerable influence, albeit unofficial, over public opinion. They were devoted to furthering the cause of exploration and, therefore, were anxious to present such enterprises to the public in the best possible light. Explorers, ever touchy and always aggressive, had to be handled with care to prevent the kind of public squabbling that would make both themselves and the science of geography look ridiculous. Yet it was difficult to avoid taking sides in disputes and nearly impossible to keep them private. Often enough news of some quarrel would reach the press, but the leak would have been much more damaging but for the efforts of men like Bowman.

But despite his dislike of controversy, Bowman was entirely sympathetic to Stefansson in the Amundsen quarrel and did not try to persuade him not to answer Amundsen's charges. He even took the trouble to point out the best ways of refuting them. Since Amundsen's arguments were weakest on the subject of living on the ice, Bowman counselled, "you can attack him there not only with your own experience but with that of Storkerson. I always felt your criticism of Amundsen was strongest when you dealt with his limited experience on ice in the Arctic."[22]

Bowman offered Stefansson several ideas for an article or book on the subject. He said he preferred the suggestion of a small book to a series of magazine articles because a book would "give the permanent answer to [Amundsen's] charge and that is the important thing, not whether Amundsen momentarily holds the stage."[23]

Rudolph Anderson was gratified by Amundsen's attacks because Amundsen had "an international reputation as a doer of deeds far beyond anything that Stefansson ever claimed." Now, as Anderson told Amundsen, the anti-Stefansson faction would be supported by a famous explorer who could not be dismissed as merely "jealous scientists." Anderson had much to say about Stefansson and the ignorance or duplicity of those individuals who supported him. He likened Stefansson to Frederick Cook as a case of mental deterioration. It was Anderson's charitable view that Stefansson was deranged, which explained both his ridiculous theories and his attacks on others. "Stefansson is the outstanding humbug in the exploration world at the present time—a persistent, perennial, and congenital liar who for years has made his living by sheer mendacity and skill in handling words."[24]

The Amundsen dispute faded away but occasionally there were lesser ones. The discovery of Salomon Andrée's remains in 1930 once more stirred up the "friendly Arctic" argument in the press. In 1897 Andrée had made an effort to reach the North Pole in a balloon. His fate had been unknown until his corpse was discovered in 1930 on White Island (north of Southampton Island and west of Foxe Channel). Experts speculated on the cause of death of the three members of the expedition. Stefansson believed they might have died of carbon monoxide poisoning; others surmised that, like Bernhard Hantzsch in 1911, they had died from trichinosis caused by eating undercooked polar bear meat. At any rate, the Swedish expedition had certainly met a tragic end. The London *Week-End Review* commented that "Stefansson's theory ["friendly Arctic"], which has been growing in popularity lately will receive a damaging blow."[25]

Stefansson responded in a letter to the London *Times*. Andrée's story was being used to support traditional views that in reality it contradicts, he argued. What is so threatening about a cold climate? Had Andrée's balloon gone down in the sea, the Swedes would not have lasted a minute. Then he went on to mention some of the long arctic journeys that had been made in the past, and he likened the prevailing view of the North to the current world alarm over a few cases of parrot fever.[26]

The relationship between Knud Rasmussen, the Danish ethnologist-explorer, and Stefansson shows two men of equal generosity. Stefansson applauded Rasmussen's achievements: "I am in the habit of saying that (with, I hope, the exception of myself) you are the only explorer who has written about the Eskimo and who has understood them." Command of the Eskimo language is necessary, he reminded Rasmussen, "and others don't have it."[27]

In his long reply, Rasmussen returned the compliment: "for many years I have known and admired your magnificent work in the Arctic." He indicated to Stefansson that his book about "white Eskimos" had stirred his interest and congratulated him on his efforts to encourage domestication of Canadian musk-oxen.[28] The two great ethnographers met only once, briefly, on one of Rasmussen's rare visits to the States. Stefansson cordially offered his hospitality to the Dane and any help that he might desire.

Among active explorers Stefansson was closest to George H. Wilkins, who later became Sir Hubert. Wilkins was one of the participants in the Canadian Arctic Expedition, but he left the expedition before its conclusion to join the armed forces, later going on to explorations of his own. Wilkins's pioneering air flights over Antarctica and the Arctic brought him much acclaim and a knighthood. Throughout his career the resourceful Australian kept in close contact with Stefansson, who encouraged him in all of his activities.

Of all Wilkins's projects, the one dearest to Stefansson's heart was Wilkins's plan to navigate a submarine to the North Pole, and once there to bring the vessel to the surface. Stefansson suggested this voyage to Wilkins and convinced him that a submarine could break through the sea ice at the Pole in the same manner as a surfacing whale.

When the announcement of the proposed polar voyage of the decommissioned *Nautilus* was made in 1931, the news was greeted with derision. Prominent naval men labelled the project dangerous folly that had no chance of success. Admiral Hugh Rodman led the attack:

Having spent the greater portion of my professional life at sea, some 30 odd years, part of which have been spent in Arctic circles where there is more or less ice at all times, and being familiar with the limitations of submarines, I am thoroughly convinced that the expedition headed by Sir Hubert Wilkins to try to dive under the Arctic ice cap some 1500 miles in a submarine is hazardous, foolhardy, fraught with danger and difficulties that will be all but impossible to overcome, and in my opinion is bound to meet with disaster. Even if he should be successful and accomplish his mission, I can't see that anything that he will learn that is new about the Arctic can be of any use or assistance to mankind at large in any way or shape at all.[29]

Polar explorer Donald MacMillan also believed that Wilkins was wasting his time. He told a *Philadelphia Ledger* reporter that surface vessels had a hard time with pack ice and a submarine would have no chance at all.

Stefansson came to Wilkins's defence in press interviews in which he stressed the practicality and the scientific value of the voyage. "It is the only one of the 25 submarine expeditions planned in this century which pursues new ideas rather than being a confirmation of old ones."[30] Stefansson also asked the New York *Times* to commission Wilkins to write articles on his work, urging the newspaper's editor and others to read Wilkins's book, *Under the North Pole,* to find out what the expedition was all about.

This book, for which Stefansson wrote an introduction that summarized the history of submarine navigation and other portions of the text, was most unusual. As a means of stirring interest in the venture for the purpose of raising money, it was published before Wilkins made his attempt on the Pole. E. B. White of the *New Yorker* lampooned the book and the voyage in verse:

> *The Nautilus that must not fail,*
> *Whose book awaited publication;*
> *The only book to go on sale*

Before *the actual exploration.*[31]

The *Nautilus* was primitive and in poor repair even by submarine standards of the day. Wilkins managed to navigate her to the Arctic, but got nowhere near the Pole. Stefansson was not surprised; he had already commented publicly that he doubted her ability to perform effectively.

But when he was interviewed by Lowell Thomas after Wilkins returned, Stefansson proved a sturdy defender of his friend. Stefansson admonished Wilkins's critics, arguing, somewhat speciously, that the expedition's backers gained what they had wanted. "For the first time in history northern conditions have been studied from a new angle."[32]

However, despite his disclaimer, Wilkins's venture had failed. Another *Nautilus*, the American atomic-powered submarine, voyaged under the ice twenty-seven years later from Bering Strait to the north of Norway. Her sister ship, the *Skate*, continued under the ice to the North Pole, surfaced briefly, and then submerged and continued on, confirming Stefansson's long-cherished contention that a submarine had only to follow the custom of beluga whales he had seen breaking through ice to the surface.

After the *Skate's* successful voyage, her captain, James Calvert, was given a copy of *Under the North Pole*. Calvert had not previously known of the earlier effort. He cabled a congratulatory message at once to Wilkins: "The majority of your aims and predictions of nearly thirty years ago were realized this summer. The men of the *Skate* send a sincere salute to a man who has many times shown the way."[33] Wilkins sent the cable on to Stefansson, reminding him that he was first to suggest that a submarine voyage to the Pole was possible.

Wilkins had proposed a winter voyage to the Pole, but he died suddenly of a heart attack before Calvert could discuss the matter with him. Calvert later consulted Stefansson about the problems involved and, in 1959, made another successful voyage. Stefansson was gratified to receive a letter from Calvert, written by the captain from the North Pole, thanking him for his help, and describing the memorial service held at the Pole for Wilkins.

Stefansson's friends assumed they were doing him a favour by reporting derogatory public remarks made by other explorers. Stefansson explained to William Hobbs, who had detected a note of disrespect in Donald MacMillan's statement that blond Eskimos did not exist, that the dispute was one of terminology and, so, of no consequence. Hobbs, an excitable man, had even hired a stenographer to record MacMillan's exact language so that Stefansson could defend himself more effectively. But Stefansson's sensibilities were not so sensitively attuned to public criticism as Hobbs supposed.

As a polar explorer, MacMillan had earned a fair share of publicity himself, and he was anxious to be known as Peary's companion. He had taken part in an earlier Peary expedition, returning afterwards to the Arctic to confirm Peary's discovery of "Crocker Land." But, instead his journey showed that it did not exist. Whether for this or for other reasons, Peary's family had difficulty warming to MacMillan and actively resisted his efforts to be a spearcarrier in the Peary cause. MacMillan's Crocker Land Expedition occurred contemporaneously with the much-honored Canadian Arctic Expedition but was not much appreciated. One sponsor, the American Geographical Society, refused to publish the findings MacMillan had submitted for a scientific report, and another, the American Museum of Natural History, neglected to recognize him as well.

An explorer must accomplish some goal in order to please his sponsors or else suffer the ignominity of rejection. Jousting with Stefansson did nothing for MacMillan's cause, nor did it bother Stefansson, who remarked mildly, "It is easy to understand why he might have a personal feeling against me—unjustified perhaps but human nevertheless."[34] Stefansson admitted that he sometimes "oversold the merits of Arctic lands and seas" in his lectures and writings, when he expounded his favourite theme too strenuously and enthusiastically.[35] And he knew that he was too much the entrepreneur to please everyone.

MacMillan would never understand Stefansson's propaganda or his jokes about the "hardship school" of exploration. As he expostulated to Marie Peary in complaining about the "friendly Arctic" theme: "When I think of your Dad struggling back over the Greenland ice cap in 1895, followed by two starving men and one emaciated dog, of his frozen feet—and the stumps of his toes, of the Big Lead in 1906, I boil at that word 'friendly' when applied to a country where even Eskimos starve!"[36]

Stefansson had described his "living off the land" innumerable times as superior to Peary's outmoded sledging method—to Peary himself as well as to others. To him, this crucial point should not be obscured in a profitless debate. For all MacMillan absorbed of his theories, Stefansson might have been talking to a stump: all MacMillan heard was "bunk"—and an insult to the memory of Peary, a dead man who "cannot defend himself."[37]

CHAPTER 21

The North Pole Controversy: Among Friends

STEFANSSON had a stock response to the question asked with irritating persistence by journalists and lecture audiences: "Have you ever been to the North Pole?" His invariable reply was that since he was not a tourist the journey did not interest him. Once the geographical record had been attained, there were more pressing reasons for travelling in the Arctic. Nevertheless, the polar record was a matter in which he had been personally involved, and sometimes the controversy caused him anxiety and even embarrassment.

Walter Sullivan, science editor for the New York *Times,* called on Stefansson at Dartmouth in March 1959 for an interview about Robert E. Peary in anticipation of the fiftieth anniversary of Peary's discovery of the North Pole. Sullivan hoped to get a fresh slant on the old controversy, and he was not disappointed because Stefansson did have a revelation to make.

To Sullivan's question, "did Peary really get there?" Stefansson replied impatiently that Peary probably had reached the Pole or come close. Except for one point, Peary's record was clear enough, although some experts were involved in petty haggling over a possible error of five or ten miles in the position of the Pole. Years earlier, when *The Friendly Arctic* was published, Stefansson did not express doubts about Peary's achievement, but he emphasized that the most important contribution was that Peary had developed the system by which he, or anyone else, could reach the Pole. The confusion surrounding Peary's record arose from his published narrative of the journey, *The North Pole.* Stefansson explained to Sullivan why the book contained inconsistencies that provoked the critics. It was simple: Peary had employed a ghostwriter, A.E. Thomas, and had neglected to check his work. Thomas knew that there were mistakes and made an effort to iron out the text with Peary, but the explorer was under stress at the time and discouraged because of the uproar over Cook's competing claim and so could not give the narrative proper attention.

In fact, Stefansson confided, Peary had suffered a mental breakdown, and his condition, which in those days would have been considered a disgrace, was kept secret. Much of the subsequent controversy would have been prevented had Peary's illness been acknowledged, but Peary's wife extracted a promise of silence from Stefansson for her lifetime, and according to Stefansson, her daughter Marie "practically exacted the same pledge." The family's determination to maintain silence over Peary's illness bothered Stefansson for a long time. "I think they are both wrong," Stefansson told Sullivan. They "are no real friends of the reputation of their husband or father."[1]

The controversy affected Stefansson, as it did others in his circle, for a number of reasons. In a real sense, explorers and students of exploration lived in the shadow of the polar scandal in much the same way that victims of McCarthy's "Red Scare" in the 1950's now live. Slanderous charges and disputes create deep divisions among colleagues, loyalties are severely tested, and amidst the rancor and discord, there often seems no way of determining the truth to a degree that would satisfy everyone. If the comparison to McCarthyism seems far-fetched, we have only to look at the occasions between 1908 and Sullivan's interview with Stefansson in 1959 when the aging explorer was called upon to address the Peary question. Tiresome as the issue may have become for Stefansson, he had to confront it again and again. For more than fifty years, Stefansson carried a share of the burden the controversy imposed on all those who were concerned with polar exploration. At times he had been optimistic enough to believe that the ghosts might be laid by certain conciliatory actions, but the controversy resisted all such efforts; the matter just stirred up too much emotion, and each side was irretrievably committed to its position.

Stefansson met Peary for the first time in 1907 and 1908, when he carried a message to Peary from some of his Seattle acquaintances concerning Frederick Cook's climb of Mt. McKinley. The people in Seattle who were interested in exploration doubted

Cook's claim to have conquered the mountain and thought Peary should be aware of the suspected fraud because they thought Cook might have ambitions to aim for the North Pole record. As it turned out, Peary did not pay particular attention to the warning.

When Stefansson heard about the North Pole controversy in 1910—a full year after it erupted—he was in the Arctic, and the news disturbed him. If Cook actually had reached the Pole, Stefansson felt he had unfairly stolen a march on Peary, taking the well-deserved credit Peary had earned for his perseverance. Cook had stepped in, as Stefansson put it, to "snatch deftly the wages of another man's toil."[2]

Stefansson subsequently wrote to Peary, describing his theories about living off the land and explaining the flexibility his hunting methods gave him in his explorations. Peary, a touchy man before and after his North Pole troubles, and not known for his graciousness to other explorers, appeared to respect Stefansson's efforts in the Arctic and found occasion to quote Stefansson's opinion that some unsuccessful adventures in exploration indicated incompetence. In 1912 Peary gave the younger explorer a boost by making recommendations to societies that might consider sponsoring Stefansson's new expedition, and after the Canadian Arctic Expedition returned, Peary contributed to the honours bestowed on Stefansson by his presence at the National Geographic Society dinner and by the gracious remarks he made at the time.

Peary died in 1920, and Stefansson was among his honorary pallbearers. By that time, Stefansson had formed a firm friendship with Marie Peary, the explorer's daughter, who was born in the Arctic during one of Peary's expeditions. During their friendship of several years, Marie and her mother talked to Stefansson about Peary's career and the effect the polar controversy had had on his health. Stefansson assured them that he would help preserve Peary's reputation against the attacks of Cook and others.

William Herbert Hobbs and Donald MacMillan, a member of Peary's expedition to the Pole, were among other Peary friends who venerated his cause and liked nothing better than the opportunity to defend it. Hobbs and Stefansson became good friends, but MacMillan and Stefansson did not hit it off; neither had much regard for the other's field achievements, and MacMillan sometimes found occasion to criticize Stefansson publicly.

In a letter to Hobbs written soon after Peary's death, Stefansson referred for the first time to Peary's use of a ghost writer in *Secrets of Polar Travel,* a book written some years after *The North Pole.* Stefansson had been more concerned to explain that although the book argued that it was impossible to find food far out on sea ice, Peary had agreed in conversation that the reason he seldom sighted seals might have been that he had no reason to look for them. Although Stefansson was always concerned about any difference of opinion on the subject of subsistence on sea ice that might undercut his own reputation, he cared about Peary's standing as well and would willingly avoid areas where their opinions conflicted. He warned Hobbs, who was preparing a paper on Peary, not to mention Peary's ignorance of the Eskimo language, and he indicated that he had deleted a reference to Peary's linguistic shortcomings from *The Friendly Arctic* because "it would hurt Mrs. Peary's feelings."[3]

But Stefansson did not think that the inquiry of critics into Peary's record would harm him much, even if they were to question the explorer's attainments. The Peary family, wife and daughter, thought otherwise, and they proved to be as sensitive to criticism as Peary himself. Every critic was assumed to have evil intentions. Even friends, as Hobbs was to find later to his deep regret, were denied access to Peary's papers.

In 1922 Stefansson heard rumours of a plot to impugn Peary's record involving Roald Amundsen. Someone had told him that Amundsen's proposed expedition in the *Maud* might be part of a plan to discredit both Peary and Cook. Stefansson believed that Peary's friends could forestall Amundsen by conceding that Peary had indeed made some mistakes and then defending his spectacular discovery of the Pole.

A year later, Isaiah Bowman, another Peary supporter, asked Stefansson to comment on some questions that had been raised. Stefansson could see no reason to doubt Peary's word—he believed him to be honest and capable of successfully accomplishing whatever he set out to do. The burden of proof, in his opinion, rested on those who contested Peary's claim, and Stefansson had not seen any arguments of substance that could refute Peary's entitlement to the polar record. On the issue of Peary's having sighted Crocker Land, Stefansson was able to distinguish a visual error (confusing clouds and land) from logistical errors (in route and turning point) based on mathematical computations and sextant observations. Stefansson stoutly defended Peary: "[The] one is really a question of whether Peary may have been deceived; the other is a question of whether he may have been a liar. The first possibility we might readily admit, but the second no one is likely to admit who knew him well."[4]

A few years later, after he visited Cook in prison, Amundsen created a sensation by telling the press that Cook's claim seemed to him to be as good as Peary's. Stefansson reacted to this news by sending a telegram to the Associated Press offering to answer Amundsen's charges by disclosing arguments that would refute Cook's claim.

A different aspect of the controversy erupted when J. Gordon Hayes became interested in Peary in the mid-1920's, and he started a correspondence with Stefansson. Hayes published a paper on Peary to which Stefansson politely demurred, remarking that he would not accept Hayes's conclusions "because I know much evidence that hasn't been published and wish it would be released." Hayes then published his *Robert Erwin Peary* in 1929, and in it he quoted Stefansson's statement that he, Hayes, had the best of the argument "insofar as the published evidence was concerned."[5] By deleting Stefansson's clearly stated reservations, Hayes gave a false impression of Stefansson's real opinion. This garbled quotation caused Stefansson a good deal of trouble when his friends Hobbs and Marie Peary read it several years later.

Hayes's book was not the first to attack Peary.[6] As early as 1911, an Englishman named W. Henry Lewin published a book entitled *Did Peary Reach the Pole?* Then, in 1917, Thomas F. Hall, an American mariner and Cook partisan, published his book, *Has the North Pole Been Discovered?* Both authors answered their little questions with a resounding "no" insofar as Peary's claim was concerned. These books had few readers but inconsistencies in Peary's narrative still disturbed a number of people, and they confided their doubts to Stefansson. These sceptics included the well-known British arctic authority, Sir James Wordie, a scientist with Shackleton and a leading exponent of British polar exploration. He told Stefansson that after rereading Peary's books, he felt some doubts about his achievements. Wordie pointed out errors in Peary's ice observations and his more serious mistakes in navigation. The latter he termed "so bad that future critics are certain to turn it down as false."[7] Wordie's opinion carried some weight with Stefansson. He was a recognized expert associated with the Scott Polar Research Institute, and he was not a wild-eyed partisan of Dr. Cook.

Although he was a friend of Peary and his family, Stefansson saw no conflict of interest in exchanging letters with men who held different views. He was very gracious to Thomas F. Hall and encouraged Hall's proposed sequel to his 1917 book: "Don't forget your promise of volume II...just because there may be a hard word or two in it [for me]. There is no pose about this with me...I shall not mind in the least."[8]

There was no year during the 1920's and 1930's in which Stefansson was not called upon at some point to discuss the Peary case. The dispute grew lively in 1934 after an English professor from Yale, Henshaw Ward, published an article that was critical of Peary in the *American Mercury*. Charles Angoff, editor of the magazine, invited Stefansson to comment. Stefansson replied tartly that "I neither want to debate with him [the author] nor discourage you from publishing." Many of Peary's friends, Stefansson told Angoff, tried to forestall any criticism of him because they feared injury to his reputation. Stefansson, however, always urged full disclosure for the same reason that "I am Jeffersonian in the criticism of government. Free speech is less likely to endanger the government than suppression."[9]

Ward's article prompted an exchange of letters. Stefansson suggested that Ward make a complete study of the polar controversy. Ward visited Stefansson in New York and reported him to be "a kindly, patient, scholarly soul. He was wearing a blue blouse-apron as he worked amidst his polar library of 10,000 volumes."[10] Stefansson told Ward that A.E. Thomas was Peary's ghost writer and suggested that Ward confirm this discovery with Thomas himself. Stefansson, however, asked Ward to keep his name out of it.

By this time, Ward had become afflicted with the familiar tendency to paranoia that was common to partisans of Cook and Peary, although, unlike most Peary critics, he did not support Cook either. (He considered both men to be fakes.) Ward simply could not understand Stefansson's attitude. "Why," he wondered, "should Stefansson, who wants Peary defended, also want me to secure a story that would damn Peary?" Why did Stefansson tell him about Thomas and then tell him that the Peary family would never admit to the existence of a ghost writer? "Perhaps," Ward speculated, "he is mean and designing." However, like a good scholar, Ward reread Stefansson's book, *The Standardization of Error,* which he termed "a kind of satire on our ignorance and hypocrisy...He [Stefansson] seems incapable of working plainly or directly."[11]

Unlike Ward, who considered Thomas's role a sensational discovery, Stefansson saw nothing scandalous about Peary having employed a ghost writer. Indeed, he thought the revelation would enable critics to understand parts of the book that were otherwise inexplicable.

Marie Peary and Stefansson were still good friends, and she appreciated most of his criticism of Ward's article (Stefansson had sent her a copy). But she questioned his suggestion to Ward that some unbiased writer ought to get at "the truth." The truth, she insisted is known: "You make me awfully mad sometimes."[12] She did not know, of course, that Stefansson had already told Ward about Thomas.

Stefansson explained that neither he nor Donald MacMillan could write about her father without being accused of bias, while anyone else who was "open-minded, clear-minded, and not lazy" could put forward Peary's case in a favourable light.[13] In Stefansson's opinion, Ward seemed a reasonable man and a fair scholar, and, therefore, a critical article written by Ward, once he had examined all the evidence, would not preclude a finding in Peary's favour.

This explanation, however, did not satisfy Marie Peary, and she showed Stefansson's letter to Henshaw Ward to W.H. Hobbs, who immediately telephoned Stefansson to give him a dressing down. During that conversation, as reported by Stefansson to Isaiah Bowman, Hobbs took the position that the Peary question "has long ago been settled, that only men of ill will study it after such settlement, that Ward is therefore obviously of ill will, and that I am giving aid and comfort to the enemy."[14] Stefansson told Bowman that his efforts to convince Hobbs that Ward seemed open-minded fell on deaf ears. Hobbs suspected malice and would not accept Stefansson's suggestion that Ward had probably formed his opinions from a reading of J. Gordon Hayes's book and that he would give a sounder opinion after doing further research.

Bowman had approved the letter to Ward, and he commiserated with Stefansson: "Hobbs surrounds a problem in which he is intensely interested with a large degree of emotion."[15]

Stefansson brought the simmering "ghost writer" issue to a boil when he told Marie Peary that he intended to write an article about it. Hobbs, who by then had read Hayes's book, tore into Stefansson violently.[16] Only a towering passion and the deepest conviction of his own righteousness could explain why he risked violating their long friendship. Stefansson answered at once, explaining that Hayes had quoted only part of his statement. "I was hoping to convince Hayes that in his own interest he had better not launch his then contemplated book attack on Peary; Hayes would necessarily get the worse of the argument if and when it were decided to reply rather than to continue ignoring the attacks."[17]

When Hobbs replied, it was with disdain: In "allying yourself with the Hayes crowd in all your public writing...and writing the introduction to Mirsky's book, you have done much harm to the cause; your explanation is to me wholly unsatisfactory. If you carry out your proposal to write that Peary's *North Pole* was ghost-written, against all internal evidence to the contrary, you can count me out of any friendly association." How could Stefansson lend support to "vicious attacks" on Peary? "I am not built that way and cannot tolerate it in my friends." Poor angry Hobbs should have known by then that the ghost-writing disclosure did not "run against all internal evidence," which he certainly would discover in the course of his research on Peary.[18]

In reply to this blast, Stefansson struggled to settle the argument on the basis of what would be best for Peary's reputation. There was nothing wrong in Peary's reliance on a ghost writer, he insisted. Furthermore, Thomas's work and other pressures on Peary accounted for most of the debatable points in the book. He argued that it would be in Peary's favour to admit the circumstances of publication, adding that denying the facts deprives Peary of a valid defence and gives his opponents the appearance of criticizing him justly. "I believe it the greatest disservice to Peary's memory to use on his side even in the smallest detail the truth-selecting devices of an advocate," Stefansson asserted. "He will not occupy the place he deserves in history till his record is fully and impartially studied and published."[19]

Marie Peary's fear of the revelation that her father employed a ghost writer was not entirely unreasonable. She knew that some people would assume "that if Peary passed off a book which he did not write as his own, he [also] might well claim to discover the Pole when he didn't." Less reasonably, however, Marie also insisted that evidence of Thomas and Peary's publisher actually proved that the explorer wrote what she referred to as "the technical parts" of the book. Even if she could not convince Stefansson, she intended to persevere in this position with the proposed publishers of Stefansson's article, and she told him emphatically that "it will only be published against our expressed wishes, an act of deliberate unfriendliness of which I cannot believe, after the evidence of so many years, that you are capable."[20]

After receiving Marie Peary's ultimatum, Stefansson poured out his frustration to another friend: "These last days I have felt between grief and despair though becoming more convinced the more I looked into it that, through unwillingness to use the Thomas-Morrow defense [William Morrow was the editor of *The North Pole* and had explained Thomas's part in it], the Peary family are, so far as possible with a sound case, delivering the Admiral's reputation into the hands of his enemies."[21]

Stefansson sent an extract of this letter to Marie Peary, declaring that it was his "last statement on this subject." He reminded her that it had been understood for many years between them that he was to give his best efforts to Peary's defence if the occasion ever came, and he warned her, "the occasion in my judgment is here." He urged Marie to send him definite word. "I have been devoting practically my whole time and energy to this now for several weeks and don't want to spend any more time if the result is merely to be the growth of animosities and the splitting of forces."[22]

Marie replied with the definite word: her father did not need a champion, she thundered, and, to his dismay, she dismissed her erstwhile friend. Although Marie Peary did not give Hobbs credit for it, his intransigence pleased her more than did Stefansson's appeal for full disclosure.

Meanwhile, Hobbs prepared to enter the lists against Hayes, Ward, and William Shea (another writer who was supposed to be writing an exposé of Peary) by writing a biography of Peary himself. It was an unfortunate decision, which would only add one more biased and unreliable tome of special pleading to the Cook-Peary bibliography.[23] Hobbs was a distinguished geologist and a competent writer, yet he was foolish to commit himself to biographical research without the assurance of Marie Peary that the Peary papers would be opened to him. And he was even more foolish to push on when the terrible truth finally dawned. But in January of 1935, Hobbs felt pleased with himself and could analyse Stefansson's fuss over the Thomas disclosure with confidence. According to Hobbs, Stefansson got himself into a bad hole when he told Hayes that he had had "the best of the Peary argument."[24] As an excuse, Hobbs explained, Stefansson had invented the ghost writer story.

A month later, Hobbs mellowed a little towards Stefansson. He agreed with Marie Peary that Stefansson was really loyal to her father, "and if he would only distinguish between intellectually honest attacks and blackmail he would be a great asset." He eventually apologized to Stefansson, but maintained that the latter had harmed Peary's reputation, and he advised him sternly, "it is more than ever important that you print in some good magazine an article which sets forth your *real position*."[25]

Marie Peary later reaffirmed her trust in Stefansson, but subsequent events indicate she might not have been entirely confident about him after all. She had been worried about Cook ever since 1930, when he was released from jail after his oil stock fraud conviction. After his parole period was over, it seemed likely that he would stir up the smoldering dispute once more. Indeed, it may have been Hobbs's campaign to protest Cook's parole that first caused him and Marie to question Stefansson's loyalty. Stefansson refused to join the protest, explaining: "It seems to me that as friends of Peary's we are interested in Dr. Cook's moral branding as an untruthful person, not in his physical incarceration." Stefansson offered to defend Peary whenever it was necessary, but he hoped Hobbs would "understand sympathetically this distinction which I make between Dr. Cook as a human being and as a candidate for a position among explorers."[26]

As Hobbs laboured over his book, he was, as he described it, "terribly set back" when Marie told him her mother would not allow him to use Peary's papers. Such documents should not be hidden away, he argued, but to no avail. Marie complained to Stefansson that she was "having a devil of a time with Hobbs who is trying to browbeat me into letting him go over all of Dad's papers, correspondence as well as records and diaries. But I am not the browbeaten type." Hobbs put a good face on the matter to Marie, agreeing that the biography would be stronger "without any claim of connection with the family."[27]

Biographers tend to develop animosities toward other writers who differ in their assessments of their subjects. Hobbs's venom towards Peary's critics, however, upset even his friends. In 1935 the deaths of three of Peary's critics within a month was a cause for Hobbs to celebrate. When General Adolphus Greely died in October, Hobbs crowed, "We certainly should rejoice over the demise of that old humbug." Then Ward died: "Hurrah," exulted Hobbs, noting with delight that Ward's book against Peary is "apparently in no completed condition." November brought the best news of all: Hobbs heard that Hayes "is soon to die from cancer, so we are not likely to have much more trouble from him."[28]

A year after Hayes's death, Hobbs published his biography of Peary. Isaiah Bowman told Marie Peary that Hobbs's emotions had coloured his facts and judgments, and that although nothing new was brought to light in the book, "it will help Peary's reputation." Bowman had earlier followed Stefansson's lead in urging Marie to allow free access to her father's papers, but now he said the book "shows he would have simply confused issues if allowed to use" them.[29] Hobbs's efforts to maintain the existence of Crocker Land dismayed Bowman and Stefansson. But the book did venerate Peary and held its place for years as the standard biography.

Stefansson, of course, was expected to review the book, and although he undoubtedly remembered Hobbs's glowing review of *The Friendly Arctic* years earlier, he could not bring himself to do so. "Hobbs," Stefansson fretted, wrote like an attorney defending "an innocent client in such a way as to prevent the jury from being unanimous in their verdict of 'Not Guilty.' "[30] He quietly suggested to Hobbs that his publisher might issue a promotional statement over Stefansson's signature, since it would be some time before he would be able to review the book.

In 1930 Marie Peary denounced Stefansson again on two counts. At the instigation of Richard Finnie, Stefansson and others in the Explorers Club decided that Matt Henson, Peary's black travelling companion to the Pole, had been neglected, and they remedied the oversight by awarding him a medal. Congress was also petitioned to give Henson the Distinguished Service Medal. Bob Bartlett, who had not gone the entire way to the Pole as Henson had, was the only companion Peary had recommended for this medal. Bartlett, however, was a white man. Marie was outraged: Henson had not been entirely loyal to Peary, yet Peary, in her opinion, had amply rewarded him by securing an appointment for him as messenger with the U.S. Custom House in Manhattan.[31] Was the Explorers Club questioning her father's generosity? she demanded. The award, she raged, amounted to "reverse race hysteria."[32]

For Marie Peary and her mother, the worst was yet to come. The Explorers Club invited them to a meeting on 6 April 1939 for the formal unveiling of Peary's portrait, on the occasion of the anniversary of Peary's discovery of the Pole. Peary was to be honoured both for his achievement and for being a past president of the club.

To the mortification of the Peary women, an entire row of portraits of past presidents was unveiled at the same time—and there was Cook's portrait next to Peary's! Marie blamed Stefansson for this "trickery," even though he had missed the unveiling—by design, she supposed.[33] After some months' silence, Marie lashed out again at Stefansson for championing Cook and Henson and protested to her friends that "no one ever yet got a direct, clean cut statement from him."[34]

As the years passed, the tension between Marie, Hobbs, and Stefansson over the Peary issue did not diminish. In 1944 a publisher suggested to Stefansson that he should write a book on Cook, and he or someone else must have mentioned the suggestion to Marie. Her explosion was predictable: "I am just as horrified as Professor Hobbs." Why, she raged, should Stefansson waste his time dignifying a charlatan by writing a book on him? "I have always defended you indignantly against those who said you were a seeker after publicity," she reminded Stefansson, "but now I am beginning to wonder."[35]

There is a lesson to be learned in examining the effect of the Peary-Cook affair on Stefansson's career: the foregoing only touches on some of the highlights. The polar controversy still rumbles on today, even though all of the combatants discussed here have been dead for years. In 1973 a scholarly treatment of the controversy proved devastating to the reputations of both Peary and Cook, and yet a determined band of Cook champions, the Doctor Frederick A. Cook Society, has met on several occasions in upstate New York in an effort to rehabilitate Cook's tarnished reputation.[36]

Peary's correspondence is now available to researchers in the Center for Polar Archives in the National Archives, and the facts underlying *The North Pole* are becoming clearer. Thomas's role as Peary's ghost writer was limited because the only resource material he had was a series of articles that Peary narrated in 1909-10 for *Hampton's Magazine*. These articles were written by Elsa Pedersen, who used only the records that Peary made available to her at the time.[37]

Walter Sullivan's interview with Stefansson on the fiftieth anniversary of Peary's discovery of the Pole also commemorated the fifty years of Stefansson's dilemma in trying at once to serve truth, defend Peary's reputation, and avoid offending the Peary family. And Stefansson loyally kept trying, but his efforts at diplomacy only succeeded in arousing suspicion in both pro- and anti-Peary camps. Perhaps his quandary was the inevitable consequence of such a tangle of competing aims.

CHAPTER 22

Projects and Books

STEFANSSON'S integrity of purpose was reflected in his manner of living: he had no hobbies and he took no vacations. He felt that his work was so enjoyable that he preferred doing it to anything else.

Other people's ideas of what constituted recreation also puzzled Stefansson. Although hunting had been essential for survival in the Arctic, the notion of hunting for sport was lost on him, and he never fired a rifle after 1917. Conversation and study were his joys, and before he went to sleep at night he indulged himself by reading lighter books—often detective fiction. Occasionally he would see a play or movie, attend a lecture or, under great compulsion, a concert. Sports bored him, although the record shows that he watched football games in college. His time was not difficult to account for, filled as it was with people, books, writing, and the heavy drain of constant travel.

Stefansson had important work during the 1930's, and he no longer professed a yearning for exploration in the field. Contracts with the government gave him a magnificent opportunity to compile a comprehensive picture of northern lands. At one point he planned to write five books: a book of general information about the North, followed by four guidebooks on Alaska, Canada, Greenland, and the Soviet Union north of 62 degrees latitude. These plans were not entirely realized, but he did publish some books in the 1930's and later completed *The Arctic Manual,* which was published in 1940.

Stefansson always earned a good income, but his book-buying, salaries for his staff, and living expenses absorbed whatever he made. In 1940 he earned about $22,000. However, only $3,000 of this amount came from lecturing, which earlier had been his chief source of income. The rest came from book royalties, magazine articles, government consulting fees for work on his polar bibliography and reports on northern countries.

His ever-expanding library was the centre of Stefansson's world. From the late 1930's the collection was housed in three adjoining four-room apartments in the Village. He and his staff of librarians welcomed anyone interested in polar research, as well as his many acquaintances from around the world. At age sixty he struck observers as "a formidable figure, tall and heavy, with rough features and an abundant, swirling shock of grey hair." Behind his tortoise-shell glasses, his eyes would glint with amusement when he would discuss "one of the many fallacious ideas he thinks are abroad in the world today. He wears a patient smile and rather resembles a friendly evangelist."[1]

Stefansson would receive his visitors seated behind a desk that was placed on a low platform. As he talked, or when he needed a reference, he would stalk around the library to find the book or magazine article that would verify his point. Books were everywhere, even under the kitchen sink and stacked between spices and baking soda on his kitchen shelves.

Stefansson also played a role in the development of polar aviation as a consultant to Pan American Airways. Pan American became interested in northern routes in 1932, after acquiring Alaska Airways, Pacific International Airways, and the North Atlantic operations of Transamerican Airlines. The airline retained Stefansson to advise them on routes to Europe via Greenland and Iceland and to assist in negotiations with the Norwegian, Swedish, Icelandic, and Soviet governments for servicing polar flights. He also helped Charles Lindbergh prepare for a survey of possible air routes through Alaska to Asia. Consulting was an ideal occupation, because he could easily fit it in without any conflict with his lecture engagements and writing.

Stefansson often joked about the modesty that people seemed to expect of explorers, and he denied having any claim to that over-rated virtue himself. He insisted that he was not a hero and therefore should not be required to appear modest. But joking aside, he did regard himself as an expert on all matters relating to the Arctic and did not hesitate to set out his credentials as a preliminary to any discussion. No other explorer, not even Peary, had wintered as many years in the North as he, and his field work formed the basis of his claim to expertise. It was not easy for him to admit that any of his projects were misdirected, even those that miscarried, like the Wrangel Island colonization scheme and the Baffin Island reindeer experiment; that they may have been ill-conceived or inadequately prepared, he would never admit. A more self-effacing demeanour might have been commendable in some instances, but given the virulent attacks he had suffered, his reluctance to admit error can perhaps be understood. He always responded to criticism with the relish of a good debater and skilled advocate. When he argued on subjects that were within his field of expertise, he would deploy all the gifts of persuasion at his command, and those gifts were formidable.

Polar exploration entered a new phase after Stefansson retired from field work. New technology, particularly aircraft, supplemented or replaced the dog team. The commencement of the age of polar exploration by air did nothing to reduce public interest in exploration or to stop the rivalry among adventurers. On the contrary, if anything the competition became more intensified, as if all participants understood that the new technology would soon chart all unknown areas on the map. Sweeping flights over both poles would finally put an end to the grand old game. If a man wanted to enter the sweepstakes for the sake of glory, now was the time for him to get moving!

Polar rivalry, as always, was intensified by the press. Wilkins, Richard Byrd, and Lincoln Ellsworth were leading newsmakers, and they were given every encouragement by the papers to discuss their future plans and comment on the achievements of others. Stefansson, as might be expected, was frequently in the news. He was interviewed often because he was readily available, and although he was gracious enough in his remarks about other explorers, an aura of controversy continued to hover over him. In a word, Stefansson made good copy.

All that Stefansson learned about the North reinforced his early fascination with the comprehensiveness of knowledge. Truth and unity existed, yet there was such a yawning gap between intellectual truth and the popular conception of it. Why is this so? he asked himself again and again. He wanted to explore in order to reveal this mystery, and the question to him was almost more important than discovering new lands. What were the impediments to understanding truth?

In his lectures and in his delightful book, *Adventures in Error* (1936), Stefansson took up the question of these comfortable beliefs. He had great fun exposing some simplistic popular images of the North and its peoples. Eskimos, he observed, were studied in the early grades of school in most countries. "In my youth," he remarked ironically, "I learned many strange things concerning them." There was some confusion concerning geographical location, but it was generally agreed that all Eskimos were alike and lived in the same place. "The Eskimos are a godsend to the schools. From their simplicity you can get a parallel to the simplicity of our own remote ancestors and also a contrast to the multiplicities of civilization." Eskimoland is simple too—it is always cold, just as lands to the south are always hot. These truths impress "upon the child-mind that there is a balance and symmetry in nature, which has been a favorite doctrine since Greek times."[2]

According to our educators, Stefansson continued, the Eskimo's growth is stunted by the cold. "In their bitter struggle to eke out the scantiest of livings they cower, wrapped in furs, inside huts of snow which give them bare shelter from the furious Arctic blizzards." He added that they live on blubber and drink oil, with which they also grease their bodies. Meat is eaten raw and, strangely enough, they thrive on a diet that is not balanced. "But, marvelous to relate, in spite of all these things, the Eskimos are a jolly, happy little people. They serve thus a double moral purpose." They help us, and, "the gruesome view of their land, of their life, makes us better contented with ours; we see from their happiness under conditions of misery that really it isn't so bad, in comparison, to be poor and jobless down here. We should all, therefore, be contented and happy."[3]

Stefansson went on to relate the hoax perpetuated by an Icelandic woman, Olaf Krarer, after she came to America. Krarer was a dwarf, but she was able to get a job as a waitress in a town in North Dakota. The townsfolk did not know much about Iceland, yet they "knew" it was inhabited by Eskimos. Krarer, a proud Nordic woman, disputed the local theory, but to no avail. Finally, she stopped protesting, and one day she was offered five dollars to speak about the Eskimo to young people in a church group. She accepted the invitation, did some hasty research, and concocted a story about her childhood. She was well received and soon went on to bigger things—the lecture platform and the circus. As an "Eskimo" she made a fair living for herself, but, what was more important, was a lasting influence on American education and thought.

Stefansson told how he had discovered a similarity between the stories that Krarer told and the peculiar views about Eskimos that were held in Teachers' College at Columbia University. Naturally, he wanted to track down the source of these curious theories, and he was eventually successful. He found a book entitled *Eskimo Stories,* in which the author acknowledged her debt to Krarer's childhood memories. What amused Stefansson most was that the author of *Eskimo Stories* was an educator who had found nothing to question in these and other bits of nonsense. Other would-be educators were just as gullible. A major New York publisher who had no suspicions either kept the book in print and selling briskly for forty years.

Stefansson's research into this hoax was thorough, as it was in the case of another fable that caught his eye about the same time. The latter was the amazing story of a best-selling book entitled *Thirty Years in the Golden North* by Jan Welzl. The book purported to be the memoir of an arctic character who lived on the New Siberian Islands during the winter and ventured forth every spring on trading and prospecting journeys as far east as the Yukon valley. While the Book of the Month Club was considering *Thirty Years* for inclusion in its list, the editor of the American edition asked Stefansson to read and comment on it. Stefansson offered to endorse it if it were promoted as a parody. The editor protested that the book was not a parody at all, but the genuine reminiscences of an actual person. If this were so, Stefansson innocently inquired, then why did the writer choose the uninhabited New Siberian Islands as a residence? He pointed out some of the more extravagant of the author's tall tales:

During the great frost, spittle freezes before it has reached the ground and it makes a curious cracking noise as it drops....On our island Eskimo girls are mature as a rule at the age of six....She generally has her first child between six and eight....After the child is born, the mother's breasts swell and from that time onwards the Eskimo woman has milk all her life. That is why she will nurse at any time and anybody, often adults come and feed on her milk.[4]

Then there were Welzl's experiences as a mail carrier. He assured his readers that he was accustomed to fastening twenty-four sledges together and harnessing a team of 350 dogs. The lead dog would be a good half mile in front of the first sledge and a thirty-man crew would man the sledges. At times the author seemed to be parodying Stefansson, for instance, when he claimed that he had suffered from scurvy twice because of his exclusively meat diet: "You have to be careful and never eat half-raw meat or else you'll catch all sorts of complaints....It is a good thing to preserve meat in vinegar, which drives out all the gamey taste, or so the polar settlers believe."[5]

Welzl rounded out his scurvy story with a real whopper: "I have heard that it is a good thing to eat raw potatoes for scurvy. But we put hot mashed potatoes between our teeth, keep them there for half an hour, carefully spit them out so as not to spit the teeth with them, and so on the whole day. This does a lot of good."[6]

Then there was the threat of frostbite: according to Welzl, often a man's nose would become frozen and he would ask someone to pull it off! However, there was a remedy for this disfigurement—a local prophet would graft skin taken from Eskimo children on the spot. Generally the children would die as a result of the operation, but, he said, no one seemed to mind.

Curious things would happen when men died. "Few people die a natural death. But when they die, a black bird, which they call the 'death bird,' comes flying up....It flies up, squats down and screeches three times, and then flies away. Before very long somebody in the neighborhood dies."[7]

After writing his review, Stefansson was astonished to find that the book's "respectable publisher" did not withdraw it immediately, and he was even more surprised when the book was selected by the Book of the Month Club. In the opinion of one of the club's judges, "the preposterous story was a genuine account of experiences that might have taken place." This same judge reviewed the book for the Saturday Review of Literature, and Stefansson reported gleefully, "he cited as impressive, incidents described in Welzl's book that would make anyone familiar with the Arctic roar with laughter."[8]

Other reviewers were equally gullible. The New Republic found the book "as striking a record of arctic adventure as has ever been written and gives a more intimate and solid feeling of arctic life than even the best books on arctic exploration though it lacks the breadth and intelligence of their observation."[9]

With the help of the Book of the Month Club, 150,000 copies

of Welzl's book were sold. By this time, however, Stefansson was annoyed. The incident reflected prevailing misconceptions about the North that he had devoted all his energies to correcting. Not only did the book reinforce hoary myths, but its very acceptance as an authentic memoir emphasized the reluctance of the public to have its more fantastic illusions corrected. Sometimes it seemed to a disillusioned Stefansson that people actually preferred familiar, cherished myths to the truth—even when confronted with their patent irrationality.

Jan Welzl was a real person—a Czech who lived in Dawson City, Yukon Territory. He had had an adventurous life in the North. Apparently on a trip to his homeland he had given a garbled interview to a couple of journalists, who then concocted *Thirty Years in the Golden North* on the basis of his account. In time Welzl heard about the best seller and wrote Stefansson asking for help. Welzl had received no payment or royalties from the book, and he was aged and destitute. With his usual generosity, Stefansson wrote to the book's American and European publishers; both denied any obligation.

Also during these years of depression, under the supervision of the U.S. Army Air Corps, Stefansson was commissioned in 1935 to use his library and staff to compile a report on living and military operating conditions in the Arctic. In three years a report of some two million words was submitted. A secondary product was a book of general information, *The Arctic Manual*, published in 1944.

Aside from the Arctic information compilations, Stefansson worked for the American government on other projects in the 1930's and during World War II. He was always keen for ideas to develop his library and staff into a major research centre along the lines of the Scott Polar Research Institute in Cambridge, England, but he found that government interest in the project was difficult to maintain. For a time, a scheme for co-ordinating information on navigating the Northwest Passage occupied Stefansson, U.S. Navy Commander Edward H. Smith, and Richard S. Finnie, but no headway could be made against the indifference of Canadian and American officials. Canadians had historic reasons for being suspicious of American interest in their territorial waters, and neither the U. S. State Department nor the military commands were sufficiently intrigued to promote the concept of a co-ordinated northern transportation system resembling that of the Soviets over the Northeast Passage.

In 1938-39, another project that was even more dear to Stefansson's heart was an abortive effort of the Explorers Club, the Works Progress Administration [W.P.A.], and the Stefansson library to produce an arctic bibliography. The W.P.A. had supported many scholarly and artistic programmes during the Depression, including state guidebooks and post office murals. Initially, the idea for the bibliography seemed a good one to New York area officials. In its second year, over one hundred clerical workers were employed on the project. Stefansson exulted at the prospect of compiling this monument of bibliographic information, beginning with the earliest references to the Arctic in classical literature and continuing to the present. Then, out of the blue, the W.P.A. cancelled the project, the New York director having decided that bibliographical work was an esoteric boondoggle.

Stefansson reacted to this obstacle, as he usually did, by going over the head of the man in charge. He won the battle briefly with the help of friends in Washington, but lost in the end when the local officials prevailed. Stefansson blamed himself for the misfortune, realizing that he should have made more of an effort to convince the W.P.A. supervisor of the bibliography's worth. His defeat at the hands of lower level bureaucrats was not a unique experience for him either in the United States or Canada; he lost as many battles as he won.

In the fall of 1940, the U.S. War Department asked Stefansson to serve as consultant to General Simon Bolivar Buckner, the newly appointed head of the Alaska Defense Command, who sought his advice on aspects of the arctic environment that might affect military construction. Stefansson flew from Seattle to Juneau and then on to Anchorage where he met Buckner. With Buckner's encouragement, Stefansson once more urged the government to establish a centre of arctic studies that would utilize his polar library, and this time the idea caught on. In October 1941 he was offered a contract to advise the Office of the Coordinator of Information. His first memorandum dealt with petroleum resources for Alaska, and it was the genesis of what became the famous Canol project, a pipeline built during the war to carry oil from Norman Wells to Whitehorse and Skagway. The Canol project proved to be very expensive for what it actually accomplished, and Stefansson later was careful to claim credit only for the conception of the idea.

Stefansson was also disappointed by the route the American and Canadian governments chose for the Alcan highway linking

Canada and Alaska. He had argued that the road should run from Edmonton to Norman Wells, then down the Mackenzie River valley, crossing over to Dawson and then following the Yukon River to Whitehorse. Instead, in 1942, the army chose a rugged route connecting the already established air bases for ferrying planes to Alaska and Siberia, pushing the construction through at breakneck speed. The road was a far cry from the Great Circle Route that Stefansson advocated, and it was equally unsatisfactory to Alaskans, who urged a route nearer the coast to avoid cutting southeastern Alaska off from the interior. In spite of much criticism, the road, now called the Alaska Highway, was built at a cost of $138 million. Stefansson sardonically praised its scenic virtues and liked to point out its value to tourists who, when they arrived in Alaska, would consume freight that had been shipped by rail all the way to the Pacific Coast, then north by sea—an uneconomic system that served to maintain the dominance of coastal cities over Alaskan trade.

By invading the Aleutian Islands, the Japanese demonstrated that they had a greater understanding of the realities of northern geography than did the American military. Although the Japanese intended to create no more than a diversionary campaign, the result was a vast build-up of Alaskan defences which, supplemented later by the Distant Early Warning stations along the Bering Sea and Arctic coasts, substantially developed the territory.

In 1942 Stefansson was asked to advise the Quartermaster General's office about the possible use of pemmican for military rations. This assignment particularly pleased him, and he and some others set up an experiment to establish the value of fatty pemmican as a weather ration for the tropics. They proved the value of pemmican as an emergency ration, at least to their own satisfaction, but professional nutritionists and family doctors protested. In the end, the military decided to retain its traditional diet in spite of all the evidence of pemmican's high food value and the obvious advantage of its slight bulk. "The armed forces went to a great deal of trouble to get my advice, but made no effort to take it," complained Stefansson, afterwards observing that most experts shared similar experiences with the military.[10] Stefansson and others were asked to advise the Quartermaster General on arctic clothing as well, and those less controversial recommendations met with less resistance.

Another consulting assignment, this time in 1943 for the Army Air Force, called for a visit to air bases of the North Atlantic Wing, travelling from Maine to Labrador and across the Canadian Arctic to Frobisher Bay. This time, Stefansson's advice was sought on northern rescue techniques and emergency pemmican rations. After writing reports covering his various observations, Stefansson was dispatched to Camp Buckley, Colorado, where he joined his friend the mountaineer, naturalist, and painter Belmore Browne in giving a mountain-climbing course to officers. This was not Stefansson's first military work in Colorado; earlier that same year he had given instruction in camping techniques to mountain and winter warfare troops at Camp Hale.

Stefansson's diaries of these journeys resemble, both in detailed observation and lively curiosity, those he had kept during his exploration years in the Arctic. The diaries also reveal his interest in the people he met and worked with such as Browne, Captain Alan Innes-Taylor, a Canadian who had wide northern experience with the RCMP, and who also handled Richard Byrd's dogs in Antarctica, and other professionals whom he encountered in his travels.

Stefansson's wartime assignments, along with his research work, writing, and speaking, kept him busy enough. As with the work he had done in the 1930's, there were frustrations with the government, but his was a small role, as he well realized. Had the Arctic loomed larger in defence plans, he might have been asked to take on more responsibility and sacrifice some of his independence. As chief of a major northern bureau of government for instance (had such a government department existed), he would have had the chance to push his innovative programmes through. Even then, his frustrations would probably have been greater than his accomplishments. If Stefansson had been a citizen of the Soviet Union and in good favour (which would have been highly unlikely), he might have headed the General Administration of the Northern Sea Route. The original Soviet supervisor of this department was Otto Yulievich Schmidt, who, according to Stefansson's information, was virtually the ruler of all the territory north of 62 degrees latitude. Schmidt's responsibilities included air, sea, and land transportation; building radio stations and scientific and administration centres; surveying rivers and harbours; and laying out sea traffic lanes for northern shipping. His department was brilliantly successful, but it is unlikely that Stefansson would have envied him the task of managing a vast bureaucracy. In any event, there was never any real danger that either Canada or the United States would attempt to duplicate the Siberian effort, or that if such a department were contemplated, that Stefansson would have been a candidate for director.

The academic world had more appeal to one of Stefansson's scholarly persuasion, and he admitted to having had "several narrow escapes from the pack ice of academic life."[11] But an administrative position or a professorship would not have given him a greater opportunity for doing what he wished to do, and such an appointment might even have curtailed his proselytizing for northern development. In any case, no American university showed much interest in northern studies during the pre-World War II years, nor did any in Canada until much later. So, happily, Stefansson managed to escape both academy and bureaucracy. As a freelancer, he had more freedom, although less financial security; but for a confident man who loved his work and was well-accustomed to making his own way, it was a good occupation.

At war's end, Stefansson, now sixty-six, kept up his customary pace. In 1946 he published *Not by Bread Alone,* a treatise that reviewed the theory and practice of western civilization on the subject of diet. He drew upon his personal experiences in the Arctic and in an experiment at Bellevue Hospital for theoretical support. *The Fat of the Land,* an enlarged version of *Not by Bread Alone,* was published in 1956. There was some controversy over the theories expounded in *Not by Bread Alone* that pleased Stefansson, who would have enjoyed even more of it. Controversy helped to spread his ideas and also sold books. His central argument was that the popular belief that human beings require a balanced food intake is nonsense. In Stefansson's opinion, people could be just as healthy subsisting solely on meat.

To demonstrate his theory, Stefansson and Karsten Andersen, a veteran of the Canadian Arctic Expedition, had taken part in a yearlong experiment beginning on 28 February 1927 at New York's Bellevue Hospital. For the first six months they slept at the hospital and during the first six weeks they had to be under supervision there at all times. They were allowed to live in a house outside the city for the second six months. "The purpose of the test was to learn the truth," wrote Stefansson later. "This was a time when lean meat was looked upon by many as unwholesome. Animal protein was supposed to lead to hardening of the arteries, high blood pressure, and breakdown of the kidneys—in short, to bring on premature old age."[12]

Doctors at Bellevue observed and tested the two men for a time while they ate normal fare, and then they switched to a meat diet. In the course of the experiment, the subjects ate various cuts of meat, as much as they liked, but no other food. Their daily caloric intake varied between 2,600 and 2,800, 80 per cent of which came from fat and 20 per cent from lean meat.

Stefansson was amused to note that some of the medical men assumed that he would be unable to confine himself to the all-meat diet; they were sure the explorers' friends would sneak other food into the hospital. And, Stefansson chuckled, "personal friends, especially women, were worried that we were making ourselves ridiculous by being experimented on like animals."[13] After a year passed the doctors and other interested scientists agreed that the two men were in good health—or, at least as good as they had been before they went on the meat diet. Stefansson himself was certain that he was in better health. But he admitted, "To me this had been an anthropological and physiological study, and in it I was not impartial."[14]

Stefansson did not have any difficulty publishing his books about the diet with Macmillan. The American Meat Institute, which subsidized the experiment through the Russell Sage Foundation, distributed a number of copies for promotional purposes.

In 1947, *Great Adventures and Explorations* was published, a book that went through several printings. This anthology, which drew upon the narratives of explorers to all parts of the world, was laced with Stefansson's editorial comments. It was his nineteenth book for adults (in the 1920's he had written four children's books in collaboration with Violet Irwin and Julia Schwartz) and a labour of love. In this "outline history of the world, told by its chief discoverers from Pytheas to Peary," the author found scope for expressing his views of the men, good and bad, noble and despicable, whose discoveries had filled in the maps.[15] He pointed out the limitations of genius, vision, skill, and "even mere competence" in some explorers, but gave generous praise to more efficient explorers, early and modern.

Great Adventures is a useful summation of Stefansson's evaluation of other explorers, and it shows his fairness in assessing their achievements. Although he rated Scott's last expedition as the noblest effort in history, for example, he also mentioned what Scott knew, or should have known, about scurvy from McClintock, Nansen, and others.

CHAPTER 23

Marriage and Politics

STEFANSSON lived in New York's Greenwich Village briefly in 1907 between his first and second arctic expeditions, and he liked its atmosphere and convenient location. When he returned to New York in 1918, he lived for several years at the Harvard Club, checking into hotels when his club rooms were needed for transient members (for whom the rooms were intended), then moving back when his quarters again became available. Since he also travelled much of the time on the lecture circuit, the arrangement suited him, even though it meant frequently having to move his growing book collection and other possessions into storage.

The arrangement with the Harvard Club annoyed Stefansson's friend and advance man, D. M. LeBourdais, more than it did the itinerant bachelor. In 1925 Le Bourdais eventually talked the explorer into taking an apartment, and he found a suitable one at 17 Grove Street. Stefansson lived in the Village for the next twenty-five years, moving from Grove to Bedford Street as more space for his books was required and finally ending up at St. Luke's Place.

Stefansson's marriage in 1941 to Evelyn Baird surprised his friends, who had long since decided that he would always remain a bachelor. The couple first met in the late 1930's at Romany Marie's—a famous Greenwich Village restaurant and gathering place for artists and writers—when Evelyn was an art student. She knew who Stefansson was long before meeting him—the famous explorer and writer, tall and distinguished looking, who walked with "the rolling gait of a sailor. Hatless and coatless whatever the weather, his thick mane of white hair blowing in the wind."[1]

Many writers have recorded their reminiscences of Greenwich Village during the 1920's and 1930's. Poets and poseurs vied with painters and publishers for the cultural spotlight. In the Village, artists from other parts of the country could easily renew old acquaintances and strike up new ones, perhaps at a party in someone's apartment. Friendships were easy in the Village, invitations abounded, conversation centred in the current *cause célèbre*, artistic or political, and there was always diverting gossip about the theatre, galleries, and editorial offices.

Romany Marie's place was the heart of Village intellectual and social life. Stefansson particularly liked the atmosphere of this unique restaurant. Evenings spent there were a refreshing contrast to days occupied with research, writing, and constant meetings with scientists, politicians, military men, editors, and northern hands. Poetry and music could be heard at Marie's in a pleasantly informal setting. Although Stefansson's taste did not extend to serious concert music, hearing Paul Robeson sing or Bob Edwards accompany one of his own pieces on a ukulele fashioned from a cigar box was diverting. Harry Kemp, the tramp poet, also fascinated Stefansson. Both men were travellers, but of a vastly different order. Kemp loved to regale his listeners with recitations of his own and others' poetry, enjoying the spotlight much more than others who were more gifted.

Romany Marie liked to dress as a gypsy and pretended to be one. Born in Romania, she married Damon Marchand, and the couple ran the cafe together. Marie was a buxom, flamboyant, charming woman, invariably generous to lost souls like Eugene O'Neill, whom she fed nightly in her kitchen during his alcoholic winter of 1916-17.

Marie served only tea and coffee, caring more for the pleasure of her guests than for profit. An indigent or would-be writer, sitting over a cup of coffee all evening, was as welcome to her as a diner. Marie's place, during her reign, captured the finest spirit of Village life, and a number of people who enjoyed her generosity have recorded their impressions of the singular venture. Marie had a rare talent for matchmaking among her friends, and, of course, she had a hand in the Evelyn Baird-Vilhjalmur Stefansson romance.

In 1939, Stefansson recommended Evelyn for a job at the Iceland Pavilion of the World's Fair. This opportunity made her an admirer of the little nation that honoured Stefansson as its favourite son. In that same year she joined the staff of the Stefansson Library at

67 Morton Street. With her quick intelligence, wit, and her interests in social and political issues, she added a new dimension to his coterie. She plunged into reading books on the Arctic, learned to type, and kept Stefansson posted on New York events while he was on the lecture circuit, showing both vigour and committed enthusiasm. Obviously, her intellectual qualities appealed to Stefansson. As a young woman she had a unique driving force which has not declined: in the mid-1970's, she completed her training in psychiatric therapy and also mastered French, just as she had become a skilled writer, editor, and librarian under Stefansson's tutelage.

At the first meeting of Evelyn and Stefansson, she was married to Bil Baird, a puppeteer with whom she had toured the country. Stefansson still had a close relationship with novelist Fanny Hurst—a romance of many years' standing. But Evelyn's vivaciousness attracted him, particularly her ability to sing folk songs effectively even in languages she did not know. For a time, she sang in a Broadway restaurant, the French Casino, where she was billed as a French country girl who specialized in old French songs and the kind of modern tunes popularized by Maurice Chevalier.

Evelyn Baird was, as Stefansson wrote in *Discovery,* "a superb human being," and he also found her an extremely attractive woman.[2] As it turned out, he was not such a confirmed bachelor as he had thought. From expressions of surprise ("almost too good to be true, that we work so well together," he wrote), he began to anticipate a closer union—"a subconscious dream of mine that is developing into a reality." After some months of a close relationship he confessed to her, "I love you beyond anything I have experienced up to the limit I can conceive."[3]

By November, 1940, the couple planned to marry and move away from New York to more rustic surroundings. Stefansson wrote to Evelyn from Anchorage, Alaska, where he was advising the American military. He discussed Alaskan land prices: land seemed expensive, he wrote, "and hard to clear. In a way I wish we had a farm here but prefer Vermont for us."[4]

In 1941, after their April marriage, the Stefanssons moved to Dearing Farm in Vermont. Olive Rathbun Wilcox, still Stefansson's mainstay as secretary-business manager-editor, remained in New York where her husband taught, except for the summers they spent at their own place in Vermont. The arrangement worked well, since much of Stefansson's business had to be conducted in the city.

Shortly before they moved to Vermont, the *New Yorker,* justly famed for its biographical profiles, published a two-part piece on Stefansson by Robert Lewis Taylor. Taylor's subject was then sixty-one years old, "tall and heavy, with a barrel chest, thick gray hair, and eyes that squint slightly, as though trying to penetrate the darkness of a winter night."[5] Stefansson was accustomed to working seventy hours a week writing, lecturing, and advising on arctic matters, just as he had for the previous twenty years and would for twenty years more. A professional writer like Taylor could appreciate the explorer's enormous literary output—fourteen books and over four hundred articles by that time—and he understood Stefansson's rather singular role as an expert on the Arctic.

An interview or series of interviews is like a game in which the subject endeavours to put forward his goals effectively and accurately, knowing all the time that final control of the interview is out of his hands. The interviewer, who sometimes has the semblance of an antagonist, sympathizes with his subject's goals, but he conceives of his role as something other than that of a press agent. He faces the awful burden of having to make his articles popular, and he must, therefore, be artful as well. Given these circumstances, it often happens that the subject of an interview is appalled at a writer's treatment of him, and, as often, the writer is astonished to learn that his subject felt he had been injured.

Most readers of the *New Yorker* would read Taylor's articles with some degree of pleasure and interest, but those with more knowledge of the Arctic would be incensed by some of his exaggerations. If they were naive, they might even believe that Taylor's representations were quoted verbatim from his interviews with Stefansson.

Taylor's articles praised Stefansson and told the story of his career with reasonable accuracy. But the writer could not have known how much anguish he caused Stefansson by such superlative comments as: "he swept across the Arctic like a blizzard, almost obliterating all traces of previous explorers."[6] Similarly, Taylor described the Russian development of the Siberian North as a Klondike-like stampede triggered by Stefansson's *The Friendly Arctic*.

Stefansson was busy with projects until the end of the war, when he returned to his writer's life. In February 1947, for example, Stefansson made a short trip to the Midwest to deliver a few lectures, visit friends in North Dakota and Iowa, and attend an autograph party in Chicago at Brentano's bookstore. He dismissed the *Chicago Tribune* (Colonel McCormack's vehement and nasty mixture of chauvinism and xenophobia) in a phrase—"as bad as ever." Stefansson completed his itinerary and travelled back to New York by train with no regrets at having left America's heartland. The *Tribune,* however, listed *Great Adventurers* as number twenty-one on their best-seller list, and that was reason enough for a celebration. Stefansson and Evelyn dined at Romany Marie's to mark the occasion and saw a Russian film afterwards, as Stefansson put it, "for Evelyn's instruction."[7] Evelyn, who was studying Russian at the time, was able with her gifted ear to pick up some of the dialogue in the film.

Stefansson's chief activity during this time was directing preparations for the *Encyclopedia Arctica* from his Village headquarters. The multi-volume work gave him a wonderful chance to round up experts for particular writing assignments. Fredericka Martin, whose book, *Hunting of the Silver Fleece,* a commissioned work on Alaska's Pribilof Islands that was published in 1946, was one of many writers to call at 48 Barrow Street, one of the two Village apartments Stefansson required to house his library. Other visitors were Henry W. Elliott—the great champion of the fur seal—and Richard Geoghegen, the Fairbanks scholar and Aleut linguist. The project began to look promising as Stefansson contacted other northern enthusiasts; the undertaking, supported by an annual operating budget of $200,000 for the first two years, was an editor's (and patron's) dream. It was a scholar's dream as well. The completed *Encyclopedia Arctica* was intended to be the crowning achievement of Stefansson's career as an expert on the Arctic.

The Navy reserved the right to screen the project's staff of translators and contributors. When one translator, an American citizen who had been trained in Moscow, was under suspicion by Navy officials, Stefansson adopted the wrong tack in defending him. In Stefansson's view, scholarship was too important to give way to Cold War hysteria, and he rightly felt that the Soviet Union's information about the North would have to be included if the encyclopedia were to be useful. Although he knew that Washington instinctively mistrusted anyone who was too well-informed about the enemy, he put his own reputation on the block by reminding the Navy that he had publicly praised Soviet polar route aviators in 1937 and had otherwise taken note of northern progress in the Soviet Union before without arousing suspicion. With perhaps more confidence in officialdom's sense of humour than the times warranted, he quipped: "It was not an adequate comment on a nonstop airplane flight of 6,195 miles from Moscow by way of the North Pole to northern California to say that communism was an unsound theory and that the Soviet Union was teetering on the verge of bankruptcy."[8] Stefansson's friends in the Navy warned him that such jokes might suggest that he himself was tainted with communist sympathies, and they urged him to clear himself by firing the translator—and to try to restrain his efforts at humour in future.

In response to this admonition, Stefansson took the offensive again, appealing to General George Marshall, then U. S. Army chief of staff. Marshall agreed, Stefansson reported, that "I was right to admire the Russians' transpolar flights not on political but on engineering grounds." and that effective translators were necessary—even if they had studied in Moscow.[9] Probably the endorsement by the famed general did nothing to advance Stefansson's cause with the Navy, which, along with some other government agencies, had what they regarded as additional damaging information on him personally. As a professional lecturer, Stefansson saw nothing wrong in speaking before such groups as the American Russian Institute in New York or the National Council of American Soviet Friendship in Ottawa. He had spoken to them in the early 1940's and saw no reason not to accept further invitations from both groups in March 1947. These lectures were familiar expressions of his favourite polar themes, which included encouraging American polar development and commenting favourably on similar progress in the Soviet Union. Inevitably, certain government agents charged with investigating possible Red front organizations noted Stefansson's lectures, subscriptions to suspect journals, and cash contributions to causes sponsored by such organizations.

In fact, Stefansson was inclined to favour theoretical socialism as an economic system that was superior to capitalism, but he by no means favoured the Soviet version of communism. His commitment to socialist ideals that had their roots in nineteenth-century liberalism did not mean that he was an advocate of its contemporary application in the Soviet Union. On the contrary, he believed in freedom of thought and was acutely conscious that the Soviets disregarded that cherished principle.

For many years, Stefansson had been telling people that communistic practice by the Eskimo worked very well in fulfilling their social needs. He probably irritated individuals disinclined to find virtues in "primitive" societies more than he upset the defenders of capitalism, and his observation probably was not noted by the

Cold War warriors at all. But lecturing before Red front organizations was a different matter—who was this opportunist, suspicious officials may have asked, who extolled communism while living on U.S. government contracts? Clouds gathered over Stefansson's dream of the *Encyclopedia Arctica*. Later, he would understand the events that shaped the disaster, but he could not have prevented it.

In *New Compass of the World,* edited by Stefansson, Hans W. Weigert, and Richard Edes Harrison in 1949 (an updating of *Compass of the World* published in 1944), Stefansson contributed an excellent essay entitled "The Soviet Union Moves North." His reflections and scholarship showed a grasp of historic sources and contemporary developments for which he often was not given credit. Stefansson compared Canadian and Alaskan resource development to the situation in Siberia, emphasizing the contrasting attitudes toward resources of the three arctic countries. These differences could be explained by Russia's concern for better transportation after her devastating defeat by the Japanese early in the century and by the Soviets' overall concern for military defence, all of which served to spur development in their North.

Stefansson whimsically called attention to the Soviet system of exile which he did not recommend, except for Stalin's exile to the Yenisei Arctic. Stalin learned his geography the hard way. Now, Stefansson mused, had Canada's Prime Minister Borden and U.S. President Coolidge exiled their rivals (for instance, Mackenzie King, Franklin Roosevelt, and Harry Truman) to the Arctic, prospects for the American North might be brighter.

After reviewing and comparing all aspects of progress in the Soviet and American Norths, he concluded that "a striking picture in contrasts [emerges] from the opposite shores of the polar mediterranean." Stefansson conceded that one's temperament or philosophy might effect whatever lesson could be drawn, but he invited his readers to look to the future: we hope for peace and understanding while watching divergent national policies; he noted, "Is the Old World wise in pressing northward? Is the New World wise in holding back?"[10] These questions still seem pertinent almost forty years after they were raised. Though Stefansson was later to be tarred by some elements of the American press as a "Red Fascist," his thinking was never influenced by either communistic or fascistic ideology. He did ponder the problem of national rivalries for power, however, and he was quick to point out that a reasonable remedy for American-Canadian fears of Soviet strength would be northern development comparable to what had been achieved in Siberia.

Work was going well on the *Encyclopedia Arctica* in 1948 when the axe fell—the Navy refused to renew their contract with Stefansson. Two volumes of the *Encyclopedia* had been completed but not published; others were near completion. Stefansson was given no official explanation. Seemingly, the project was a victim of the Cold War. Stefansson had been in contact with the Soviet embassy in the hope of getting information on the Russian North, and the Navy might have feared that it would be tainted by this association. Perhaps some far-seeing admirals anticipated the intensity of the Red scare and the appearance of Senator Joseph McCarthy. Whatever the reason, when funding was not renewed, the project was doomed.[11]

Before the Navy cancelled its contract, Stefansson had received some further unfavourable publicity implying that he planned to corrupt the Boy Scouts. In January 1948, the New York *Journal-American* "exposed" what it described as an insidious conspiracy directed against the Boy Scout movement. A headline story, "REDS TO TRAIN 30 SCOUT EXECUTIVES," claimed that Stefansson, "a veteran joiner of Red Fascist groups" planned to give a course for Scout supervisors in Bethel, Vermont. The story did not make clear any of the project's circumstances except to say that Stefansson, according to the congressional committee investigating un-American activities, held membership in, or sponsored, seventy-six Communist front organizations and had published articles in "such Red Fascist publications as the *New Masses*."[12] The story did not say explicitly that Stefansson intended to infiltrate the Scouts or otherwise subvert them; still, the innuendo was clear.

What Stefansson had arranged with the Scouts appears rather more innocent. He planned to instruct adult Scout executives in field techniques that would be appropriate to camping activities. Nothing more controversial than teaching them the best means of providing suitable shelter would have been likely to emerge, but that did not matter during those first nervous days of the "Red Scare."

In 1949 the government of Iceland invited the Stefanssons to spend a month there. It was opportunity to visit the Stefansson ancestral home, keep in touch with developments, and to feel the great esteem Icelanders had for Stefansson. Four years later the

Danish government invited them to spend a summer in Greenland, and both opportunities were pleasant learning experiences.

Around this same time another bright chapter in Stefansson's career was underway. Stefansson's association with Dartmouth College in Hanover, New Hampshire, had begun in 1929 when he gave a series of four lectures there. He lectured on other occasions as well, and in 1947 he was asked to assist in the development of a polar study programme, which he managed to do in four campus visits, each of several days' duration. These and subsequent visits to Dartmouth laid the foundation for the programme which was formally established in 1953.

Albert Bradley, an alumnus of the college, agreed to purchase the Stefansson Collection for Dartmouth in 1951, and Charles P. Everitt, a well-known New York book dealer, appraised the library. The Stefanssons wished to take their part in the donation to Dartmouth, so only accepted one-half of the collection's valuation. The acquisition of the collection by Dartmouth provided the already distinguished Baker Library with a rich resource and in this one stroke elevated it to the front rank of polar libraries in the world. Over the years, additions have been made to the Stefansson collection, which continues to hold its place as a mecca for students and visiting scholars engaged in polar research.

Dartmouth's faculty included a number of scholars from various disciplines who were interested in the polar regions, and the acquisition of the Stefansson Library encouraged the development of an interdisciplinary programme. Students could specialize in regional studies, crossing over disciplinary lines to take any of a number of available courses. An Arctic seminar conducted first by Stefansson, and later by Evelyn, tied the programme together.

At Dartmouth Stefansson found a pleasant niche. He enjoyed talking to students, who greatly respected the scope of his scholarship. A colleague of the time, David C. Nutt, has described Stefansson working happily at the library, his "white shock of hair and scholarly face" visible to pedestrians on Elm Street; "his regular morning visits to the post office, his crossing the campus hatless and coatless even in winter, his frequent appearance in the front row of Convocation or Commencement exercises, and his snowhouses in the middle of the Green." Nutt also recalled Stefansson dining at the Dartmouth Inn. "Dinner companions...or perhaps those listening in from an adjoining table—could hear Stef's explicit instructions on how bacon was to be barely warmed, not to cut the fat off the meat, and to bring extra pats of butter but no potatoes or vegetables." He was still on a meat diet but learned to supplement it with "an occasional martini before dinner."[13]

After living for many years as New Yorkers, the Stefanssons found a different pace in Bethel and Hanover. Evelyn took courses in painting and other subjects at the university, performed with the theatrical group and did some writing. Stefansson did not need to take up new hobbies; he simply continued to work and travel for lecture engagements and other meetings.

There was always good converesation, the kind of stimulating exchange Stefansson had missed most during his years in the Arctic. Evelyn vividly described such occasions in her introduction to Owen Lattimore's book, *Silk, Spices, and Empire,* as "the special kind of dialogue that Owen and Stef engaged in when conditions were right."[14] "Right" conditions meant quiet, the presence of good listeners, and something to drink, either coffee or wine. At such times these two experts on Mongols and Eskimos, now close neighbours, would draw from their knowledge facts and inferences that were useful for comparison, each stirring the other intellectually as the talk went on.

The Stefanssons enjoyed other kinds of social occasions during the Dartmouth years—the receptions, dinners, and cocktail parties that are always part of an academic community's social routine—but they found that spirited and serious conversations were hard to come by in such circumstances. Stefansson, perhaps taking advantage of his advanced years and his celebrity, did not invariably please his hostesses when he would urge a group to silence in order to listen to someone who had an interesting story to tell. Hostesses could also be irritated if Stefansson should decide, as he sometimes did, that a buffet dinner offered too many carbohydrates. He would ask for a quarter of a pound of butter and a spoon, and would eat it unperturbed; he would have been astonished to learn that he had offended anyone.

A few years after moving to Dartmouth, Stefansson and Evelyn became clearly designated victims of the Red Scare. There were several reasons for which McCarthyites singled out the old polar expert. Owen Lattimore had himself been pilloried by Senator McCarthy in one of his more sensational attacks. The Stefanssons sold the Lattimore's farm for them to a buyer who, unknown to anyone at the time, had been a Communist. Then there was that habit Stefansson had of calling attention to the Soviet Union's successful development of Siberia.

The third reason for the state Senate subcommittee's attacks was owing to some confusion regarding Evelyn Stefansson's background. Someone had reported that she had been a Red agent in Hungary before emigrating to the United States. (She was, in fact, born in New York.) The slander against Evelyn originated in an anonymous letter to New Hampshire's attorney-general, apparently sent by a mentally ill or jealous woman with an imagined grievance.

In 1955 Stefansson was called to appear before New Hampshire Attorney-General Louis C. Wyman, in the course of his investigation into communist infiltration of state colleges. Stefansson freely admitted having been a member of some organizations that were listed by the federal attorney-general as being subversive, but he denied having played any role in a group such as Americans Concerned for the Settlement of Jews other than in activities that were connected with its stated purpose. Nor did he deny that he had been among the many distinguished Americans who had called for an end to witch-hunting by the House UnAmerican Activities Committee in 1949. Wyman's report did not accuse Stefansson of having ties with the Soviet Union, but it did not exonerate him either. This left the *New Hampshire Sunday News* (the Sunday edition of the notorious *Manchester News-Union Ledger*) free to blacken Stefansson and the intellectual community of Dartmouth. Headlines trumpeted the news of his alleged Red links, and the newspaper reminded readers of what had been said about Stefansson during the hearings on Lattimore. Louis Budenz, an ex-Communist who had realized the error of his ways and become a Christian, named a number of people as communist sympathizers. Budenz asserted about Stefansson: "I know from official reports that he is a communist." He pointed out that Owen Lattimore had contributed to the book on geopolitics entitled *New Compass of the World* that had been edited by Stefansson and others, a book that Budenz claimed "shows in an involved and, I should say, semi-scholarly way, that Soviet Russia is impregnable because it has control of the Heartland."[15]

The report in the *New Hampshire Sunday News* went on to observe that officials of Dartmouth College showed a "tendency to lionize Stefansson since his Red ties were publicized." Their attitude, according to the paper, belied any denial of "Stefansson's sensitive position" in dealing with "strategic Arctic information."

Dartmouth publicity, according to the paper indicated that the college had "staked out the Arctic," a region of potential power "in a strategic sense." Readers of the *New Hampshire Sunday News* were advised to clip and save its column exposing Stefansson because copies of the Wyman report "are not numerous."[16] It was noted that although Stefansson denied having any knowledge of Lattimore's communist sympathies, the latter was then under indictment for perjury before congress. (Lattimore was later exonerated of the charges against him.)

A reporter for *The Dartmouth,* the college paper, thought it strange that the *News-Union Ledger* had failed to make clear that Attorney-General Wyman was unable to find evidence of subversive influences at the college. In fact, in Stefansson's case, newspaper articles suggested just the opposite. *The Dartmouth* interviewed Wyman and asked why his report did not mention that Stefansson had admitted to being a member of some suspect organizations. "I wanted to give these people every break I could," he replied.[17]

Stefansson had nothing to hide, so he indulged himself a little by baiting his interrogator. He certainly realized that the state of affairs was anything but funny. The Lattimores had suffered intensely from Senator McCarthy's direct attacks, and the Stefanssons responded by giving their beleaguered friends their utmost sympathy. Then Wyman told Stefansson that Evelyn had to appear for questioning as well. The atmosphere of the time was such that prosecutors were permitted a great deal of latitude in their irresponsible probing for breaches of security. Stefansson watched Evelyn lose sleep during the week she had to wait for her interview, and he worried about her. "Innocent as she was, she must have feared they might set some kind of trap for her," he noted. "I imagine that the tension and uncertainty of the accused must have been similar during the Salem witchcraft hysteria, in the Know-Nothing era, and during the Palmer raids after World War I."[18]

The New Hampshire Attorney-General's reasons for suppressing the results of his investigations were obvious enough to anyone who was interested in Dartmouth. In his investigation of New Hampshire colleges and the activities of faculty members (dating back to the 1930's), Wyman had been disappointed at the negative results of his enquiry. As a good American (and a publicity-seeking politician), he hoped to share Joe McCarthy's notoriety and thus raise himself in public esteem. The problem was that New Hampshire had not been a hotbed of political subversion since the revolutionary era. Authentic witches were hard to come by, and Wyman hated to admit that his misuse of American citizens' time and money had also dashed his political hopes. *The Dartmouth* concluded that Stefansson was "cleared" by the Wyman report even though the report did not explicitly say so.[19]

The *Manchester News-Union Ledger* returned to the attack in 1959 in an editorial clamouring that to remain silent on Budenz's charges just because he was eighty years old was poor journalism. A reporter for Dartmouth's student newspaper interviewed Stefansson at the Baker Library and found the old man pleased at the renewed notoriety. He was reminded, he said, of his campaign in 1902 for superintendent of schools in North Dakota that had received national publicity because he was only twenty-three years old and thus ineligible to hold public office. The publicity, he joked, had been "my stepping stone to fame."[20]

As for Budenz, Stefansson was delighted that the charges had been publicized because Budenz had been discredited repeatedly. *The News-Union Ledger* was particularly incensed because the Institute for Pacific Relations, an organization of which Stefansson was a member, had been cited by the U.S. attorney-general as a communist front organization. Stefansson did not think the attorney-general had made good his charges against the I.P.R., but he did not care whether the organization was Red or not. He had joined it for the same reason as he had become a member of all the other organizations: because their publications were essential to his library. The U.S. government had commissioned him to do intelligence work on other northern countries during the 1930's, and it was his business to study all kinds of people, pro- as well as anti-Communists.[21]

A lifelong observer of mankind's weakness for believing in improbable and irrational concepts, Stefansson might have written more about the Red hysteria had he been younger. Yet the light ironic touch with which he treated the Welzl book and the Eskimo imposter stories in his youth might have been hard to achieve. The activities of the Red hunters were too destructive to be amusing— resembling more the intolerance of racist Nazis than the harmless ignorance that Stefansson had so gleefully parodied in *Adventures in Error* and *The Standardization of Error.*

CHAPTER 24

One Last Party

ON 31 MAY, 1961, Stefansson suffered a stroke that left his right leg paralysed from the hip down. Officials at Dartmouth College arranged convalescent facilities for him, and President John Dickey and Vice-President Orton Hicks often visited to cheer the patient. Evelyn, who had recovered from bone surgery in the same room a few months before, looked after his needs. But inactivity did not suit Stefansson, and he was soon immersed in reading the galleys of a book for which he had promised to write an introduction. By the time he had read twenty pages of galley proofs he could wiggle his toes and bend his ankle, a feat that he considered a tribute to the book as well as to the nursing staff. Within three days he could walk around the room on the arm of Evelyn or a nurse, and soon he was able to go home. Once there, Stefansson reported happily, he could pound his typewriter throughout the night and finish his work.

In March 1962, Stefansson wrote what he called a postscript to his autobiography in which he reflected on his approaching death. Although he could not describe it himself, he chuckled that he hoped "it will be seemly and perhaps pervaded by the odor of sanctity" which (recalling his Divinity School professor) "George Foot Moore, the wisest man I ever knew, suggested might be the odor of unwashed linen."[1]

One last joke, then one last serious thought. Noting that only five of the fifteen members of the Canadian Arctic Expedition's scientific staff were still alive, Stefansson reflected "As we worked together in the North, we had our agreements and our differences, and as we look to the last chapter of our lives, we shall no doubt have similar differences and arguments." He phrased his last words with care: "Whatever others may think after reading these pages, I know what I have experienced, and I know what it has meant to me." He ended his reflections with a quotation from Ecclesiastes:

Wherefore I perceive that there is nothing better, than that a man should rejoice in his own works; for that is his portion; for who shall bring him to see what shall be after him?[2]

Five months later, on a hot August day, Stefansson suffered a fatal stroke.

Evelyn recalled her husband's death in her postlude to his autobiography: "Stef's wish for a seemly death was granted." They had been giving a dinner party for some friends. Flushed "with good wine and delight in each other's company," the party had moved from the dining room to the living room for coffee. "Stef was about to take a sip when, with a trembling hand that splashed coffee, he painstakingly placed the cup back on the table. Then, in the silent language all well-married couples know, he sent a message, urgent as a cry, for help."[3] A week later he was dead.

For Evelyn "the seemliness of Stef's death was that on his last night with us, his wits were sharp, and he was able to amuse, instruct, delight, and draw each of us out, making the evening a memorable one." She thought, "perhaps Stef might have learned to love a party from the Eskimos....Any excuse would do, an out-of-town visitor was a favorite; so was good news of any sort, or even the *prospect* of good news." If the prospect did not materialize, she remembered, "you at least had the celebration. If a book contract was signed, if he received an advance from a publisher, if a royalty check fatter than expected arrived, if it was publication day of a new book, a celebration was called for. 'Bookdays' were as important as birthdays in our family."[4] And, of course, Stefansson's last party had been on a "bookday"—the party celebrated the completion of *Discovery*.

An existing autobiography is the most fascinating of documents. There is so much to ponder in what a man chooses to record of his own life and the emphasis he places on critical events. Stefansson wrote *Discovery* when he was in his eighties, working in the midst of that mass of arctic documentation, much of which had been accumulated by his own efforts. In this last of his many books, Stefansson showed no inclination towards historical revision; nor did he make any effort to create a legend of himself. He had always been a careful scholar as well as a fluent writer, and these attributes are evident in *Discovery*.

There are a few minor errors in the book, but very few, thanks to Evelyn Stefansson's editing and the enormous quantity of material available—particularly the thousands of letters dating back to Stefansson's youth. He forgot that some correspondence had passed between Shackleton and him prior to Shackleton's abortive attempt to head a proposed Canadian government expedition to the Beaufort Sea in 1920, and he made a curious slip in his discussion of pemmican when he remarked that he only knew of its value at secondhand because he had always depended upon hunting when he was in the Arctic. He also erred in recalling that Desbarats encouraged him to lecture after returning from the Canadian Arctic Expedition. Yet in the summary of eighty active years, he and Evelyn were remarkably successful.

Stefansson's autobiography is an honest book. The old explorer did not try to conceal his disappointments and setbacks, nor even his small vanities, yet the image he projected in the book did not appeal to everyone. One Canadian northern enthusiast, for example, found the account of Stefansson's early years delightful and humorous—as indeed it is—but he disliked the writer's tone when he described the Canadian Arctic Expedition. The book, he said "too often sounds like the ramblings of an angry embittered old man. This Stef certainly was not."[5]

But Stefansson was consistent, not nostalgic, and he reaffirmed his life's achievements and confessed his biases in his book. *Discovery* shows Stefansson as he saw himself, and it does not distort history.

Stefansson died on 26 August 1962. At the time, Evelyn Stefansson received many messages of condolence, and a number of writers were moved to define for themselves those qualities that distinguished a remarkable man.

One of the many people who were influenced by Stefansson was Lawrence McKinley Gould, a former president of Carleton College and distinguished scientist who did much work in Antarctica. In his Stefansson Memorial Lecture at Dartmouth, he recalled the dictum of Antarctic explorer, Apsley Cherry-Garrard: "exploration is but the physical expression of the intellectual passion...This...is what exploration should be but rarely is." To Gould, Stefansson's life was "a perfect fulfillment" of Cherry-Garrard's memorable definition.[6]

Gould's "subjective view" of the friend he admired summarizes well the qualities for which Stefansson was remembered:

Possessed of splendid health and great physical vigor, proper equipment for the explorer, he also had the curiosity, the imagination, and the capacity for careful observation which are the necessary characteristics of any good scientist. And so Stef has left us a heritage of great achievement in Arctic exploration, a brilliant record as author, lecturer, and teacher, and, as a further permanent record of his consuming intellectual concern, the Stefansson Collection—the most comprehensive library on the polar regions in the Western Hemisphere. Tradition fades, but the written record does not, and in his own works and in his library Stef has left a record of himself which will remain ever fresh.

Stef was provocative and controversial, as indeed most interesting people are. But Stef always provided such stimulating controversy! He was never guilty of the unforgivable sin of dullness.

I have known few people so tenacious of their own ideas as was Stef; but he had reason to be tenacious, for he was careful and meticulous in collecting and marshaling his facts. One soon learned that it was best to be well armed before taking Stef on in an argument or debate. But with Stef it was always fun, for he was not intolerant of other points of view. It seems to me that in my many contacts with Stef I usually agreed with him, but when I did not he was always generous, judicious, and friendly....

If I were to inquire into my own scientific genealogy the name of Stefansson would loom large in my "hereditary" background. I still have vivid memories of my first meeting with Stef. It happened more than forty years ago at the University of Michigan where Stef had come to lecture and where I was a student. Then and there "The Friendly Arctic" became a reality and my own interest in the polar regions began.

I am sure a host of other men currently interested in the polar regions could make observations similar to my own. To all of us he gave the gift of the good example of a passionate concern to have all the facts available. We shall remember him for the intellectual stimulation of his friendship, for his good humor and his great generosity with his own time, and perhaps above all his unending infectious enthusiasm.[7]

Owen Lattimore explained Stefansson's friendliness to others, his easy manner that encouraged strangers to call him "Stef" within a few minutes of meeting him. To Lattimore, this quality was "rooted in the universality of his concept of man." Stefansson saw man as "a continuum of past, present, and future," and he believed that "the study of man should be pushed back to the remotest origins." This belief enabled Stefansson to see his own life as coherent and organic, and it convinced him that "the more we know and understand...the past...the more thorough our command of ourselves in the present, and the better we shall be able to shape the future." A period of life should not be considered as a compartment of time; unity, rather than separateness, was important. Lattimore explained, "as always, he saw all three aspects of time as a continuum....With increasing age he became neither more conservative nor more sentimentally liberal, but more and more rationally and fearlessly liberal, more convinced that the future must be shaped not by the destructiveness of war but by constructive development of the individual within a collectively responsible society."[8]

Lattimore's appreciation reveals Stefansson's strength as an individual—the rational, humanitarian thrust that manifested itself in all of his thoughts and activities. His belief gave him a confidence in his dealings with people, regardless of their foibles. Although it did not render him incapable of mistakes, it was a powerful bulwark against bias and pettiness in his relationships. The fanatic devotion of some people to various creeds or "isms" was as customary in Stefansson's time as before it and since, but knowing these to be transitory fads, they neither cheered nor alarmed him very much. In his view it was to be expected that some men would accept Communism and its works without question while others were bound to elevate capitalism or nationalism to the level of religion. To Stefansson, one simply had to go on searching for the harder truths while demanding of oneself rationality and spiritual bravery against popular pressures.

There are many choices for an epitaph that would best express Stefansson's character. Most people stress his controversial nature, but the word "controversial" alone cannot adequately sum up all that he was. In the history of exploration, disputes over Stefansson's leadership and achievements do not rank highly on a comparative scale. His "friendly Arctic" theme was a complex concept that had much broader implications.

Undoubtedly Stefansson contributed to his reputation for public disputation deliberately. The young student who had been suspended from university still relished confrontations with authority as a mature man. However, examined in the light of his overall goals, his dealings with other people show that he did not seek controversy for its own sake, even though he was always aware of the value of a provocative approach in publicizing his ideas. No one who loves people and truth actually prefers controversy to amicable compromise.

Stefansson was a poor hater; he understood that people might act uncharitably in anger, disappointment, or ignorance, and he believed that they should not be blamed for doing so. He always tried to look beyond personal and public quarrels, reaching out to truth as a rational and charitable man must reach. One of his friends who was quoted in the 1941 *New Yorker* profile probably described Stefansson best, within the limitations of epigram, when he said, "he gives liberally of himself."[9]

Indeed, he gave liberally—and he had much to give; not just ideas and theories, but those intangible qualities that human character can summon—interest and concern, kindness and sympathy.

Abbreviations

Unless otherwise indicated, all manuscript material cited is in the Stefansson Collection, Baker Library, Dartmouth College (SC). Other collections are cited as follows:

NA: Center for Polar Archives, National Archives, Washington, D.C.
PAC: Public Archives of Canada, Ottawa.
PM: Pitt Museum, Oxford.
SPRI: Scott Polar Research Institute, Cambridge, England.
UO: University of Oregon Library, Eugene, Lopp Collection.
UA: Elmer E. Rasmuson Library, University of Alaska, Fairbanks.

Notes

NOTES TO CHAPTER ONE

1. Vilhjalmur Stefansson, *Discovery* (New York: McGraw-Hill, 1964), p. 10.
2. *Ibid.*, p. 11.
3. *Ibid.*, p. 12.
4. *Ibid.*, p. 13.

NOTES TO CHAPTER TWO

1. Vilhjalmur Stefansson, *Discovery* (New York: McGraw-Hill, 1964), p. 27.
2. Carl to Stefansson, 23 July 1899.
3. Stefansson to A.E. Morrison, 28 August, 1899.
4. Stefansson to Valdi Thorvaldson, 2 October 1899.
5. Stefansson to A.E. Morrison, 28 August 1899.
6. Poetry, Correspondence file, 1903-6.
7. *Ibid.*
8. *Ibid.*
9. Stefansson to ... unidentified letter, c. 1899.
10. Bertha Ferguson to Stefansson, June ?, 1899.
11. Stefansson to Valdi Thorvaldson, 2 October 1899.
12. *Ibid.*
13. *Ibid.*
14. *Ibid.*
15. Mary Brennan Clapp memoir, June 1930.

16. *Ibid.*
17. *Ibid.*
18. *Ibid.*
19. Vilhjalmur Stefansson, "English Loan-Nouns in the Icelandic Colony of North Dakota," *Dialect Notes*, 2, pt. 5 (1903): 354-62. Cited in Henry L. Mencken, *American Language* (New York: Knopf, 1937), pp. 631-32.
20. Webster Merrifield to Stefansson, 27 January 1903.
21. Stefansson to Brandjord, 12 December 1903.
22. Ejnar Mikkelsen, *Mirage in the Arctic* (London: Rupert Hart-Davis, 1955), p. 13.
23. *Ibid.*, p. 14.

NOTES TO CHAPTER THREE

1. Vilhjalmur Stefansson, *Discovery* (New York: McGraw-Hill, 1964), p. 67.
2. *Ibid.*, p. 69.
3. Stefansson diary, 13 August 1906.
4. Stefansson diary, 11 August 1906.
5. Stefansson, *Discovery*, p. 74.
6. Vilhjalmur Stefansson, *Hunters of the Great North* (New York: Harcourt, Brace, 1922), p. 52.
7. *U.S. v. Klengenberg* file. RG 60. Department of Justice, National Archives. The British ambassador to

the U.S. volunteered to have Klengenberg tried in Canada because the alleged crimes were within waters claimed by Canada, but went along with the U.S. Attorney General and the U.S. State Department's wish to treat events as the U.S.'s concern since ship and crew were American.

8. Stefansson, *Hunters,* p. 54.
9. *Ibid.*
10. *Ibid.,* pp. 55-56.
11. *Ibid.,* p. 61.
12. *Ibid.,* p. 63.
13. Stefansson, *Discovery* (New York: McGraw-Hill, 1964), p. 83.
14. Jabbertown derived its picturesque name from the medley of languages which were spoken there whenever the whaling crews landed.
15. Ejnar Mikkelsen, *Mirage of the Arctic* (London: Hart-Davis, 1955), p. 43.
16. Stefansson, *Hunters,* p. 206.
17. *Ibid.,* p. 207.
18. Stefansson, *Discovery,* p. 97.
19. *Ibid.,* p. 99.

NOTES TO CHAPTER FOUR

1. Vilhjalmur Stefansson, *Discovery* (New York: McGraw-Hill, 1964), p. 101.
2. *Ibid.,* p. 102.
3. Vilhjalmur Stefansson, *My Life with the Eskimo* (New York: Macmillan, 1921), p. 41.
4. *Ibid.,* p. 340.
5. Stefansson, *Discovery,* p. 104.
6. Stefansson, *My Life with the Eskimo,* p. 299.
7. *Ibid.*
8. *Ibid.,* pp. 299-300.
9. Stefansson diary, 19 January 1909.
10. *Ibid.,* 9 March 1910.
11. C.E. Whittaker, *Arctic Eskimo* (London: Seeley, Service, 1937), p. 70.
12. William R. Hunt, *North of 53°* (New

York: Macmillan, 1974), pp. 258-65.
13. Vilhjalmur Stefansson, *Not by Bread Alone* (New York: Macmillan, 1956), p. 175.
14. *Ibid.,* p. 94-95.
15. René Dubos, "The Medical Anthropologist," *Polar Notes,* (November 1962): 30. See also, G. Edgar Folk, Jr. and Mary Arp Folk, *Vilhjalmur Stefansson and the Development of Arctic Terrestrial Science* (Iowa City: University of Iowa, 1984), pp. 101-10.
16. Stefansson, *My Life with the Eskimo,* p. 149.
17. *Ibid.,* p. 155.
18. Vilhjalmur Stefansson, *Stefansson-Anderson Ex pedition,* p. 129.
19. *Ibid.,* p. 153.
20. Helmer Hanssen, *Voyages of a Modern Viking* (London: Routledge, 1936), p. 129.
21. Stefansson, *Stefansson-Anderson Expedition,* pp. 164, 177.
22. *Ibid.,* pp. 181-82.
23. *Ibid.*
24. *Ibid.*
25. Diamond Jenness, *People of the Twilight* (New York: Macmillan, 1928), p. 207.
26. *Ibid.,* p. 208.
27. *Ibid.,* pp. 208-9.
28. *Ibid.*
29. Stefansson, *Stefansson-Anderson Expedition,* p. 192.

NOTES TO CHAPTER FIVE

1. Vilhjalmur Stefansson, *Discovery* (New York: McGraw-Hill, 1964), p. 110. The possibility of late nineteenth-century contacts between whalers and Copper Eskimos in this region is discussed in John Bockstoce, "Contacts between American Whalemen and the Copper Eskimos," *Arctic* (December, 1975): 298-99.
2. *Ibid.,* p. 111.

3. *Ibid.*, p. 112.
4. Vilhjalmur Stefansson, *My Life with the Eskimo* (New York: Macmillan, 1921), p. 182.
5. Stefansson, *Discovery*, p. 114.
6. *Ibid.*, p. 115.
7. *Ibid.*, p. 118.
8. *Ibid.*, p. 119.
9. *Ibid.*, p. 122.
10. Stefansson, *My Life with the Eskimo*, p. 192.
11. *Ibid.*, pp. 192-93.
12. Stefansson to Percy Crews, 12 December 1910.
13. *Ibid.*
14. *Ibid.*
15. Stefansson, *Discovery*, p. 126.
16. *Ibid.*, pp. 130-31.
17. *Ibid.*, p. 131.
18. Stefansson Diary, 28 May 1912.
19. *Ibid.*
20. *Ibid.*
21. *Ibid.*
22. *Ibid.*
23. *Ibid.*, 9 June 1912.
24. Stefansson, *Discovery*, p. 132.

NOTES TO CHAPTER SIX

1. Vilhjalmur Stefansson, *Discovery* (New York: McGraw-Hill, 1964), p. 133.
2. *Ibid.*, p. 133-34. The original story as quoted here is in the *Seattle Daily Times*, 9 September 1912, page one, under the heading "AMERICAN EXPLORER DISCOVERS LOST TRIBE OF WHITES, DESCENDENTS OF LEIF ERICKSEN."
3. *Ibid.*, p. 134.
4. *New York Times*, 10 September 1912.
5. *Ibid.*, 11 September 1912.
6. *Ibid.*
7. *Ibid.*, 12 September 1912.
8. *Ibid.*, 13 September 1912.
9. Stefansson, *Discovery*, p. 135.
10. Vilhjalmur Stefansson, *My Life with the Eskimo* (New York: Macmillan, 1921), p. 193.

11. *Venice Vanguard*, 23 September 1915.
12. Stefansson, *My Life with the Eskimo*, p. 192; pp. 194-95; p. 200. Diamond Jenness's studies on the Canadian Arctic Expedition concluded against the Viking theory, as have others, although T. J. Olesen, *Early Voyages and Northern Approaches* (Toronto: McClelland and Stewart, 1963), p. 84 supports the possibility.
13. Arctic clipping book, 1912, SPRI.
14. Cited in *The Alaska Daily Dispatch*, 31 January 1913.
15. *Ibid.*
16. *Ibid.*
17. *Ibid.*

NOTES TO CHAPTER SEVEN

1. Richard S. Finnie, *Canada Moves North* (New York: Macmillan, 1942), pp. 22-23. According to Finnie, Stefansson "never complained" about the "lone-wolf" description: "Indeed, he liked the book and often recommended it as the best general account of the Canadian Arctic at the time of its publication [1942]." Finnie to author, personal communication, 20 October 1976.
2. Undated memo in LeRoy letter file, vol. 20 of Anderson papers. PAC. It is not clear why LeRoy said the Naval Service provided no coordination of provisioning. (George Phillips joined the expedition at Esquimalt, B.C. and Nome for this purpose. Phillips was an employee of the Naval Service assigned to CAE provisioning.) See Vilhjalmur Stefansson, *The Friendly Arctic*, p. 115. LeRoy's memo clearly expresses his hostility to Stefansson and his efforts to disrupt the expedition. It is my assumption that much of LeRoy's antipathy to Stefansson derived from his frustration over the prime minister's decision to place the CAE

under Naval Service direction. LeRoy had little, if any, personal contact with Stefansson. Obviously much of the information on the affairs of the expedition once it left for the field came from Chipman, who well knew what LeRoy wanted to hear about Stefansson. Stefansson had rather a high opinion of Chipman and would have been amazed had he seen the young topographer's letters to LeRoy.

3. Chipman diary, 17 December 1913, PAC. "In our personal instructions there is nothing to indicate that we are in any way responsible to anyone except the Department and the leader of the Southern Party." But Chipman was concerned about the position LeRoy left him in, as a 15 July note appended to his 30 April 1914 letter to LeRoy shows. He complained that Brock had sent his sympathies, leaving Boyd the task of "going into particulars," yet Boyd wrote "a purely personal" letter. "Evidently we are going to be *goats* but I have no fear of what this may mean." Still, Chipman would have liked something from Ottawa in writing to fall back on in case of difficulty. In the same letter, Chipman insists for the record that no scientist on the expedition had ever questioned the overall authority of Stefansson. The scientists had raised legitimate questions at times but had not "disputed authority."

4. R.M. Anderson to Mrs. Anderson, 16 July 1913, PAC.

5. Chipman to Boyd, 18 July 1913. PAC.

6. Chipman diary, 10 July 1913. PAC.

7. Jenness to Balfour, 3 July 1913. PAC.

8. Chipman diary, 10 July 1913. PAC.

9. Chipman to Boyd, 19 July 1913. PAC.

10. Copy of Jenness's contract attached to letter to Balfour, 3 July 1913. PM.

11. Jenness to Balfour, 3 July 1913. PM.

12. O'Neill to LeRoy, 17 July 1913. PAC.

13. Stefansson, *Discovery*, pp. 153-54; Stefansson, *Friendly Arctic*, p. 115.

NOTES TO CHAPTER EIGHT

1. William Laird McKinlay, *Karluk* (London: Weidenfeld & Nicolson, 1976), p. 34.

2. *Ibid.*, p. 35.

3. *Ibid.*

4. *Ibid.*, p. 36.

5. *Ibid.*, p. 37.

6. R.M. Anderson, "Preliminary History of the Canadian Arctic Expedition," and Mrs. Anderson to McKinlay, 26 January 1922, PAC.

7. R.M. Anderson, "Preliminary History," PAC.

8. *Ibid.*

9. McKinlay, *Karluk*, p. 12.

10. *Ibid.*, p. 40.

11. Robert A. Bartlett, *Last Voyage of the Karluk* (Boston: Small, Maynard, 1916), pp. 45, 67.

12. Williamson to Stefansson, 30 April 1959.

13. McKinlay, *Karluk*, p. 52.

14. John Hadley's memoir, p. 3.

15. Williamson to Stefansson, 17 May 1959.

16. Hadley's memoir, p. 4.

17. *Ibid.*

18. Olaf Swenson, *Northwest of the World* (New York: Dodd, Mead, 1944), p. 104.

19. Fred Maurer, "The Drift," in *World Magazine*, 6 June 1915, p. 5.

20. McKinlay, *Karluk*, p. 68.

21. *Ibid.*, p. 70.

22. Hadley's memoir, p. 6.

23. McKinlay, *Karluk*, p. 76. Eventually the men reached the shore of Herald Island and died there in their tent, possibly of monoxide poisoning. Louis Lane discovered their remains on 29 September 1924.

24. Hadley's memoir, p. 10. For these

and other unfavourable comments on Bartlett's conduct, Hadley is the sole source.

25. Bartlett, *Last Voyage*, p. 127.
26. Hadley's memoir, p. 10.
27. Bartlett, *Last Voyage*, p. 128.
28. Hadley's memoir, p. 12. The text is confusing. It appears that Bartlett is referring to Chief Mate Anderson's party, yet this seems unlikely. Storkerson, on reading this version of the events, recalled that Hadley had said that Bartlett used the expression when Mackay's party left. (Storkerson's annotation on Hadley's memoir, 5 September 1919.)
29. Maurer, "The Drift," p. 7.
30. *Ibid.*, p. 8.
31. *Ibid.*, p. 9.
32. *Ibid.*, p. 10.
33. *Ibid.*, p. 11.
34. *Ibid.*
35. Bartlett, *Last Voyage*, p. 167.
36. Hadley's memoir, as published in Vilhjalmur Stefansson, *The Friendly Arctic* (New York: Macmillan, 1921), p. 711.
37. Maurer, "The Drift," p. 12.
38. McKinlay, *Karluk*, p. 98.
39. *Ibid.*
40. *Ibid.*
41. Hadley's diary, 25 June 1914. PAC.
42. *Ibid.*, 30 June 1914.
43. Hadley's memoir, p. 26. All citations of Hadley's memoir refer to the account written for Stefansson at Herschel. As explained elsewhere, this report different in some respects from the version printed in Stefansson, *The Friendly Arctic*. Thus, including the diary, there are three accounts in existence by Hadley. His diary is in the Public Archives of Canada, Ottawa.
44. "Magnus At Large," *The Mail*, n.d. [1976?]. Magnus Magnusson wrote the introduction to McKinlay's book.
45. Maurer, "The Drift," p. 15.
46. *Ibid.*, p. 16.

NOTES TO CHAPTER NINE

1. George Wilkin's autobiography, pages unnumbered.
2. *Ibid.*
3. *Ibid.*
4. Stefansson to Desbarats, 24 October 1913. CAE letter Digest.
5. Stefansson, *The Friendly Arctic*, pp. 93-94.
6. Stefansson, *The Friendly Arctic*, p. 97.
7. *Ibid.*, p. 98. Stefansson, however, was not as personally detached as his published narrative might indicate. In a letter to a friend, he described Anderson as a "different man" from the one with whom he had worked earlier. Still, he remained fond of Anderson and "owed him much for our last work together." But he thought Anderson was jealous, "though I tried to make him prominent and got him his present job." Anderson told Stefansson that such favours were done for an ulterior motive, but Anderson did not speculate about what that motive might be. In reply to Anderson's expressed concern about handicapping the Southern Party, Stefansson could only insist that he had the interests of the Southern Party "as much at heart as those of the Northern Party," (Stefansson to Phillips, 14 February 1914).
8. Stefansson, *The Friendly Arctic*, p. 113.
9. *Ibid.*, p. 120.
10. Chipman to Boyd, 19 December 1913. PAC.

NOTES TO CHAPTER TEN

1. Vilhjalmur Stefansson, *The Friendly Arctic*, (New York: Macmillan, 1932), pp. 145-46.
2. *Ibid.*, p. 55, p. 145; Stefansson diary, 22 March 1914.
3. Stefansson diary, 26 April 1914.
4. *Ibid.*

5. Stefansson, *The Friendly Arctic*, p. 197.
6. *Ibid.*, p. 206, quoting the diary for 19 May 1914.
7. Stefansson diary, 19 May 1914.
8. Stefansson, *The Friendly Arctic*, p. 236.
9. *Ibid.*, p. 140.
10. Draft biography of Ole Andreasen written by Stefansson for his *Encyclopedia Arctica* project.
11. George Wilkins, Autobiography (unpublished), pages unnumbered.
12. *Ibid.*
13. George Wilkins, quoted in Stefansson, *The Friendly Arctic*, p. 277.
14. George Wilkins, *Autobiography* (unpublished), pages unnumbered.
15. *Ibid.*
16. Stefansson, *The Friendly Arctic*, p. 277.
17. Vilhjalmur Stefansson, *Discovery*, (New York: McGraw-Hill, 1964), p. 188.
18. *Ibid.*, p. 180.
19. Stefansson diary, 26 November 1914.
20. *Ibid.*
21. *Ibid.*

11. Stefansson to Peary, 19 January 1914.
12. Stefansson to Desbarats, 14 January 1914.
13. *Ibid.*
14. Quoted in Richard Diubaldo, *The Canadian Career of Vilhjalmur Stefansson* (London: University of Western Ontario, 1972), p. 107.
15. A. C. Doyle to Stefansson, 13 February 1914. CAE Letter Digest.
16. Stefansson to Mrs. Anderson, 8 February 1914.
17. *Ibid.*
18. *Ibid.*
19. *Ibid.*
20. *Ibid.*
21. Stefansson to Ed Deming, 1 February 1914.
22. *Ibid.*, 28 September 1914.
23. Stefansson to Charlotte Rudyard, 14 September 1914.
24. *Ibid.*
25. *Ibid.*
26. *Ibid.*
27. *Ibid.*

NOTES TO CHAPTER ELEVEN

1. Stefansson to Mrs. Anderson, 16 February 1915.
2. *London Star*, 13 December 1914.
3. Stefansson to Mrs. Anderson, 16 February 1915.
4. Adams to Stefansson, 14 March 1914.
5. Stefansson to Dellenbaugh, 13 April 1914.
6. Ed Deming to Stefansson, 13 April 1914.
7. Undated clipping, *Catholic Register*.
8. Stefansson to the *Catholic Register*, 6 November 1915.
9. *Ibid.*
10. Diamond Jenness, *Life of the Copper Eskimo* (New York: Johnson Reprint Corp., 1970), p. 11.

NOTES TO CHAPTER TWELVE

1. Anderson to Stefansson, 12 August 1915, CAE Letter Digest.
2. Chipman to Boyd, 6 January 1914. PAC.
3. Anderson's diary, 17 January 1916. PAC.
4. *Ibid.*
5. *Ibid.*, 27 July 1908.
6. Stefansson to Anderson, 27 August 1915, CAE Letter Digest.
7. Stefansson to Desbarats, 13 February 1914, CAE Letter Digest.
8. Chipman to Boyd, 28 June 1915, PAC.
9. *Ibid.*
10. *Ibid.*
11. *Ibid.*
12. Anderson's diary, 17 January 1916. PAC.
13. Chipman to LeRoy, 30 April 1914. PAC.
14. *Ibid.*

15. Stefansson, *My Life With The Eskimo*, (New York: Macmillan, 1931), p. 117. Apparently, Stefansson offered to take mother and child "outside" and support them, but Pannigabluk preferred to remain in the Arctic. It is hard to imagine that he neglected to do so, for he was invariably generous to Eskimos even where he had no obligations to them. Pannigabluk's family took pride in their relationship to Stefansson. Georgina Stefansson in "My Grandfather, Dr. Vilhjalmur Stefansson," (Ottawa: *North*, 1961) makes it clear that, despite gossip among whites, the Eskimos concerned were satisfied. Had it been otherwise, Pannigabluk had ample occasion to complain, but she did not.
16. Chipman to LeRoy, 30 April 1914. PAC.
17. *Ibid.*
18. Stefansson to Mrs. Anderson, 16 February 1915. PAC.
19. *Ibid.*
20. *Ibid.*
21. *Ibid.*
22. *Ibid.*
23. Mrs. Anderson to Stefansson, 26 March 1914. CAE Letter Digest.
24. Stefansson to Mrs. Anderson, 16 February 1915.
25. *Ibid.*
26. *Ibid.*
27. *Ibid.*

NOTES TO CHAPTER THIRTEEN

1. Vilhjalmur Stefansson, *The Friendly Arctic* (New York: Macmillan, 1921), p. 330.
2. *Ibid.*, p. 367.
3. *Ibid.*, pp. 373-74.
4. Stefansson to Ed Deming, 4 July 1915.
5. *Ibid.*, 28 December 1915.
6. Stefansson, *The Friendly Arctic*, p. 375.

7. R. C. McConnell to G. J. Desbarats, 3 November 1914. PAC. Reference to the "condemned *Karluk*" here echoed that of other Geological Survey members. The *Karluk* had in fact been inspected before the voyage by experts and declared to be sound.
8. Stefansson to Deming, 28 December 1915.
9. Stefansson, *The Friendly Arctic*, p. 367.
10. *Ibid.*, p. 372.
11. *Ibid.*, 20 April 1916.
12. *Ibid.*, 29 May 1916.
13. *Ibid.*, 13 September 1916.
14. *Ibid.*, 7 October 1916.
15. Harold Noice, *With Stefansson in the Arctic* (New York: Dodd, Mead, n.d.) pp. 29-30, 52, 30.
16. *Ibid.*, p. 30.
17. Stefansson diary, 3 November 1916.
18. *Ibid.*
19. *Ibid.*, 18 August 1917.
20. *Ibid.*
21. Stefansson, *The Friendly Arctic*, p. 672.
22. Joseph Bernard, "Arctic Voyages," Unpublished manuscript, Rasmussen Library, University of Alaska, p. 520.
23. *Ibid.*, p. 58. Nelson's great sea victory at Copenhagen was achieved after he had been ordered to discontinue action.
24. August Masik, *Arctic Night's Entertainment* (London: Blackie, 1935), pp. 124-25.
25. *Ibid.*, pp. 128-29.
26. *Ibid.*, p. 138. August Masik died in Seattle in 1976 at the age of 88.
27. Stefansson, *The Friendly Arctic*, p. 685.
28. Stuck to Wood, 15 May 1918.
29. Chipman scrapbook, clipping, 4 February 1915. PAC. The report was probably made by D'Arcy Arden rather than "D'Ardier."
30. *The Citizen*, Ottawa, 25 November 1916.
31. *Ibid.*
32. *Ibid.*

NOTES TO CHAPTER FOURTEEN

1. Alexander Graham Bell to Stefansson, 25 November 1916.
2. Draft of Stefansson autobiography, 19 January 1962, p. 871.
3. Desbarats to Stefansson, 13 September 1918. In *Discovery*, p. 212, Stefansson said that Desbarats had urged him to "tell the public what our expedition had been like." This is misleading as Desbarats clearly wanted an official report for the public and not lectures.
4. *Ibid.*
5. Stefansson to Desbarats, 19 September 1918.
6. Desbarats to Stefansson, 3 October 1918.
7. Stefansson to Desbarats, 16 October 1918.
8. *Ibid.,* 13 November 1918.
9. Roald Amundsen, *My Life as an Explorer* (New York: Doubleday, Page, 1927), p. 130.
10. Stefansson to Desbarats, 17 January 1919; Anderson's letter to Bowman was dated 6 November 1918; it is remarkable for the invective and innuendo with which he seemed to think Bowman would be in accord.
11. From Storkerson's account of his drift on the sea ice, published as an appendix to Vilhjalmur Stefansson, *The Friendly Arctic* (New York: Macmillan, 1932), pp. 701-2.
12. Vilhjalmur Stefansson, *Discovery* (New York: McGraw-Hill, 1964), p. 222.
13. Vilhjalmur Stefansson, *Not by Bread Alone* (New York: Macmillan, 1956), p. ii.
14. Stefansson to Desbarats, 10 September 1919.
15. *Ibid.,* 19 December 1919.
16. Betty Brainerd to Stefansson, 1918 (n.d.); 30 October 1918; 31 October 1918; Stefansson to Betty Brainerd, 30 October 1918. NA.
17. Betty Brainerd to Stefansson, 13 September 1919. NA.
18. *Ibid.,* 12 December 1923.
19. Draft of Stefansson's autobiography, 18 January 1962, p. 876.
20. *Ibid.,* p. 877.
21. Stefansson to W. H. Hobbs, 21 January 1920; Stefansson to Louis J. de Milhau, 11 January 1922.
22. Clippings, Keedick case.
23. Arctic scrapbook, SPRI.
24. *Ibid.*
25. *New York Herald Tribune,* 15 October 1931.
26. *Montreal Daily Star,* 15 October 1931.
27. Stefansson, *The Standardization of Error,* (New York: Norton and Co., 1927), p. 11.
28. Stefansson folder, University of Washington Library, Special Collections.
29. Stefansson to Charlotte Rudyard, 30 October 1919.
30. Stefansson, *Discovery,* p. 226.
31. Constance Skinner to Stefansson, 30 December 1921. NA.
32. *Ibid.,* 2 February 1923; 8 January 1923. NA.
33. *Ibid.,* 8 November 1924; 18 March 1924. NA.
34. Elizabeth Hanes to Stefansson, 15 June 1921; Fanny Hurst to Stefansson, 1923. NA.
35. Marjorie Holmes to Stefansson, 6 June 1923. NA.
36. Peggy Fletcher to Stefansson, 9 June 1923; 6 June 1922. NA.
37. *Ibid.,* 6 April 1922. NA.
38. *Ibid.,* 3 July 1924. NA.
39. Constance Lindsay Skinner to Stefansson, 6 October 1925, NA; V.S. Pritchett, *Midnight Oil* (London: Chatto and Windus, 1976), p. 219.
40. Fanny Hurst to Stefansson, 30 May 1924. NA.
41. *New York Times,* 23 February 1968.
42. Fanny Hurst to Stefansson, 11 January 1939. NA.
43. Charles P. Everett, *The Adventures of a Treasure Hunter,* (Boston: Little, Brown, 1951) p. 262.

44. Stefansson autobiography, draft, 29 March 1962, p. 77.
45. *Ibid.*, 17 May 1962, p. 89.

NOTES TO CHAPTER FIFTEEN

1. T. C. Fairley, *Sverdrup's Arctic Adventures* (London: Longmans, Green, 1959), p. 278.
2 Stefansson, *Discovery*, pp. 229-30.
3. Stefansson outlined his recommendations in a memo to Meighen dated 30 October 1920, in which he referred to a meeting on 2 October with Meighen, Loring Christie, and John Rutherford (chairman of the royal commission established to review the North's economic potential). Meighen also consulted former prime minister Robert Borden, among others. Borden favoured Stefansson's plans in a memo of 3 November 1920, Meighen papers, PAC.
4. Stefansson to Meighen, 8 January 1921; Harkin to Stefansson (n.d.), Harkin papers, PAC.
5. Stefansson to Harkin, 2 February 1921, Harkin papers, PAC.
6. Stefansson to Harkin, 12 April 1921, Harkin papers, PAC.
7. Harkin to Cory, 19, 25 April 1921, Harkin papers, PAC.
8. Harkin to Stefansson, 31 May 1921, Harkin papers, PAC.
9. Harkin to Cory, 18 July 1921, Harkin papers, PAC.
10. Stefansson's note on an undated news clipping, Harkin papers, PAC.
11. Harkin's notebook, vol. 2 (unnumbered), Harkin papers, PAC.
12. Meighen to Sir James Lougheed, 5 February 1921, Meighen papers, PAC.
13. Shackleton to Stefansson, 17 April 1920. Shackleton thanks Stefansson for his "generous promise of assistance in the event of turning my wandering feet, for a change, to the Far North." On 4 May 1920, after

returning home, Stefansson wrote again asking Shackleton to keep in confidence what Stefansson had related of his polar expedition plans, and reaffirmed what he had said in conversation—that Shackleton's northern exploration was welcome: "My attitude is that no competition in this field can be harmful, and if you still continue interested I shall be glad to give you any information by correspondence." Stefansson also indicated that his own expedition was likely to be approved. (Stefansson wrote later that Shackleton's statement "that I voluntarily conceded to him preference in that field surprised me very much." Stefansson to Armstrong, 7 March 1921, Meighen papers, PAC.)

Years after these events, Stefansson still recalled that he had been double-crossed by Shackleton, but he confused some of the details. In his autobiography, *Discovery*, pp. 237-39, he recalled that he had not offered to help Shackleton because he was totally unaware of Shackleton's plans to explore in the North. Perhaps the confusion is only over the point at which Shackleton revealed his intentions. It does appear, however, that Stefansson was far more generous in offering help than was called for by exploration tradition; his reward was Shackleton's determined effort to convince Meighen that he, Stefansson, had retired from exploration.

14. Shackleton to Meighen, 5 April 1921, enclosed Stefansson's letter to Shackleton of 15 April, 1920. Shackleton must have hoped that Meighen would take his word about Stefansson's intentions rather than reading the letter, but the Englishman's audacity did not prevail. Stefansson's letter confirmed his own exploration plans and Shackleton's bold misrepresentation. Meighen papers, PAC.

15. *Ibid.*
16. Meighen to Shackleton, 9 May 1921, Meighen papers, PAC. In his book, *Stefansson and the Canadian Arctic* (1978), Richard Diubaldo accepts Shackleton's argument to Meighen that the government had made a commitment, and he criticizes Meighen for dodging the promise on the pretense that Shackleton had not completed his preparations. Whether Shackleton was ready or not probably would not have mattered, but his own (unsubstantiated) claim that he was prepared is not convincing authority that Meighen's information was wrong. Diubaldo's sympathy for Shackleton is remarkable ("Shackleton, even if he had been trying to outmanoeuvre Stefansson, was shabbily treated by the Canadian government—or at least by Meighen" [p. 169]) considering his lack of sympathy for Stefansson who, after all, had originated the expedition idea and had been given definite assurances by the government official who was responsible.
17. Bernier to Meighen, 29 July 1921, Meighen papers, PAC.
18. T. C. Fairley, *Sverdrup's Arctic Adventures,* pp. 289-90.
19. Stefansson, *Discovery,* p. 239. See *also* note 13.
20. Stefansson to Meighen, 23 February 1922, Meighen papers, PAC.
21. Stefansson to Hugh Keenleyside, 3 November 1949, Harkin papers, PAC. Harkin was given the letter and wrote his comments on the margin. Stefansson obviously felt that his role in urging Canada to establish sovereignty over the Arctic Islands had not been fully acknowledged. This would still appear to be true even after consultation with the Harkin and Meighen papers in the Public Archives of Canada. It is not clear whether it was money, Shackleton's rivalry, or some other circumstances that determined the course of events. Nor it is evident that Harkin's attitude was generally shared by leading government officials. Although I have been told that Ottawa in the 1920's was a small and petty place, the Byzantine devices suggested by Harkin confound the mind.
22. W.T. Lopp, Report to Hudson's Bay Reindeer Company, 7 April 1925. University of Oregon Archives.
23. Stefansson to Mackenzie King, 5 October 1923.
24. Stefansson to Carl Lomen, 20 June 1927. University of Alaska Archives.
25. Dr. Peter Lent, Alaska Cooperative Wildlife Research Unit, University of Alaska, conversation with author, 17 June 1974.

NOTES TO CHAPTER SIXTEEN

1. Vilhjalmur Stefansson, *The Friendly Arctic,* (New York: Macmillan, 1932), p. xviii.
2. *Ibid.,* p. xix.
3. *Ibid.,* p. xxiv.
4. Years later John Teal, a young friend of Stefansson's, began research with musk-ox in Vermont and later at the University of Alaska. The project was carried on until the mid-1970's when the animals were moved from the campus to selected native villages.
5. Stefansson, *The Friendly Arctic,* p. xxv.
6. *Ibid.,* p. 20.
7. *Ibid.,* p. 580.
8. Neil M. Clark, "Ships North to Alaska's Coast," *Montana* (Fall 1973): 36.
9. London *Express,* 4 March 1902.
10. Stefansson, *The Friendly Arctic* (New York: Macmillan, 1921), p. 258.
11. Anthony Fiala, *Fighting the Polar Ice* (New York: Doubleday, Page, 1906), pp. 3, 7.

12. Trevelyan Miller, *World's Greatest Adventure* (Philadelphia: Winston, 1930), p. 8.
13. Stefansson, *The Friendly Arctic*, p. 114.
14. *Ibid.*
15. *Ibid.*, p. 98.
16. Dellenbaugh, *Nation*. CAE clipping file.
17. W.H. Hobbs, *Journal of Geology*, February-March 1923. CAE clipping file.
18. *Geographical Review*, April 1922. CAE clipping file.
19. *Montreal Standard*, 21 January 1922.
20. *Ibid.*
21. Morris Zaslow, *The Opening of the Canadian North: 1870-1914*, (Toronto: McClelland and Stewart, 1971), p. 276.
22. Diamond Jenness, "The Friendly Arctic," *Science* (7 July, 1922): 8.
23. Vilhjalmur Stefansson, "The Friendly Arctic," *Science*, (30 March 1923): 369.
24. Burt M. McConnell and Harold Noice, "The Friendly Arctic," *Science*, (30 March 1923): 370.
25. *Ibid.*, pp. 371-72.
26. *Ibid.*, p. 372.
27. *Ibid.*, p. 373.
28. *Ibid.*
29. Stefansson to Burnham, 21 August 1922.
30. Charles Camsell, "The Friendly Arctic," *Science*, (8 June 1923): 666.
31. Brock to Camsell, 24 April 1923, PAC.
32. Camsell to Prince, 26 April 1923, PAC.
33. *New York Times*, 14 and 15 January 1922.
34. *Ibid.*, 16 January 1922.
35. *Ibid.*, 17 and 18 January 1922.
36. *Ibid.*, 19 January 1922. The *Times* was certainly right about the controversy. See the author's book, *To Stand At The Pole* (New York: Stein and Day, 1981), for a discussion of controversies concerning Elisha

Kent Kane, G.W. DeLong, A.W. Greely, E.B. Baldwin, Robert Peary, and Frederick Cook.

NOTES TO CHAPTER SEVENTEEN

1. Late in 1921, Mrs. Rudolph Anderson decided that she had gathered enough evidence about Stefansson to ruin his reputation. She was sure she could prove dramatically that he was not a Canadian citizen and that therefore his whole career was based on fraud and imposture. Mrs. Anderson's accomplice in the published attack was a "Mrs. Martin," who had been commissioned by the Andersons to write several articles based on material that Mrs. Anderson pulled together. The other source was a long interview with Rudolph Anderson, for which he had prepared a thirty-four page memorandum. On 14 January 1922 Mrs. Anderson boasted in a letter to William Laird McKinlay: "This morning the first round was fired in the Canadian papers, 132 of them. It will be followed by others." She also referred to an interview her husband had given a newsman in Iowa two months earlier. "Stefansson," she wrote, "had been there a short time before knocking Dr. Anderson in his home state," and so, according to her, Anderson was merely trying to set the record straight. Mrs. Anderson urged McKinlay to write magazine articles about the expedition, assuring him that Stefansson "is discredited as a scientific man," although he "is still a popular hero in U.S.A. They know him better in Canada." (Mrs. Anderson to W.L. McKinlay, 14 January 1922.)

   Anderson's memorandum is an interesting document. The biologist intended it to be his complete answer to articles Stefansson had written in *Harpers, Maclean's,* and *World's*

Work, as well as The Friendly Arctic. Anderson argued that Stefansson's case for an Arctic rich in natural resources ignored the frequent deaths of northern travellers, "including a considerable percentage of the men who have, unfortunately, been associated with Mr. Stefansson." It was the judgment of Anderson and others that what he described as Stefansson's "romantic tales" were responsible for many deaths, "and if allowed to pass unchecked [they] will be responsible for many more in the future." Anderson reviewed the history of the Canadian Arctic Expedition as he recalled it. His report was predictably subjective, and like Stefansson's own, it revealed his conviction that he had been invariably correct and judicious in his conduct, whereas his chief adversary had been gravely in the wrong. The closest Anderson came to being charitable was when he wrote that he was "inclined to think...Mr. Stefansson's mental balance was not on [an] even keel during the whole of the time of the expedition." (R.M. Anderson, memorandum on Stefansson, The Friendly Arctic, 3 April 1922, pages unnumbered (PAC).)

2. Pedersen to Stefansson, 8 March 1922.

3. Stefansson to Pedersen, 12 January 1916; Stefansson to Tilton, 21 January 1916.

4. Vilhjalmur Stefansson, The Friendly Arctic (New York: Macmillan, 1932), pp. 47-48.

5. Stefansson to Phillips, 19 January 1914; Stefansson to Perry, 19 January 1914.

6. R.M. Anderson, memorandum on Stefansson, The Friendly Arctic, 3 April 1922.

7. Diamond Jenness, Dawn in Arctic Alaska (Minneapolis: University of Minnesota, 1957), p. 7. Jenness's diary in the Public Archives of

Canada, Ottawa, reflects the same point of view as his book.

8. Robert Bartlett, Last Voyage of the Karluk (Boston: Small, 'Maynard, 1916), p. 29.

9. Ibid., pp. 34-36.

10. William Laird McKinlay, Karluk (London: Weidenfeld and Nicolson, 1976), p. 30. It is unlikely that McKinlay had missed Bartlett's discussion of the hunting party in Last Voyage of the Karluk.

11. Mrs. Anderson to Bartlett, 2 January 1922; Mrs. Anderson to McKinlay, 14 January 1922. I have not found any letters from Bartlett to Mrs. Anderson, but in a letter to McKinlay, 9 February 1922, PAC, she wrote "It is Hadley's account [in The Friendly Arctic] that makes Bartlett so mad."

12. Stefansson, Discovery (New York: McGraw Hill, 1964), pp. 216-17.

13. Harold Harwood, Bartlett: The Great Canadian Explorer (New York: Doubleday, 1977), p. 15, p. 17, also criticizes Bartlett's preparations.

14. Stefansson to Desbarats, 12 January 1916.

15. John Hadley's memoir, p. 8.

16. Stefansson to Desbarats, 12 January 1916.

17. Ibid. According to Bartlett, Stefansson did not know at the time he was writing that some Karluk personnel were too ill for strenuous travel. However, even when Stefansson heard Bartlett's counterargument, he remained unconvinced.

18. Vilhjalmur Stefansson, Adventure of Wrangel Island (New York: Macmillan, 1925), p. 63.

19. McKinlay to Mrs. Anderson, 8 February 1922, PAC.

20. R.M. Anderson, memorandum on Stefansson, The Friendly Arctic, pp. 8-9, PAC.

21. Stefansson, The Friendly Arctic, p. 704.

22. Stefansson to Williamson, 21 May 1959.
23. Williamson to Stefansson, 17 May and 11 June 1959.
24. *The Citizen*, Ottawa, 7 October 1976.
25. McKinlay, *Karluk*, p. 161.
26. *Ibid.*, p. 162.
27. *Ibid.*, pp. ix-x.
28. Some of the correspondence between Mrs. Anderson and McKinlay cited elsewhere shows where McKinlay got much of his information.

NOTES TO CHAPTER EIGHTEEN

1. Vilhjalmur Stefansson, *Discovery* (New York: McGraw-Hill, 1964), p. 254.
2. Vilhjalmur Stefansson, *The Adventure of Wrangel Island* (New York: Macmillan, 1925), p. 80.
3. Stefansson, *Discovery*, p. 255.
4. Stefansson, *Adventure*, p. 120.
5. *New York Times*, 20 March 1922.
6. Stefansson, *Adventure*, p. 283.
7. Stefansson to Mackenzie King, 10 July 1923, PAC.
8. Stefansson to Batterbee, 30 July 1923, PAC.
9. *Ibid.*
10. *Ibid.*
11. Stefansson, *Adventure*, p. 162.
12. *Ibid.*, p. 167.
13. *Ibid.*, p. 286, pp. 294-95.
14. *Montreal Standard*, 9 September 1923.
15. Unidentified Toronto newspaper, 15 September 1923. Wrangel Island Scrapbook.
16. Stefansson, *Adventure*, p. 294. Canadian historian Richard Diubaldo has effectively shown how embarrassing the international incident was for the government and the procrastination of King and Meighen after the ire of the Soviet Union and the apprehension of the United States were aroused.

Diubaldo's reasoning and documentation are a little shakey in going on to find that Stefansson's motives were mercenary rather than patriotic or adventurous. Stefansson would have preferred a reimbursement of his expenses for the colony to a lease, and without a lease he had no chance of making money from the project. Anyone reflecting on Stefansson's life should notice that profit making was not a conspicuous motivation in any of his endeavors. Diubaldo misread Stefansson's letter to O.S. Finnie, 3 May 1922, that shows Stefansson's preference and clear statement to the government. See Richard Diubaldo, "Wrangling over Wrangel Island," *Canadian Historical Review* 48(3): 209, 211. *See also* Diubaldo, *Stefansson and the Canadian Arctic* (Montreal: McGill-Queen's, 1978), p. 170.
17. Wrangel Island Scrapbook. The Andersons had intensified their press efforts, particularly with the Ottawa *Citizen*.
18. John Irvine Knight, in Stefansson, *Adventure*, p. xix.
19. The Lomen papers at the University of Alaska indicate that the U.S. Government agreed to pay the claim. Mark Jerome Seidenberg, an American citizen residing in Los Angeles, who holds a quit claim deed to the island from Ralph Lomen, believes that the claim was not paid. As an item of peripheral interest, an American right wing group announced in September 1977 that Wrangel Island was an American territory and demanded that the U.S. assert its claim to sovereignty against the Soviet Union.

NOTES TO CHAPTER NINETEEN

1. *Times Literary Supplement*, 29 March 1923.

2. Ottawa *Citizen*, 4 December 1929.
3. Vilhjalmur Stefansson, *Discovery* (New York: McGraw-Hill, 1964), p. 296.
4. *Ibid.*, p. 297.
5. *Ibid.*
6. Diubaldo, *Stefansson and the Canadian Arctic*, p. 251.
7. Calvin White memorandum.
8. Rudolph Anderson to Harkin, 27 September 1920. Anderson papers, PAC. Anderson's letter ran to twelve pages.
9. Richard Finnie, *Canada Moves North* (New York: Macmillan, 1942), p. 2.
10. Kenneth Rea, *The Political Economy of the Canadian North* (Toronto: University of Toronto Press, 1966), p. 3.
11. *North* (November-December 1973): 2.
12. Richard Finnie, "North American Arctic Petroleum Development," *Polar Notes*, (1971): 21-41.
13. Laurence F. Jones and George Loun, *Pathfinders of the North* (Toronto: Pitt, 1970), pp. vii-viii.
14. David Judd, "Canada's Northern Policy: Retrospect and Prospect," *Polar Record* 14, no. 92 (1969): 595.
15. *Ibid.*
16. *Ibid.*
17. *Ibid.*, pp. 593, 602.
18. *Dallas Morning News,*, 8 August 1985.

NOTES TO CHAPTER TWENTY

1. Ottawa *Journal*, undated clipping (March 1926?). Cited in Stefansson to Isaiah Bowman, 15 March 1926.
2. Stefansson, *The Friendly Arctic* (New York: Macmillan, 1943), p. v.
3. *Ibid.*, p. 278.
4. Vilhjalmur Stefansson, *Unsolved Mysteries of the Arctic* (New York: Macmillan, 1939), p. 38.
5. *Ibid.*, p. 38.
6. Fridtjof Nansen, *Farthest North* (London: Newnes, 1898), p. 232.
7. Stefansson to J. Gordon Hayes, 5 February 1927. His praise of Nansen also appeared in the *New York Herald Tribune* (3 February 1929) and on occasion in other publications.
8. Stefansson, *Discovery* (New York: McGraw-Hill, 1964), p. 136.
9. Stefansson to J. Gordon Hayes, 5 February 1927.
10. *Ibid.*
11. Ottawa *Journal, op. cit.*
12. *Ibid.*
13. *Explorers Club Tales*, p. 19.
14. *Ibid.*
15. *Ibid.*, p. 21.
16. *Ibid.* Amundsen was not usually as arrogant as his statement suggests, but his ego did meet the demands of the exploration endeavour. His reaction to encountering King William Island Eskimos should be compared with Stefansson's feelings on meeting the Copper Eskimo. "This was a truly thrilling moment in the lives of these poor savages," Amundsen wrote. "No one of them had ever seen a white man before." ("Amundsen Answers His Critics," *World's Work* [July 1927]: 284).
17. Carl Lomen to Frank Dellenbaugh, 17 October 1927; Stefansson, *The Friendly Arctic*, p. 7.
18. Arctic Scrapbook, 1927-28. SPRI. Reviewers did not pay particular attention to Amundsen's slurs on Stefansson, perhaps because his attacks on Umberto Nobile concerning the then recent flight of the *Norge* were more interesting.
19. *Ibid.*
20. W.H. Hobbs to Stefansson, 21 November 1927. Roland Huntford, *Scott and Amundsen* (New York: Putnam's Sons), p. 573, describes Amundsen's autobiography as "an unbalanced work" reflecting a sharp personality change.
21. Bowman to Stefansson, 19 Sep-

tember 1927. Sir Hubert Wilkins took up some of Amundsen's errors in a letter to the Norwegian's American publisher, which he had hoped to place also in some journal. It is worthy of note that after arguing that Amundsen probably suffered a mental aberration because of his *Maud* expedition woes, Wilkins still observed that "Amundsen deserves much more credit than he will ever get for the really great work he has accomplished." Wilkins to A. Page Cooper, 6 October 1927.

22. *Ibid.*
23. *Ibid.* Stefansson's request that the American Geographical Society formally investigate the charges were ignored as was his request of the Explorers Club that it give Storkerson a medal for his ice drift which featured sea ice hunting. Stefansson to Bowman, 29 November 1927; Stefansson to Explorers Club, 1 November 1927. Later Stefansson rebuked Explorers Club members who suggested withdrawing a Club medal from Amundsen for his treatment of the Club, reminding them that the medal had not been awarded for good manners. Stefansson to Explorers Club, 10 November 1927.
24. Anderson to Amundsen, 4 March 1926. PAC.
25. *Week-End Review,* 30 August 1930.
26. London *Times,* 3 September 1930.
27. Stefansson to Knud Rasmussen, 13 April 1920.
28. Rasmussen to Stefansson, 11 May 1920.
29. Statement of Admiral Hugh Rodman.
30. Statement for Fox Movietone news.
31. *The New Yorker,* 28 March 1931, p. 24.
32. Statement for National Broadcasting Company, 6 October 1931.
33. Stefansson, *Discovery,* p. 301.
34. Stefansson to W.H. Hobbs, 7 March 1923.

35. Stefansson autobiography, draft, p. 89.
36. MacMillan to Marie Peary Stafford, 1932, n.d. NA.
37. *Ibid.*

NOTES TO
CHAPTER TWENTY-ONE

1. Taped interview, Stefansson by Walter Sullivan, 10 March 1959; Sullivan's article is in New York *Times,* 6 April 1959, p. 26:3.
2. Stefansson diary, 13 September 1910 to 30 January 1911. Notes on unnumbered pages in first part of diary.
3. Stefansson to W.H. Hobbs, 17 September 1920.
4. Stefansson to Isaiah Bowman, 20 December 1923.
5. Stefansson to J. Gordon Hayes, 5 February 1927. Hayes's failure to quote Stefansson's full comment may not have been an effort to deceive his readers. He knew that Stefansson did not wish to be quoted on any matter that the Peary family considered to be personal. Yet the quotation was taken out of context without his approval, and it injured Stefansson.
6. L.P. Kirwan, *History of Polar Exploration* (New York: Norton, 1960), p. 361, described Hayes's book as unbalanced and biased.
7. James Wordie to Stefansson, 12 May 1922.
8. Stefansson to Thomas F. Hall, 24 June 1938.
9. Stefansson to Charles Angoff, 29 May 1934.
10. Henshaw Ward to Commander Wood, 4 October 1934. NA.
11. Henshaw Ward diary, 2, 6 October, 1934. NA.
12. Marie Peary Stafford to Stefansson, 25 September 1934.
13. Stefansson to Marie Peary Stafford, 28 September 1934.

14. Stefansson to Isaiah Bowman, 8 November 1934.
15. Isaiah Bowman to Stefansson, 9 November 1934.
16. W.H. Hobbs to Stefansson, 2 January 1935. See also note 5 above.
17. Stefansson to W.H. Hobbs, 4, 7 January 1935.
18. W.H. Hobbs to Stefansson, 8 January 1935. The "Mirsky book" to which Hobbs referred was Jeannette Mirsky's, To The North (New York: Viking, 1934), which for many years has been the most popular American book on polar exploration. It is a lively, well written chronicle, and in recent years has appeared in paperback. Mirsky consulted Stefansson during her research and she altered her views on the Cook-Peary controversy as a result of her reading and their discussions. Originally, Jeanette Mirsky had given Cook credit for all he claimed to have achieved (except for reaching the Pole) and in Stefansson's view she accepted much that was dubious. Mirsky's book upset Cook enough to compel him to bring a lawsuit against her, in spite of which Marie Peary Stafford described the book as "horrid," and Hobbs found Stefansson's introduction harmful. (Stefansson to Marie Peary Stafford, 15 October 1934; Marie Peary Stafford to Stefansson, 4 January 1935.)
19. Stefansson to W.H. Hobbs, 10 January 1935.
20. Marie Peary Stafford to Stefansson, 11 January 1935.
21. Stefansson to Balmer, 15 January 1935.
22. Stefansson to Marie Peary Stafford, 15 January 1935.
23. Hobbs's biography remained the standard work in the United States until John Edward Weems's, Peary: The Explorer and the Man (London: Eyre & Spotteswoode, 1967), appeared.
24. W.H. Hobbs to Wise, 20 January 1935. NA.
25. W.H. Hobbs to Marie Peary Stafford and to Stefansson, 12 February 1935. NA.
26. Stefansson to W.H. Hobbs, 20 January 1930.
27. W.H. Hobbs to Marie Peary Stafford, 15 May 1935; 4 June 1935, NA. Marie Peary Stafford to Stefansson, 31 March 1935.
28. W.H. Hobbs to Marie Peary Stafford, 24 October 1935 and 22 November 1935. NA.
29. Isaiah Bowman to Marie Peary Stafford, 27 February, 12 March 1935. NA.
30. Stefansson to Isaiah Bowman, 9 March 1937; Isaiah Bowman to Stefansson, 27 July 1937, gives Bowman's opinion on the book.
31. Marie Peary Stafford to Lawrence Gould, 6 December 1939. Both Peary and Marie were incensed by Matt Henson's statements that Peary's crippled condition had required him to ride in the sledge on the final approach to the Pole. Stefansson apparently accepted Henson's version and cited it as the kind of inconsistency in reporting that occurs in ghost-written books. In Robert Peary, The North Pole (New York: Stokes, 1910), Peary asserts that he was moving under his own power all the way. In my view Stefansson was too charitable in assuming that Peary would not have concealed his weakness in the published narrative.
32. Ibid.
33. Marie Peary Stafford to Stefansson, 19 November 1939, NA.
34. Marie Peary Stafford to Lawrence Gould, 9 December 1939, NA.
35. Marie Peary Stafford to Stefansson, 15 June 1944, NA.
36. Dennis Rawlins, Peary at the Pole: Fact or Fiction? (Toronto: Musson, 1973). Whether the Cook Society still exists I do not know, but members of the group were active in the

mid-1970's. There have also been a number of journalistic attempts to restore Cook's reputation, usually at the expense of Peary's, and a recent American TV drama following the same line. See William R. Hunt, *To Stand at the Pole* (New York: Stein & Day, 1981).

37. The Peary correspondence in the National Archives makes the story comprehensible. Reading it, Stefansson learned about Thomas, but not about Pedersen. His argument for Peary would have strengthened had he known then that Peary had two ghost writers.

NOTES TO CHAPTER TWENTY-TWO

1. The *New Yorker,* 25 October 1941, p. 27.
2. Vilhjalmur Stefansson, *Adventures in Error* (New York: Robert M. McBride, 1936), p. 244.
3. *Ibid.*
4. Jan Welzl, *Thirty Years in the Golden North* (New York: Macmillan, 1932), pp. 190, 221.
5. *Ibid.*, p. 186.
6. *Ibid.*, p. 286.
7. *Ibid.*, p. 300.
8. Stefansson, *Discovery*, p. 305.
9. *Ibid.*
10. Stefansson, *Discovery*, p. 343. Later tests refuted Stefansson's conclusions. See G. Edgar Folk, Jr., *Vilhjalmur Stefansson and the Development of Arctic Territorial Science* (Iowa City: University of Iowa, 1984), pp. 85-100.
11. *Ibid.*, p. 247.
12. *Ibid.*, p. 288.
13. *Ibid.*, p. 289.
14. *Ibid.*, p. 292.
15. Vilhjalmaur Stefansson, *Great Adventures & Exploration,* (London: Robert Hale, 1947), p. xi.

NOTES TO CHAPTER TWENTY-THREE

1. Stefansson, *Discovery* (New York: McGraw-Hill, 1964), p. 391.
2. *Ibid.*, p. 337.
3. Stefansson to Evelyn Baird, 16 November 1939; 13 May 1940. NA.
4. *Ibid.*, 1 November 1940. NA.
5. *The New Yorker,* 18 October 1941, p. 26.
6. *Ibid.*, pp. 26, 30.
7. Stefansson diary, 3 February 1947; 15 February 1947.
8. Stefansson, *Discovery*, p. 364.
9. *Ibid.*, 3 December 1923. NA.
10. Weigert, Hans W., et al. *New Compass of the World* (London: Harrap, 1949), p. 24.
11. In time the *Encyclopedia Arctica* was published on microfilm (Ann Arbor: University Microfilms, 1944).
12. New York *Journal-American,* 12 January 1948.
13. Nutt, "Stef at Dartmouth," *Polar Notes* (November 1962): 31, 36.
14. Owen Lattimore, *Silk, Spices, and Empire,* p. ii.
15. *New Hampshire Sunday News,* 16 January 1955.
16. *Ibid.*
17. *The Dartmouth,* 17 February 1955.
18. Stefansson, *Discovery*, p. 374.
19. *The Dartmouth,* 20 January 1955.
20. Stefansson interview tape, 12 November 1959.
21. *Ibid.*

NOTES TO CHAPTER TWENTY-FOUR

1. Stefansson, *Discovery* (New York: McGraw-Hill, 1964), p. 387.
2. *Ibid.*, p. 389.
3. *Ibid.*, p. 390.
4. *Ibid.*, p. 391.
5. *New York Times,* 13 September 1964.

6. Lawrence McKinley Gould, "Vilhjalmur Stefansson: A Subjective
   View," *Polar Notes* (November
   1962): 2. At this writing, Gould is
   still working. He made his latest Antarctic field trip in 1976-77 at eighty
   years of age and was an active
   teacher and researcher at the University of Arizona.
7. *Ibid.*
8. Owen Lattimore, "Some Apprecia-
   tions," *Polar Notes* (November
   1962): 40.
9. *The New Yorker*, 25 October 1941,
   p. 76.

Bibliography

PRIMARY SOURCES

The Stefansson Collection at Dartmouth College is the most important single source of documentation. The correspondence is well arranged by date in the general correspondence files, but there is also a card catalogue for easy access. All materials on some major topics, like the Wrangel Island colony, are grouped together for convenient reference. There is also a letter digest to correspondence on the Stefansson-Anderson Expedition and the Canadian Arctic Expedition.

Much of the Stefansson Collection material on the CAE is duplicated in the CAE collection of the Public Archives of Canada in Ottawa. The Public Archives has all the original diaries kept on the expedition, all official correspondence, memos, and so forth, and the photographic record of the expedition. As my specific chapter note references indicate, I have also used other related collections at the Public Archives, including the Rudolph Anderson, Kenneth Chipman, J. B. Harkin, Arthur Meighen, Charles Camsell, J.T. Crawford, W. L. Mackenzie King, and the Geological Survey collections.

The Center for Polar Archives at the National Archives in Washington has a small collection of Stefansson's personal correspondence, some Peary papers, and the C. Henshaw Ward papers. I have also used the Lomen Collection at the University of Oregon; a letter from the Pitts Museum, one from the University of Washington Suzzallo Library, Special Collections, and very useful correspondence and clipping books in the Scott Polar Research Institute at Cambridge, England.

Archival Material

Dartmouth College, Baker Library, Stefansson Collection
  General correspondence
  Papers and manuscripts

National Archives, Center for Polar Archives
  Marie Stafford Papers
  Vilhjalmur Stefansson Personal Correspondence
  C. Henshaw Ward Papers

Pitt Museum, Oxford

Public Archives of Canada, Manuscript Division
  Mrs. Rudolf Anderson Collection
  Canadian Arctic Expedition Papers
  Chipman Papers
  Harkin Papers
  Meighen Papers

Scott Polar Research Institute
  Pedersen-Swithinbank Correspondence
  Press Cuttings — Arctic

SECONDARY SOURCES

Amundsen, Roald. *The Northwest Passage.* 2 vols. London: Archibald Constable, 1908.
———. *My Life as an Explorer.* New York: Doubleday, Page, 1927.
Anderson, J.R.L. *The Ulysses Factor.* London: Hodder & Stoughton, 1970.
Bartlett, Robert A. *Last Voyage of the Karluk.* Boston: Small, Maynard, 1916.
———. *The Log of Bob Bartlett.* New York: Blue Ribbon, 1928.
Bernard, Joseph. *Arctic Voyages.* Unpublished manuscript, Rasmuson Library, University of Alaska.
Birket-Smith, Kaj. *The Eskimos.* London: Methuen, 1955.
Bockstoce, John. "Contacts Between American Whalemen and the Copper Eskimos." *Arctic* 28, no. 4 (1975):298-99.
Brower, Charles D. *Fifty Years Below Zero.* London: Robert Hale, n.d.
Camsell, Charles. [Letter to the Editor]. *Science* 57(1923):665-66.
Carlson, William S. *Lifelines through the Arctic.* New York: Duell, Sloan, and Pearce, 1962.

Caswell, John E. *Arctic Frontiers*. Norman, Oklahoma: University of Oklahoma Press, 1956.

Catalogue of the Stefansson Collection on the Polar Regions in the Dartmouth College Library. Boston: G.K. Hall, 1967.

Clark, Neil M. "Ships North to Alaska's Coast." *Montana the Magazine of Western History* 23, no. 4 (1973):32-41.

Cook, Dr. Frederick Albert. *My Attainment of the Pole*. New York: The Polar Publishing Co., 1911.

———. *Return From the Pole*. Annotated by Frederick J. Pohl. New York: Pellegrini & Cudahy, 1951.

Corner, George W. *Dr. Kane of the Arctic Seas*. Philadelphia: Temple University Press, 1972.

Courtauld, Augustine. *From the Ends of the Earth: An Anthology of Polar Writings*. London: Oxford University Press, 1958.

Davis, Robert, and Zannis, Mark. *Genocide Machine in Canada*. Montreal: Black Rose Books, 1973.

Diubaldo, Richard J. "Wrangling over Wrangel Island." *Canadian Historical Review* 48, no. 3 (1967):201-26.

———. *Stefansson and the Canadian Arctic*. Montreal: McGill-Queen's University Press, 1978.

Dodge, Ernest S. *Northwest By Sea*. London: Oxford University Press, 1961.

Dunbar, Moira. *Arctic Canada From the Air*. In collaboration with Keith R. Greenaway. Ottawa: Queen's Printer, 1956.

Eames, Hugh. *Winner Lose All: Dr. Cook and the Theft of the North Pole*. Boston: Little, Brown, 1973.

Ellsworth, Lincoln. *Beyond Horizons*. London: Heinemann, 1938.

Enterline, James Robert. *Viking America*. New York: Doubleday, 1972.

Everett, Charles. *Adventures of a Treasure Hunter*.

Fejes, Claire. *People of the Noatak*. New York: Knopf, 1967.

Fiala, Anthony. *Fighting the Polar Ice*. New York: Doubleday, Page, 1906.

Finnie, Richard. *Canada Moves North*. New York: The Macmillan Company. 1942.

———. *Lure of the North*. Philadelphia: McKay, 1940.

Fisher, Margery and James. *Shackleton*. London: Barrie, 1957.

Folk, G. Edgar and Mary Arp Folk, *Vilhjalmur Stefansson and the Development of Arctic Terrestial Science*. Iowa City: University of Iowa, 1984.

Franklin, Sir John. *Narrative of a Journey to the Shores of the Polar Sea in the Years 1819-20-21-22*. London: Dent, 1819.

———. *Narrative of a Second Expedition to the Shores of the Polar Sea in the Years 1825, 1826, and 1827*. London: John Murray, 1828.

Freuchen, Peter. *Arctic Adventure: My Life in the Frozen North*. New York: Farrar & Rinehart, 1935.

———. *I Sailed with Rasmussen*. New York: Viking Press, 1961.

———. *Book of the Eskimos*. New York: Fawcett World Library, 1961.

———. *Book of Arctic Exploration*. New York: Coward-McCann, 1962.

Gillingham, D.W. *Umiak!* London: Museum Press, 1955.

Greely, A.W. *Handbook of Polar Discoveries*. Boston: Little, Brown, 1907.

Grierson, John. *Sir Hubert Wilkins, Enigma of Exploration.* London: Robert Hale, 1960.

Gruber, Ruth. *I Went to the Soviet Arctic.* New York: Simon & Schuster, 1939.

Hall, Charles Francis. *Life With the Esquimaux.* Edmonton: Hurtig, 1970.

Hanford, Roland. *Scott & Amundsen.* New York: G.P. Putman's, 1980.

Hanson, Earl P. *Stefansson, Prophet of the North.* New York: Harper & Brothers, 1941.

Hanssen, Helmer. *Voyages of a Modern Viking.* London: Routledge & Sons, Ltd., 1936.

Harrison, Alfred H. *In Search of a Polar Continent.* London: Arnold, 1908.

Hayes, J. Gordon. *Conquest of the North Pole.* New York: Macmillan, 1934.

Hearne, Samuel. *A Journey to the Northern Ocean.* Toronto: Macmillan, 1958.

Henson, Matthew A. *A Black Explorer at the North Pole.* Toronto: Ryerson Press, 1969.

Hinton, A. Cherry, and Godsell, Philip H. *Yukon.* Philadelphia: Macrae Smith, 1955.

Hobbs, William Herbert. *Peary.* New York: The Macmillan Company, 1936.

Hudson, Will E. *Icy Hell.* London: Constable and Company, Ltd., 1937.

Hunt, L.A.C.O. Review of LeBourdais's "Stefansson, Ambassador of the North." *North* (1975).

Hunt, William R. *North of 53°.* New York: Macmillan, 1974.

——— "Cold Glory: Values of Polar Exploration." *Polar Notes* (1975):43-53.

——— *To Stand at the Pole.* New York: Stein and Day, 1981.

Hurst, Fannie. *Anatomy of Me.* New York: Doubleday, 1958.

Jenness, Diamond. "The Friendly Arctic." *Science* 56(1922):8-12.

——— *People of the Twilight.* New York: Macmillan, 1928.

——— *Dawn in Arctic Alaska.* Minneapolis: University of Minnesota Press, 1957.

——— *Life of the Copper Eskimo.* New York: Johnson Reprint Corp., 1970.

Joerg, W.L.G. *Problems of Polar Research.* New York: American Geographical Society, 1928.

Jones, Kenneth. "How Canada Almost Claimed Wrangel Island." *Canadian Geographic:* 57-63.

Jones, Lawrence F., and Lonn, George. *Pathfinders of the North.* Toronto: Pitt Publishing Company, 1970.

Kane, Elisha Kent. *The U.S. Grinnell Expedition in Search of Sir John Franklin.* New York: Harper & Bros., 1854.

——— *Arctic Explorations in the Years 1853, '54, '55.* Philadelphia: Childe & Paterson, 1856.

Kirwan, L.P. *History of Polar Exploration.* New York: Norton, 1960.

Lamb, G.F. *Franklin, Happy Voyager.* London: Benn, 1956.

LeBourdais, D.M. *Northward on the New Frontier.* Ottawa: Graphic Publisher's Limited, 1931.

———. *Canada's Century.* Toronto: Methuen, 1951.

———. *Stefansson, Ambassador of the North.* Montreal: Harvest House, 1963.

Lomen, Carl J. *Fifty Years in Alaska.* New York: McKay, 1954.

Loomis, Chauncey. *Weird and Tragic Shores.* New York: Knopf, 1971.

Lotz, Jim. *Northern Realities.* Chicago: Follett, 1971.

McClintock, F. Leopold. *The Voyage of the Fox in Arctic Seas*. London: Murray, 1908.

McCracken, Harold. *Roughnecks and Gentlemen*. New York: Doubleday, 1968.

MacDonald, R. St. J. *The Arctic Frontier*. Toronto: University of Toronto Press, 1966.

McFee, William. *The Life of Sir Martin Frobisher*. London: John Lane, The Bodley Head, 1928.

MacInnes, Tom, ed. *Klengenberg of the Arctic*. London: Cape, 1932.

MacKay, Douglas. *The Honourable Company*. Toronto: McClelland & Stewart, 1949.

McKinlay, William Laird. *Karluk*. London: Weidenfeld & Nicolson, 1976.

MacMillan, Donald B. *Four Years in the White North*. Boston: Hale, Cushman, & Flint, 1933.

———. *How Peary Reached the Pole*. Boston: Houghton Mifflin, 1934.

Malaurie, Jean. *The Last Kings of Thule*. New York: Dutton, 1982.

Maskik, August, and Hutchison, Isobel W. *Arctic Nights' Entertainment*. London: Blackie, 1935.

Mencken, H.L. *The American Language*. New York: Knopf, 1937.

Miller, Trevelyan. *World's Greatest Adventure*. Philadelphia: Winston, 1930.

Mirsky, Jeanette. *To The North*. New York: The Viking Press, 1934.

Montgomery, Richard G. *"Pechuck," Lorne Knight's Adventures in the Arctic*. Caldwell, Idaho: Caxton Printers, 1948.

Morison, Samuel Eliot. *The European Discovery of America: the Northern Voyages A.D. 500-1600*. New York: Oxford University Press, 1971.

Mowat, Farley. *The Polar Passion*. Toronto: McClelland & Stewart, 1967.

Nansen, Fridtjof. *Farthest North*. London: Newnes, 1898.

Nanton, Paul. *Arctic Breakthrough*. Toronto: Clarke, Irwin, 1970.

Neatby, L.H. *Conquest of the Last Frontier*. Athens, Ohio: Ohio University Press, 1966.

Nobile, Umberto. *My Polar Flight*. London: Muller, 1961.

Noice, Harold. *With Stefansson in the Arctic*. New York: Dodd, Mead, 1924.

———, and Burt McConnell. "The Friendly Arctic." *Science 57* (1922):369-73.

North. Government of Canada, Department of Indian and Northern Affairs, Ottawa, *passim*.

Oleson, Tryggvi J. *Early Voyages and Northern Approaches 1000-1632*. Toronto: McClelland & Stewart, 1963.

Oswalt, Wendell H. *Eskimos and Explorers*. Novato, Ca.: Chandler & Sharp, 1979.

Pearl, Raymond. "The Friendly Arctic." *Science 55*(1922):320-21.

Peary, Robert E. *Northward Over the "Great Ice."* New York: Stokes, 1898.

———. *Nearest the Pole*. New York: Doubleday, Page, 1907.

———. *The North Pole*. New York: Stokes, 1910.

———. *Secrets of Polar Travel*. New York: Century, 1917.

Phillips, R.A.J. *Canada's North*. Toronto: Macmillan, 1967.

Polar Notes. Stefansson Collection, Dartmouth College, *passim*.

Polar Record. Scott Polar Research Institute, Cambridge University, *passim*.

Polar Times. American Polar Society, New York.

Putnam, George Palmer. *Mariner of the North*. New York: Duell, Sloan & Pearce, 1947.

Rae, Dr. John. *Narrative of an Expedition to the Shores of the Arctic Sea in 1846-47*. London: Boone, 1850.

———. *Rae's Arctic Correspondence, 1844-1855*. London: Hudson's Bay Record Society, 1953.

Rasky, Frank. *Polar Voyages*. Toronto: McGraw-Hill Ryerson, 1976.

Rasmussen, Knud. *Across Arctic America: Narrative of the Fifth Thule Expedition*. New York: G.P. Putnam's Sons, 1927.

Rawlins, Dennis. *Peary at the North Pole: Fact or Fiction?* Toronto: Musson, 1973.

Rea, D.J. *Political Economy of the Canadian North*. Toronto: University of Toronto Press, 1968.

Renner, Louis L. "A Footnote to Stefansson's 'The Friendly Arctic.'" *Alaska Journal* (1974):203-4.

Sater, John E. *The Arctic Basin*. Montreal: Arctic Institute of North America, 1963.

Starokadomskiy, L.M. *Charting the Russian Northern Sea Route*. Montreal: Arctic Institute of North America and McGill-Queen's, 1976.

Steele, Harwood. *Policing the Arctic*. London: Jarrolds, 1936.

Stefansson, Georgina. "My Grandfather, Dr. Vilhjalmur Stefansson." *North* 8, no. 4 (1961):25.

Stuck, Hudson. *A Winter Circuit of Our Arctic Coast*. New York: Scribner's, 1917.

Sverdrup, Otto. *Sverdrup's Arctic Adventures*. Toronto: Longmans, 1959.

Swenson, Olaf. *Northwest of the World*. New York: Dodd, Mead, 1944.

Todd, A.L. *Abandoned*. New York: McGraw-Hill, 1961.

Traprock, Walter E. *My Northern Exposure*. New York: Putnam's, 1922.

Turley, Charles. *Nansen of Norway*. London: Methuen, 1933.

———. *Roald Amundsen, Explorer*. London: Methuen, 1935.

Victor, Paul-Emile. *Man and the Conquest of the Poles*. New York: Simon & Schuster, 1963.

Villarejo, Oscar M. *Dr. Kane's Voyages to the Polar Lands*. Philadelphia: University of Pennsylvania Press, 1965.

Weems, John Edward. *Race for the Pole*. New York: Holt, 1960.

———. *Peary: The Explorer and the Man*. London: Eyre & Spottiswoode, 1967.

Weigert, Hans W., Stefansson, Vilhjalmur and Harrison, Richard Edes, eds. *New Compass of the World*. New York: Macmillan, 1944.

Welzl, Jan. *Thirty Years in the Golden North*. New York: Macmillan, 1932.

———. *Quest for Polar Treasures*. New York: Macmillan, 1933.

Whalley, George. *The Legend of John Hornby*. London: Murray, 1962.

Whittaker, C.E. *Arctic Eskimo*. London: Seeley, Service, 1937.

Wilkins, George H. *Flying the Arctic*. New York: Putnam's, 1928.

———. *Under the North Pole*. New York: Brewer, Warren and Putnam, 1931.

Wilkinson, Doug. *Arctic Fever*. Toronto: Clarke, Irwin, 1941.

Wonders, William C. *Canada's Changing North*. Toronto: McClelland and Stewart, 1972.

————. *The Arctic Circle*. Ontario: Longman, 1976.
————. *The North*. Toronto: University of Toronto Press, 1972.
Wright, Noel. *Quest for Franklin*. London: Heinemann, 1959.
Wright, Theon. *The Big Nail: The Story of the Cook-Peary Feud*. New York: John Day, 1970.
Zaslow, Morris. *The Opening of the Canadian North: 1970-1914*. Toronto: McClelland and Stewart, 1971.
————. *Reading the Rocks*. Toronto: Macmillan, 1975.

WORKS BY VILHJALMUR STEFANSSON

BOOKS

My Life with the Eskimo. New York: Macmillan, 1913.
Anthropological Papers. New York: American Museum of Natural History, 1914.
The Friendly Arctic. New York: Macmillan, 1921.
Hunters of the Great North. New York: Harcourt, Brace, 1922.
The Northward Course of Empire. New York: Harcourt, Brace, 1922.
The Adventure of Wrangel Island. New York: Macmillan, 1925.
My Life with the Eskimo (abridged). New York: Macmillan, 1927.
The Standardization of Error. New York: W.W. Norton, 1927.
Adventures in Error. New York: Robert M. McBride, 1936.
The Three Voyages of Martin Frobisher. (in collaboration with Eloise McCaskill). London: Argonaut Press, 1938.
Unsolved Mysteries of the Arctic. New York: Macmillan, 1938.
Iceland: The First American Republic. New York: Doubleday, Doran, 1939.
The Problem of Meighen Island. New York: Privately printed for Joseph Robinson, 1939.
Ultima Thule. New York: Macmillan, 1940.
Greenland. New York: Doubleday, Doran, 1942.
The Friendly Arctic (new edition). New York: Macmillan, 1943.
Arctic Manual. New York: Macmillan, 1944.
Compass of the World (with Hans W. Weigert). New York: Macmillan, 1944.
Not by Bread Alone, 1946. (Enlarged edition issued under the title *The Fat of the Land*.) New York: Macmillan, 1956.
Great Adventures and Explorations (in collaboration with Olive Rathbun Wilcox). New York: Dial Press, 1947.
New Compass of the World (with Hans W. Weigert and Richard Edes Harrison). New York: Macmillan, 1949.

The Fat of the Land. (Revised, enlarged edition of *Not by Bread Alone.*) New York: Macmillan, 1956.
Northwest to Fortune. New York: Duell, Sloan and Pearce, 1958.
Cancer: Disease of Civilization? New York: Hill and Wang, 1960.
Discovery. New York: McGraw-Hill, 1964.

Publications of United States Government

The Air Corps, United States Army: Arctic Manual, 2 vols., 1940.
The U.S. Navy, Hydrographic Office: Sailing Directions for the East Coast of Greenland and Iceland, 1943. (H.O. No. 75.)
Sailing Directions for Northern Canada, 1946. (H.O. No. 77.)
Sailing Directions for Baffin Bay and Davis Strait, 1947. (H.O. No. 76.)

Books for Younger Readers

(In collaboration with Violet Irwin), Kak, the Copper Eskimo, 1924, The Shaman's Revenge, 1925, The Mountain of Jade, 1926; (In collaboration with Julia Schwartz), Northward Ho!, 1925

Other

Microfilm Edition of Encyclopedia Arctica, 1944

ARTICLES, BOOK REVIEWS, AND LETTERS TO THE EDITOR
TO JANUARY 1960

1901   "*Vacation Tragedy.* A Play." *The Student* 14(4):43-45.
1903   "English Loan-Nouns Used in the Icelandic Colony of North Dakota." *Dialect Notes* 2(5):354-62.
1904   "The Newer Literature of Iceland." *Poet Lore* 15(1):62-76.
        "A North Dakotan at Harvard." *The Student* 17(3):4-6.
        "Present-Day Literature of Iceland." *Poet Lore* 15(2):126-38.
1906   "Icelandic Beast and Bird Lore." *Journal of American Folklore* 19(75):300-308.
        "The Icelandic Colony in Greenland." *American Anthropologist* 8(2):262-70.
1907   "Report of the Mikkelsen-Leffingwell Expedition." *Bulletin of the American Geographical Society:* 607-20. Map.

1908 "The Anglo-American Polar Expedition." *Harper's Monthly Magazine* 116(693):327-42. Illustrated.

"The Home Life of the Eskimo." *Harper's Monthly Magazine* 117(701):721-30. Illustrated.

"Ice Conditions at the Western End of Amundsen's North-West Passage." *Bulletin of the American Geographical Society* 40(1):26-27.

"On the Mackenzie River." *Bulletin of the American Geographical Society* 40(3):157-68. Illustrated.

"A Preliminary Report of an Ethnological Investigation of the Mackenzie Delta." Government of Canada, Department of Mines, Geological Survey Branch, *Summary Report* 26:190-202.

"The Stefansson-Anderson Arctic Expedition." *American Museum Journal* 8(7):101-6.

"Suitability of Eskimo Methods of Winter Travel in Scientific Exploration." *Bulletin of the American Geographical Society* 40(40):210-13.

"Theory and Treatment of Disease among Mackenzie River Eskimos." *Journal of American Folklore* 21:43-45.

"Wintering among the Eskimos." *Harper's Monthly Magazine* 117(697):38-48. Illustrated.

1909 "The Eskimo Trade Jargon of Herschel Island." *American Anthropologist* n.s. 2(2):217-32.

"News from the Museum's Explorers." *American Museum Journal* 9(5):109-12.

"Northern Alaska in Winter." *Bulletin of the American Geographical Society* 41(10):601-10.

1910 *The American Museum Journal* 10(4):108-9.

"An Ethnologist in the Arctic." *Harper's Monthly Magazine* 117(717):455-63. Illustrated.

"'Turning Kogmollik' for Science." *American Museum Journal* 10(7):216-19.

"Underground Ice in Northern Alaska." *Bulletin of the American Geographical Society* 42(5):337-45. Illustrated.

1911 "The Indian and Civilization." *New York Independent* 71:1434-38. Illustrated.

"Stefansson and Anderson in the Canadian Arctic." *Bulletin of the American Geographical Society* 43(10):771-75.

"Work among the Arctic Eskimos." Government of Canada, Department of Mines, Geological Survey Branch. *Summary Report, Sessional Paper No. 26.* pp. 389-90.

1912 "The Eskimo and Civilization." *American Museum Journal* 12(6):195-204. Illustrated.

"Life With the Eskimos." Newspaper unidentified.

"On Eskimo Work, 1908-1912." *Summary Report of the Geological Survey Department of Mines:* 488-96.

"My Quest in the Arctic." *Harper's Monthly Magazine* 126(751):3-13. Illustrated, map.

"Quotations from an Explorer's Letters." *American Museum Journal* 12(1):3-14. Illustrated.

"Some Details of Mr. Stefansson's Geographical Work." *Bulletin of the American Geographical Society* 44(9):660-63.

"Stefansson's Own Story of his Discoveries." *The [New York] Sun,* 15 September, the fourth magazine section, pp. 1-2. Illustrated, map.

"The Story of the Blond Eskimos." *Illustrated Outdoor World and Recreation,* n.s. 48(1):10-14. Illustrated, map.

"The Technique of Arctic Winter Travel." *Bulletin of the American Geographical Society* 45(5):340-47.

"White Eskimos and the Franklin Expedition." *Harper's Weekly* 56(2914):20.

1913 "The Canadian Arctic Expedition." *Geographical Journal* 42(1):49-53. Illustrated.

"The Distribution of Human and Animal Life in the Western Arctic America." *Geographical Journal* 41(5):449-60. Illustrated.

"Isolating the Blond Eskimo." *Literary Digest* 46(1):22-23.

"Misconceptions About Life in the Arctic." *Bulletin of the American Geographical Society* 45(1):17-32.

"My Quest in the Arctic." *Harper's Monthly Magazine.* 126(752):176-87; 126(753):348-59; 126(754):512-22; 126(755): 671-84; 126(756):888-900. Illustrated, maps.

"On Christianizing the Eskimos." *Harper's Monthly Magazine* 127(761):672-82.

"Religious Beliefs of the Eskimo." *Harper's Monthly Magazine* 127(762):869-78.

"Seeking a New Continent." *Harper's Weekly* 57(2940):8-9. Illustrated, map.

"Victoria Island and the Surrounding Seas." *Bulletin of the American Geographical Society* 45(2):93-106. Map.

1914 "Prehistoric and Present Commerce among the Arctic Coast Eskimos." Canada. Department of Mines, Geological Survey, *Museum Bulletin no. 6* (Anthropological Series no. 3):1-29. Map.

"The Stefansson-Anderson Arctic Expedition of the American Museum; Preliminary Report." *Anthropological Papers of the American Museum of Natural History* 14(1):146. Illustrated, map.

"Stefansson's Expedition." *Bulletin of the American Geographical Society* 46(3):184-91. Map.

1918 "The Activities of the Canadian Arctic Expedition from October, 1916, to April, 1918." *Geographical Review* 6(4):354-69. Map.

"The Fall of a Meteor in Northern Canada." *Geographical Review* 6(3):282-83.

"Letter from Mr. Stefansson." *Geographical Journal* 52(4):248-55.

"Observations on Three Cases of Scurvy." *Journal of the American Medical Association* 71(21):1715-18.

"Original Observations on Scurvy and My Opinion of the Medical Profession." *Medical Review of Reviews* 24(5):257-64.

"Polar Regions. Mr. Rasmussen's Expedition to Northern Greenland." *Geographical Journal* 52(1):63.

1919   "The Blessings of Civilization." *Churchman* 119(9):276-78.

"Colonel Roosevelt as Explorer." *American Review of Reviews* 59(2):165-66.

"'Living Off the Country' as a Method of Arctic Exploration." *Geographical Review* 7(5):291-310. Illustrated.

"Man Can Live on Meat Alone." *Physical Culture* 42(2):23-24, 64-66.

"Solving the Problem of the Arctic." [Six articles.] *Harper's Magazine*. Illustrated, maps.

    "A Record of Five Years' Exploration." 138(827):577-90.

    "Ways and Means of Life on the Ice." 138(828):721-35.

    "Drifting to Banks Island—the Arrival of the Mary Sachs." 139(829):36-47.

    "Hunting Caribou and Building Snow Houses." 139(830):193-203.

    "Our First Discovery of New Land." 139(831):386-98.

    "Conclusion—Further discoveries of New Land." 139(833):709-20.

1920   "Food Tastes and Food Prejudices of Men and Dogs." *Scientific Monthly* 11(12):540-43.

"Health, Wealth and Enjoyment in the Far, Far North." *The Maple Leaf* 2(1):11-14.

"Hudson Stuck, Explorer. Reminiscences of a Fellow Explorer." *The Churchman* 122(19):11-12. Illustrated.

"Peary." *New Republic* 22(274):27-28.

"The Region of Maximum Inaccessibility in the Arctic." *Geographical Review* 9(9):167-72.

"Robert Edwin Peary." [Memorial meeting at the Explorers Club, New York City, 12 March 1920, Vilhjalmur Stefansson presiding.] In Minutes, 22 p., Address, pp. 5-8.

"Temperature Factor in Determining the Age of Maturity among the Eskimos." *Journal of the American Medical Association* 75(10):669-70.

"Tribute to Peary." *New York Times*, 21 February, p. 1.

1921   "The Canadian Arctic Expedition of 1913 to 1918." *Geographical Journal* 58(4):283-305. Map.

"The North That Never Was." *World's Work* 43(2):188-200. Illustrated.

"Northward the Course of Empire: The Fallacy of an Idea about Northern Lands." *World's Work* 43(1):35-40.

"Our North That Never Was." *Maclean's Magazine* 34(24):16, 45-48. Map.

"Plover Land and Borden Land." *Geographical Review* 11(2):283-91. Illustrated, map.

1922   "The Arctic as an Air Route of the Future." *National Geographic*

42(2):205-18. Illustrated, map.

"Canada's Caribou Crop." *Maclean's Magazine* 35(2):27, 35-36.

"Far North Really Liveable." *Maclean's Magazine* 35(3):23-24, 43-44.

"The Fruitful Arctic." *World's Work* 43(3):313-26. Illustrated.

"Human Flight a Triumph of Pure Reason." *U.S. Air Service* 7(11):18. Illustrated.

"The Livable North." *World's Work* 43(4):440-48. Illustrated.

"A North Polar Parody." *New York Times,* 1 October, pp. 4, 12, 25-29.

"Popular Science from Unfamiliar Sources." *Literary Digest International Book Review* 1(1):30-31, 90. Illustrated.

"Property among the Eskimos." *World Tomorrow* 5(4):100-101.

"Sir Arthur Conan Doyle." *Outlook* 131(1):26-27. Illustrated.

"Some Erroneous Ideas of Arctic Geography." *Geographical Review* 12(2):264-77.

"What Do You Know That Isn't So?" *Collier's* 70(27):11. Illustrated.

1923   "The Adventure of Wrangell Island." *Spectator* 131(4964):215-16.

"Educated Ignorance." *Collier's* 71(8):25. Illustrated.

"Facts That Are Not So." Publication unknown. pp. 793-801. Illustrated.

"The Friendly Arctic." *Quarterly Review* 5(1):1-5.

"The Friendly Arctic." *Science,* n.s. 57(1471):368-69, and (1484):666.

"Go North, Young Man!" *Popular Science Monthly* 102(1):23-25. Illustrated.

"The History and Importance of Wrangel Island." *Spectator* 130(4954):958-59 and (4955):998-1000.

"Is It Cold Enough for You?" *Collier's* 72(18):33.

"A Letter from Stefansson to Joseph Kennedy." University of North Dakota, *School of Education Record* 9(1):4.

"The Musk Ox in Arctic Islands." *Nature* 112(2816):590.

"The Mythical Wolf Pack." *Collier's* 71(16):27. Illustrated.

"Polar Temperatures and Coal Measures." *Nature* 112(2805):162-63, and (2813):472-73.

"Popular Errors." *Spectator.*

"That Primitive People Have Simple Languages." 131(4969):378-80.

"That the Further North the Colder." 131(4970):416-17.

"That You Cannot Live without Vegetables." 131(4971):545-55.

"Transpolar Commerce by Air." *U.S. Air Service* 8(3):9-14.

"Wrangel Island." *Spectator* 130(4957):1079.

1923-24   "Alaska, a Vast Territory and Its Possibilities." *Countries of the World:* 38-58. Illustrated.

"The Arctic Lands, Today and Tomorrow in the Far North." *Countries of the World:* 259-86.

1924   "Adventure of Wrangell Island." *The Premier Magazine.* 2(11):499-

511; 2(12):623-33; 3(1):99-110; 3(2):210-16; 3(3):432-40. Illustrated, maps.

"Arctic Air Routes to the Orient." *The Forum* 72(6):721-32. Map.

"Attacking Pet and Popular Beliefs." *Current Opinion.*

"Belief in Possibilities of Central Australian Desert." *New York Times,* 28 December.

"Every Science an Exact Science." *The American Mercury* 1(3):309-14.

"The Great Central Desert in Australia." *New York Times,* 16 September.

"How I Talk to My Public." *Life* Australia: 113-14. Illustrated.

"Mr. Stefansson's Comments." *Geographical Journal* 63(6):524-25.

"Popular Errors." *Spectator.*
   "That the Ostrich Hides His Head in the Sand." 132(4985):43-44.
   "That Frostbite is Cured by Snow." 132(4987):118-19.
   "That Eskimos Drink Oil." 132(4989):194-96.

"Survey of Central Australia." *New York Times,* 7 August.

1924-25   "100° Above Zero in the Arctic." *The Forum* 74(5):795-96.

1925   "Air-Craft Opening Empire of the North." *Aero Digest* 6(2):73-75. Illustrated.

"Amundsen Aerial Expedition to the North Pole." *New York Times,* 24 May and 20 June.

"The Arctic: Its Changing Phases." *Current History* 23(2):155-70. Illustrated.

"Comparing New York's Boat Wave with Those of the Equator." *New York Times,* 21 June.

"New Farm Animals." *Country Gentleman* 90(37):21, 158.

"The Norse Discovery of the Western World." *New York Masonic Outlook* 2(2):35-38. Illustrated, map.

"Our [New York] Heat Waves Worse Than the Equator's." *New York Times,* 21 June, p. 4. Illustrated.

"Pioneering on a Far-Off Frontier." *Country Gentleman* 90(35):14, 147, 151-52. Illustrated.

"Six Elusive Poles Intrigue the Explorer." *New York Times,* 26 July, p. 3. Illustrated, map.

"Spend Your Vacation at the North Pole." *Collier's* 26(2):5-6. Illustrated.

"When the World Will Starve." *World's Work* 50(6):639-44. Maps.

"Where There Are No Lodges." *New York Masonic Outlook* 2(3):74-76, 96. Illustrated.

"Who Will Fly across the Arctic?" *Spectator* 135(5079):753.

1926   "Circling the World Becomes a Vivid Sport." *New York Times,* 1 August, p. 4. Illustrated, map.

"Comments on Norge's Flight across the North Pole and Congratulations to Leaders." *New York Times,* 16 May.

"Detroit Arctic Expedition." *Michigan Engineer* 44(3):11-17.

"Food from Our Frozen Desert." *American Review of Reviews*

73(2):199-200.

"Life in Polar Seas." *The Forum* 75(5):786-87.

"Living by Forage in Arctic Exploration." *Geographical Review* 16(2):9-15.

"More Celebrities Tell Why They Never Married." *Saint Louis Post Dispatch*, 6 November.

"Norse Discovery of America Again Debated." *New York Times*, 19 September, p. 4. Illustrated.

"Norse Voyages to America are Retraced." *New York Times*, 18 July, p. 4. Illustrated, map.

"The Pageant of America." *The Forum* 76(5):798-99.

"Passing the Buck to Posterity." *Birth Control Review* 10(9):269-71; 10(10):310-12; 10(11):340-42, 354.

"Polar Pastures." *Forum* 75(1):9-20.

"Possibilities of Polar Flight." *New York Times*, 17 May.

"The Short Road to Asia." *The Lincoln*, pp. 10-11. Map.

"The Standardization of Error." *Psyche*, pp. 101-8.

"Success of Richard E. Byrd's Polar Flight." *New York Times*, 10 May.

"What Amundsen Has Proved: The Earth is a Sphere, Not a Cylinder." *World's Work* 52(3):241-49. Maps.

"Where Weather Is Made." *Country Gentleman* 91(7):12, 62. Illustrated.

"Why Do People Go to the Arctic?" *Success Magazine* 10(6):73. Illustrated.

"The World's Meat Supply from the Arctic." *Literary Digest* 88(7):21-22. Illustrated.

1927   "Across Arctic America, Narrative of the Fifth Thule Expedition." *Canadian Historical Review* 8(3):247-51.

"The Airplane and the Arctic." *Harper's Monthly Magazine* 155(929):595-604.

"The Arctic Flying of Captain Wilkins and Lieutenant Eielson." *Science* 65(1691):523-25.

"Arctic Skylarking." *The Forum* 77(2):305.

"Are Explorers to Join the Dodo?" *The American Mercury* 11(41):13-18.

"De-Bunking the Arctic." *The [New York] World*, 26 June. Illustrated.

"The Friendly Eskimo." *The Mentor* 15(1):36-40.

"Knud Rasmussen Knows the Eskimo Inside and Out." *New York Times Book Review*, 10 April, pp. 3, 19.

"New Polar Trails." *The Forum* 77(1):54-64.

"Noashak's Growing Up." *American Girl* 10(3):12-13, 42. Illustrated.

"Well-Oiled Esquimaux." *The Forum* 77(3):469-70.

"The Wolf-Pack." *American Mercury* 11(43):327-30.

1928   "Arctic Annals." *Saturday Review of Literature* 5(14):291-92.

"Arctic Danger Spots and Seasons." *The Outlook* 149(7):258-259, 278. Map.

"Ben Eielson—Arctic Explorer." *The Outlook* 149(10):378-79. Illustrated.

"The 'Blond' Eskimos." *Harper's Monthly Magazine* 156(932):191-98.

"Both Ends of the Earth." *The Living Age* 335(4333):9-11, 77. Maps.

"By Air to the Ends of the Earth." *Natural History* 28(5):451-62. Illustrated, maps.

"Canada's Arctic Air Lanes." *Maclean's Magazine* 41(18):7, 53, 58. Maps.

"An Explorer's View of the Arctic Disaster." *The Outlook* 149(14):532-35. Illustrated.

"Flying North." *The Outlook* 150(4):852, 878. Map.

"Greenland's Icy Interior as an Air Way Station." *New York Times Magazine*, 16 September, pp. 12-13, 20. Illustrated.

"A Half Chapter for an Autobiography." *The Frontier* 8(3):150-53.

"Notes on Arctic Flying." *Geographical Journal* 71(2):167-71.

"Over the Top of the World: The Story of Sir Hubert Wilkins." *The American Magazine* 106(3):46-47, 103-4, 106, 108, 110. Illustrated, map.

"The Republic of Greenland." *Forum* 80(2): 250-66. Illustrated.

"The Resources of the Arctic and the Problem of their Utilization." *American Geographical Society Special Publication* no. 7, pp. 209-33.

"Santa Claus' Reindeer." *Panorama* 1(13):10.

"The SOS Enters the Icebound Arctic." *Buffalo Evening News*, 28 July, p. 3. (Reprinted in *New York Herald Tribune*, 29 July, pp. 16-17, 27. Illustrated.)

"Taktuk, an Arctic Boy." *Saturday Review of Literature* 5(6):350.

"The True Adventurer." *Saturday Review Of Literature* 5(8):117-18.

"Wilkins Blazes Trail of an Arctic Airway." *New York Times*, 29 April, p. 3. Illustrated, map.

1929   "Antarctic Calls to Map-Makers." *Seattle Post-Intelligence*, 27 January, p. 3M. Illustrated, map.

"Capt. Wilkins Has Solved Greatest Problem of Antarctic Region, Declares Stefansson." *Boston Advertiser*, 13 January, pp. 1, 4. Illustrated.

"Defense of Nobile." [Reprinted in] *World Today* 54(3):229-36.

"Flight in the Arctic Regions." *Mechanical Engineering* 51(11):807-12. Illustrated, maps.

"Icelandic Independence." *Foreign Affairs* 7(2):270-81. Map.

"Nansen—King of the North." *New York Herald Tribune*, 3 February, pp. 6-7.

"The Question of Living by Forage in the Arctic." *Arktis* 2(1):11-15.

"Some Problems of Arctic Travel: After a Forced Landing." *Geographical Journal* 74(5):417-33.

"Teaching the Truth about the Arctic." *American Childhood* 14(5):5-

8, 62-63. Illustrated.

"That 'Frozen' North!" *Maclean's* 42(22):3-4, 59-61. Illustrated, maps.

"The Theoretical Continent." *Natural History* 29(5): 465-80. Illustrated, maps.

"What We Gain from Polar Exploration." *Redbook Magazine* 53(1):59-61, 145-48. Illustrated.

1929-30   *The Canadian Elk Series.* October 1929—June 1930.

1930   "Abolishing the Arctic." *School and Community* 16(2):105-11.

"Eskimos." *Teachers World* 39(1098):74-75. Illustrated.

"The Eskimo's Modern Dwelling." *Canadian Elk Magazine* 5(10):5. Illustrated.

"The Eskimo's Surroundings." *Canadian Elk Magazine* 5(11):6-7. Illustrated.

"The Friendly North." *Grolier Society,* pp. 5-16.

"How Andrée Lived and Died." *Sphere* 123(1603):64-65. Illustrated, map.

"The Little Eskimo." *Canadian Elk Magazine* 5(12):7-8. Illustrated.

"Man in Greenland." *Geographical Review* 20(4):657-63.

"Savages Are Pleasant People." *Redbook Magazine* 54(5):43-47, 114-17. Illustrated. Reprinted in condensed form in *Reader's Digest* 17(97):64-66.

"Spring in the Arctic." *World News:* 6-7. Illustrated.

"The Truth about the Arctic." *Teacher's World* 38(1096):1013, 1037, 1050. Illustrated.

1931   "An Arctic Mystery." *Saturday Review of Literature* 7(24):497-99.

"Chat with Stefansson." *Town Tidings* 5(8):24-26.

"Dogs in Harness." *Home Geographical Monthly* 1(2):1-7. Illustrated.

"The Eskimo Word 'Iglu.'" *Science,* n.s. 73(1889):285-86.

"How Did Andree Die?" *Spectator* 146(5354):177-78.

"Wilkins Submarine a Scientific Laboratory Diving Like a Whale in Arctic Ice Lanes, Says Stefansson." *New York American,* p. 2-E. Illustrated.

1932   "Hakluyt or Hoax?" *Saturday Review of Literature* 8(51):825, 828. Illustrated.

"Stefansson Foresees Competing Airmail Lines across Atlantic within Four Years." *New York American,* pp. E-3, E-4. Illustrated, map.

"Which is Happier?" *Redbook Magazine* 59(5):62-65. Illustrated.

1933   "The Anthropometry of the Western and Copper Eskimos, Based on Data of Vilhjalmur Stefansson." *Human Biology* 5(3):313-17. Map.

"Blue Eyes for Brown." *Science* 77(1990):191-92.

"The Eskimo World." *Yale Review* n.s. 22(3):617-19.

1934   "Castaways in the Arctic." *New York Herald Tribune Magazine,* 18 March, pp. 3, 27. Illustrated.

"A Defense of the Arctic." *All's Well* 12(1):39-40.

"An Eskimo Discovery of an Island North of Alaska." *Geographical*

Review 24(1):104-14. Illustrated, map.
"Knud Rasmussen." *Geographical Review* 24(2):336-37.
"Via North Pole, Please!" *The Passing Show,* 10 February, pp. 8, 11. Illustrated, map.

1935 "Adventures in Diet." *Harper's Monthly Magazine,* Part I, 171(1026):668-75; Part II, 172(1027):46-54.
"Byrd Has Advanced American Claims to Antarctic Dependency." *New York American,* 24 February, p. 4-E. Illustrated, map.
"Ellsworth Adds 5 Islands, 3 Fiords, Some Mountains to the Antarctic Map." *New York American,* 19 February, p. 5-E. Illustrated, map.
— [somewhat revised]. *Leiv Eiriksson Review,* pp. 3, 8-9. Illustrated.
"Impressions of Iceland." [Brochure for Showing of Paintings by Emile Walters.] Kleeman Galleries.
"Introduction to the Cheyne Articles." *Bulletin of the Geographical Society of Philadelphia* 33(4):97-98.
"My Visit to the Stone Age." *Blue Book* 61(4):126-30. Illustrated.
"Stefansson Backs Ellsworth Chances." *New York American,* 8 December, p. [?]. Illustrated, map.

1936 "Adventures in Diet." *Harper's Monthly Magazine* 172(1028):178-89. Reprinted in two installments and abridged in *Montana Wool Growers News Letter* 10(7):22-23, (8):21-22, (9):21-22, (10):20-22, (11):6-9, and (12):6-8, 18, 23. Also reprinted and abridged in *Oral Hygiene* 26(2):202-10. Illustrated, map.
"A Letter from Stefansson." *Natural History* 37(5):380-81.

1937 "Adventures in Error." *Book Digest of Best Sellers* 1(3):81-93.
"The Background of the Trans-Polar Flights." *Research Bulletin of the Soviet Union* 2(8):83-84.
"Food of the Ancient and Modern Stone Age Man." *Journal of the American Dietetic Association* 13(2):102-19.
"King of the North." *Blue Book* 64(5):130-33.
"My Adventures on the Polar Ice." *Personal Adventure Stories* 1(1):18-23. Illustrated.
"The Near Way is North—By Plane." *The Rotarian* 50(6):17-21. Illustrated.
"A Prophesy Fulfilled." *Soviet Russia Today* 6(5):8. Illustrated.
"The Soviet Flyers May Still Be Alive." *The Explorers Journal* 5(4):3-4.
"We Chew Far More Than Our Ancestors." *Scientific American* 156(1):56.
"Why the Russians Want the North Pole." *Liberty* 14(38):11-12. Illustrated, map.

1938 "American-Soviet Friendship." *Soviet Russia Today* 7(3):24-25.
"Thoughts on the Arctic." *International Quarterly* 2(2):7-12.

1939 "The American Far North." *Foreign Affairs* 17(3):508-23. Map.
"The Diet of Eskimos." *Medical Record* 150(4):9-10.
"A Dilemma in Vitamins." *Science* n.s. 89(2317):484-85.
"The Disappearance of the Greenland Colony." *Natural History*

43(1):7-12, 34-37.
"The Friendly Soviet Arctic." *Soviet Russia Today* 8(4):17-19. Illustrated.
"I Believe." *Omnibook Magazine* 2(1):26-28.
"Lessons in Living from the Stone Age." *Harper's Monthly Magazine* 179(1070):158-64.
"The Lost 9000." *Canadian Magazine* 91(1):35-38. Illustrated.
"The Problem of Meighen Island." [Intended as the third chapter, but suppressed in publication of *Unsolved Mysteries of the Arctic*. Privately printed for Mr. Joseph Robinson.] 71 pp.
— *The Northman*, 3 October, pp. 2, 10.

1940   "Iceland Has a Way!" *The Rotarian* 56(5):8-12. Illustrated, map.
"Russia's 'Menace' to Alaska." *New Republic* 103(21):686-87.
"A Ten-Year Program of Arctic Study." *Proceedings of the American Philosophical Society* 82(5):897-919. Map.

1941   "Alaska." *Teachers' Handbook*. 21 p.
"Alaska, American Outpost No. 4." *Harper's Monthly Magazine* 183(1093):83-92. Map.
"Blueprint for Hemisphere Defense." *University of Chicago Round Table* 174:1-21. Map.
"The Colonization of Northern Lands." *Yearbook of Agriculture*, pp. 206-16. Map.
"Front Line Road to Alaska." *[Toronto] Star Weekly*, pp. 2, 11. Illustrated, map.
"Iceland and America." *Scholastic* 39(5):8, 39. Illustrated.
"Mystery of Arctic Weather." *Science Digest* 9(6):23-27.
"The Not-So-Frozen North." *Everyday Reading* 9(10):119-20.
"Routes to Alaska." *Foreign Affairs* 19(4):861-69. Map.
"Was the Diomede Scare a Japanese Plant?" *Alaska Life* 4(2):3, 16-18.
"What Is the Western Hemisphere?" *Foreign Affairs* 19(2):343-46. Map.

1942   "Arctic Supply Line." *Fortune* 26(1):64-66, 154, 156, 158. Map.
"The North That Never Was." *Reader's Digest* 40(238):84-86.
"The Northwest Spouts Oil." *[Toronto] Star Weekly*, 7 February, p. 7. Illustrated.
"Spotlight on Asia." *Talks* 7(3):31.
"The Untapped Wealth of Alaska." *Science Digest* 71(6):71-74.

1942-43   "Man's Path of Progress Leads North." *A Forum of the Future*, pp. 34-35. Illustrated.

1943   "Do You Know This Greenland?" *Natural History* 51(2):95-99. Illustrated.
"The Meat Diet." *War Department, Office of the Quartermaster General*, 6 July, 2 p.
"Post-War Opportunities." *Pic* 13(11):7-9.

1944   "The Arctic Link." *Canadian Affairs* 1(12):3-9. Map.
"The Diet of Explorers." *Military Surgeon* 95(1):1-3.

"Pemmican." *Military Surgeon* 95(2):89-98.

"10th Anniversary Birobidjan." *Jewish Autonomous Region* 10th Anniversary [Ambijan] Committee, p. 1. Illustrated.

"Wonders of the Northland." *Reader's Digest* 45(272):27.

1945   "The Arctic Frontier." *Think* 11(10):17-19. Illustrated.

"Arctic in Fact and Fable." *Headline Series,* 51:95 p. Illustrated, map.

"Living on the Fat of the Land." *Harper's Monthly Magazine* 191(1142):70-76.

"The Mediterranean of the Future." *Travel* 85(2):11-15, 31. Illustrated, map.

"See Your Dentist Twice a Year." *Atlantic Monthly* 176(5):61-66.

"The Standardization of Error." *Dunker Doings,* year 2, nos. 42-60, 18 installments, one page each.

1946   "Canada the Link—USA to USSR." *The Rotarian* 69(5):22-25. Illustrated, map.

"Explorer Stefansson Gives Farmers Ideas." *The Vermonter* 51(8):8, 24, 30.

"Farming without Barns." *Harper's Monthly Magazine* 192(1148):53-56. Reprinted, slightly abridged, in *Reader's Digest* 49(292):85-87.

"New Farm Animals for Vermont." Offprint in Stefansson Collection, Baker Memorial Library.

"Primitive People Are Far from Simple." *Redbook Magazine* 86(5):32-33, 128, 131-34. Illustrated.

"Safety for Adventurers." *National Safety News* 54(4):88-89, 132, 134, 136, 138. Illustrated.

1947   "Alaska in the Air Age." *Classroom Clipper* 3(4):3-5. Map.

"Bibliography of Arctic Books." *Across the Top of the World,* U.S. Department of the Navy, pp. 49-71.

"The Ethnic Issue." Reprint of speeches made in a forum before the Jewish Theological Seminary of America, pp. 61-75.

"Musk-Ox, Digested." 2½ p.

"How Eskimos Keep Cool." *Science Digest* 22(1):81-85.

"Logbook for Grace." *Natural History* 56(6):245. Illustrated, reprint from February 1922. *Reader's Digest* 50.

"Our Neglected Arctic." *Science Illustrated* 2(1):17-21, 112-15. Map.

"Polar Facts and Fancy." *Minneapolis Star-Journal.* Illustrated, maps.

     "What to Expect from Byrd's Adventure." 3 March.

     "Arctic Holds Key to Third World War." 4 March.

     "Safety, Speed to Make Arctic Hub of Aviation." 5 March.

     "Farms, Mines, Oil Promised by Rich Arctic." 6 March.

"The Polar Regions in Fact and Fancy." *St. John's Telegram.*

     "Operation High Jump." 3 March.

     "North Pole—Air Hub of the World." 4 March.

     "Arctic Weather Awaits Exploration." 8 March.

"What about the Polar Regions?" *Indianapolis Star,* 27 February.

Illustrated.

"Winnipeg Tribune Series." *Winnipeg Tribune*. Illustrated.

"Uranium Deposits Sought in Antarctic." 1 March, pp. 1, 5.

"North Pole Forms Air Hub of the World." 3 March, pp. 1, 5.

"Stefansson Urges North Colonization." 4 March, p. [?].

"Arctic Wealth Awaits Exploration for Peace." 5 March, p. [?].

1948   "Encyclopedia Arctica." *Arctic* 1(1):44-46.

1949   "Economic Utilization of Wildlife through Partial or Complete Domestication." *Transactions of the Fourteenth Annual North American Wildlife Conference*, pp. 31-35.

"Eskimo Houses." *Alaskan Churchman* 44(2):6-8. Illustrated.

"Twenty Questions about the Arctic." *Forest and Outdoors* 45(2):14-15, 27. Illustrated, map.

1950   "The Andree Mystery." *Master Detective* 42(6):38-41, 78-86. Illustrated.

"The Arctic." *Air Affairs* 3(2):391-402.

1951   "Claims to Polar Discovery." *Saturday Review of Literature* 34(49):26. Illustrated.

"De Mensura Orbis Terrae, Geographical Treatise of the Irish Monk Dicuil, Written A.D. 825." *American Philosophical Society*, Yearbook 1951, pp. 232-53.

"Isaiah Bowman (1878-1950)." *American Philosophical Society*, Yearbook, 1951, pp. 291-94.

"Stefansson on Snowhouses." *Natural History* 60(3):98, 143.

1952   "The Mackenzie River—Coronation Gulf Eskimos: Their Concept of the Spirit World, and of Immortality." *Divinity School Bulletin*, Harvard University 50(10):5-28.

"Military Rations: Pemmican." Research Development Associates, Food and Container Institute, Inc., *Activities Report* 3(4):241-51. Illustrated.

"Scott: Scott's Last Expedition." *Invitation to Learning* 2(3):266-72.

1954   "Americans from Norseland." *Saturday Review of Literature* 37(33):18. Illustrated.

"Arctic Controversy: The Letters of John Rae." *Geographical Journal* 120(4):486-93.

"Ice Island Priorities." *Explorers Journal* 32(4):28-29, 52-54.

"Kipling and Vermont." *Vermont History* 22(4):245-53.

"Rae's Arctic Correspondence." *The Beaver*, Outfit 284:35-37.

1955   "Clothes Make the Eskimo." *Natural History* 64(1):32-41, 51. Illustrated.

"How Hot Can You Stand It?" Co-written with Olive Wilcox. *Natural History* 64(10):528-31. Illustrated.

1956   "Causes of Eskimo Birth-Rate Increase." *Nature* 178(4542):1132.

"From the Pioneer West to the Arctic." *Westerner's Brand Book* 13(8):57-58. Reprinted in *The Maple Leaf* pp. 7-10.

"Natural Cold Storage." United States Navy, Chief of Naval Operations, 22p.

"A Word Common to the Natives of Alaska, Canada, Greenland, and Brazil." *Nature* 178(4540):1008.

1958 "An All-Meat Diet." *Everybody's Poultry Magazine* 63(3):32.

"Eskimo Longevity in Northern Alaska." *Science* 127(3288):16-19.

"Fabulous Formula Diet—Stone Age Style." *Ladies' Home Journal* 75(11):4, 46.

"Letter to Linda M. Goolsby." *Jr. High-Lites* 1p. mimeographed.

"Man's Meat." *Gourmet* 18(1):10, 11, 21, 22, 24.

1959 "Eating for Weight Loss." *New York Times*, 12 September, p. 20.

"The Most Unforgettable Character I've Met [Sir Hubert Wilkins]." *Reader's Digest* 75(447):95-101.

"What's in a Name?" *Christian Science Monitor* 51(96):22

1960 "What Changes Will the Sixties Bring?" *Esquire* 53(1):68.

Index